Arthur .

Papers on Tir.

Arthur N. Prior
Papers on Time and Tense

NEW EDITION

Edited by

PER HASLE
PETER ØHRSTRØM
TORBEN BRAÜNER
JACK COPELAND

OXFORD
UNIVERSITY PRESS

OXFORD

UNIVERSITY PRESS

Great Clarendon Street, Oxford OX2 6DP

Oxford University Press is a department of the University of Oxford.
It furthers the University's objective of excellence in research, scholarship,
and education by publishing worldwide in

Oxford New York

Auckland Bangkok Buenos Aires Cape Town Chennai
Dar es Salaam Delhi Hong Kong Istanbul Karachi Kolkata
Kuala Lumpur Madrid Melbourne Mexico City Mumbai Nairobi
São Paulo Shanghai Taipei Tokyo Toronto

Oxford is a registered trade mark of Oxford University Press
in the UK and certain other countries

Published in the United States
by Oxford University Press Inc., New York

British Library Cataloguing in Publication Data

Data available

Library of Congress Cataloging-in-Publication Data

Prior, A. N. (Arthur N.), 1914–1969.
Papers on time and tense / Arthur N. Prior.—New ed. / edited by Per Hasle . . . [et al.].
p. cm.
Includes bibliographical references and index.
1. Modality (Logic)   2. Tense (Logic)   I. Hasle, Per F. V.   II. Title
BC199.M6 P7 2002   160—dc21   2002029796

ISBN 0–19–925606–3
ISBN 0–19–925607–1 (Pbk.)

1 3 5 7 9 10 8 6 4 2

Printed in Great Britain by Biddles Ltd.,
Guildford and King's Lynn

CONTENTS

EDITORS' INTRODUCTION

The first edition of Prior's *Papers on Time and Tense* was published in 1968, just one year before Arthur Norman Prior died at the age of only 55 years old. This book should be seen as a continuation of his two books *Time and Modality* and *Past, Present and Future*. Together the three books form the core of Prior's foundation of modern temporal logic. Whereas the first two books introduce the basic ideas of temporal logic, this third volume suggests a number of open questions within the field and also establishes various connections to other philosophical topics, such as investigations into individual identity and the notion of action.

Unlike Prior's first two books on temporal logic, *Papers on Time and Tense* should not be seen as an attempt to introduce the ideas of temporal logic in a rounded and well-balanced way. It should be viewed rather as work in progress. For this reason it was natural for Prior, only a year after the first edition, to consider a new edition extended with some additional papers. Prior wrote a list of contents and a preface for the projected edition. Unfortunately, because of his sudden death in October 1969, Prior was never able to carry out his plan. In producing this second edition, the editors have attempted to realise Prior's intentions. The papers in the edition are exactly those that Prior included in his list. We have, however, taken the liberty of changing the logical notation. Prior used Polish notation, still rather common in the 1960s. But – as Dr. Mary Prior has put it – the battle between Polish and Russellian notation is over, and Russellian notation has clearly won. We assume that the change of notation will make Prior's work accessible to a larger audience. This is also the view of Dr. Mary Prior, who emphasises that it is more important for the ideas of her late husband to be accessible than for the original form of his formulae to be preserved in the new edition.

In this volume we have made "Editors' notes" where we have been able to add useful information about Prior's text. We have made a clear distinction between these editorial notes and Prior's own footnotes.

In the first edition of the book Prior published a bibliography of tense logic. He intended to update this bibliography in the second edition. There is, however, no information available about the additions that Prior intended to make. We have made no attempt to carry out the kind of updating which Prior intended in 1969. We have instead compiled a complete bibliography of Prior's own writings. This work has been carried out mainly by Per Hasle, and a closer description of it is found in the introduction to the bibliography. In this connection we must mention the *Nachlass* of A.N. Prior, which is deposited in the Bodleian Library, Oxford. Thorough studies of these papers have played a crucial role in the compilation of the new bibliography. A detailed overview and description of the papers kept in the Bodleian Library can be found at 'The WWW-site for Prior-studies' (www.hum.auc.dk/prior).

Per Hasle has also made and edited an interview with Dr. Mary Prior, which has been included in this volume. The interview is concerned partly with the life of the Priors, and partly with the philosophical and logical views of Arthur Prior. It supplements the major papers on Arthur Prior's life and work. For closer information, see the introduction to the interview.

Acknowledgements

First, and above all, we wish to thank Mary Prior for her forthcoming and helpful answers to questions on her late husband Arthur N. Prior's work and life, and her kind support in all manners.

We are indebted to several distinguished researchers, who have written on Prior and/or have known him personally. We want to thank Kit Fine for supporting this work and taking an interest in it. We also thank Nuel Belnap, Robert Bull, Anthony Kenny, Storrs McCall, Peter McKenzie, Thomas Müller, William Newton-Smith, Martin Prior, and Alberto Zanardo for kind assistance and stimulating discussions.

We wish to thank those institutions and bodies who have supported or otherwise helped our work:

Balliol College for a gracious offer of accommodation while working on Prior's papers;

Aarhus University Research Foundation for a grant towards the construction of the aforementioned 'WWW-site for Prior-studies';

The Centre for Cultural Research at the University of Aarhus, and in particular its director from 1998–2000, Niels Ole Finnemann, for practical and moral support of the project;

The staff of the Bodleian Library in the Department for Western Manuscripts, and especially in the Modern Papers Reading Room, for kind assistance when working with Prior's papers there. A special thanks to Colin Harris in this connection.

We also wish to thank three junior researchers who have contributed to the new bibliography and the production of the WWW-site:

Ms. Tine Kleif, who with enthusiasm and great skill helped organise and finalise the descriptions, on which the WWW-site is founded, and who laid a significant piece of ground-work for the new bibliography presented in this volume; and Mr. Henrik Gylling Møller, who with similar enthusiasm has been responsible for the final technical construction of the WWW-site. Finally, we must mention Ms. Helene Løchen Stenrud, who put the final touches to the bibliography in this volume. She thus followed in the footsteps of her countryman Olav Flo, the Norwegian who published the first bibliography of Prior's work.

PER HASLE
PETER ØHRSTRØM
TORBEN BRAÜNER
JACK COPELAND

PRIOR'S PREFACE
TO THE SECOND EDITION

The first nine of these papers are of a comparatively discursive and non-symbolic sort, and develop in various ways, and with various problems immediately in view, a certain way of looking at time and temporal reference. There follow eleven papers which are either themselves of a more technical character, in which the philosophical attitudes expressed in some of the first nine are at once presupposed and made more precise, or so presuppose these more technical developments that they cannot be placed earlier.

Thirteen of these papers appeared in the first edition of this book, and the rest have appeared since. There is inevitably some community of content between all of these papers and my two books *Time and Modality* and *Past, Present and Future*, but I have tried to select items which will in some way extend or clarify what is said in those books, and I have excluded papers whose content has now been wholly absorbed in them. I have also omitted items whose content has been absorbed in the papers that have been included, though I shall mention below what these items are.

Of the nine 'philosophical' papers, the first three are concerned with the nature of temporal succession in the most general sense. The first, 'Changes in Events and Changes in Things', was originally published by the University of Kansas, having been delivered as the Lindley Lecture in that university in 1962. Much of its contents had already been given in a course of W.E.A. lectures[1] in York towards the end of the preceding year, and one of its central ideas had been earlier developed in a short discussion note entitled 'Time after Time' which appeared in *Mind*, Vol. 67, No. 266 (April 1968), pp. 244–6. In this paper ('Changes in Events and Changes in Things') I exploit a certain notion of propositions, facts and events as 'logical constructions' which I have elsewhere developed in connexion with individual speech and belief contexts, notably in the papers 'Berkeley in Logical Form', *Theoria*, Vol. 21, Nos. 2–3 (1955), pp. 117–22; 'Is the Concept of Referential

---

[1] *Editors' note*. A series of adult education lectures, regularly given on Wednesdays. (The program can be found in Prior's Papers at the Bodleian Library, Box 7.)

Opacity Really Necessary?', *Acta Philosophica Fennica*, Fasc. 15 (1963), pp. 189–99; 'Oratio Obliqua', *Proceedings of the Aristotelian Society*, Supplementary Volume 37 (1963), pp. 115–26; and 'Intentionality and Intensionality', ibid., Supplementary Volume 42 (1968), pp. 91–106.

The second paper, 'Fugitive Truth', first appeared in *Analysis*, Vol. 29, No. 1 (October 1968), pp. 5–8, and deals with a minor but vexing semantic point arising out of the first.

The parallel between tense-formation and *oratio obliqua* is also drawn in the third paper included here, 'On Spurious Egocentricity'. This was first published in *Philosophy* for October 1967, and was first delivered at the University of Keele in 1960, apart from the last section, which arises out of the discussion which took place there. But this and the preceding two papers are closely related to Chapter I of *Past, Present and Future*.

There follow four papers on the general topic of time and determinism. The first of these, 'The Formalities of Omniscience', originally appeared in *Philosophy* for April 1962, having been read a year or two before that at a philosophical conference at Spode House in Staffordshire. It has obvious connexions with Chapter VII of *Past, Present and Future*. I place it first in this group because it reflects the general point of view of 'Changes of Events and Changes in Things' rather more immediately than do the two which follow it, though these were delivered earlier. The paper on 'Contemplation and Action', which has not previously been published, was given at an East-West philosophical 'working party' at University House, Canberra, in 1957 (the proceedings of which, including the discussion of this paper, are informally reported in the *Australasian Journal of Philosophy* for May 1958; I include part of this discussion). The one after it, 'The Consequences of Actions', was part of a symposium on this subject at the Joint Session of the Mind Association and the Aristotelian Society at Aberystwyth in 1956, and was published in the thirtieth Supplementary Volume of the *Proceedings of the Aristotelian Society*. The fourth paper in this group, 'Limited Indeterminism', is not concerned (as the preceding three are) with fore-knowledge or with deliberation, but with a rather more metaphysical aspect of the determinism-indeterminism controversy, and has close links with the two papers that come after it. It was first delivered at the conference of the Mid-Western Division of the American Philosophical Association at Detroit in 1962, and was published in the *Review of Metaphysics*, Vol. 16, No. 1 (September 1962), pp. 55–61.

The next two papers are on the general topic of time, existence, and identity, discussed in Chapter VIII of *Past, Present and Future*. The first, 'Identifiable Individuals', appeared in the *Review of Metaphysics*, Vol. 13, No. 4 (June 1960), pp. 684–96. The puzzle about creation out of nothing which forms one of its central topics had been earlier discussed in 'Creation in Science and Theology', in the astronomical journal *Southern Stars*, Vol. 18, No. 4 (December 1959), and the notion of 'logical illusion', which is brought in incidentally, is more fully discussed in 'On a Family of Paradoxes', *Notre Dame Journal of Formal Logic*, Vol. 2, No. 1 (1961), pp. 16–32.

The second paper in this group, entitled 'Time, Existence, and Identity', appeared in the *Proceedings of the Aristotelian Society* for 1965–6, pp. 183–92, and concerns a problem ('Can one thing become two?') which I had discussed earlier in 'Opposite Number', *Review of Metaphysics*, Vol. 2, No. 2 (December 1957), pp. 196–201.

Many of the more formal pieces that follow begin from E.J. Lemmon's 'stratified' version of the logic of tenses, in which we first develop a calculus which does not reflect any special assumptions about the earlier-later relation, and on this we superimpose further postulates which reflect whatever special assumptions about that relation we may regard as true or interesting. This technique is fairly straightforwardly illustrated in Paper X, 'Recent Advances in Tense Logic' which first appeared in the *Monist*, Vol. 53 (1969), pp. 325–39, and Paper XII,[2] 'The Logic of Ending Time', which first appeared in the first edition of this book. I have appended to it, as a note, a correction which first appeared in a note entitled 'Time and Change', in *Ratio*, Vol. 10 (1968), pp. 173–7. Modifications of Lemmon's technique to cope with certain special problems are developed in Paper XIII, 'Stratified Metric Tense Logic', which first appeared in *Theoria*, Vol. 33 (1967), No. 1, pp. 28–38; and Paper XIV, 'Now', which first appeared in *Noûs*, Vol. 2, No. 2 (May 1968), pp. 101–20, though I give it here with modifications first mentioned in '"Now" Corrected and Condensed', *Noûs*, Vol. 2, No.

---

[2] *Editors' note.* In order to make sure that the idea of instants as propositions is presented properly before it is used, we have renumbered the paper 'Tense Logic and the Logic of Earlier and Later' as number XI. In consequence, the numbers (but not the order) of the 3 following papers have also been changed.

4.[3] The 'Now' paper offers a solution to some problems raised in Paper III.

Paper XII, 'The Logic of Ending Time', also expounds in passing the view (my own, not Lemmon's, and first adumbrated in Appendix B of *Past, Present and Future*) that the logic of the earlier-later relation is something to be embedded in tense logic rather than vice versa. This reversal is the main topic of Paper XI, 'Tense Logic and the Logic of Earlier and Later' (first published in the first edition of this book). Here I move through a succession of calculi in which tense logic is first dominated by the theory of the earlier-later relation and then progressively 'takes over'.

In Paper XV, 'Tensed Propositions as Predicates', first published in the *American Philosophical Quarterly*, Vol. 6 (1969), pp. 290–7, I move through the same series of calculi, but present them in a new way in which the dominance of the theory of the earlier-later relation is maintained throughout. This is a non-polemical paper in which my aim is to do the best I can for the opponents of my own point of view, i.e. for those who hold that tensed propositions are not genuine propositions at all, but mere predicates which are tenselessly attachable to instants. The same is true, in a different way, of the three papers which follow – Paper XVI, 'Quasi-propositions and Quasi-individuals', which first appeared in the first edition of this book; Paper XVII, 'Egocentric Logic', which first appeared in *Noûs*, Vol. 2, No. 3 (1968), pp. 191–207; and Paper XVIII, 'Worlds, Times and Selves', which first appeared in *L'Age de la Science*, No. 3 (1969), pp. 179–91. In this group of papers, I concede that there is a way of treating not only predicates attachable to instants but any predicates at all as if they were complete propositions. The resulting 'logic of selfhood' is one which some philosophers might well wish to use in formalizing a broadly idealistic point of view which I would myself repudiate. I might repeat here what I said in *Past, Present and Future*, p. 59, about the formal logician's job being rather like that of a lawyer; he has to help philosophers of all kinds – not only his own – to make as good and clear a case as they can. These three papers (on the logic of selfhood) are not very technical, and would have been placed in the 'informal' group had they not depended so heavily on the two which immediately precede them. The second and third of them,

---

[3] *Editors' note.* Prior's amalgamation of the two texts has not been found. But the editors have incorporated the corrections suggested by Prior.

however, each finish with brief developments of new formal calculi, which have turned out since I produced them to have some mathematical interest.

Paper XIX, 'Tense Logic for Non-permanent Existents' (which first appeared in the first edition of this book) is mainly about technicalities, but is also heavily laden metaphysically. In it, I detect substantial and questionable metaphysical assumptions even in Lemmon's 'non-committal' basis for tense logic, and make suggestions for its revision. The philosophical motivation for this revision of Lemmon's basic system is connected with the problems about individuality and existence raised in Paper VII and at the end of Papers I and XVI, and discussed more fully in Chapter VIII of *Past, Present and Future*.

In Paper XX, 'Modal Logic and the Logic of Applicability', first published in *Theoria*, Vol. 34 (1968), pp. 183–202, I consider whether tensed propositions can still be treated as predicates of instants even when they are given this more complicated logic, and conclude that as far as tensed *propositional* logic is concerned they can, though only if we adopt a somewhat non-standard predicate logic, which however can be independently justified. But as far as tensed *predicate* logic is concerned this move does not seem to work.

I wish to thank the editors of *L'Age de la Science*, *American Philosophical Quarterly*, *Analysis*, *Australasian Journal of Philosophy*, *Noûs*, *Philosophy*, *Proceedings of the Aristotelian Society*, *Ratio*, *Review of Metaphysics*, and *Theoria*, and the Philosophy Department of the University of Kansas, for permission to republish the papers originally published by them.

This collection is dedicated to the memory of Edward John Lemmon, who died in July 1966 in California, at the age of 36.

A.N.P.
Oxford, 1969

I
CHANGES IN EVENTS AND CHANGES IN THINGS

The basic question to which I wish to address myself in this lecture is simply the old one, does time really flow or pass? The problem, of course, is that genuine flowing or passage is something which occurs *in* time, and *takes* time to occur. If time itself flows or passes, must there not be some 'super-time' in which it does so? Again, whatever flows or passes does so at some *rate*, but a rate of flow is just the amount of movement in a given *time*, so how could there be a rate of flow of time itself? And if time does not flow at any rate, how can it flow at all?

A natural first move towards extricating ourselves from these perplexities is to admit that talk of the flow or passage of time is just a metaphor. Time may be, as Isaac Watts says, *like* an ever-rolling stream, but it isn't really and literally an ever-rolling stream. But *how* is it like an ever-rolling stream? What is the literal truth behind this metaphor? The answer to this is not, at first sight, difficult. Generally when we make such remarks as 'Time does fly, doesn't it? – why, it's already the 16th', we mean that some date or moment which we have been looking forward to as future, has ceased to be future and is now present and on its way into the past. Or more fundamentally, perhaps, some future *event* to which we have been looking forward with hope or dread is now at last occurring, and soon will have occurred, and will have occurred a longer and longer time *ago*. We might say, for example, 'Time does fly, I'm already 47' that is, my birth is already that much past, 'and soon I shall be 48', i.e. it will be more past still. Suppose we speak about something 'becoming more past' not only when it moves from the comparatively near past to the comparatively distant past, but also when it moves from the present to the past, from the future to the present, and from the comparatively distant future to the comparatively near future. Then whatever is happening, has happened, or will happen is all the time 'becoming more past' in this extended sense; and just this is what we mean by the flow or passage of time. And if we want to give the *rate* of this flow or passage, it is surely very simple – it takes one exactly a year to get a year older, i.e. events become more past at the rate of a year per year, an hour per hour, a second per second.

Does this remove the difficulty? It is far from obvious that it does. It's not just that an hour per hour is a queer sort of rate – *this* queerness, I think, has been exaggerated, and I shall say more about it in a minute – but the whole idea of events changing is at first sight a little strange, even if we abandon the admittedly figurative description of this change as a *movement*. By and large, to judge by the way that we ordinarily talk, it's *things* that change, and events don't change but *happen*. Chairs, tables, horses, people change – chairs get worn out and then mended, tables get dirty and then clean again, horses get tired and then refreshed, people learn things and forget them, or are happy and then miserable, active and then sleepy, and so on, and all these are changes, and chairs, tables, horses and people are all what I mean by things as opposed to events. An accident, a coronation, a death, a prizegiving, are examples of what we'd call events, and it does seem unnatural to describe these as changing – what these do, one is inclined to say, is not to change but to happen or occur.

One of the things that make us inclined to deny that events undergo changes is that events *are* changes – to say that such and such an event has occurred is generally to say that some thing has, or some things have, changed in some way. To say, for instance, that the retirement of Sir Anthony Eden occurred in such and such a year is just to say that Sir Anthony then retired and so suffered the change or changes that retirement consists in – he had been Prime Minister, and then was not Prime Minister. Sir Anthony's retirement is or was a change concerning Sir Anthony; to say that it itself changes or has changed sounds queer because it sounds queer to talk of a change changing.

This queerness, however, is superficial. When we reflect further we realize that changes do change, especially if they go on for any length of time. (In this case we generally, though not always, call the change a *process* rather than an event, and there are other important differences between events and processes besides the length of time they take, but these differences are not relevant to the present discussion, so I shall ignore them and discuss changes generally, events and processes alike.) Changes do change – a movement, for example, may be slow at first and then rapid, a prizegiving or a lecture may be at first dull and afterwards interesting, or vice versa, and so on. It would hardly be too much to say that modern science began when people became accustomed to the idea of changes changing, e.g. to the idea of acceleration as opposed to simple motion. I've no doubt the ordinary measure of acceleration, so many feet per second per second, sounded queer when it was first used, and I think it still sounds queer to most students when they first encounter it. Ordinary speech is still resistant to it, and indeed to the expression of anything in the nature of a comparison of a comparison. We are taught at school that 'more older', for example, is bad English, but why shouldn't I say that I am more older than my son than he is than my daughter? And if we have learned to talk of an acceleration of a foot per second per second without imagining that the second 'second' must somehow be a different kind of 'second' from the first one – without imagining that if motion takes place in ordinary time, acceleration must take place in some super-time – can we not accustom ourselves equally to a change of 'a second per second' without any such imagining?

Changes do change, then, but this does not leave everything quite simple and solved. For there's still something odd about the change that we describe figuratively as the flow or passage of time – the change from an event's being future to its being present, and from its being present to its being more and more past. For the other changes in events which I have mentioned are ones which go on in the event *while it is occurring*; for example, if a lecture gets duller or a movement faster then this is something it does *as it goes on*; but the change from past to still further past isn't one that occurs while the event is occurring, for all the time that an event is occurring it isn't past but present, in fact the presentness of an event just *is* its happening, its occurring, as opposed to its merely having happened or being merely about to happen. We might put it this way: the things that change are *existing* things, and it's while they exist that they change, e.g. it's existing men, not non-existent men, that get tired and then pick up again; Julius Caesar, for example, isn't now getting tired and picking up again, unless the doctrine of immortality is true and he exists now as much as he ever did. And such changes as the change in the rate of movement are similarly changes that go on in events or processes while they exist, that is, while they exist in the only sense in which events and processes do exist, namely while they are occurring. But getting more and more past seems to be something an event does when it *doesn't* exist, and this seems very queer indeed.

We may retrace our steps to this point by looking at some of the literature of our subject. Professor C.D. Broad, in the second volume of his *Examination of McTaggart's Philosophy*, says that the ordinary view that an event, say the death of Queen Anne, is in the indefinitely distant future and then less and less future and then present and then goes into the more and more distant past – this ordinary story, Broad says, cannot possibly be true because it takes the death of Queen Anne to be at once a mere momentary thing and something with an indefinitely long history. We can make a first answer to this by distinguishing between the history that an event *has*, and the bit of history that it *is*. The bit of history that Queen Anne's death is, or was, is a very very short bit, but that doesn't prevent the history that it has from being indefinitely long. Queen Anne's death is part of the history of Queen Anne, and a very short part of it; what is long is not this part of the history of Queen Anne, but rather the history of this part of her history – the history of this part of her history is that first it was future, then it was present, and so on, and this can be a long history even if the bit of history that it is the history *of* is very short. There is not, therefore, the flat contradiction that Broad suggests here. There is, however, the difficulty that we generally think of the history of a thing as the sum of what it does and what happens to it *while it is there* – when it ceases to be, its history has ended – and this does make it seem odd that there should be an indefinitely long history of something which itself occupies a time which is indefinitely short.

But if there is a genuine puzzle here, it concerns what is actually going on also. For whatever goes on for any length of time – and that means: whatever goes on – will have future and past phases as well as the immediately present one; its going on is in fact a continual passage of one phase after another from being future through being present to being past. Augustine's reflections, in the eleventh chapter of his *Confessions*, on the notion of a 'long time', are relevant here. Just when, he asks, is a long time long? Is it long when it is present, or when it is past or future? We need not, I think, attach much importance to the fact that Augustine concentrates on so abstract a thing as a 'time' or an interval; his problems can be quite easily re-stated in terms of *what goes on* over the interval; in fact he himself slips into this, and talks about his childhood, a future sunrise and so on. When, we may ask, does a process go on for a long time – while it is going on, or when it lies ahead of us, or is all over?

Augustine is at first driven to the view that it is when it is present that a time is long, for only what *is* can be long or short (paragraph 18). We can give the same answer with processes – it is when they are going on that they go on for a long time. But then, as Augustine points out, there are these phases. A hundred years is a long time, but it's not really present all at once, and even if we try to boil down the present to an hour, 'that one hour passes away in flying particles'. 'The present hath no space' (20). Augustine had apparently not heard of the 'specious present', but even if he had it would not have helped him much – most of the happenings we are interested in take longer than that. He tries out the hypotheses that the past and the future, and past and future events, in some sense after all 'are' – that there is some 'secret place' where they exist all the time, and from which they come and to which they go. If there is no such place, then where do those who foresee the future and recall the past, discern these things? 'For that which is not, cannot be seen' (22).

Well, Augustine says, he doesn't know anything about that, but one thing that he does know is that wherever 'time past and to come' may 'be', 'they are not there as future, or past, but present. For if there also they be future, they are not yet there; if there also they be past, they are no longer there. Wheresoever then is whatsoever is, it is only as present' (23). Of course there are present 'traces' or images of past things in our memories, and present signs and intentions on the basis of which we make our future forecasts (23, 24), and sometimes Augustine seems satisfied with this – past, present, and future, he says, 'do exist in some sort, in the soul, but otherwhere do I not see them' (26). But sometimes he seems far from content with this – *that which* we remember and anticipate, he says, is different from these signs, and is *not* present (23, 24) – and, one must surely add, is *not* 'in the soul'.

It is time now to be constructive, and as a preparation for this I shall indulge in what may seem a digression, on the subject of Grammar. English philosophers who visit the United States are always asked sooner or later whether they are 'analysts'. I'm not at all sure what the answer is in my own case, but there's another word that Professor Passmore once invented to describe some English philosophers who are often called 'analysts', namely the word 'grammaticist', and that's something I wouldn't at all mind calling myself. I don't deny that there are genuine metaphysical problems, but I think you have to talk about grammar at least a little bit in order to solve most of them. And in particular, I would want to maintain that most of the present group of problems about time and change, though not quite all of them, arise from the fact that many expressions which look like nouns, i.e. names of objects, are not really nouns at all but concealed verbs, and many expressions which look like verbs are not really verbs but concealed conjunctions and adverbs. That is a slight over-simplification, but before we can get it stated more accurately we must look more closely at verbs, conjunctions, and adverbs.

I shall assume that we are sufficiently clear for our present purposes as to what a noun or name is, and what a sentence is; and given these notions, we can define a verb or verb-phrase as an expression that constructs a sentence out of a name or names. For instance, if you tack the verb 'died' on the name 'Queen Anne' you get the sentence 'Queen Anne died', and if you tack the phrase 'is an undertaker' on the name 'James Bowels' you get the sentence 'James Bowels is an undertaker', so that this is a verb-phrase. I say 'out of a name *or names*' because some verbs have to have an object as well as a subject. Thus if you put the verb 'loves' between the names 'Richard' and 'Joan' you get the sentence 'Richard loves Joan'; this verb constructs this sentence out of these two names; and the phrase 'is taller than' would function similarly. Logicians call verbs and verb-phrases 'predicates'; 'died' and 'is an undertaker' would be 'one-place' predicates, and 'loves' and 'is taller than' are 'two-place' predicates. There are also expressions which construct sentences, not out of names, but out of other sentences. If an expression constructs a sentence out of two or more other sentences it is a conjunction, or a phrase equivalent to a conjunction. For example 'Either – or –' functions in this way in 'Either it will rain or it will snow'. If the expression constructs a sentence out of one other sentence it is an adverb or adverbial phrase, like 'not' or 'It is not the case that' or 'allegedly' or 'It is alleged that', or 'possibly' or 'It is possible that'. Thus by attaching these expressions to 'It is raining' we obtain the sentences

> It is not raining;
> It is not the case that it is raining;
> It is allegedly raining;
> It is alleged that it is raining;
> It is possibly raining;
> It is possible that it is raining.

One very important difference between conjunctions and adverbs, on the one hand, and verbs, on the other, is that because the former construct sentences out of sentences, i.e. the same sort of thing as they end up with, they can be applied again and again to build up more and more complicated sentences, like 'It is allegedly possible that he will not come', which could be spread out as

It is said that (it is possible that (it is not the case that (he will come))).

You can also use the same adverb twice and obtain such things as double negation, alleged allegations and so on. Verbs, because they do not end up with the same sort of expression as what they start with, cannot be piled up in this way. Having constructed 'Queen Anne died' by the verb 'died' out of the name 'Queen Anne', you cannot do it again – 'Queen Anne died died' is not a sentence.

Turning now to our main subject, I want to suggest that putting a verb into the past or future tense is exactly the same sort of thing as adding an adverb to the sentence. 'I *was* having my breakfast' is related to 'I am having my breakfast' in exactly the same way as 'I am *allegedly* having my breakfast' is related to it, and it is only an historical accident that we generally form the past tense by modifying the present tense, e.g. by changing 'am' to 'was', rather than by tacking on an adverb. In a rationalized language with uniform constructions for similar functions we could form the past tense by prefixing to a given sentence the phrase 'It was the case that', or 'It has been the case that' (depending on what sort of past we meant), and the future tense by prefixing 'It will be the case that'. For example, instead of 'I will be eating my breakfast' we could say

'It will be the case that I am eating my breakfast',

and instead of 'I was eating my breakfast' we could say

'It was the case that I am eating my breakfast'.

The nearest we get to the latter in ordinary English is 'It was the case that I *was* eating my breakfast', but this is one of those anomalies like emphatic double negation. The construction I am sketching embodies the truth behind Augustine's suggestion of the 'secret place' where past and future times 'are', and his insistence that wherever they are, they are not there as past or future but as present. The past is not the present but it *is* the past present, and the future is not the present but it *is* the future present.

There is also, of course, the past future and the future past. For these adverbial phrases, like other adverbial phrases, can be applied repeatedly – the sentences to which they are attached do not have to be simple ones; it is enough that they be sentences, and they can be sentences which already have tense-adverbs, as we might call them, within them. Hence we can have such a construction as

> 'It will be that case that (it has been the case that (I am taking off my coat))',

or in plain English, 'I will have taken off my coat'. We can similarly apply repeatedly such *specific* tense-adverbs as 'It was the case forty-eight years ago that'. For example, we could have

> 'It will be the case seven months hence that (it was the case forty-eight years ago that (I am being born))',

that is, it will be my forty-eighth birthday in seven months' time.

To say that a change has occurred is to say at least this much: that something which was the case formerly is not the case now. That is, it is at least to say that for some sentence *p* we have

> It was the case that *p*, and it is not the case that *p*.

This sentence *p* can be as complicated as you like, and can itself contain tense-adverbs, so that one example of our formula would be

> It was the case 5 months ago that (it was the case only 47 years ago that (I am being born)), and it is not now the case that (it was the case only 47 years ago that (I am being born)),

that is, I am not as young as I used to be. This last change, of course, is a case of precisely that recession of events into the past that we are really talking about when we say that time flows or passes, and the piling of time-references on top of one another, with no suggestion that the time-words must be used in a different sense at each level, simply reflects the fact that tense-adverbs *are* adverbs, not verbs.

An important point to notice now is that while *I* have been talking about words – for example about verbs and adverbs – for quite a long time, the sentences that I have been using as examples have *not* been about words but about real things. When a sentence is formed out of another sentence or other sentences by means of an adverb or conjunction, it is not *about* those other sentences, but about whatever they are themselves about. For example, the compound sentence 'Either I will wear my cap or I will wear my beret' is not about the sentences 'I will wear my cap' and 'I will wear my beret'; like them, it is about me and my headgear, though the information it conveys about these is a little less definite than what either of them would convey separately. Similarly, the sentence 'It will be the case that I am having my tooth out' is not about the sentence 'I am having my tooth out'; it is about me. A genuine sentence about the sentence 'I am having my tooth out' would be one stating that it contained six words and nineteen letters, but 'It will be the case that I am having my tooth out', i.e. 'I will be having my tooth out', is quite obviously not a sentence of this sort at all.

Nor is it about some abstract entity named by the clause 'that I am having my tooth out'. It is about me and my tooth, and about nothing else whatever. The fact is that it is difficult for the human mind to get beyond the simple subject-predicate or noun-verb structure, and when a sentence or thought hasn't that structure but a more complex one we try in various ways to force it into the subject-predicate pattern. We thus invent new modes of speech in which the subordinate sentences are replaced by noun-phrases and the conjunctions or adverbs by verbs or verb-phrases. For example, instead of saying

(1)   *If* you have oranges in your larder you have been to the greengrocer's,

we may say

(2)   Your having oranges in your larder *implies* your having been to the greengrocer's,

which looks as if it has the same form as 'Richard loves Joan' except that 'Your having oranges in your larder' and 'Your having been to the grocer' seem to name more abstract objects than Richard and Joan, and implying seems a more abstract activity than loving. We can rid ourselves of this suggestion if we reflect that (2) is nothing more than a paraphrase of (1). Similarly

(3)   It is now six years since it was the case that I am falling out of a punt,

could be re-written as

(4)   My falling out of a punt has receded six years into the past.

This suggests that something called an event, my falling out of a punt, has gone through a performance called receding into the past, and moreover has been going through this performance even after it has ceased to exist, i.e. after it has stopped happening. But of course (4) is just a paraphrase of (3), and like (3) is not about any objects except me and that punt – there is no real reason to believe in the existence either now or six years ago of a further object called 'my falling out of a punt'.

What I am suggesting is that what looks like talk about events is really at bottom talk about things, and that what looks like talk about changes in events is really just slightly more complicated talk about changes in things. This applies *both* to the changes that we say occur in events when they are going on, like the change in speed of a movement ('movement' is a *façon de parler*; there is just the moving car, which moves more quickly than it did), *and* the changes that we say occur in events when they are not going on any longer, or not yet, e.g. my birth's receding into the past ('birth' is a *façon de parler* – there's just me being born, and then getting older).

It's not all quite as simple as this, however. This story works very well for me and my birth and my fall out of the punt, but what about Queen Anne? Does Queen Anne's death getting more past mean that *Queen Anne* has changed from having died 250 years ago to having died 251 years ago, or whatever the period is? – that *she* is still 'getting older', though in a slightly extended sense? The trouble with this, of course, is just that Queen Anne doesn't exist now any more than her death does. There are at least two different ways in which we might deal with this one. We might, in the first place, say that our statement really is about Queen Anne (despite the fact that she 'is no more'), and really is, or at least entails, a statement of the form

It was the case that p, and is not now the case that p,

namely

It was the case that it was the case only 250 years ago that Queen Anne is dying, and is not now the case that it was the case only 250 years ago that Queen Anne is dying,

but we may add that this statement does not record a 'change' in any natural sense of that word, and certainly not a change in Queen Anne. A genuine record of change, we could say, must not only be of the form above indicated but must meet certain further conditions which we might specify in various ways. And we could say that although what is here recorded *isn't* a change in the proper sense, it is *like* a change in fitting the above formula. The flow of time, we would then say, is merely metaphorical, not only because what is meant by it isn't a genuine change; but the force of the metaphor can still be explained – we use the metaphor because what we call the flow of time does fit the above formula. On this view it might be that not only the recession of Queen Anne's death but my own growing older will not count as a change in the strict sense, though growing older is normally *accompanied* by genuine changes, and the phrase is commonly extended to cover these – increasing wisdom, bald patches, and so on.

But can a statement really be *about* Queen Anne after she has ceased to be? I do not wish to dogmatize about this, but an alternative solution is worth mentioning. We might paraphrase 'Queen Anne has died' as 'Once there was a person named "Anne", who reigned over England, etc., but there is not now any such person'. This solution exploits a distinction which we may describe as one between *general facts* and *individual facts*. That someone has stolen my pencil is a general fact; that John Jones has stolen my pencil, if it is a fact at all, is an individual fact. It has often been said – for example, it was said by the Stoic logicians – that there are no general facts without there being the corresponding individual facts. It cannot, for example, be the case that 'someone' has stolen my pencil, unless it is the case that some specific individual – if not John Jones, then somebody else – has stolen it. And in cases of this sort the principle is very plausible, indeed it is obviously true. I have read that some of the schoolmen described the subject of sentences like 'someone has stolen my pencil' as an *individuum vagum*, but of course this is a makeshift – forcing things into a pattern again. There are no 'vague individuals', and if a pencil has been stolen at all it has been stolen not by a vague individual but by some quite definite one, or else by a number of such. There are vague statements, however, and vague thoughts, and the existence of such statements and thoughts is as much a fact about the real world as any other; and when we describe the making of such statements and the entertaining of such thoughts, we do encounter at least partly general facts to which no wholly individual facts correspond. If I allege or believe that someone has stolen my pencil, there may be *no* specific individual with respect to whom I allege or believe that *he* stole my pencil. There is *alleged or believed to be* an individual who stole it, but there is *no individual who is alleged or believed* to have stolen it (not even a vague one). So while it is a fact that I allege or believe that someone stole it, there is no fact of the form 'I allege (or believe) that X stole it'. The one fact that there is, is no doubt an individual fact in so far as it concerns me, but is irreducibly general as far as the thief is concerned. (There may indeed be *no* thief – I am perhaps mistaken about the whole thing – but this is another question; our present point is that there may be no one who is even said or thought to be a thief, though it is said or thought *that there is* a thief.)

Returning now to Queen Anne, what I am suggesting is that the sort of thing that we unquestionably do have with 'It is said that' and 'It is thought that', we also have with 'It will be the case that' and 'It was the case that'. It *was the case that someone* was called 'Anne', reigned over England, etc., even though *there is not now anyone* of whom it was the case that *she* was called 'Anne', reigned over England, etc. What we must be careful about here is simply getting our prefixes in the right order. Just as

(1)   I think that (for some specific X (X stole my pencil))

does not imply

(2)   For some specific X (I think that (X stole my pencil)),

so

(3)   It was the case that (for some specific X (X is called 'Anne',
        reigns over England, etc.))

does not imply

(4)   For some specific X (it was the case that (X is called 'Anne',
        reigns over England, etc.)).

On this view, the fact that Queen Anne has been dead for some years is
not, in the strict sense of 'about', a fact about Queen Anne; it is not a
fact about anyone or anything – it is a *general* fact. Or if it is about
anything, what it is about is not Queen Anne – it is about the earth,
maybe, which has rolled around the sun so many times since there was a
person who was called 'Anne', reigned over England, etc. (It would
then be a *partly* general fact – individual in so far as it concerns the
earth, but irreducibly general as far as the dead queen is concerned. But
if there are – as there undoubtedly are – irreducibly partly general facts,
could there not be irreducibly wholly general ones?) Note, too, that the
fact that this fact is not about Queen Anne, cannot itself be a fact about
Queen Anne – its statement needs rephrasing in some such way as
'There is no person who was called "Anne", etc., and about whom it is a
fact that, etc.'
    On this view, the recession of Queen Anne's death into the further
past is quite decidedly not a change in Queen Anne, not because we are
using 'change' in so tight a sense that it is not a change at all, but
because Queen Anne doesn't herself enter into this recession, or indeed,
now, into any fact whatever. But the recession *is* still a change or quasi-
change in the sense that it fits the formula 'It was the case that p, but is
not now the case that p' – this formula continues to express what is
common to the flow of a literal river on the one hand (where it was the
case that such-and-such drops were at a certain place, and this is the
case no longer) and the flow of time on the other.

II
FUGITIVE TRUTH

I have argued elsewhere[1] that present-tensed utterances, and tensed utterances generally, do not normally refer to themselves, and therefore not to the time of their own utterance, or at all events do not refer to the time of their utterance *as* the time of their utterance. It is nevertheless necessary to refer to the time of their utterance when we are not *using* but *mentioning* such sentences, and discussing their truth-conditions. For example, the sentence 'I am about to go home', or 'I am now about to go home', is true if and only if the person who utters it *is* about to go home at the time at which he utters it.

In this connexion, some curious puzzles have been raised by Dr. A. J. Kenny.[2] One is that it would seem to be impossible to utter any true sentence reporting, in the present tense, an instantaneous event. For the utterance of a sentence always takes some finite time, and during part of the time when we say, e.g., 'Eclipse is now just past the winning-post', Eclipse will *not* be *just* past the winning-post but an appreciable distance past it. Moreover, Kenny has pointed out, if 'Eclipse *was* just past the winning post' is to be analysed as 'It was the case that Eclipse *is* just past the winning post', and 'It was the case that *p*' in general *is* true if and only if *p was* true, then even 'Eclipse *was* just past the winning-post' cannot ever be true either.

There are two points to be made here. In the first place, 'It was the case that Eclipse is just past, *etc.*' is not *about* the sentence 'Eclipse is just past, *etc.*' but is, rather, a more complicated sentence about Eclipse. And the rule for its truth is not the one just given, but rather that 'It was the case that *p*' is true if and only if it was the case that *p*; and we may be able to say this truly even if we can never say truly that *p* (not because it is never the case that *p* but because saying that *p* takes too long). The relation between the complex and the simple sentence could be like that between 'For some *x*, I have never said anything about *x*', and some specific sentence of the form 'I have never said anything

---

[1] See, e.g., *Past, Present and Future*, pp. 10–15.
[2] In commenting, at a meeting in 1967, on my paper 'Tense Logic and the Logic of Earlier and Later', this volume pp. 117–38.

about x' – any such specific sentence is self-refuting, yet its existential generalisation could be, and in fact is, perfectly true.

However, we need not admit that even the present-tense 'Eclipse is just past the post' can never be uttered with truth. Kenny's puzzle is a variant of one which bothered some medieval writers, e.g. Buridan. It would seem, Buridan pointed out, that a self-contradictory sentence, e.g. 'Socrates is sitting down and Socrates is not sitting down', may very well be true since Socrates may be sitting down while we utter the first part of it but may stand up while we utter the second part[3,4]. It is clear that we need to make our conventions a little more explicit at this point. We understand a sentence as being true if and only if what it says is the case *throughout* the time when it is being uttered, or if and only if what it says is the case at *some* instant within the period of its utterance, or if and only if what it says is the case at the *last* moment of its utterance, or if and only if what it says is the case at the *first* moment of its utterance – or, if its utterance has no first moment or no last one, if and only if what it says is the case at the last moment before it begins, or at the first moment after it ends. If the sentence contains the word 'now', and is supposed true if things are as it says they are while 'now' is being said, exactly the same problems arise, since even 'now' takes some time to say; and there are the same alternative solutions. It is in general best to avoid the first suggested conventions, since either of them, when we adopt it for a given sentence, forces the other on us for its negation. There is in fact no satisfactory way of referring in the present tense to a temporal boundary (which is what an instantaneous event always is) except *by* a temporal boundary. And even with this there are ambiguities – must the sentence cease leaving the man's mouth, or must it begin entering the hearer's ear (or his consciousness), just as the horse ceases passing the post? However we decide this point, it will be by good luck

---

[3] Buridan, *Sophismata*, Ch. 7, Soph. 4.

[4] *Editors' note*. Buridan made a distinction between two kinds of negation. The statement 'S is non-P' is true if and only if it is not the case that 'S is P' is true throughout every part of the present, whereas the statement 'S is not P' is true if and only if it is not the case that 'S is P' is true throughout any part of the present. If the statement 'Socrates is sitting down and Socrates is not sitting down' should be counted as true in Buridan's context, it should be read as 'Socrates is sitting down and Socrates is not-sitting-down'.

as well as good management that the speaker gets it exactly right, if he does. But it is not *impossible* that he should do so.

These solutions, with all their disadvantages, are not unnatural or *ad hoc*; they are the ones we adopt when we are confronted with Kenny's problem in practical life, e.g. in giving a running commentary on a race. And the problem *is* one that arises in practical life: it is not a pseudo-problem generated by an eccentric view about the relations between truth and time.

But there is a similar problem, Kenny has observed, about the validity of inferences. Suppose we run through the following *modus ponens* aloud, with Socrates before us:

> If Socrates is sitting, he is not standing
> Socrates is sitting
> Therefore Socrates is not standing.

The first premiss is true at all times, and the second might be true because Socrates is sitting at the last moment of its utterance; yet the conclusion might be false because Socrates *is* standing at the last moment of *its* utterance. This is again a type of puzzle which was not unknown to medieval logicians, who were tempted to say that an inference is valid if and only if its premisses cannot all be true and its conclusion false, but who resisted this temptation precisely because of exceptions of the sort mentioned by Kenny. One rather nice example given by Buridan is this:

> Om-nis sy-la-ba est plu-res lit-te-rae
> (Every syllable consists of several letters)
> Ergo, Nul-la syl-la-ba est u-ni-ca lit-te-ra
> (Therefore no syllable consists of a single letter).[5]

Here the premiss, when uttered, is true (if understood as referring to syllables in the argument), but the conclusion, when uttered, is false, since it contains the one-lettered syllable *u* in *unica*. Again, he supposes God to make the premiss 'All sentences are affirmative' true by annihilating all negative ones, and then some logician spoils His good work by drawing, and enunciating, the conclusion 'No sentence is

[5] Buridan, *Sophismata*, Ch. 8, Soph. 1.

negative'. Buridan's solution is to add to the definition of validity the proviso 'with the premiss and conclusion *simul formatis*'. This is a somewhat unrealistic provision; with spoken arguments in particular, the premiss and conclusion never *are* completed simultaneously. But for other reasons Buridan considers that the definition of validity needs more radical revision anyway. It must be changed at least to: An inference is valid if and only if things cannot (at any time) be as its premisses say they are without at the same time being as its conclusion says they are.

My own answer would be that logic is not really about inference but about implication, i.e. about the truths that make inferences valid, and that in leaving pure logic for applied, as we do when we use an implication to guide an inference, it needs to be observed that, if our inference is not to lead us astray, the state of affairs we are arguing about must not alter while we are arguing about it. Since most of our arguments, when they are not about what does not alter anyway, are about what has happened before the argument started or will happen after it ends, this proviso seldom bothers us. But a semantics which studies the truth-conditions of written or spoken sentence tokens, and the conditions under which arguments involving these are safe or valid, is bound to notice these complications; it was one of the merits of medieval semantics that it did not ignore them.

There is, however, a genuine difficulty, which I do not know how to solve, about the representation of past-tense facts as the former being-the-case of the present tense ones. Since the present is an instant, the only past-tense facts which we can represent by 'It was the case that *p*' or 'It has been the case that *p*', where *p* is in the present tense, are facts about what was the case at an instant or a succession of instants. This covers much more than the strictly instantaneous, i.e. what is the case at one instant only, or at an instant but not at any neighbouring instant. Whatever *goes on for* a period of time can be fitted into this pattern, since it *is going on at* each instant in the period. But what *takes* time eludes this representation. Consider such simple examples as 'I gave a lecture', 'I ate my breakfast', 'I went to London', or simply 'I moved'. It makes no sense to speak of these as referring to what was the case at an instant, and it seems to me implausible to represent what is here stated as somehow constructed out of what was the case at a succession of instants. I can indeed *be moving* (eating, lecturing) at an instant, and I can therefore say 'It was the case that I am moving (eating, lecturing)', i.e. that I am in the course of or in a state or condition of moving (eating, lecturing); but these forms seem to be parasitic on the others. It is, in short, not what is the case at an instant, but what most signally and irreducibly is not, that presents the hardest problem for the tense-logician.

III
ON SPURIOUS EGOCENTRICITY

1. It is frequently said that words like 'now', 'then', 'ago', 'present', 'past', 'future', and the various indications of tense, are 'egocentric' or 'token-reflexive' in character. I want to suggest, on the contrary, that the apparent egocentricity or token-reflexiveness of this class of expression is deceptive. It is perhaps not easy to see how on a point of this sort deception is possible, but a parallel case may make the position clearer.

2. The 108th of the 'Miscellaneous Examples for the Exercise of Learners' appended to Whately's *Elements of Logic* runs as follows: 'He who believes himself to be always in the right in his opinion, lays claim to infallibility: you always believe yourself to be in the right in your opinion: therefore you lay claim to infallibility.' What we are intended to say about this is clearly that as a syllogism it is invalid through having four terms, 'believing oneself to be always in the right' (in the major) being a different thing from 'always believing oneself to be in the right' (in the minor); but the fact that these are different is itself a fact of some significance. It is not possible to believe anything seriously without believing that this believed thing is the case, or is true; nor can one person *A* sincerely agree with another person *B* on any matter, or sincerely pronounce *B*'s opinions to be true or right in this matter, unless *B*'s opinions coincide with his own – this sharing of *B*'s opinions or supposed opinions is a *sine qua non* of sincerity on this point, i.e. of not only saying but thinking and believing that what *B* believes is the case or is true. To that extent the phrases 'It is true that ...' and 'It is the case that ...' could well be described as 'egocentric' expressions. Yet it seems perfectly clear that this implicit reference to the opinions of the speaker is an 'inseparable accident' of the use of these phrases rather than part and parcel of their meaning. 'It is the case that *p*' just does not mean 'It is my opinion that *p*'; and 'You are right in thinking that *p*' just does not mean 'It is not only your opinion that *p*, but mine also'. For a man can unquestionably use the expression 'It is the case' and 'You are right' sincerely and seriously without for a minute imagining that he himself is always right and never wrong in his opinions (as he would have to if he thought that 'being right' simply meant 'being believed by him'). In the terms of Whately's example, 'always believing oneself to

be in the right' (i.e. in what one believes at the time) is inevitable, but if
this were because 'in the right' meant 'believed by me', then 'believing
oneself to be always in the right' would be equally inevitable; but it
isn't.

It has been often observed in this connexion that although there is a
certain absurdity in a person's saying 'I believe that grass is green but of
course it isn't really', there is no absurdity in another person's saying
about the first one 'He believes that grass is green but it isn't really'.
This difference between 'I' and 'he' in a way strengthens the temptation
to equate the meaning of 'true' with that of 'believed by me', and of
'really' with 'in my opinion'. For if we think of it this way, the
difference is easily explainable – 'I believe that grass is green but it isn't
really so' reduces to the simple contradiction 'I believe it is and I don't
believe it is', while 'He believes that it is but it isn't really' reduces to
'He believes that it is but I don't', where the contradiction disappears
through the two parts of the conjunction having different subjects. But
of course this explanation won't do – 'I believe that grass is green but it
isn't really' isn't a simple contradiction because it could quite easily
happen to be true (it would be if the observer's 'he' statement were).

There is, too, a three-   valuedness about 'believed by me' that there
isn't about 'true'. Just as I cannot sincerely pronounce a thing true, or
agree with it, without believing it, so I cannot sincerely pronounce it
false, or disagree with it, unless I disbelieve it. But what is not believed
by me is not always disbelieved by me – I might have no opinion about
it at all, might in fact never have thought about it. What is not true,
however, is false (at least where it makes sense to talk of 'truth' at all).

An egocentric theory of truth, based on the facts adduced above,
would surely be a simple *hysteron proteron*. I think true only those
opinions with which I agree, not because this agreement is what 'truth'
means, but on the contrary because 'agreeing with X' means thinking
true what X thinks true. And the absurdity of 'I believe that grass is
green but it isn't really' lies not in simple self-contradiction but in the
fact that such a statement can only be true if its utterance is insincere,
meaning by an 'insincere' utterance one in which the speaker asserts
either something that he does not believe or the contradictory of
something that he does believe. If, in the given case, he really does
believe that grass is green (so that the first clause of his utterance is
true), and it really isn't (so that the second clause is also true), he is
insincere because in saying (truly) that it isn't he contradicts his

(admitted and genuine) belief that it is. The outsider, of course, can report the two facts without either falsehood or insincerity.

3. There is another theory of truth which is sometimes confused with the egocentric theory, and does share with it an appearance of mild scepticism, but which is in fact totally different. I mean what is sometimes called the 'no-truth' theory of Ramsey and Ayer – the theory that 'It is true that grass is green', 'It is the case that grass is green', 'Grass is really green', all just amount to 'Grass is green'. There is certainly at least complete mutual entailment between these forms, and interchangeability without change of truth-value in most contexts that I can think of, including *oratio obliqua* – there is not only no difference in logical force between the propositions just cited, but none, either, between 'It is true that he believes that grass is green', 'He believes that grass is green', and 'He believes that it is true that grass is green'. The allegedly equivalent 'I believe that' will not preserve its vacuity in these contexts – 'I believe that he believes that grass is green' need not have the same truth-value as the plain 'He believes that grass is green', and still more certainly neither of these need have the same truth-value as 'He believes that I believe that grass is green'. (I say 'still more certainly' because I cannot at the time of saying them discriminate both sincerely and with truth between the first two statements, I mean distinguish them as the one true and the other false, but I can certainly thus discriminate between either of them and the third.)

One might put the 'no-truth' theory in a technical context thus: in certain symbolic systems a variable, say 'd', is used to stand indifferently for any expression which constructs a statement out of a statement, e.g. 'It is not the case that ...', 'Grass is green and ...', 'If ... then grass is green', 'It is possible that ...', 'Aristotle asserted that ...'. Thus 'd (The sky is blue)' can stand indifferently for 'It is not the case that the sky is blue', 'Grass is green and the sky is blue', 'If the sky is blue then grass is green', and so on. In expressing logical generalizations by means of such variables it is useful to include 'The sky is blue' itself, without any adornments, as being among the things that 'd (The sky is blue)' can stand for. But here there is no actual expression that has been put in the place of 'd', and we tend to feel that this is awkward. The awkwardness, if we are really worried about it, can be relieved by simply introducing an actual expression which when put for 'd' in 'd (The sky is blue)' will yield a sentence meaning no more

and no less than the plain 'The sky is blue'. If we used 'It is the case that
...' or 'It is true that ...' or 'really' or 'truly' in this way, this would be
precisely its commonest use in ordinary English.

4. There is, indeed, one common sense of 'truly' that does add
something to what is said, namely when it means 'correctly', as when
we say that someone believes (or says) truly (or with truth) that grass is
green. This certainly says more than merely that the man believes or
says the thing. But the difference doesn't refute the 'no-truth' theory,
since we can explain what 'truly' adds here, and eliminate the word
itself, by translating the remark as 'He believes that grass is green, and it
is' (and similarly with 'says'). Just as 'Truly p' or 'It is true (the case)
that p' seems a mere inflation of the plain 'p', so 'X believes (says) truly
that p, and p' seems to mean no more and no less than 'X believes (says)
that p, and p'. And the problem of eliminating 'true' from statements
like 'Everything that John believes is true', i.e. 'Whatever John believes
he believes truly (correctly)', seems completely solved by translating it
in Ramsey's manner as 'For all p, if John believes that p then p'.

It is perhaps less misleading to describe this 'no-truth' theory as the
'adverbial' theory, for it proceeds basically by giving a simple account
of 'truly' (in the two related senses that it has in 'Truly p' and in 'He
says truly that p'), and assumes that locutions in which 'true' appears as
an adjective are dispensable variations of forms in which it occurs only
as part of an adverb or adverbial phrase. It is a 'pseudo-adjective' that
can be attached with sense only to 'pseudo-nouns', namely 'that'-
clauses and their equivalents, and to 'pseudo-descriptions' like 'what X
thinks'. It has indeed been given a use, as by Tarski, as a genuine
adjective attaching to genuine nouns which designate sentences, i.e.
physical inscriptions; but this use is a highly artificial one, and need not
be considered here. And it is worth observing that Tarski himself, in
addition to his definitions of 'true sentence', has given some attention to
a function $as(p)$ which has precisely the properties of Ramsey's 'It is
true that p' (*Logic, Semantics and Metamathematics*, p. 3).

5. At almost all these points the parallel with 'now' and 'present' seems
as complete as any such parallel can be. Certainly if I say that some
process or other is 'present' or that it is 'going on now', I will be right if
and only if it is going on contemporaneously with my utterance. That is,
what is present when I say it is, is always contemporaneous with my

saying it. But this, it seems to me, is not at all because this is what 'being present' means, but on the contrary because 'contemporaneous with X' means 'present when X is present' ('going on when X is going on').

As an analogue of the sophism in Whately's exercise, we might construct this one: What is always contemporaneous with whatever is happening, must go on for ever; but always my utterances are contemporaneous with whatever is happening; therefore I never stop talking. It is bound to be true, in view of what 'contemporaneous' means, that whatever utterances are occurring (and indeed whatever events of any sort are occurring) are occurring contemporaneously with whatever is occurring. And not only is this true now but it always has been and always will be – whoever says, not only now but at any time, 'Whatever is occurring, e.g. my own talking, is contemporaneous with whatever is occurring' will say this with truth. But it by no means follows, nor is it in general true, that if I select some present occurrence A and say of it that at any time when any occurrence B was going on and was present, the one that I have selected was going on and was present contemporaneously with B.

'Was going on' and 'was present' – note these phrases. The presentness of an event can itself become past, in fact automatically does so when the event in question does. And even the *material* equivalence of 'present' and 'contemporaneous with this utterance' does not survive changes of tense (just as the material equivalence, at least in the view of the believer, of 'true' and 'believed by me' does not survive embedding in *oratio obliqua*). 'His eating his breakfast is a present fact' is true when and only when 'His eating his breakfast is contemporary with this utterance' is true; but the same cannot be said of 'His eating his breakfast was a present fact' and 'His eating his breakfast was contemporaneous with this utterance' (which is only true if the utterance is one that has gone on without interruption since whenever it was that he was eating his breakfast). (Cf. our parallel to the Whately problem.)

Again, just as there must surely be many truths which no one believes (unless it be God) and no one disbelieves, since no one has thought of them, so surely things like the solidifying of the earth were future and became present and then became past – were about to happen and then happened and then had happened – without anybody saying so or being there to say so, i.e. without there being any utterances for them to be contemporaneous with or earlier or later than. It was remarked by

McTaggart (*The Nature of Existence*, ch. xxxiii, § 313) that on the relative-to-utterance theory, 'if there were events earlier than any consciousness, those events would never be future or present, though they could be past', i.e. once consciousness, and utterances, had appeared (before then they couldn't be past either). This is surely, as McTaggart intended it to be, a sufficient *reductio ad absurdum* of this theory.

6. On the other hand, a 'no-present' theory analogous to the Ramsey-Ayer theory of truth has almost everything to be said for it. That is, 'He is eating his breakfast now' and 'He is eating his breakfast at present' seem to say no more and no less, apart from nuances of emphasis, than the plain 'He is eating his breakfast'. We can do without 'now', we can do without a present-tense copula 'is', we can do without even a special present-tense inflection of the main verb – just using the root verb-form itself, as in 'I eat' and 'They eat' in English – if we understand that this is what we have with us all the time – this is what the verb form basically means.

This equivalence of the 'presentness of the occurring of *X*' with the simple 'occurring of *X*' is preserved under tense inflection, in the way that the equivalence of 'presentness' with 'contemporaneity with this utterance' (as we saw earlier) is not so preserved. This point was remarked by Thomas Aquinas, in a comment on that curious passage in Aristotle's *De Interpretatione* (16^b 17–19) in which it is said that verbs in non-present tenses are not genuine verbs at all but only 'cases' of verbs, like the oblique cases of nouns. Thomas notes that some positive connexion with genuine verbs is still suggested by Aristotle's description, and finds this connexion in the fact that the present or presentness is indirectly referred to even in talk of past or future, for it is always a present that is past or future – 'est praeteritum quod fuit praesens, futurum autem quod erit praesens'. The same surely applies also on the other side of the 'tensing'; I mean, not only is pastness in all case past presentness, but it is also in all cases present pastness, and similarly with futurity. There are, indeed, past and future pastness too, and past and future futurity; it is just this that makes it worth saying that plain pastness and futurity are present pastness and futurity ('present' is the vacuous special case of temporal modification); but the equation given in the last sentence still holds, for past and future pastness are past and future present pastness, and past and future futurity are past and future present futurity. To put it another way: The verb *tout simple* is the present-tense verb, and this is true even if the verb in question is an auxiliary verb, with other verbs depending on it, and even if, out of the various auxiliaries there are, it happens to be 'has been' or 'will be'.

Nor do these two 'vacuity' or 'omnipresence' theories – the one about 'truly' and the one about the present – constitute a mere parallelism. They are in a sense the same theory – in the sense that they merely assert the vacuity of one and the same phrase, 'It is the case that ...' or 'It is true that ...', considered against different non-vacuous contrasting phrases. It is, on the one hand, the vacuous member of the pair of which the non-vacuous member is 'It is not the case that ...' or 'It is false that ...'. But it is also the vacuous member of a set of which other members are 'It has been the case that ...' (or 'It has been true that ...') and 'It will be the case that ...' (or 'It will be true that ...'), with variations like 'It used to be the case that ...', 'It was the case *x* hours ago that ...', etc. But the phrase 'It is the case (true) that ...' doesn't have different senses in these two settings. It carries tense with it – the present tense – just as much when it is being contrasted with 'It is not the case (is false) that ...' as when it is being contrasted with 'It has been that ...' or 'It will be that ...'. And conversely, it's no more than the same old 'multiply by one' business when we think of it as a tense-indication.

7. I have had, all the same, to express myself with caution at certain key points – I have said only that my parallel holds at 'almost' all points, and that the 'no-present' theory has 'almost' everything to be said for it. This has been necessary because colloquial English is not so streamlined as to fit in with the view I have sketched in all its uses of tense indicators. This admission is especially necessary with the simple 'now'. There are in fact uses of 'now' in which it really is synonymous with 'contemporaneously with this utterance', e.g. when the word is uttered in order to let someone know when to stop pouring water into one's whisky – here the actual utterance really has to be in the centre of one's consciousness. But this use of 'now' stands out so sharply from all its other uses that the very fact that the translation suits it is enough to show that it doesn't suit the others. But it is also unusual, it must be confessed, for 'now' to be directly dispensable with oblique tenses (as it ought to be by my account). We can drop it from 'He was now approaching the stairway' and from 'You will come to a lamp-post, and you will now see the house you want on your left'; and here 'was now'

and 'will now' really do express past presentness and future presentness; but these, like the drinker's response to 'Say when', are rather special cases. What happens more often is that 'now' gets attached in sense to a statement as a whole, no matter how subordinate the clause in which it is immediately placed. When we say, for example, 'he said he would be in London now', we do not at all mean that he proclaimed the presentness of his being in London; nor if we say 'You will always be proud of what you are doing now' do we mean that you will always be proud-of-what-you-are-doing. There is, I am inclined to think, a king of periphrastic dispensability of this 'now' – the first example is equivalent to something like 'He is now due in London', and the second to 'You are now doing something on which you will always look back with pride', and the 'now' can be dropped from both of these.

This peculiarity of having the whole sentence for its 'scope' rather than the sub-sentence in which it immediately occurs, is a peculiarity which the colloquial 'now' shares with the colloquial 'any'. What the word 'any' conveys is universal quantification, and in general it has the same logical force as 'every' – '*Any* man who looks at this will find it hard to see' is equivalent to '*Every* man who looks at this will find it hard to see'; and similarly in most cases. But not in all. 'They didn't eat any apples' is distinctly stronger in force than 'They didn't eat every apple', not equivalent to it, and similarly with 'If *any* man moves I'll shoot' and 'If *every* man moves I'll shoot'. The thing about 'any' is that it gives universal quantity to the *whole sentence* in which it occurs, even if this means that sometimes it doesn't give universal quantity to its own immediate sub-sentence, as 'every' does. It must just be admitted, I think, that this deplorable holism does infect the ordinary English use of certain words, and 'any' and 'now' are among them.

8. It may, however, be argued that I have now cut the ground from under my own feet at another point. I observed earlier that even if there might be a sort of 'illocutionary inconsistency' in my saying 'He believes that grass is green' but refusing to say 'I believe that he believes that grass is green', there would be none in my saying both of these things but refusing to say 'He believes that I believe that grass is green'. (This was supposed to show the non-equivalence of 'It is true that *p*' and 'I believe that *p*'.) One might counter this by saying that here again we are confronted merely by the 'deplorable holism' which infects the English language; it is the same with 'I' as it is with 'now' and with

'any' – even in subordinate clauses we make it refer to the speaker of the entire sentence. In a more rational language we might have used a pronoun 'self' in such a way that 'Self is sick', for example, means the same as our present 'I am sick', but 'He believes that self is sick' would mean, not the same as our present 'He believes that I am sick', but the same as our present 'He believes that he is sick'. And then, perhaps, 'He believes that self believes that grass is green' would be related to 'He believes that it is true that grass is green' exactly as 'It is true that grass is green' is to 'I believe (i.e. self believes) that grass is green'. Certainly 'He *says* that it is true that grass is green' would be related in this way to 'He says that self believes that grass is green'.

I do not think I want to quarrel with this (it is a point which was first made to me by Mr. J. Wiredu), and I am happy to throw away whatever additional force I may have stolen for my main contentions by the use of this example. The question still remains: what *is* the relation between 'It is true that *p*' and 'Self believes that *p*', whether these forms occur on their own or in subordinate clauses; and the correct answer still seems to me the one that I have given. It remains true, for instance, that the man who says 'Self believes that grass is green, but in fact it is not' (whether this man be *my*self or another), is not guilty of actual inconsistency, i.e. it is not impossible that both parts of his statement should be true, but only that both parts of it should be both true and sincere. It remains true that the prefix 'Self believes that ...' is not vacuous in the way that 'It is true that ...' is. For example, the following remark may be perfectly in order:

'He says that self believes that *p*, and that nevertheless it is not the case that *p*; and as it happens – though of course the poor twit doesn't know it – he's right both times';

but surely not the following:

'He says that *p*, and that nevertheless it is not the case that *p*; and as it happens, etc., he's right both times',

though had 'it is true that ...' replaced 'self believes that ...' in the first sentence, they *would* have been on the same footing. The proposed logic of 'self', it is worth adding, would have its own difficulties. For example,

(1)   He says rightly that self believes that *p*

would not entail

(2)   *Self* believes that *p*,

but rather

(3)   *He* believes that *p*,

since (2) would mean what is now meant by '*I* believe that *p*', which does not follow from (1) on the proposed interpretation. Somewhat similarly, if the present tense is used in formal tense calculi in the way that I propose,

(4)   He *said* rightly that it is raining

would not entail

(5)   It is raining,

but rather

(6)   It *was* raining.

In this case, however, we can preserve the normal rule that

(7)   'He *says* rightly that *p*' entails that *p*,

and if we read (4) as

(4)   It was the case that (he says rightly that it is raining),

we can derive (6) from this by (7) and

(8)   If *X* entails *Y*, then 'It was the case that *X*' entails 'It was the case that *Y*'.

Analogous moves, to explain the entailment of (3) but not (2) by (1), could possibly be worked out for a pronoun-logic, but they would be trickier.[1] In any case, as I have insisted in the previous paragraph, such possibilities do not affect my central contentions.

[1] Such moves may be carried out, for example, in the pronounless 'egocentric' logic adumbrated in Paper XVII. Alternatively, we may keep closer to ordinary speech by modifying (7), as in Hector-Neri Castañeda's '"He", A study in the logic of self-consciousness', *Ratio*, vol. 8, no. 2 (Dec. 1965), pp. 130–57). My proposed pronoun 'self' combines the properties of Castañeda's 'I', when this is so used as to be 'ineliminable for the speaker', with those of his 'he*'.

IV
THE FORMALITIES OF OMNISCIENCE

What do we mean by saying that a being, God for example, is omniscient? One way of answering this question is to translate 'God is omniscient' into some slightly more formalised language than colloquial English, e.g. one with variables of a number of different types, including variables replaceable by statements, and quantifiers binding these. In such a language, the common form of the statements

> God knows that 2+2=4
> God knows that 2+2=5
> God knows that God knows that 2+2=5

can clearly be given as

> God knows that p,

and this is going to be useful in answering our opening question.

If there is no God, it would seem that all statements of the form just given are false; but even if there is a God, it would seem that some of them are. For example, God doesn't know that 2 and 2 are 5, for the simple reason that 2 and 2 *aren't* 5.

This example is sufficient to show that one way in which we might be tempted to translate 'God is omniscient' simply will not do. I mean the translation

(1)   For every p, God knows that p.

At least, this won't do if we want to mean something *true* by 'God is omniscient'. For it is a general rule that we may pass from a universal proposition to any singular instantiation of it, and one instantiation of (1) would be the false proposition

> God knows that 2+2=5.

And we know this to be false, not by any subtle or dubious theologising, but simply by the logic of knowledge as such – if anyone thinks that 2+2=5, his state of mind isn't knowledge but error.

Still, the correction required to this first effort seems simple and obvious. When we say that anyone knows everything, it is surely understood that what we mean is that he knows everything that's true. So, as a second attempted translation of 'God is omniscient' let us put

For every p, if it is *true* that p then God knows that p,

or more simply

(2)   For every p, if p then God knows that p.

And it does seem that all the instantiations of *this* proposition are things which a believer in God's omniscience *would* wish to maintain. For example

If 2+2=4 then God knows that 2+2=4
If 2+2=5 then God knows that 2+2=5
If God knows everything then God knows that God knows everything.

These are 'instantiations' of (2) in the sense that they are formed by simply dropping the initial quantifier and putting some actual statement for the variable 'p' at the two places where it occurs, the same statement at each place. There are also 'instantiations' of (2) in a slightly more complicated sense, and all of these are, I think, propositions which a believer in God's omniscience would wish to maintain. These more complicated instantiations of (2) are ones like

(3)   For every x, if $x+2=4$, then God knows that $x+2=4$.

It is easy to see how we get instantiations of (2) like this. In place of the two 'p's after the quantifier in (2) we put, not actual statements, but *forms* of statements still containing variables, and we replace the initial quantifier 'For every p' by another one containing whatever variables occur in the replacement for 'p'.

Here is another example of the same sort: Suppose we write '*fx*' for any statement about *x*, e.g. '*f(Plato)*' for any statement about Plato. Then the proposition

(4)   For every *f*, if *f(Plato)* then God knows that *f(Plato)*

would mean that God knows everything there is to know about Plato, and this too would be an instantiation of (2). So also would

(5)   For every *f* and *x*, if *f(x)* then God knows that *f(x)*,

which asserts in plain English that God knows everything about everything.

Again, suppose we introduce a variable *d* which stands for any expression which, attached to a statement, forms a statement, for example, 'It is not the case that ...', 'Johnny believes that ...', and so on. Thus a formula like '*d(2+2=5)*' can stand indifferently for such statements as

    It is not the case that 2+2=5
    Johnny believes that 2+2=5
    I wish it were the case that 2+2=5

and so on; and also for such statements as

    1+1=3 and 2+2=5
    Either my name is Percy or 2+2=5
    If my name is not Percy then 2+2=5

and, for that matter, for such statements as

    If 2+2=5 then 2+3=6
    Either 2+2=5 or my name is Percy
    That 2+2=5 is less surprising than that my name is Percy

in which the expression substituted for '*d*', and making a statement by being attached to '2+2=5', isn't attached to '2+2=5' by being *prefixed* to it but rather by being as it were wrapped around it. And among the instantiations of the proposition (2) is this:

(6)   For all d, if $d(2+2=5)$ then God knows that $d(2+2=5)$.

This could be a way of translating something rather puzzling that some of the schoolmen used to say, namely that there *is* a sense in which God knows even false propositions;[1] for He *understands* them just as completely as He understands true propositions, and of course as part of this complete understanding He understands or knows that they are false. He knows, we might say, all truths into which the idea of 2 and 2 being 5 in any way enters, e.g. the truth that it is not the case that 2+2=5, that some idiotic boy believes that 2+2=5, and so on.

But now we must raise a deeply controversial point. In this statement that for every p, if p then God knows that p, are we to understand this verb 'knows' as a verb in the present tense, or are we not? Many very reputable philosophers, e.g. St. Thomas Aquinas, have held that God's knowledge is in some way right outside of time, in which case presumably the verb 'knows' in our translation would have to be thought of as tenseless. I want to argue against this view, on the ground that its final effect is to restrict *what God knows* to those truths, if any, which are themselves timeless. For example, God could not, on the view I am considering, know that the 1960 final examinations at Manchester are now over; for this isn't something that He or anyone could know timelessly, because it just isn't true timelessly. It's true now, but it wasn't true a year ago (I write this on August 29th, 1960) and so far as I can see all that can be said on this subject timelessly is that the finishing-date of the 1960 final examinations is an earlier one than August 29th, and this is *not* the thing we know when we know that those examinations are over. I cannot think of any better way of showing this than one I've used before,[2] namely, the argument that what we know when we know that the 1960 final examinations are over can't be just a timeless relation between dates because this isn't the thing we're *pleased* about when we're pleased that the examinations are over. In any case it seems an extraordinary way of affirming God's omniscience if a person, when asked what God knows *now*, must say 'Nothing', and

---

[1] See, e.g., Ockham, *Tractatus de Praedestinatione*, etc., ed. P. Boehner (Franciscan Institute, 1954), pp. 56, 101B.

[2] A.N. Prior, 'Thank Goodness That's Over', *Philosophy*, Jan. 1959, p. 17. Cf. C.D. Broad, *Examination of McTaggart's Philosophy*, Vol. II, Part I, pp. 266–7.

when asked what He knew yesterday, must again say 'Nothing', and must yet again say 'Nothing' when asked what God will know tomorrow.

Of course if we take the 'knows' in our translation to be the ordinary present-tense 'knows', then we must regard the 'is' in the thing it's a translation *of*, namely 'God is omniscient', as the ordinary present-tense 'is', and if we want to translate the belief that God's omniscience is a permanent and unalterable thing we must expand our (2) to this:

(7)   It is, always has been, and always will be the case that for all p, if p then God knows that p.

We may further note that even with respect to what God is said in both formula (2) and formula (7) to know *now*, the statements over which the variable 'p' may range include not only present-tense but past-tense and future-tense ones, and tenseless ones also, if any such there be. For example, we can infer by instantiation from both (2) and (7) the following propositions:

> If there were living organisms a million years ago, God knows that there were living organisms a million years ago;

and

> If there will be living organisms a million years hence, God knows that there will be living organisms a million years hence.

Omniscience as here defined, in other words, covers *fore*-knowledge of whatever will be, that is, *knowledge at every moment of whatever at that moment will be*.

But now I want to raise a subtler point. Is the believer in God's omniscience committed to the following proposition:

(8)   For all p, if (it is the case that) p, God has always known that it would be the case that p

(for example, if I now scratch my head, has God always known that I would scratch my head on this occasion?) The first thing to be said about this proposition is that it *isn't* a simple logical consequence of

God's omniscience in the sense of our proposition. It does follow from proposition (7) that

(9)   If, at any time, it was the case at that time that it would be the case that *p*, then God knew at that time that it would be the case that *p*.

But this is not enough to give us proposition (8), unless we supplement it by

(10) For all *p*, if (it is the case that) *p* then it has always been the case that it would be the case that *p*.

If (10) is true, and God is omniscient in the sense of proposition (7), then (8) is true. And contrariwise if (10) is false, then (8) must be false also. For if (10) is false, that means that in some cases in which it *is* the case that *p*, it nevertheless *hasn't* always been the case that *p* would be the case, and if this hasn't always *been* true, then clearly neither God nor anyone can have *known* it to be true. So that at this point everything really depends on whether for every *p* that *is* the case, it has always been the case that it would come to pass that *p*, or as I sometimes loosely put it, whether whatever *is* the case *has always been going to be* the case. This proposition, together with God's omniscience, *does* yield the conclusion that with respect to whatever is now the case, God has always known that it would be the case; but that conclusion, i.e. our proposition (8), does *not* follow from God's omniscience alone. And my own view would be that, whatever may be the case with the doctrine of God's omniscience itself, proposition (8) is not true, nor is proposition (10). And on both these points, I mean the denial of the logical proposition (10) and even of the theological proposition (8). I rather think that, for what this is worth, I have St. Thomas Aquinas on my side, though this involves some very tricky questions of exposition.

Let's look, anyhow, at a bit of what Thomas has to say about these matters in his *De Veritate*, Question 2, Article 12, 'Whether God knows singular future contingents'.[3] He begins by stating some twelve

---

[3] Directly on the maxim that *id quod est verum in praesenti, semper fuit verum esse futurum*, it is worth also glancing at *Summa Theologica*, Part I, Question 16, Article 7, Objection 3 and answer.

arguments for the negative, of which I think the most persuasive is the seventh, which begins like this: given any true proposition of the form 'If p then q', if the antecedent p is absolutely necessary, then the consequent q must be absolutely necessary also. The point of this *necessarium absolute*, and the sort of necessity with which Thomas is contrasting it, is obvious enough. If I make a statement of the form 'If p then necessarily q', I may not mean that from the truth of p we can infer that q is in itself a necessary truth, i.e. I may not mean 'If p then necessarily-q'; I may only mean that the truth of q – it could quite well be the *contingent* truth of q – *necessarily follows* from the truth of p, i.e. I may only mean 'If p then necessarily-q'. This is not an absolute but a merely conditional necessity of q; in fact not really a necessity of q at all, but only a necessary connexion between q and something else. Nevertheless we can legitimately infer the necessity of q in itself if we are given not only its necessary following from p, but also the necessity of p in itself. What necessarily follows from something necessary is itself necessary. That's the first premiss that Thomas's imaginary objector uses here, and Thomas himself, we shall find, quite explicitly assents to it.[4]

Now here, the objector goes on, is a true proposition of the form 'If p then q': 'If anything is known to God, then that thing will be'. This perhaps needs filling out a little; it is clear from the context that what the objector has in mind is any proposition of the general form 'If it has come to God's knowledge that X will happen, then X *will* happen'. But the antecedent of this, at least if it's true at all, is necessary, if only because it's *past*, and so beyond anyone's power to prevent – *quod fuit, non potest non fuisse*, 'What has been, cannot now not have been'.[5] So anything that follows from this necessary, i.e. now-unpreventable, truth, must itself be now-unpreventable. From this in turn it follows – the corollary is too obvious for Thomas to bother drawing it explicitly – that whatever *isn't* now-unpreventable *hasn't* yet come to God's knowledge. That's against proposition (8); it is clear that a similar argument could be used to show, against proposition (10), that whatever *has already come to be* part of what is to come is now-unpreventable, and so

---

[4] Stock sources for this law in Aristotle are *An. Pr.* I, Ch. 15, 34a, 23, and *An. Post.* I, Ch. 6, 75a, 1–11.

[5] The main stock source for this is the *Nicomachean Ethics*, VI, 1139b. See also *De Caelo* I, 283b 13.

whatever isn't yet unpreventable hasn't yet come to be part of what is to come.

The general point of this type of argument might be brought out by using a few symbols. Suppose we use '$X \equiv Y$' to assert that the propositions X and Y are logically equivalent, i.e. inferable from one another; this equivalence having the usual properties of symmetry (if $X \equiv Y$, $Y \equiv X$) and transitiveness (if $X \equiv Y$ and $Y \equiv Z$, $X \equiv Z$) and also the property that if $X \equiv Y$ then $f(X) \equiv f(Y)$, where f is any logical function, e.g. 'Not'. Let us, further, include among logical functions of a proposition p the functions 'Necessarily p' (or 'Now-unpreventably p'), symbolised as 'Lp'; 'It was the case n time-units ago that p', written '$P(n)p$'; 'It will be the case n time-units hence that p', written '$F(n)p$'; and 'God knows that p', written 'Gp'. It is easy to show that if we have the logical equivalence

$$P(n)p \equiv LP(n)p$$

('It was the case that p if and only if it now-unpreventably was the case that p') and any logical equivalence of the form

(i) $X \equiv P(n)Y$

we can prove

(ii) $X \equiv LX$

for we have $X \equiv P(n)Y \equiv LP(n)Y \equiv LX$. Thus if we have

(iii) $p \equiv P(n)GF(n)p$

('p is the case if and only if n time-units ago God knew that p would be the case n time-units later'; i.e. approximately proposition (8)), then we have

$$p \equiv P(n)GF(n)p \equiv LP(n)GF(n)p \equiv Lp$$

while if we have

(iv) $p \equiv P(n)F(n)p$

('p is the case if and only if it was the case n time-units ago that p would be the case n time-units later'; i.e. approximately proposition (10)), then we have

$$p \equiv P(n)F(n)p \equiv LP(n)F(n)p \equiv Lp$$

And if we have

(v) $p \equiv Gp$

('p if and only if God knows that p'), then we can derive (iii) from (iv) and *vice versa* (my earlier point about the deductive equivalence of (8) and (10), given God's omniscience); for by (v), $F(n)p \equiv GF(n)p$, and so $P(n)F(n)p \equiv P(n)GF(n)p$.

I wish I knew where Thomas got this seventh objection from. It was developed very powerfully *after* Thomas by the fifteenth-century anti-Occamist Louvain philosopher Peter de Rivo;[6] and Peter de Rivo knew, but so far as I can discover Thomas did not know, Cicero's *De Fato*, in which a very similar argument is put into the mouth of Diodorus the Megarian.[7] In the absence of any better theory, I would suggest that perhaps Thomas himself constructed this argument against the theological proposition (8) on the pattern of the analogous argument against the logical proposition (10) which he found in Aristotle's *De Interpretatione*, and enlarged upon (and so far as I can see accepted) in his commentary on that work, Book I, *Lectio* 13. But wherever Thomas got the argument from, it seems to me, with one slight modification that I'll discuss later, entirely conclusive. Thomas treats it, too, with the respect it deserves, and brushes aside three ways of dealing with it which he considers inadequate before putting forward an answer of his own.

There are some, he tells us, who argue that the antecedent of this conditional, despite its expressing a truth about the past, is contingent. For, these people say, it has a reference to the future, and that sort of

---

[6] See L. Baudry's excellent collection of texts, *La Querelle des Futurs Contingents (Louvain, 1465–75)*, Vrin, 1950, e.g. p. 70.

[7] Cicero, *De Fato*, VII, 14.

truth about the past isn't always unpreventable – we do sometimes say truly that a thing was going to happen, and then when the time comes it doesn't. Thomas admits this sense of 'going to happen' – we do sometimes say that a thing was going to happen when we mean that everything was so to speak pointing that way – but even in this sense of 'going to happen', Thomas points out, if it's ever true that a thing was going to happen, then it cannot by that time not have been going to happen in that sense, even though perhaps by this time it isn't happening and it's clear that it never will.

Others, again, say that the proposition 'It has come to God's knowledge that X will happen' is contingent because it's a compound proposition with a contingent component, like 'Peter is a white man' – Peter cannot but be a man, but he needn't be white, and so needn't be a white man. To this Thomas replies that the necessity or contingency of a proposition doesn't depend on the character of its subject-matter but on the nature of the main 'link' in its construction; e.g. 'I believe that man is an animal' and 'I believe that Peter is running' are equally contingent though the thing believed is necessary in the one case and contingent in the other. I'm not sure that this rule of Thomas's always works; with simple conjunctions like 'Peter is an animal and Peter is running' the modality of the whole *does* depend up to a point on the modality of the bits; but the point perhaps is that what we have here isn't that sort of combination but rather the sort in which there is definitely a principal clause ('It has come to God's knowledge ...') and a subordinate one, and here the pastness and consequent 'necessity' of the principal clause does seem to settle the matter.[8]

While I think Thomas was right on the main point here, I ought to mention that this is what was called in question by most of the writers subsequent to him who considered this argument and were not satisfied with his handling of it; for example, the fifteenth-century Occamists. They held that an element of futurity even in a subordinate clause could destroy the sort of necessity which normally attaches to past-tense truths, and in fact made such truths essentially future in sense even if

---

[8] On these two very different ways in which a proposition may be compounded out of past-tense and future-tense elements, see Peter de Rivo in Baudry, *op. cit.*, p. 339.

past in form.[9] If, to construct a new example, my own future choice and
nothing else can cause me to start smoking tomorrow, then my own
future choice and nothing else can cause it to *have been* the case
yesterday that I would start smoking in two days' time from then; and
this fact that is directly about yesterday and only indirectly about
tomorrow, if it is a fact at all, is as much a contingent fact as the one that
is directly about tomorrow. Nor have Occamists hesitated to ascribe a
like contingency to God's foreknowledge. But I must confess to a
difficulty here. I think I can attach intelligible senses to the phrases 'was
true yesterday' and 'was *the case* yesterday' which give the Occamist
results; but I cannot find any such sense for 'was *known* yesterday'. I
can by my free choice, not exercised until tomorrow, cause a person's
guess, made yesterday, to have been a correct one (I do this simply by
deciding to do what he guessed I would); and I can by the same act
convey the same retrospective verification to another person's guess,
made right now, that the first person's guess *was* a correct one. It is so
to speak still open to this latter guess, despite its past-tense subject
matter, either to turn out to have been correct or to turn out not to have
been correct; its present correctness, if it does turn out to have been
correct, is thus entirely contingent. But while contingent futures, and
contingent future-infected pasts, can in this way be correctly or
incorrectly guessed, I cannot see in what way they can be 'known'; or to
put it another way, I cannot see in what way the alleged knowledge,
even if it were God's, could be more than correct guessing. For there
would be *ex hypothesi* nothing that could *make* it knowledge, no present
ground for the guess's correctness which a specially penetrating person
might perceive.[10] So if we talk this way, while we do get my proposition
(10) in a rather trivial way, I don't think we get my proposition (8),
because I don't think we get the thing that ties the two together, namely

---

[9] See Ockham himself on this, *op. cit.*, pp. 5–6C, and Ferdinand of Cordova in
Baudry, *op. cit.*, p. 159. For what seems to be a very similar view, see Ryle's
Dilemmas, 'It Was to Be'.

[10] I owe much in this paragraph to Professor J.M. Shorter. Cf. also, on the
negative point, Jonathan Edwards on the Will, Part II, Sect. XII, Observation II.
But this is a frequently repeated Thomist point too – that there can logically be
no *knowledge* of the future, for one who is still awaiting its actualisation, but
what he can gather from its already present causes. (See, e.g., *De Malo*, XVI
7.)

God's omniscience, except in the weak sense that He *knows whatever is knowable*, this being no longer coextensive with what is true. This conclusion (that you don't get omniscience this way) seems confirmed by the fact that Ockham, who I suppose was the classical exponent of the point of view I've just been sketching, was driven to assert that 'it is impossible to express clearly the manner in which God knows future contingencies'.[11]

Returning now to Thomas: he goes on to consider a third way of answering his 'seventh objection', namely by arguing that a necessary antecedent of a true conditional *can* have a contingent consequent, as in, for example, 'If the sun shines this tree will flower'. The sun cannot but shine; but something *could* interfere with its influence on the tree so that it doesn't flower after all. Only where the connexion between antecedent and consequent is immediate, without the possibility of anything intervening to frustrate it, does the rule really hold. So it is argued; but Thomas argues on the contrary that it is only where there is no possibility of frustration that the conditional is strictly true. 'If the sun shines the tree will flower' is for this reason *not* true; if it *were* true, the necessity of its antecedent *would* be conveyed to its consequent.

Once again I think Thomas is right, but there is something that ought to be added here to obviate a misunderstanding. Some writers on these topics have thought it important to insist that no sort of knowledge, not knowledge of what is to come any more than knowledge of what has been, actually *causes* the truth of that which is known. Thomas doesn't insist on this, I think because in the case of divine foreknowledge he doesn't believe it is true. Personally I do think it is true, but not very relevant to the argument we are considering. For a conditional proposition such as 'If it has come to God's knowledge that *X* will be, then *X* will be', doesn't require for its truth, or for its conveying necessity from its antecedent to its consequent, that its antecedent should *causally bring about* its consequent. It is enough that the former cannot be the case without the latter being the case, regardless of why this is so. And in fact if we like to say that it is because *X* will be that it can be known that it will be, rather than *vice versa*, this means more than ever that *X*'s future coming to pass is beyond prevention, since it has already *had consequences* which its opposite could not have (I take

---

[11] Ockham, *op. cit.*, p. 15.

this point from Jonathan Edwards,[12] who reproduced this Objection 7 in the eighteenth century for a different purpose – not to show that God cannot know future contingencies, but to show that, just because God does know all the future, none of it can *be* contingent).

What, then, with all these lines of escape stopped up, are we left with? Nothing, Thomas thinks, but to accept the objector's conclusion; only with a careful elucidation of the exact sense in which it is true. Here I must do a little re-translating of his Latin. Above, I have used the phrase 'has come to God's knowledge' to render Thomas's *est scitum a Deo*, because this translation brings out the pastness of the *scitum*, on which the objection as stated so heavily depends. But in fact what is *scitum a Deo* is necessarily so whether this *scitum* expresses a *past* fact or an *eternal* one, and this point is explicitly admitted by Thomas when he restates this objection in the *Summa Theologica*, Part I, Question 14, Article 13 (Objection 2). His answer to the argument, however, requires him to insist that what *is* in fact expressed, so far as we may suppose the antecedent to be true at all, is not proper pastness but eternity. And his answer consists in simply admitting that what is known to God *is* unalterable in the form in which God knows it; for God does not see the future contingent fact as future but as present. It is, he says, nearer the truth to say that if God knows a thing it *is*, than that if He knows it, it *will be*. At an earlier point, where he is neither stating nor answering an objection but simply setting out his own view, he argues thus: The contingent, considered as future (*ut futurum est*) cannot be the object of any sort of knowledge which cannot fall into falsehood; so since the divine knowledge neither does nor can fall into falsehood, God could not possibly have any knowledge of future contingencies if He knows them *as* future. Divine *fore*knowledge of such events is, in fact, out; as He knows them, they are not still to come, but already there. This (which is what I had in mind when I said earlier that Thomas denies not only the logical proposition (10) but even in a way the theological proposition (8)) is a doctrine taken over from Boethius; its import is perhaps illuminated by the comment of an earlier follower of Boethius, namely Anselm, who observes that the unchanging 'presence' which on this view all things have to God, is in some ways less like our own

---

[12] Edwards, *op. cit.*, Observation III, Corollary I, discussion of Whitby. My attention was first drawn to this section in Edwards, and the resemblances between its opening argument and Thomas's Objection 7, by Mr. J.C. Thornton.

present than our past. Looking back over what *has* happened, we can distinguish what was bound to happen as it did from what could have happened otherwise, though of course none of it *can now*, by the time we look back on it, have happened otherwise. It is in some such way as this that God distinguishes necessities and contingencies even though there is no contingency left in the latter in the form in which they reach His gaze.

For myself, I cannot wholly agree either with the objection or with Thomas's answer to it. I do agree with both that in some sense in which we *can* alter the future we *cannot* alter the past. But there is an objection to this that the future is precisely whatever it is that does come to pass after our alleged alteration has taken place, so what we alter *isn't* the future after all, and the real future can no more be altered than the past can. What I want to say to this – and as far as it goes I think it is Thomist doctrine too – is that nothing can be said to be truly 'going-to-happen' (*futurum*) until it is so 'present in its causes' as to be beyond stopping; until that happens, neither 'It will be the case that *p*' nor 'It will be the case that not *p*' is strictly speaking true. What Thomas says is that neither of them is true *determinate*; and what this appears to mean is that though they somehow share truth and falsehood between them, neither is as yet definitely attached to either proposition rather than the other.[13] I don't myself now think – though I once did – that this complication is necessary; it is enough to distinguish (as Thomas did not) between the form 'It will be that it is not the case that *p*' (which commits one to the futurition of not-*p*) and the form 'It is not the case that it will be that *p*' (which could also be true if it is simply as yet undetermined whether it is *p* or not-*p* that the future holds). Writing '*F*' for the simple 'It will be that', '~' for 'Not', and '*X* v *Y*' for 'Either *X* or *Y*', I would say that we have at this stage

$$\sim(Fp \lor F\sim p)$$

('Neither it-will-be-that *p* nor it-will-be-that not-*p*'). And this state of affairs we can alter, changing it to

---

[13] See, especially, the latter part of Part I, *Lectio* 13, in his *Peri Hermeneias* commentary.

$Fp \lor F{\sim}p$

when it is in our power to decide one way or the other and we do so. But what is past cannot be thus altered, for it is *always* the case that either p *has been* the case or not-p has, i.e. we always have

$Pp \lor P{\sim}p$

and there can be no question of changing from this to its opposite or *vice versa*. Moreover, with respect to any specific past time, say n time-units ago, we have

$P(n)p \lor P(n){\sim}p$

but for some future times we have, on the contrary,

${\sim}(F(n)p \lor F(n){\sim}p)$.

Let us now put '$MF(n)p$' for the assertion that p is one of the things that *can* happen n time-units hence, and take this to mean that it *isn't* yet settled that p will *not* be the case that time; i.e.

(vi) $MF(n)p \equiv {\sim}F(n){\sim}p$.

We can similarly define 'It can be that p *has* happened n time-units ago', $MP(n)p$, as ${\sim}P(n){\sim}p$; but there is a very big difference between this case and the preceding. For 'It *isn't* the case that p was then *not* the case' is true only of those times of which it *is* the case that p then *was* the case,[14] i.e. we have

(vii) $MP(n)p \equiv P(n)p$

---

[14] At least the theory of future contingencies provides no exceptions to this. For the possibility of other exceptions, see *Summa Theologica*, Part I, Question 16, Article 7, Objection 4, and answer; and my own *Time and Modality*, Ch. 4, and 'Identifiable Individuals', *Review of Metaphysics*, June 1960, pp. 692, 695–6.

whereas 'It isn't (yet) the case that p will then not be the case' can be true of 'thens' of which it isn't yet the case, either, that p will then *be* the case, i.e. we do *not* have as a law

$$MF(n)p \equiv F(n)p.$$

So I want to say that 'It can be that X' is logically equivalent to the simple X where X is a past-tense proposition, but not where it is a future-tense. Thomas and his objector would, I think, agree with this, but they say, further, that 'It *must* be that X' is equivalent to the simple X where X is in the past tense and not where it is future; and this difference I cannot myself obtain in any straightforward way.[15] What I have succeeded in formalising is in fact not quite the Aristotelian-Thomist account of this whole situation, but a slight modification of it that you get in C.S. Peirce, who says that the past is the region of 'brute fact', while the future divides into the necessitated, for which alone we have either $F(n)p$ or $F(n){\sim}p$, and the merely possible, for which we have neither.[16]

Still, with this position also the proposed distinction between past and future can be shown to break down if we equate p either with $P(n)F(n)p$ or with $P(n)GF(n)p$, at least if we also admit (as all writers that I know of do) that

(viii) $p \equiv F(n)P(n)p$

i.e. a proposition *is* true if and only if it *will* be the case at any given time hence that it *was* the case that interval of time before. For on these assumptions we have

$$MF(n)p$$

$\equiv {\sim}F(n){\sim}p$	[vi]
$\equiv F(n)P(n){\sim}F(n){\sim}p$	[viii]
$\equiv F(n){\sim}P(n){\sim}{\sim}F(n){\sim}p$	[vii]
$\equiv F(n){\sim}P(n)F(n){\sim}p$	$[{\sim}{\sim}p \equiv p]$
$\equiv F(n){\sim}{\sim}p$	[iv]

[15] For the difficulty here, see my *Time and Modality*, p. 97.
[16] *Collected Papers* of C.S. Peirce, 5, 459.

$\equiv F(n)p$ $[\sim\sim p \equiv p \ ]$

('$\equiv F(n)\sim P(n)GF(n)\sim p$' may be inserted after the fourth line by (v) and removed by (iii)). Intuitively, the argument proceeds thus: suppose it is now possible that a certain thing, say p, should come to pass n time-units hence. Then it *will* be true when that time comes (whatever actually happens then) that this thing *was* possible now. That is, it *will* be false then that the thing *was* at this present time booked to fail to come to pass. But if this will be false then, it will also be false then that it *is* failing to come to pass (for on the hypothesis that we are considering, if it were then failing to come to pass, it *would* now have been going to fail). But if it will then be *false* that is *isn't* coming to pass, it will be *true* that it *is* coming to pass. That is, from the mere possibility of a future event we can by these steps infer that it will actually occur. On this view also, then, the reality of future contingency is incompatible with our proposition (10), and by the same type of argument with proposition (8).

There is an interesting, and formally rather beautiful, relation between the 'tense logic' here advocated and the 'Occamist' tense logic mentioned earlier as an alternative to Thomas's. We can formalise the Occamist system by having one set of variables, say 'p', 'q', 'r', etc., for statements generally, and a special further set, say 'a', 'b', 'c', etc., restricted to statements with no trace of futurity in them. We might then have '$a \equiv La$' as a law but not the more general '$p \equiv Lp$' and not even '$P(n)p \equiv LP(n)p$', though we would have '$P(n)a \equiv LP(n)a$'. Certain functions of the 'A-variables' would be substitutable for them in laws (would constitute 'A-formulae'), others not. For example, '$P(n)a$' as well as the plain 'a' (and '$\sim a$') would count as an A-formula, and be substitutable for 'a' in laws, but '$F(n)a$' would not, nor would '$P(m)F(n)a$', though both of these would be substitutable for 'p'. ('$P(n)a$' would be an A-formula because formed by prefixing '$P(n)$' to an A-formula, but '$P(m)F(n)a$' would not, because the formula to which the '$P(m)$' is here prefixed isn't one.) '$LF(n)a$' and '$LP(m)F(n)a$' are of course well-formed, and propositions of this form could sometimes be true; and there is a case for counting as an 'A-formula', i.e. as not having *proper* futurity, any formula at all that begins with 'L', even ones like '$LF(n)a$'. (Such assertions 'haven't proper futurity' because whether it is or is not necessary that $F(n)a$ must depend solely on factors now in being, which either do or do not now leave open an alternative future, n time-units hence, to a.) And earlier I have in effect sketched a case for taking the same line with 'G', and for having in this sort of system the law '$a \equiv Ga$', but not '$p \equiv Gp$'.

The laws of this system would include both '$\sim P(n)p \equiv P(n)\sim p$' ('It is not the case that p was then so, if and only if it was then the case that not-p') and '$\sim F(n)p \equiv F(n)\sim p$' ('It is not the case that p will then be, if and only if it will then be that not p'), and of course the substitutions of 'a' for 'p' in these. But whereas they will include '$\sim LP(n)a \equiv LP(n)\sim a$' by the law '$a \equiv La$', the fact that '$P(n)a$' and '$P(n)\sim a$' are A-formulae, and a preceding equivalence, these giving us the chain

$$\sim LP(n)a \equiv \sim P(n)a \equiv P(n)\sim a \equiv LP(n)\sim a,$$

they will not include '$\sim LF(n)a \equiv LF(n)\sim a$' (the chain breaks because '$F(n)a$' and '$F(n)\sim a$' are not substitutable for 'a' in '$a \equiv La$').

Suppose now we remove the Occamist's functor 'F' from the system and replace it by another 'F' equivalent to the Occamist's 'LF'. Assuming that there is no way of forming 'non-A' propositions out of the A ones except by the use of the Occamist 'F', in this new system none but A-propositions will be formulable, so no variables need be used but A-variables; or if you like, the P-variables can be treated as A-variables. Because we had '$a \equiv La$' in the old system, we will have '$p \equiv Lp$' in the new one; in fact there will be no use in it for the operator 'L'. And we will have '$\sim P(n)p \equiv P(n)\sim p$' in the new system as in the old; but we will *not* have '$\sim F(n)p \equiv F(n)\sim p$', for the new '$F$' is the old '$LF$', and we didn't have '$\sim LF(n)a \equiv LF(n)\sim a$'. We will, though, now have '$p \equiv Gp$', since we had '$a \equiv Ga$' in the old.

The 'new' system is in fact precisely the 'Peircean' or near-Aristotelian system advocated above. So it could be said, and indeed it has been said (e.g. by Professor Shorter), that the system advocated is merely the Occamist one robbed of its means of expressing contingent truths. I would reply that in an important sense of 'truths' there are no contingent truths; once a thing reaches the status of a 'truth' there can be no going back on it; though there are 'contingencies', i.e. matters of which it is not yet true either that they will be the case or that they will fail to be the case. This is of course a terminological difference rather than one of substance, but being a difference as to what we shall count as a 'truth', it affects what we mean by 'God knows all truths', and so could (and in my view should) affect what truth-value we attach to this statement.

There is, we may observe at this point, an even more direct way of getting '$p \equiv Lp$' than the method of Thomas's Objection 7. For the schoolmen commonly contrasted the contingency of the future with the necessity not only of the past but also of the present – not only what *has been* the case cannot now not have been the case, but what *is* the case cannot now not *be* the case. But it is plausible to say that the functor 'It is the case that ...' makes no difference to the truth or falsehood of *anything* to which it is prefixed, so that *all* propositions are equivalent to ones which are of the present tense in their principal clause. Thomas seems to admit this when, commenting on *De Interpretatione* 16^b 17-19, he equates *est praeteritum* and *fuit praesens*, and *est futurum* and *erit praesens* – putting 'Sp' for 'It is the case that p', we have '$Sp \equiv p$' and in particular '$SPp \equiv Pp \equiv PSp$' and '$SFp \equiv Fp \equiv FSP$'. And this, given '$Sp \equiv LSp$', gives '$Fp \equiv SFp \equiv LSFp \equiv LFp$', thus breaking down the above difference between future and present. The Occamist answer to this is presumably to replace 'p' by 'a' in the law '$Sp \equiv LSp$' (there is then no need for him to alter '$p \equiv Sp$'); the Peircean admits the conclusion but gets the reality of future and unreality of present and past contingency in another way.

As to Thomas's own answer to his real or imaginary objector, I can only say this: I simply cannot see how the presentness, pastness or futurity of any state of affairs can be in any way relative to the *persons to whom* this state of affairs is known.[17] What makes this quite impossible to stomach is precisely the truth that both Thomas and his objector insist on, namely that the future has an openness to alternatives which the past has not; such openness is just not the sort of thing that can be present for one observer and absent for another – either it exists or it doesn't, and there's an end to it; and so either a thing has already occurred or it hasn't, and there's an end to *that*. But the presentness, pastness or futurity of states of affairs does of course vary with *time*, i.e. it is itself a tensed matter – what *was* future or present, *is* now and *will be* past, and so on.[18] So I don't understand what is meant by saying that contingent future occurrences are neither contingent nor future *as* God

---

[17] Cf. Scotus, as given in Ockham, *op. cit.*, p. 53 and n.
[18] Cf. McTaggart, *The Nature of Existence*, Ch. XXXIII, Sects. 305, 330; and my own 'Time after Time', *Mind*, April 1958, pp. 244–6.

sees them, though I do understand what would be meant if it were said that they are neither contingent nor future *when* God sees them. How, in fact, could God *know* a state of affairs to be present and beyond alteration, until it *is* present and beyond alteration (for if He sees it as present when it is not, surely He is in error)? But to know that something is so when it is so, is surely not foreknowledge. So when I try to set out to myself what Boethius and Thomas – and later on, Peter de Rivo (and even Peirce[19]) – are saying here, I find that either I cannot understand what I am saying, or I slip into something which I certainly *can* understand, but which is surely too trivial altogether to express the intention of these writers. Still, with this trivial thing, so far as it goes, I do agree; I agree, that is, that God, or let us say any omniscient being, knows what is happening when it is happening; and of course I agree also with the negative admission of Thomas and of Peter de Rivo that God *doesn't* know future contingencies literally *when* they are still future and contingent, and that it is impossible that He or anyone else should know them in this way. But (and this is what Thomas himself says[20]) this is only because there is not then any truth of the form 'It will be the case that *p*' (or 'It will be the case that not *p*'), with respect to this future contingency *p*, for Him to know; and *nihil potest sciri nisi verum.*

[19] C.S. Peirce, *op. cit.*, 4, 67.
[20] *De Veritate*, Question 2, Article 13, Objection 1 and answer.

V
CONTEMPLATION AND ACTION

It would be easy to cavil at this title 'Contemplation and Action' if it is meant to suggest some kind of contrast, as surely it is. For whatever contemplation is, it is among other things a kind of action, for it is something which men do. One might meet this easily enough, of course, by revising the title to 'Contemplation and Other Actions'. But it is not as simple as this – there are contexts in which 'Contemplation and Action *is* the right antithesis. If we are going to talk about the merits of different kinds of life, then contemplation is one among the various things we may habitually put our time to, and we ought to talk about 'contemplation and other actions', or, better, about 'contemplation and other activities'. But if we have before us some sort of image of a man at some cross-roads, first viewing the situation, sizing it up, and then making up his mind what to do about it, a contrast between 'contemplation' and 'action' is entirely in order; we can almost *see* the dividing-line between the two. And I propose to concentrate on this, the topic which the title properly suggests.

In this context one makes a sharp distinction between contemplation and action because one makes a distinction between what is within one's power and what is not. The shape of the future depends on what *we* do with what is *given* to us, or to be a little less anthropomorphic, on what *we* do with what is *there*; and by 'what is *there*' we mean basically what has already happened, together with what is already being carried forward, as it were, by a certain momentum from the past, too great for us to stop or divert.

We make this distinction all the time, do we not? Even in public life, we set up 'fact-finding commissions', whose job is as it were purely contemplative – setting the situation clearly before whatever body it is that does the quite different thing, acting. And a good deal of practical wisdom consists, or at all events seem to consist, in ascertaining just where we can do no more than contemplate, and where our freedom of action begins. Moreover, there seems to be some sort of *inconsistency* between being an object of contemplation and being an object of action; if there is something anywhere to be seen and contemplated, then that is beyond being determined by our action, while if there is something which we can bring about or prevent by our action, then that thing is to that extent opaque to the contemplative eye. I can look in the larder now and see what is there, and over what I shall see I have no control; I can perhaps also look in an almanac and 'see' where the moon will be at 9 o'clock tomorrow night; but I cannot in the same sense 'see' what I shall eat for supper tonight – I may eat what is in the larder, or eat out, or not eat at all; but it is not a question of *finding out* what I shall do, but of deciding. In order to decide rationally, there is no doubt much that I must find out, for example, what restaurants will be open and whose they are, but I would be in a hopeless position if one of the things I had to find out was *how I shall decide*.

At this point, then, contemplation and action seem as sharply distinguished as they could be. But reflection suggests that it is not as simple as all that. This 'momentum' from the past at least sometimes carries human actions along with it as well as other things, and this lack or possible lack of freedom in our choices is not just a speculative matter. In sizing up the situations before us we include an estimate of how other people will decide, and they in turn treat our decisions thus. And at some points we do seem even explicitly to treat our own decision thus; e.g. when we say 'I prefer political candidate X to either Y or Z, but he hasn't a chance of gaining enough votes, so if I vote for him I'll only weaken the chances of Y'; or even this: 'I prefer X to either Y or Z, and so do most people, but they're afraid to vote for him because they think they'll do no more by it than splitting the votes for Y; so if I vote for him, etc.' How nice (and contemplative) the 'they' is here! – 'I would vote for him if I thought it would do any good; but unfortunately *they* won't vote for him because *they* don't think it would do any good; so it won't do any good, and I can't vote for him'. Still, this is a rational consideration, isn't it, when one is deciding how to vote?

Nevertheless, the direct 'I'll find out how I'm going to decide, and then decide that way' has an odd sound; and no wonder, for the grammar of 'decide' is such that it would be just as sensible to say 'I'll find out how I'm going to decide, and then decide the other way'. The first, indeed, looks as if it *could* be true, while the second could not, if the words 'and then' were taken quite literally as expressing temporal succession and nothing more. But if I really do *find out what I am going to do*, can I really be said, after having found this out, to *decide* to do it? and consequently can I be said to have *found out what I am going to decide*? The answer to these questions seems to me quite clearly No. Contemplation and action at this point really are incompatible.

But might not *somebody else* find out how I am going to decide? This is not so easy to answer. The person might tell me his findings, but then I might not believe him, or might at any rate not know that he is right, and so not myself 'find out' what I shall do; and so I might still really 'decide' after this other person had found out. He might, too, tell me falsely what he had found with the very idea of making me do the other thing to prove him wrong, this other thing being what he foresaw all along that I should do. I could not rationally think of myself as 'deciding as he had *found out* that I would not decide', but only as 'deciding as he had *thought* that I would not decide'; but he might really have found out, nevertheless (i.e. found out that I would decide, not as he said, but as I did decide).

If one takes this view, however, one is committed to the view that action, in the sense of decision, presupposes a certain amount of ignorance – ignorance of what might in principle be known, and perhaps even *is* known to someone other than the agent. A man may, of course, on this or any view, 'know how he will act' *after* he has decided; but it is not 'decision' if he knows it before (there may still be *effort* in this case, but that is another thing). From this it seems to follow that the power to make decisions is something not entirely desirable. For if, say, someone has found out what I shall do and has told me, it would be better for me to know that what this man says is true and so cease to be able to 'decide' about it, than for me to remain in my ignorance and then decide as the man said I would and knew I would. 'Poor chap!' he might well say, 'I knew what he would do, and told him, but he still had to go through all that business of deciding'.

But I fancy that part of our feeling that this would be a proper reaction on the wiser man's part, arises from a suspicion, it may be even a conviction, that in such a case the 'business of deciding' would have something spurious about it – in the view of the other man's knowledge, it all seems shadow-play and not real deciding; I would think this about it myself if the man convinced me later that he really did know what I was going to do. Suppose, again, that the man says I will do X and just because he says so I do Y; and then he says 'I knew you would do that; in fact I knew that my saying you would do the other thing would make you do that, and that was why I said it'. My first reaction would no doubt be to say, 'Look here, if I'd known that I wouldn't have done it'. But this would rather disprove my freedom than prove it – the other man knew all that too. I would be left feeling, I think, a rather push-button creature; or at least I would feel that my behaviour on the occasion in question had been push-button behaviour and not the 'decision' I had taken it to be at the time.

So I want to say, now, that 'how I shall decide' is something which not only cannot be known beforehand (cannot be 'contemplated') by myself, but cannot be known beforehand by anyone else either, because if it is a genuine decision there is *nothing to be known* beforehand about which way it will go. This much, it seems to me, is involved in the way we ordinarily use the verb 'decide'. It is therefore a consequence of this ordinary use of the verb 'decide' that we cannot consistently talk of 'contemplating' a person's future decisions (either one's own or someone else's). Or rather, we cannot contemplate *specific* future decisions, e.g. 'the decision that Jones is going to make, to have tea in town tonight'; though one can contemplate such decisions described *generically*, e.g. I can contemplate 'the decision that Jones is going to make about whether to have tea in town tonight or not', and reflect about it that if he does not make it before 4.30 p.m. he will be too late for the last bus in by tea-time. I cannot contemplate the decision Jones is going to make to have tea in town tonight, because there is just no such thing as the decision Jones is going to make to have tea in town tonight; nor any such thing as the decision he is going to make not to have it. After it is all over, the decision Jones is going to make about whether to have etc. *will have become* either a decision-to-have or a decision-not-to, and will then be contemplatable as such. Or alternatively, Jones *is* going to have tea in town tonight, or he is not going to, and I can contemplate that (whichever it is), but *in this case there is just no (future) 'decision' about it.*

All this is I think involved in the ordinary use of 'decide'. It is also implied in much that we ordinarily say that 'decisions' in this sense do from time to time occur. Whether this is really so I do not know; the fact that it is commonly assumed, and the assumption reflected in common speech, is no argument one way or the other.

To sum up: It may be said that contemplation without action is impotent and action without contemplation is blind; but such impotence and blindness are inescapable if contemplation is to be contemplation and action action. Only it is possible that there is in fact no action but only happening, some of which feels like action but isn't.

Extract from discussion of this paper (involving J.L. Mackie, K. Baier, and J.A. Passmore):

Mackie: I agree that it is absurd to say 'I know that I shall do X, so now I decide to do it'; it is like 'I know the solution to this problem, so now I shall proceed to solve it'. But there's nothing wrong with 'I know the solution to this problem, and now *he* will proceed to solve it'; nor is there with 'I know that he will do X, and now he will decide to do it'.

Prior: Solving a theoretical problem and deciding what to do are alike in that each is the closing of a gap, and cannot take place if the gap is already filled. With the problem-solving it's just a gap in a man's knowledge; in the other case it's a *gap in the facts*. When it isn't yet the case that I am going to do X, and isn't yet the case that I'm going to refrain from doing X, my decision is needed to make one of these things the case. But if it isn't yet the case that I shall do X I can't know that I shall do X, *and neither can anyone else*; similarly with the other alternative.

Baier: But 'being the case' isn't the sort of thing that it makes sense to attach a time-qualification to.

Prior: Why not? – in common speech we say that whereas yesterday Jones was a hungry man today this is no longer the case.

Passmore: In common speech we also say 'I know how he is going to decide'.

Prior: Common speech has a strong and a weak sense of 'decide'.

Mackie: Suppose you take yourself to be making, over a long period, a series of 'decisions', and then I suddenly come forth with a certain Mr. Smith, who all the time has been predicting what you will do, and has been right every time. Would this give you any inclination to withdraw the claim to have been making decisions?

Prior: Yes.

Mackie: So that it *might* be that you never make decisions at all, in your sense of 'decision'?

Prior: Yes.

VI
THE CONSEQUENCES OF ACTIONS

In Moore's *Principia Ethica* it is repeatedly affirmed that our duty is that action which, of all the alternatives open to us, will have the best total consequences. Moore himself emphasizes in this work the practical impossibility of finding out with any certainty what our duty is, given this definition of 'duty'. I do not want to go into that; what I want to do now is to argue that there is not merely a practical impossibility in finding out what our duty in this sense is, but something more like a logical impossibility in there *being* such a thing as a duty in this sense.

My argument is dilemmatic. Either determinism is true or it is not. If determinism *is* true then there are not really (though there may seem to be) a number of alternative actions which we could perform on a given occasion; the one action that we can perform is the one that we do perform. Hence whatever we in fact do is the best possible action (the one with the best possible total consequences) because it is the *only* possible action; so that whatever we in fact do is our duty, in Moore's sense of 'duty'. Moore himself saw this horn of the dilemma (and indeed it is a commonplace that determinism presents problems of this sort); but it has another horn which so far as I know he did *not* see. Suppose that determinism is *not* true. Then there may indeed be a number of alternative actions which we could perform on a given occasion, but none of these actions can be said to have any 'total consequences', or to bring about a definite state of the world which is better than any other that might be brought about by other choices. For we may presume that other agents are free beside the one who is on the given occasion deciding what he ought to do, and the total future state of the world depends on how these others choose as well as on how the given person chooses; and even if there were not other people to spoil one's calculations there would still be oneself, with one's own future choices, or some of them, undetermined like this present one (unless a man decides that it is too risky for him to have any further free-will, and on this very ground finds it to be his duty to do away with himself). And while I speak here of one's calculations being spoilt, the trouble of course goes deeper than that – it's not merely that one cannot calculate the totality of what will happen if one decides in a certain way; the point is rather that there *is* no such totality.

The conclusion seems clear. If determinism is true, then whatever we do is our duty in Moore's sense of 'duty', and if determinism is not true then nothing at all is our duty in this sense. Hence, if we use the term 'duty' in this way, either whatever we do is our duty or nothing at all is our duty, and either way there cannot be any duty that we have failed to perform. We are driven, in a word, to a version of what Professor G.E. Hughes calls the Principle of Continuous Moral Rectitude. This principle is, indeed, only deduced with a certain proviso. It is possible that someone should fail to perform a duty in the sense of *Principia Ethica* if this agent (i) is free, and (ii) is the only free agent there is, or at least the only free agent there will be from the time he makes his decision, and (iii) himself acts freely only once in the course of his existence. This complex supposition is of course one which no reasonable person would make, but it is of some interest that this supposition alone prevents the deduction of the Principle of Continuous Moral Rectitude from Moore's definition of 'duty'. For such moral solipsism would amount to treating oneself as a kind of God (with the problem about whether to tie one's own hands or not with which God is traditionally beset); and one of Butler's criticisms of Utilitarianism was precisely that it involved a rash assumption of a divine prerogative.

It is not only over the position of *Principia Ethica*, however, that this sword hangs. Our deduction would obviously be equally possible if we equated 'doing our duty' with securing the best possible total consequences, not by definition as in *Principia Ethica*, but synthetically as in Moore's later *Ethics*. And our paradox is only slightly mitigated if we adopt a position which is not as a whole Utilitarian at all, but which admits the securing of the best possible consequences as one among a number of prima facie duties. For if we ascribe a certain finite weight or degree of stringency to a prima facie duty which either is something that is always automatically performed or is just nothing at all, a senseless or indeterminate element is introduced into the whole complex of prima facie duties of which our duty *sans phrase* is supposed to be the resultant.

It really is necessary, I think, for the Utilitarian, and even for the man who makes the maximization of goodness a prima facie duty, to climb down a little here, but how little can we make it? Taking the non-determinism horn first, perhaps we can say that if determinism is not true, it suffices to speak of a duty to do what will *probably* have the best total consequences of all the actions open to us. We can only take this line, however, if we are prepared to talk about objective probabilities; that is, if we are prepared to argue that '*p* is probable' need not merely mean 'We don't know that *p* will be true, but what evidence we have is more in favour of it than against it', but may mean something more like '*p* is not yet either going to be the case or not going to be the case, but is more like going to be the case than not'.

What about the determinist horn? Even apart from my use of it to construct this paradox, many determinists are irritated by the suggestion that their position is incompatible with the view that there are alternative possible courses open to us in given situations. They will insist that there are numerous quite ordinary senses of 'possible' in which determinism is not at all incompatible with this. Moore in his *Ethics* gives the example of two ships, one of which *could* be going at 20 knots and the other of which could not, though neither of them is in fact doing so, and neither of them would be credited with free will. It is clear that we arrive at this sort of possibility by deliberately leaving certain factors out – as far as the construction of its engines, say, is concerned, this ship which is not doing 20 knots *could* be doing 20 knots – that is, in circumstances which are quite ordinary, though they do not in fact obtain at this moment, ships with that sort of engine *do* go at 20 knots. And so far as I can see, all the senses of 'could' which the determinist admits are of this general type. But while this may help the determinist in some of his troubles, it surely does not help him here. For how can we seriously estimate the *total* consequences of an action when we have deliberately left out of account certain of its surrounding circumstances? At least some of the features of the situation which results after my action are bound to be due to the very factors which in the end made me act as I did, and which I therefore had to ignore when making my decision, and treating it *as* a decision.

What is substantially the same point might also be expressed as follows: even on a determinist view, the succession of situations which follow one another after a given action has been performed is never the result of that action alone, but of that action together with an infinity of other concurrent happenings. It is quite impossible to draw a sharp line and say that everything on one side of it is a consequence of the action, and everything on the other side a consequence of other things; and therefore impossible to arrive at a set of total consequences of the action. What makes it momentarily appear to be possible is that we do sometimes say of an action *X*, 'If *X* had not been done, *Z* would not have happened'. But this is not such a simple hypothetical as it seems – in practice what we always mean is 'If X had not been done, but Y had been as it actually was, Z would not have happened'. This would still enable us to describe Z in ordinary parlance as a 'consequence' of X; but when it comes to specifying X's *total* consequences the antecedent of our hypothetical must be 'If X had not been done, but *everything* else had been as it actually was...', and on a determinist view this is an impossible supposition. The notion of the *total* consequences of an action seems thus to suffer from an incurable incoherence which renders it useless for ethical theory or for any other sort of theory.

Now this really ought, so far as I can see, to be the end of the matter. But I am aware that abstract logic is for some reason a little suspect these days; so out of deference to this attitude, let us shut up our Moore for a while, and take down Mother Goose.

> For want of a nail
>   The shoe was lost;
> For want of a shoe
>   The horse was lost;
> For want of a horse
>   The rider was lost;
> For want of a rider
>   The battle was lost;
> For want of a battle
>   The kingdom was lost;
> And all for the want
>   Of a horse-shoe nail.

In these lines we are asked, in effect, to assent to the validity of the following sort of reasoning: The fate of the kingdom depended on that battle (it was what is called a 'decisive' battle); one more good cavalryman in the field would have saved the day; we'd have had Bayard Bloggs there if his horse hadn't been crippled through the loss of a shoe; the shoe would have held out if it had had one more nail in it; so that nail lost us the kingdom, and plague take all careless blacksmiths. Well, no doubt the smith's negligence was most reprehensible – we all know the importance in warfare of what is called a 'high standard of maintenance' – but it is surely a little hard to place on his shoulders *the* responsibility for the loss of the kingdom. If Bayard Bloggs's absence could make that much difference, the battle was clearly a close go, and an extra cannon might have turned the scale as well; perhaps we would have had it too, if the horse that was pulling it hadn't given in through exhaustion; that horse would have been in better fettle if it had been better fed; it would have been better fed if its master hadn't had that bout of 'flu, which he would not have had if he hadn't been courting Mary Jane on Ilkley Moor without a hat; he'd have had the hat if his brother Bert hadn't borrowed it; so the whole thing was Bert's fault really, rather than the blacksmith's.

The loss of the kingdom *was*, all the same, a 'consequence' of the blacksmith's negligence, even if it was what we would call a 'remote' consequence; and it would certainly be included among its 'total' consequences by those who use this phrase. But so would much else; for example, if the horse, too late for the battle because of its injury, became the ancestor of a breed of racehorses which brought more renown and profit to the kingdom than it had ever had before it was conquered – this must stand among the 'consequences' of the blacksmith's negligence also, though it would hardly be considered a ground for conferring a knighthood on a man. Sooner or later, in fact, the consequences of the blacksmith's negligence – and also those of Bert's borrowing the hat – will include the entire international situation.

So far, I should say, our reflection on the nursery story has uncovered nothing that tells *against* Moore's account of what duty is. In considering concrete cases one always becomes acutely aware of how little anyone *knows* about the consequences of one's actions; but this is only part of the general problem of 'duty and ignorance of fact', which has nothing specially to do with Utilitarianism, and was allowed for by Moore anyway. Our responsibility is to do our duty as far as we can see it, and unless something is a duty whether we can find it out or not, we cannot even 'do our duty as far as we can see it', for there is nothing for us even to start looking for. If the blacksmith's foresight had extended to the breed of racehorses, perhaps he *would* have deserved a knighthood.

But what about Bert's borrowed hat? A disciple of Moore could say, I think, that that was one of the things the blacksmith needed to know about in order to know his duty fully, but it did not make that duty any the less his, the blacksmith's, duty. There is a passage in Kierkegaard's

Purify Your Hearts which is perhaps relevant here.[1] Kierkegaard says that too many people listen to sermons as if they were theatrical performances – as if the preacher were a sort of actor, to be subjected after the service to discerning dramatic criticism. In fact, he says, it is we, the listeners, who are the actors, and the preacher is rather a kind of prompter; the responsibility of each of us is to look to *our own* acting, rather than judge anyone else's. So the blacksmith must not judge the hat-borrower, but simply see to his own duty in the circumstances that the hat-borrower has placed him in; and the hat-borrower similarly *vis-à-vis* the blacksmith.

But wouldn't a man go mad if he really tried to take the whole responsibility of everything upon himself in this way? And I suppose I tell you, now, that the blacksmith's negligence in the matter of the nail was a result of sheer intolerable fatigue, brought about by the absence of the young man who usually assisted him. And where was this young man? Why, away at the wars, of course – and in that very battle of which we have been speaking. (To anyone complaining of the deterioration of his standards of workmanship, the blacksmith would have said, 'Don't you know there's a war on?') The blacksmith *couldn't* have gone on and on and on shoeing soldiers' horses as he was expected to without his assistant by his side; but if this same assistant had been out of the battle, perhaps even Bayard Bloggs on his charger could not have saved the day. This surely puts the blacksmith's duty, in Moore's sense of 'duty', in a very queer light indeed. The urgency of equipping Bayard Bloggs's horse satisfactorily – its being a matter which *could* decide the battle – depends in part on the very thing that makes it impossible that the blacksmith *should* perform his duty. It is difficult to resist the temptation to cry out at this point, 'But surely we cannot suppose the smith to know about this twist to the thing', as if that were relevant to the present discussion. Of course it is not relevant – whether we can suppose the smith to know about it or not, the whereabouts of his assistant is one of the factors that makes the smith's actual or

---

[1] *Editors' note.* It seems that Prior used the following translation: *Purify Your Heart! A 'Discourse for a Special Occasion' the first of three 'Edifying Discourses in a Different Vein'* published in 1847 at Copenhagen, by S. Kierkegaard. Translated from Danish by A.S. Aldworth and W.S. Ferrie, The C.W. Daniel Company, Ltd., London 1937.

objective duty what it is (on Moore's view of the matter) and at the same time determines his capacity to perform it.

Of course when we bring up this sort of thing we are ceasing to take the blacksmith seriously as a person who *has* duties. The responsibility has passed now to somebody like the Minister in charge of manpower; and I don't know whether even this is taking it far enough back. For the Minister also is in an awkward position. We have some inclination to say that the military disaster was a consequence of his drafting the blacksmith's assistant, so that the blacksmith was too tired to notice the missing nail, Bloggs could not arrive on time, and so on. But if he had *not* drafted the blacksmith's assistant, we would have been inclined to call the defeat a consequence of *this* fact. There is something that seems to bear on this sort of dilemma in the *Prior Analytics*. Aristotle argues that q cannot ever be necessitated both by p and not-p, because

(1) p necessitates q, and not-p necessitates

entails

(2)   not-q necessitates not-p necessitates q

by contraposition of the first conjunct; and this in turn entails

(3)   not-q necessitates q

by hypothetical syllogism, but (3) is a fantastic proposition. This is nowadays generally written off as an error, and with some senses of 'necessitates' it *is* an error, but how does it work out in the present case? We suppose that defeat is a consequence of the drafting of the blacksmith's assistant, but would equally have been a consequence of not drafting him. Then we can say both that to avoid defeat the Minister should not have drafted the blacksmith's assistant, and that if he had not drafted him defeat would have followed, so that defeat would have followed from his avoiding defeat. This conclusion certainly sounds odd; yet something like it seems to express exactly how the Minister *is* placed. Whichever measure he might take, and *rationally* take, to avoid defeat, will result in defeat – this *is* the fix he is in, is it not? And of course the upshot of the whole matter, both formally and concretely, is that defeat is inevitable.

It is inevitable, anyway, if the only pieces that the Minister is free to move are Bloggs and the blacksmith's assistant, and he certainly could be in that position at some stage. But if we are to regard the defeat as in any sense capable of being weighed against other alternatives, i.e. against the consequences of other alternative previous courses, we must say that either the Minister himself at an earlier stage, or somebody else, might have disposed the country's forces in a way that would not have left the position so desperate. If only, earlier on, the Minister had taken a *little* less whisky at that diplomatic party –. But a man must relax sometimes, mustn't he? – I mean, even to do his work effectively he must. What has been done with the blacksmith can be done with the Minister too, and it is clear that we should soon be back where we were before. The notion of 'total consequences', in short, will not work any better in the concrete than it will in the abstract; and the concrete case perhaps makes it clearer than ever that it is even more unworkable on the determinist hypothesis than on the indeterminist one. The indeterminist can approximate to it with the notion of '(objectively) probable total consequences', but the determinist cannot sort out one action from another sufficiently sharply to give us even that.

VII
LIMITED INDETERMINISM

My main business here is the examination of a certain argument of Jonathan Edwards. There seems to be something of an 'Edwards revival' among at least a section of American philosophers, and this is a piece of New World patriotism with which I have considerable sympathy. Edwards was, as it happens, one of the first philosophers I ever heard of, and I still think he bears reading. For there is in his work, beside his crude rationalistic psychology, and beside the half-submerged predestinarian fervour that is so strangely echoed and transmuted in Herman Melville's *Mardi* and *Moby Dick*, a certain metaphysical *logic* with which we may still grapple profitably. In particular, his treatise on the will has three closely reasoned excursuses which raise wide philosophical issues in a way that is still intriguing: the discussion of knowledge and contingency in Part II, Section XII; that of the identity of the nonexistent in Part IV, Section VIII; and the discussion in Part II, Section III, on which I wish to concentrate now.

The general question to which Edwards here addresses himself is 'whether any event whatsoever, and *volition* in particular, can come to pass *without a cause* of its existence', and among other arguments for a negative answer he has a *reductio ad absurdum*, arguing that if an act of will can occur without a cause, then anything at all, no matter how fantastic, can occur without a cause. There is, he says in effect, an inner contradiction in the notion that uncaused events are bound always to be acts of will. We must note, however, in following his argument through, that his language is not quite that which I have just used, and in particular he does not speak primarily of what 'occurs' but rather of what 'begins to be'. He says,

> What is self-existent must be from eternity...: but as to all things that *begin to be*, they are not self-existent, and therefore must have some foundation of their existence without themselves. That whatsoever begins to be, which before was not, must have a Cause why it then begins to exist, seems to be the first dictate of the common and natural sense which God hath implanted in the minds of all mankind.

Then he immediately subsumes what we might be inclined to regard as a different and less radical sort of change under this one as a special case.

> This dictate of common sense equally respects substances and modes, or things and the manner and circumstances of things. Thus, if we see a body which has hitherto been at rest, start out of a state of rest, and begin to move, we do as naturally and necessarily suppose there is some Cause or reason of this new mode of existence, as of the existence of a body itself which had hitherto not existed. And so if a body, which had hitherto moved in a certain direction, should suddenly change the direction of its motion; or if it should put off its old figure, and take a new one; or change its colour: the beginning of these new modes is a new Event, and the mind of mankind necessarily supposes that there is some Cause or reason of them.

Then, after some of the usual remarks about the dependence of all but the most immediate forms of knowledge upon the acceptance of this principle, he argues that if there is a single uncaused event or thing there is no reason why there should not be an indefinite number. And indeed, he says, the advocates of free-will do hold that millions of uncaused events, namely volitions, are occurring all the time. But this argument can be developed qualitatively as well as quantitatively. There is not the least reason why uncaused events should be all of one *kind*, if there are uncaused events at all.

> If it were so, that things only of one kind, *viz.* acts of the will, seemed to come to pass of themselves; ...this very thing would demonstrate that there was some Cause of them, which made such a difference between this Event and others, and that they did not happen contingently. For contingence is blind, and does not pick and chuse for a particular sort of Events. Nothing has no choice. This No-Cause, which causes no existence, cannot cause the existence which comes to pass, to be of one particular sort only, distinguished from all others. Thus, that only one sort of matter drops out of the heavens, even water, ...shows that ...something besides mere contingence has a hand in the matter. If we should suppose Non-entity to be about to bring forth; and things were coming into existence, without any Cause or Antecedent, on which the existence,

or kind, or manner of existence depends; or which could at all determine whether the things should be stones, or stars, or beasts, or angels, or human bodies, or souls, or only some new motion or figure in natural bodies, or some new sensations in animals, or new ideas in the human understanding, or new volitions in the will; or any thing else of all the infinite number of possibles; then certainly it would not be expected, although many millions of millions of things are coming into existence in this manner, all over the face of the earth, that they should all be only of one particular kind, and that it should be thus in all ages.

And it just won't do – this is the nerve of his argument – to say that it is the peculiar and special *nature* of volitions to start into being without a cause, for *nothing has any nature until it is there, so that whatever a thing's nature may explain or permit, it cannot explain or permit the thing's starting to be.*

If any should imagine, that there is something in the sort of Event that renders it possible for it to come into existence without a Cause, and should say, that the free acts of the will are existences of an exceeding different nature from other things; by reason of which they may come into existence without any previous ground or reason of it, tho' other things cannot; ...I would observe, that the particular nature of existence, be it never so diverse from others, can lay no foundation for that thing's coming into existence without a Cause; because to suppose this, would be to suppose the particular nature of existence to be a thing prior to the existence; and so a thing which makes way for existence, with such a circumstance, namely, without a cause or reason of existence. But that which in any respect makes way for a thing's coming into being, or for any manner or circumstance of its first existence, must be prior to the existence. The distinguished nature of the effect, which is something belonging to the effect, cannot have influence backward, to act before it is. The peculiar nature of that thing called volition, can do nothing, can have no influence, while it is not. And afterwards it is too late for its influence: for then the thing has made sure of existence already, without its help.

Hence Edwards concludes that

It is ... as repugnant to reason, to suppose that an act of the will should come into existence without a cause, as to suppose the human soul, or an angel, or the globe of the earth, or the whole universe, should come into existence without a cause. And if once we allow, that such a sort of effect as a Volition may come to pass without a Cause, how do we know but that many other sorts of effects may do so too?

It is clear that this argument, if it is any good at all, will apply not only to those who say that the nature of acts of will is such that they (and they only) can occur causelessly, but also to anyone who says that the nature of *any* sort of event, say an electron's 'jumping' from one of a limited set of orbits to another, is such that events of this sort, and of this sort only, can occur causelessly. But *is* the argument any good?

Let us begin at, or at least near, the beginning, with Edwards's subsumption of all happenings, or anyhow of all changes, under the idea of the 'beginning to be' either of concrete objects or of abstract ones. It is easy to dismiss this as a mere quirk of language – a bit of harmless philosophical pedantry. And no doubt it is easy to attach a harmless sense to the statement that my headache, say, began to exist an hour ago – what does this mean but that an hour ago my head started to ache? And again, no modern writer on causation would deny that it is, as Edwards says, common sense to look for the cause of an event of this sort (one's head starting to ache), and not just to look for causes when we are confronted (if we ever are) with the absolute beginning-to-be of a 'thing'. Indeed, what seems odd to modern readers is not that Edwards should thus extend the principle of causation to motions, accelerations, colour-changes and the like, but that he should feel that this required special justification – that he should regard it as an 'extension' at all – that he should take something else, the beginning-to-exist of a 'thing', as his paradigm of what requires a cause, and so feel obliged to interpret, for example, the imparting of an acceleration as giving 'existence' to a new 'mode of motion'.

But this inversion, I would contend, is not just a bit of 'quaintness' or backwoodsmanship – it is of the very first importance, and his argument depends on it. And so, at the risk of myself falling into philosophical pedantry, I shall proceed to knock it down. I have admitted that we can, if we like, describe a head's starting to ache as a headache's starting to exist; but what must be insisted upon, if we are to answer Edwards, is that this change of key is *not* metaphysically illuminating but metaphysically obfuscating. This 'existence' and this 'starting to exist' of things like headaches is a purely Pickwickian and eliminable existence and starting-to-exist, and we explain what is meant by a headache's starting to exist by saying that it just means a head's starting to ache, not vice versa. Behind this view is, of course, the assumption that the world consists not of events, such as headaches, but of things, such as heads, which act and interact and change. And a remoter part of this underlying assumption is that how things behave – that is, what events occur – is determined partly by their natures or dispositions, and partly by what happens to them.

Given this metaphysical apparatus, it seems perfectly possible to say that some things, but not all things, have alternative possibilities of reaction to one and the same stimulation. It is 'open', we might say, to a disturbed electron to jump to orbit A, and equally open to it to jump to orbit B, but perhaps not open to it to jump to orbit C. In other words, its dispositions may be such that with certain provocations it will 'jump to orbit A or to orbit B', without having any determinate disposition to jump to orbit A, or any to jump to orbit B. Its jumping to orbit A rather than to orbit B, which we can call if we like the coming-to-be of a jump to orbit A rather than of one to orbit B, will then be a circumstance without a cause. And it may be that the only circumstances without causes are the ways that electrons jump from orbit to orbit. But the explanation of this fact will lie, not in the nature of those non-existent or not-yet-existent jumps, but in the nature of the *existing* electrons (and of other existing things). A similar explanation holds, if the only uncaused circumstances are the ways people choose; or if the only ones are of this sort *or* the preceding. We cannot and do not need to say that it is the nature of 'volitions', or of certain volitions, which makes their coming-to-be possible but not necessary, and the nature of other non-existent or not-yet-existent occurrences which makes their coming-to-be either necessary or impossible. It is rather that there are certain already-existing objects which have certain capacities, and some which lack them, and none which have certain other capacities. Persons, say, have the power, without the necessity, of doing X in certain circumstances; for oysters, on the other hand, doing X may be necessary or impossible; and Y, say turning into a dragon, may be something which no existing object has the power to do.

Don't be misled by this last way of talking either. A 'capacity' is not a *relation* between an object and a sort-of-action. '*A* is capable of *Y*-ing' is only superficially of the same form as '*A* loves *B*', with 'is capable of' in place of 'loves' and '*Y*-ing' in place of '*B*'. 'Is capable of' is not, to use a Polish technicality, that sort of functor. The real functor here is 'is capable of –ing', and what goes in the gap is not a noun but a verb. 'Is capable of –ing' is something like 'believes that someone –', where the gap could be filled by, say, 'smokes', or 'has magical powers'. In the strict sense of 'are', there 'are' no actions and no capacities, but things that act and things that are capable of acting. And, I repeat, it is *their* limitations – the limitations of actually present things, not those of still absent events – which, while leaving some alternatives possible, do not leave all alternatives possible.

We really have, I think, now driven away the spectre which Edwards has been dangling in front of us. But it is important to remember how we have done it. We have done it by falling back on a metaphysic of 'substances' endowed with capacities and dispositions, and our line of escape would hardly be open to someone (let us say Professor Hartshorne) who believes that objects are logical constructions out of events rather than vice versa. And it seems to me that this apparent dependence of the distinction between a limited and an unlimited indeterminism on this metaphysic of substances endowed with capacities, is a definite argument in favour of such a metaphysic. For the distinction between limited and unlimited indeterminism *is* one which it seems prima facie possible to make.

If we adopt a 'substance' metaphysic, for this or any other reason, we must of course do it properly, and be prepared to wear its further trimmings and trappings. Substance-talk, for example, is *tensed* talk. The use of the 'earlier' and 'later' relations in making temporal references belongs basically to the event-and-process language, and if it is made fundamental we get a world-picture of events arranged in an unchanging string. If events are logical constructions out of 'things acting', then '*A*'s hitting *B* is (tenselessly) a later event than *C*'s hitting *D*' means simply that it is, has been, or will be the case (and sooner or later it's 'has been') that (i) *A* is hitting *B* and (ii) it has been the case that *C* is hitting *D*.

We must note further that as regards the causeless starting-to-be of things themselves, we have implicitly allowed Edwards's point to stand. I understand that there are astronomers, Hoyle for example, who believe that immense numbers of hydrogen atoms are all the time starting to exist all over the place, with a certain regularity in their distribution. It is no part of Hoyle's theory that this process is causeless, but I want to be more definite about this, and to say that if it *is* causeless, then what is alleged to happen is fantastic and incredible. If it is possible for objects – objects, now, which really *are* objects, 'substances endowed with capacities' – to start existing without a cause, then it is incredible that they should all turn out to be objects of the same sort, namely hydrogen atoms. The peculiar nature of hydrogen atoms cannot possibly be what makes such starting-to-exist possible for them but not for objects of any other sort; for hydrogen atoms do not have this nature until they are there to have it, i.e. until their starting-to-exist has already occurred. That is Edwards' argument, in fact; and here it does seem entirely cogent, leaving us with no alternatives but that either this starting-to-exist is caused (and a very strange sort of causation this must be; but that is another story), or it is a mis-categorization to treat hydrogen atoms as 'substances with capacities'.

VIII
IDENTIFIABLE INDIVIDUALS

I want to examine some of the things that Professor N.L. Wilson says about the identity of individuals in his paper on 'Substances without Substrata';[1] and then I want to raise a few further problems of my own.

We can best begin from Wilson's 'simple little puzzle' about Caesar and Antony: 'What would the world be like if Julius Caesar had all the properties of Mark Antony and Mark Antony had all the properties of Julius Caesar'.[2] Wilson's own approach to an answer is indirect – he begins by telling us not what such a world would *be* like but what it would *look* like. 'Clearly the world would look exactly the same under our supposition.' But this assumes that the question 'What would such a world look like?' is a proper one; which it surely is not. For his answer to it is meaningless until he specifies *to whom* this supposed world would look as he says it would. It *would* look exactly the same to him or to me; but would it have looked the same to Caesar or to Antony? In fact Julius Caesar had the experiences of being called 'Julius Caesar', being murdered on the Ides of March, and so on; so I don't see how this alternative course of events could possibly have looked the same to Julius Caesar; or – using a similar line of argument – to Mark Antony. So I cannot agree that, as Wilson goes on to say, 'our attempt to describe a distinct possible world has produced just the same old world all over again'.[3] I am not, indeed, convinced that even a world which looked to *everyone* just as the actual one does would necessarily *be* the same world (since no one sees everything); but even putting this doubt aside, since the world mentioned *wouldn't* look to everyone as the actual world does, it wouldn't be the same even by Wilson's own standards (unless, indeed, he is a solipsist, and equates how the world is with how it looks to *him*).

Wilson then goes on[4] to consider a peculiarly perverse person who maintains that what has just been supposed is in fact the case, i.e. who seriously contends that in fact it *was* Antony, not Caesar, who was

[1] *Review of Metaphysics*, 12, 4 (June 1959), pp. 521–39.
[2] *Ibid.*, p. 522.
[3] *Ibid.*, p. 523.
[4] *Ibid.*, p. 524–5.

murdered on the Ides of March, etc., and Caesar, not Antony, who dallied on the Nile with Cleopatra. With regard to such a person, Wilson says that 'it would seem at least plausible to suppose' that he 'is really not guilty of historical error, but is using the words 'Caesar' and 'Antony' with significations we attach to 'Antony' and 'Caesar' respectively'.[5] I don't disagree with Wilson at this point, except that he seems to me not half emphatic enough. I would say that what he suggests is even more than 'plausible', and that there is nothing else we *can* suppose such a man to be doing unless it be flatly contradicting himself. For Wilson explicitly includes being called 'Julius Caesar' and 'Mark Antony' respectively among the properties which are supposed to be interchanged;[6] and while he doesn't say so, we can fairly assume that when he says 'called "Julius Caesar" ' he means 'called "Julius Caesar" *by most people*', and similarly with being called 'Mark Antony'. But it is impossible consistently to maintain that the man whom most of us call not 'Caesar' but 'Antony' is the man who really had the experience (among other experiences) of being called by most of us not 'Antony' but 'Caesar'. It really is absurd to say, 'It isn't the person we all call "Julius Caesar" that we all call "Julius Caesar", but it is rather the different person whom we don't call "Julius Caesar" but "Mark Antony" whom we call "Julius Caesar" '. So certainly the most charitable thing to think of a man who says or implies this is that he is using names in an idiosyncratic way.

But why is this ridiculous person brought into Wilson's story at all? Apparently the argument is that because such a man must at best be supposed to be using language in an odd and private way, and at worst contradicting himself, this is all that we can suppose about a man (myself, for example) who says that Caesar *could* have been named 'Antony', and Antony 'Caesar', and each had the other's properties. This sounds deplorably like the following argument which was discussed (and trounced) by William of Ockham: 'I am going to sit down tomorrow, so God, whose thoughts are always true, thinks that I am going to; but I could have been not going to, so God could have

[5] *Ibid.*, p. 526.
[6] *Ibid.*, p. 522.

been wrong.'[7] The obvious answer is that if I had not been going to sit down, God would not have thought I was going to. And analogously, if Caesar had been called not 'Caesar' but 'Antony', then 'Antony' and not 'Caesar' is what we would have called him, so that we would *not* under those circumstances have described the situation by saying (in the manner of Wilson's eccentric gentleman) 'The person we call "Antony" is not really Antony but Caesar'. Nevertheless the person we would in the imagined circumstances be calling 'Antony' would be the person whom in the actual circumstances we call 'Caesar', and in the actual circumstances the correct and only way to describe the imagined circumstance is as 'one in which it is not Antony but Caesar who is called "Antony" '.

I have, nevertheless, my own qualms about this supposed exchange. In the first place, there is quite certainly at least one property of Antony's which it makes no sense to suppose Caesar exchanging with the corresponding property of his own, namely the property of *being Antony*. For if we do attempt to include this property among those exchanged, and so suppose that all of Antony's antics and experiences characterize someone who *is Antony*, and similarly all of Caesar's characterize someone who *is Caesar*, this is indeed to suppose things to be exactly as they are.

Properties which *entail* being Caesar or being Antony, as the case may be, are also obviously to be exempted from the exchange if it is to be an exchange at all. For example, Antony had the complex property of 'dallying with Cleopatra, and not dallying with Cleopatra without being Antony'; clearly no one but Antony can be consistently supposed to have this property, though someone else can easily be supposed to have the simpler property of dallying with Cleopatra. But this is a comparatively trivial extension of my last point; I have more vexing worries.

As Wilson himself suggests, one way in which his question may be put is by asking whether there is a 'possible world', distinct from the actual one, in which Caesar has all of Antony's properties (with, of course, the exceptions just mentioned) and Antony all of Caesar's. It is clear that any such possible world must *contain* both Antony and

---

[7] William of Ockham, *Tractatus de Praedestinatione et de Praescientia Dei et de Futuris Contingentibus*, ed. P. Boehner, Franciscan Institute, St. Bonaventure, N.Y., 1945, pp. 19 ff.

Caesar, that is to say the actual Antony and Caesar; and it is here that our new troubles begin. When we talk about 'possible worlds' we frequently do so as if each such world were a complete and separate idea in the mind of God (or some such place); and when thinking of them in this way I find it difficult to believe that *any* merely possible world can contain individuals identifiable as our Julius Caesar and our Mark Antony. My objection here is not at all the Leibnizian one that Caesar is or is defined by the sum of his properties, so that any individual with different properties (including relational properties; and so any individual set in a different world) could not have been Caesar. On the contrary, I am away over on the other side of this fence; and it is just because Caesar *isn't* a property or collection of properties, that it is impossible as it were to detach his identity from the *Caesar that is* and attach it to a merely imaginary person in a merely imaginary world.

The feeling to which I have given voice may be in some way misguided; but it is worth giving way to it sufficiently to let it drive us into considering a somewhat different way of talking about possible worlds, namely thus: We might say that a possible world is (i) one of the alternative possible future outcomes of the present actual state of affairs; or by a natural extension (ii) anything that *was* a possible world in the preceding sense, i.e. an outcome of some *past* state of affairs which *was* possible at the time, though it may by now have been excluded by what has actually taken place instead. Or finally, (iii) we may use the phrase for anything that constitutes a 'possible world' in the sense of (i) or (ii), together with its past, so that a possible world in this last sense is a *total course of events* which either is now possible or was possible once. And perhaps the more abstractly 'possible' worlds considered in the last paragraph may be comprehended in the present sort, inasmuch as, for any abstractly possible world *W*, if you wipe out *enough* of the actual past you will presumably reach a state of affairs of which *W* would have been a possible outcome. This would seem to be so, at all events, if going back far enough takes you to the creative *fiat* of God.

However it may be with this last speculation, 'possible worlds' in our second sense undoubtedly include some in which the actual Julius Caesar figures; namely, at the very least, all those which constitute alternative possible continuations of his actual life-story. And there is a possible world in which Julius Caesar is called 'Antony', i.e. Julius Caesar could have been called 'Antony'; since possible sequels to parts of his life include, for example, adoption by Antony's family. But of course this is only a very minor tinkering with the actual, and remains so even if we go on to suppose a different upbringing to have made rather a different man of him. Can we not go further and suppose Caesar to have had the whole of Antony's life, including being born to Antony's parents?

It is always a useful exercise (and one insufficiently practised by philosophers), when told that something was possible, i.e. could have happened, to ask '*When* was it possible?' '*When* could it have happened?' So if Caesar could have had different parents, when could he have had them? *After* his birth, indeed after his conception – indeed, *at or after* his conception – it was clearly *too late* for him to have had different parents. But why not before? Do not the possible worlds in which Caesar figures include alternative sequels to what happened before he existed, in which we have him *entering* the stage at a different point? My difficulty here is that *before* Caesar existed (whether we suppose his conception or some other event to constitute the start of his existence) there would seem to have been no individual identifiable as Caesar, i.e. the Caesar we are now discussing, who could have been the subject of this possibility.

But this line of argument, it may be objected, proves too much. For if, before Caesar existed, there was no individual identifiable as Caesar to be the subject of the possibility of being born to *Mark Antony's* actual parents, neither was there an individual identifiable as Caesar to be the subject of the possibility of being born to *Julius Caesar's* actual parents. So there cannot have been at that time any such possibility as that of Caesar's being born to these parents. Yet in due course this non-possible thing actually happened!

Let's repeat this paradox, so that it is quite clear what is being said. Julius Caesar, i.e. a certain now-identifiable individual, did at a certain time begin to exist. But before that time, the possible outcomes of what was going on did not include the starting-to-exist of *this* individual. However, they did include the possibility that there should be *an* individual born to these parents, who would be called 'Caesar', would be murdered on the Ides of March, and so on; and this possibility was in fact realized when Caesar was born and underwent all these things.

Is this really so outrageous and unparalleled? Some of the schoolmen made a puzzle of the sentence *Equus tibi promittitur*.[8] There are two ways in which I may promise you a horse: I may promise you a particular horse, or I may just 'promise you a horse' without undertaking to let you have any horse in particular. In the former case, there is a horse-that-I-have-promised-you, but in the latter case there is none, though any horse whatever that I make over to you will constitute a fulfilment of my promise. I may even say as I hand it over, 'Here is the horse I promised you', but it is my handing it over in fulfilment of my promise that makes it that – it wasn't that when I promised (I could not truly say of this or any horse, 'This *was* the horse I promised you'); nor would it make sense for you to raise a doubt on the point and ask, 'But is *this* the horse you promised me? – are you sure it's *this* one?' With the other sort of promise, this question would of course be entirely in order. And what I want to say now is that the possibility that *an* individual should begin to exist and do and undergo such-and-such things, is like a promise of the second kind. *Any* individual's starting to exist and doing and undergoing the things in question will constitute a realization of this possibility; yet one cannot say of any individual that what was possible was that *he* should begin to exist and do and undergo these things; there just cannot be a possibility of that sort (which would correspond to a promise of the *first* kind) except with respect to what already exists (and so no possibility, of this sort, of existence itself).

Put it this way: Suppose there is some person living before the existence of Caesar or Antony who prophesies that there will begin to be a person who will be called 'Caesar', who will be murdered, etc., and another person who will be called 'Antony', who will dally with Cleopatra, etc. And then suppose this prophet to say, 'No, I'm not sure now that it *will* be like that – perhaps it is the *second* of the people I mentioned who will be called "Caesar" and will be murdered, etc., and the first who will be born later and be called "Antony"', etc.' This, it seems to me, really would be a spurious switch; and after Caesar and Antony had actually come into being and acted and suffered as prophesied, it would be quite senseless to ask 'Are these, I wonder, really the two people he meant?' and if possible more senseless still to

[8] See, e.g., W. Burleigh, *De Puritate Artis Logicae Tractatus Longior*, ed. P. Boehner (Franciscan Institute, St. Bonaventure, N.Y., 1955), pp. 13 (*Dubium* 2), 14, 15.

ask, 'Is it – if either of them – our man's first prophecy, or his suggested alternative, that has now come to pass?' 'The (merely) possible', as Peirce said, 'is necessarily general', and 'it is only actuality, the force of existence, which bursts the fluidity of the general and produces a discrete unit'.[9]

Wilson, one feels at first, has read into our present condition, in which it really does mean something different to say that Caesar did and suffered this and that and to say that Antony did, the indeterminacy on this point which obtained before Caesar and Antony existed, when we could speak and think only of suppositious individuals. But one's second thought is that maybe Wilson is not all that far out, since in order fully to imagine an interchange of Antony's and Caesar's properties we must as it were pass through this Limbo in which their identities are lost, and then we can never regain them. Or, to drop the metaphor: in filling in the details of this supposed exchange, we must look back to the time before either Caesar or Antony existed, and as alternative futures to *this* time the two histories mentioned by Wilson really are indistinguishable.

But could not even God Himself have launched Julius Caesar into being, or arranged his coming into being, at a different time and under different circumstances? I doubt it; and I am not the first to have doubted it either. Thomas Aquinas doubted it; and though I have read what he has to say on this subject again and again, I am still not sure what his final opinion really amounts to. The relevant passages are in his *Quaestiones Disputatae de Potentia Dei*, Q. 3, *De Creatione*, Articles 1 to 3. The immediate subject here is the creation of the world out of nothing, but much that is said bears equally upon the bringing into being of any individual subject that was not there before. Like any good writer on this topic, Thomas insists that when we speak of *creatio ex nihilo*, we don't mean that 'nothing' was some sort of *material*, no doubt very tenuous, out of which the world was made. That the world was made out of nothing just means that it *wasn't made out of anything*; and indeed in this sense God was 'made out of nothing' too – there was nothing *He* was made out of, because He wasn't made at all. But, as Thomas nicely puts it, this manner of speaking is not usual, and the world was made out of nothing in the narrower sense of being indeed

---

[9] C.S. Peirce, *Collected Papers*, 4, 172. Cf. my *Time and Modality*, p. 114.

made, but not made out of anything.[10] But what was it of which it was possible, before it was made, that it should be made? Nothing, Aquinas says – it was possible that there should be a world, and God had the power to make a world, but there was nothing that had the power of being made.[11] But if creation was a gift of existence, he imagines an objector asking, *to what* was existence given? If to nothing, then nothing was created. If to something, then it must have had its own existence before the existence was given.[12] To this Aquinas answers that in creation 'God at the same time gives being and provides that which receives being';[13] an answer which I do not fully understand, but it is at least clear that Aquinas has *not* said, and has very deliberately not said, that the world somehow existed before it did exist in order to receive (and before that be capable of) existence.

'Is Creation a Change?' he asks next,[14] and answers that although the unreflective may regard it as the most radical change conceivable, it is not properly speaking a change at all. For in what is properly called change, one and the same subject must first have this or that true of it, and then not ('one same thing must be otherwise than it was before') – for example, if at one time X is Z, and at another time Y is not Z, there need be no change here ('two contraries if referred to different subjects can exist simultaneously'). But we do not have any one subject X first being Z and then not, or first not being Z and then being Z, when X begins to be; for before it was, there was just no X. But is not this itself a change in the wider sense in which there is change if at one time P and not Q is true, at another time Q and not P? Thomas answers that there can be nothing like this with the creation of the world, since before the world there was no time. My own answer would be that 'Once X was not, and now it is' cannot mean 'Once X's non-being was the case and now its being is', but can only mean 'It *is not* the case that X *was*, but it *is* the case that X *is*', and this does not express a change but two contrasting present facts (note the tense of the two main verbs).[15]

[10] Art. 1, ad Obj. 7.
[11] Art. 1, ad Obj. 2.
[12] Art. 1, Obj. 17.
[13] Ad Obj. 17.
[14] Art. 2.
[15] Cf. my *Time and Modality*, pp. 34–5.

In Article 3 Thomas goes further and says that being created is not properly speaking a *passion* in a thing, i.e. something that it has done to it, and insists that not only must a finite being *be created* in order to *be*, but any being must *be* in order to *be created*. ('This relation' – i.e. being created – 'is an accident, and considered in its being, is subsequent to the thing created.')[16] So on Thomas's view, whatever else is obscure, it seems clear that there can be no question, even for God, of grabbing hold of *Caesar* and bringing him from nothingness to being at some arbitrary time. Expressions like 'launching' Caesar into being, and Caesar 'entering' upon the stage of existence, would certainly have been recognized by Thomas as the metaphors they are, and as misleading metaphors to the extent that their literal performance would involve Caesar's existing-before-he-existed. And this seems very close indeed to the admission that it is only once he exists that Caesar is an identifiable individual, and that God did not and could not 'create Caesar' in any sense in which, He having said, 'Let there be a man, with properties X to Z', and there then starting to be a man with those properties, one could intelligibly ask 'But was *this* the man you wanted?' or intelligibly say 'This – this and no other – *was* the man God intended'.

To stop at this point, however, even with this remarkable theological reinforcement, would be to forget where we began. Let us leave both God and Caesar out of it for a moment; could not *I* have been born when and where Mark Antony was and had all his properties and experiences? As each of us puts this question to himself, it will seem clear that the thing is at least logically possible, i.e. not a self-contradictory supposition, and discernibly different from the actual state of affairs. We have already, in fact, in Section I, imagined Caesar putting this question to himself and having to give this answer. We may reflect also that if the theories of pre-existence and transmigration had been true, Caesar *would* have existed before his conception and so could have waited and been born to Mark Antony's parents at Mark Antony's time, and Mark Antony, also pre-existing, could have been born a little earlier to the people who in fact had Julius Caesar as their child; and we do not *know* that doctrines of pre-existence and transmigration are *not* true. Even if most of us regard it as so unlikely that belief in it is not a 'live option', it seems at least logically possible that it should be true.

---

[16] Art. 3, ad Obj. 3.

I have no wish to maintain that we cannot be mistaken as to what is logically possible. On the contrary, to fall into error on this subject is extremely easy. For example, the following imagined sequence of events is one which most people will be inclined to regard as logically possible: A certain Mr. X has a very low opinion of the intelligence of a colleague, Mr. Y, and the two of them are walking down a corridor and eventually separate into adjacent rooms; Mr. Y, as he thinks, into Room 7, and Mr. X, as he thinks, into Room 8. It is towards 6 o'clock and Mr. X reflects for a while, as he often does, on the incurable stupidity of Mr. Y, and at precisely 6 o'clock the thought occurs to him that whatever is being thought at 6 o'clock that night in Room 7 is false. That is all that he thinks at that time, and there is no one else in the room with him. But unfortunately, owing to some inadvertence, it is he himself who has gone into Room 7, and Mr. Y is in fact in Room 6. Most readers who have followed me so far will, I think, have found this chain of events a possible one, however curious. Yet it is easy to demonstrate that what I have described is incompatible with the most elementary logical laws. For what Mr. X takes to be the case must either be the case or not be the case. And it cannot be the case, for if it were, i.e. if it were the case that nothing thought at 6 in Room 7 is the case, then it would not be the case, since it is itself thought at 6 in Room 7. And since it thus cannot be the case that nothing thought at 6 in Room 7 is the case, then the fact must be that *something* thought at 6 in Room 7 is the case. But this true thought in Room 7 cannot be the one we know about, since that, as we have just seen, is false. So there must be some other thought than this one occurring at 6 in Room 7; but our hypothesis was that it was the only one. Our hypothesis as a whole, therefore, is implicitly self-contradictory, exactly as the hypothesis that there is a barber who shaves all those people and only those people who do not shave themselves is implicitly self-contradictory. Yet I must confess that I still feel, and I suspect that this is true of other people also, that there could be a Mr. X and Mr. Y behaving internally and externally exactly as I have said; so great is the force of certain 'logical illusions'.[17]

I doubt, however, whether it is necessary to bring in the hypothesis of 'logical illusion' to explain the apparent logical possibility of an exchange of properties between Antony and Caesar, or even between

[17] Cf. my 'Epimenides the Cretan', *Journal of Symbolic Logic*, Vol. 23, No. 3 (September 1958), pp. 261–6.

Antony and me. What *is* necessary is to distinguish logical possibility from the sort of possibility that we have been considering hitherto, and to get their relation straight. The distinction we want is made, for example, by the fifteenth-century scholastic philosopher Ferdinand of Cordova,[18] when describing a certain argument for the 'necessity' of correctly predicted future events. What is in question, he says, is not that 'logical necessity' which arises from a certain relation between a proposition's terms, but rather that 'truth which can no longer be prevented' which Aristotle was thought (by the propounders of the argument) to have required for a proposition to be counted 'already true'. If this distinction be kept clearly in view, it will be profitable to look again at the other horn of my dilemma about the *time* at which it was possible for Caesar to have had other parents. Once he was already born, I suggested, it was too late for him to have any chance of having had other parents. The 'necessity' here hinted at is of Ferdinand of Cordova's second sort; but the proposition that *this* person (the one we know as 'Julius Caesar') should have had those other persons (the ones who were in fact the parents of Mark Antony) as his parents, is certainly 'possible' in the sense of containing no internal inconsistency, and moreover is different in sense from the proposition that *that* person (the one we know as 'Mark Antony') had those persons as his parents.

In making this distinction, it is tempting to say that logical necessity and possibility are independent of the passage of time; and that about this sort of possibility the question '*When* was it possible?' need not and in fact cannot sensibly be asked. This, however, seems to be over-simplification. For there can be no truths, not even logical truths, that are distinguishably 'about' Caesar and Antony until there are such persons to be the subjects of these truths. Hence, while the passage of time may eliminate 'possibilities' in the sense of alternative outcomes of actual states of affairs, and cause that to be no longer alterable which once might have been otherwise, with 'logical' possibilities the opposite change occurs. For as new distinguishable individuals come into being, there is a multiplication of the number of different subjects to which our predications can be consistently attached, and so a multiplication of distinguishable logical possibilities. What was once just a possibility that 'someone' should have such-and-such a history, and 'someone else'

---

[18] In L. Baudry's *La Querelle des Futurs Contingents*, J. Vrin, Paris, 1950, p. 139.

should have such-and-such another history, can now be replaced by the distinct possibilities that X should have had the first history and Y the second, and that Y should have had the first and X the second. We must also accept the slightly odd result that it is logically possible that Julius Caesar *should have been* the son of Mark Antony's parents, even though before he existed it was not logically or in any other way possible that he should *come to have* those people, or any other people, as his parents. One must, in other words, take very seriously the present tense of the main verb in 'It is logically possible that Julius Caesar should have, etc.', just as one must take it very seriously (*v.s.* on creation and change) in 'It is not the case that Julius Caesar existed in 200 B.C.'

IX
TIME, EXISTENCE, AND IDENTITY

For some years now a number of us have been working on what is called 'tense logic', in which an attempt is made to give something of the rigour of modern logical systems to a language whose sentences resemble those of natural languages in being, in some cases at least, true at one time and false at another. In such a language it is possible to have rudimentary tense-inflections, notably Fp for 'It will be the case that p', which is, of course, true whenever p itself is going to be true at some future time, and Pp for 'It has been the case that p', which is true whenever p has been true at some past time. The extensions of *propositional* calculus which we obtain by adding such modifiers to the usual $\sim p$ ('It is not (now) the case that p'), $p \supset q$ ('If p then q'), $p \lor q$ ('Either p or q'), $p \land q$ ('Both p and q'), etc., are now fairly well understood, but we encounter serious problems when we attempt to introduce the same inflections into *predicate* logic, with quantification over individual variables.

To see where the difficulty lies, something should first be said about what these individual variables are supposed to stand for. In a logic with tenses, it is natural to let them stand for the 'things' of ordinary speech, that is, 'substances' in the old sense, or what W.E. Johnson calls 'continuants', objects such that we can say of each one of them that once it had such and such properties and did and suffered such and such things, that now it – the very same object – has such and such other properties and does and suffers such and such other things, and in the future it – the very same object – will have different properties again, and do and suffer different things. Tables and chairs and horses and men are typical 'individuals' of the sort intended; we may say of such-and-such a man, for example, that once he was a boy and now he is grown-up and some day he will be old, or that yesterday he was ill and now he is on the mend and tomorrow he will be quite better. And while in general these individual objects have parts – men have arms and legs and so on – and these parts are objects of a sort, we do *not* say that they have *temporal* parts or phases, in the way that processes and histories do. My boyhood, for example, is not a part of me, though it is a part of my history; and it is not the case that one part of me was a boy in New Zealand while another part of me is a man in England; it is I who was that boy, and I – the same I – who am the man.

This language is surely well enough understood, and most of the time fairly easily handled. When, however, we allow such 'substances' or 'continuants' to be the 'values' that the variables x, y, etc., can take in formulae like 'For some x, it was the case 40 years ago that x is a boy in New Zealand', we are soon compelled to take account, in one way or another, of the fact that most individuals of this sort have been in existence, and will be in existence, for a finite time only, and that the individuals in existence at any given time are not entirely the same as the individuals in existence at other times. We might, indeed, attempt to argue on physical or metaphysical grounds that tables and chairs and horses and men are not genuine individual continuants but only collections of these, the real continuants being certain ultimate 'simples' which exist throughout all time and merely get rearranged in various ways. Or we might argue that there is only a single genuine individual, the Universe, which gets John-Smithish or Mary-Brownish in such-and-such regions for such-and-such periods. But, prima facie at least, this is *not* how things are, and it ought to be at least possible to develop a tensed predicate logic which does not depend for its validity on any such assumptions. And, in fact, this is not only possible, but has been already done, in a variety of ways.

One very natural way of proceeding is to say, when we have a tense-operator such as 'It will be the case that' followed by a quantifier such as 'For some x', that the objects that are relevant to the verification of the quantified propositions are the ones which will be in existence at the time to which the tense-operator takes us. If I say, for example, that it will be the case that for some x, x is flying to the planet Mars, what I mean is that something *then* existing (whether it already exists now or not) will be flying to the planet Mars. If, on the other hand, we have a quantifier right at the beginning of a sentence, we can suppose it to be governed by the operator 'It is the case that', i.e. 'It is now the case that', which can be prefixed to any tensed sentence without making any difference to what is said. So the form 'For some x, it will be the case that x is flying to the planet Mars' may be taken to mean 'Something which now exists will be flying to the planet Mars'.

That, at all events, is one way of handling this problem, and we now have a fair idea of what sort of tensed predicate logic we will get if we do it this way. We might argue, on the other hand, that it is just as easy to refer to what once existed, and perhaps just as easy to refer to what is going to exist, as to what exists now, and we might use *all* such objects, whether they exist now or not, as values of our variables, and if what we mean by 'Something' is 'Something that now exists' we must explicitly say so. For example, we may take both of the foregoing forms, namely,

'It will be the case that, for some x, x is flying to the moon'

and

'For some x, it will be the case that x is flying to the moon'

to mean merely that something that exists or has existed or will exist will fly to the moon, and the stronger form must be written as

'For some x, x now exists and it will be the case that x flies to the moon'.

This sort of tensed predicate logic is also fairly well developed now.

I have an uneasy feeling, however, that both these forms of tensed predicate logic operate with too crude and stark a notion of the beginning-to-be and ceasing-to-be of individuals. It is as if at one moment these individuals are just not there, and at another they are. In the real world it seldom seems as simple as this, although neither is it as simple as it would be if the only individuals were permanent 'ultimate simples', or if there were only a single genuine individual, also permanent. To quote what I have said elsewhere, 'Very roughly, it would seem that countable "things" are made or grow from bits of stuff, or from other countable "things", that are already there. The precise logic of this process hasn't been worked out yet, and until it has been, it seems likely that any tensed predicate logic can only be provisional in character.'

I shall not attempt in this paper to do anything like filling this gap, but I want to say enough to indicate that not only what I have called 'stark starting to be', but also kinds of 'starting to be' which are much less 'stark', present serious logical problems. The obvious alternative to something's starting to be *without* antecedents is its starting to be *with* antecedents, and it is tempting to describe this as *one thing becoming another thing*. But what could this be, if it is neither a case of one thing simply ceasing to exist and a quite different thing starting to exist (maybe in roughly the same locality), nor a case of some one thing radically changing in its qualities or nature? It is not at all clear that there could be anything in between these two, but at least one kind of change which does not seem to fall under either description, and which is in any case worth investigating, would be *one thing becoming two things*. There do seem to be at least approximations to this in nature, e.g. the 'multiplication by division' of unicellular organisms, and still closer approximations to it seem to be easily imaginable, e.g. conscious organisms which divide in two and retain after division a clear memory of their undivided state.

If anything does, in fact, happen which could be reasonably described as one individual thing becoming two individual things, it is natural to ask whether this would be consistent with the generally accepted laws of the logic of identity. These are, primarily, the two laws which may be expressed as follows (using the form '$x=y$' for 'x and y are one and the same individual thing'):

1. $x=x$,
2. $x=y \supset (\varphi x \supset \varphi y)$.

The first states that anything is the same individual as itself; the second, that if x and y are one and the same individual thing, then if anything at all is true of x, that thing must be ipso facto true of y (we would be inclined to say its being true of x is its being true of y, since x is y). The second law is sometimes called 'Leibniz's law', or 'the indiscernibility of identicals'. From these two, certain others easily follow. In the first place, ordinary commutation takes us from 2. to

3. $\varphi x \supset (x=y \supset \varphi y)$.

If in this we let our 'φ-ing' be 'being identical with x', i.e. if we substitute $=x$ for φ, we obtain

4. $x=x \supset (x=y \supset y=x)$,

which by detachment of 1. yields

5. $x=y \supset y=x$,

asserting that identity is symmetrical. Again, if in 3. we let our 'φ-ing' be 'z's being identical with', i.e. if we substitute $=z$ for φ, we obtain

6. $z=x \supset (x=y \supset z=y)$,

asserting that identity is transitive. And if in 2. we let our 'φ-ing' be 'being identical with z', i.e. if we substitute $z=$ for φ, we obtain

7. $x=y \supset (x=z \supset y=z)$,

asserting that if x is identical both with y and with z, then y is identical with z.

It formerly seemed to me that the basic laws 1. and 2. would be compatible with one thing's becoming two, if we were prepared to adopt a slightly non-standard tense-logic.[1] The difficulty which seemed to demand this was the following one: law 2. merely states that (i) if x is now the very same individual as y, then whatever now goes for x now goes for y. It does not state that (ii) if x was once the very same individual as y, then whatever now goes for x now goes for y. We could infer from (i), however, that (iii) if x was once the very same individual as y, then it was once the case that whatever went for x went for y, and in a metric tense-logic (with $P(n)p$ for 'It was the case the interval n ago that p', and $F(n)p$ for 'It will be the case that the interval n hence that p') we would infer that (iv) if x was once the very same individual as y, then whatever then went for x, then went for y, too, or symbolically

8. $P(n)(x=y) \supset (P(n)(x \supset P(n)(y)).$

Now let us suppose that the individual x is no longer identical with y (x and y being the two things which some one thing has become), and that x is now φ-ing. Then in any ordinary tense-logic it would follow that it was the case the interval n ago that it would be the case the interval n later that x is φ-ing, i.e. we have

9. $\varphi x \supset P(n)F(n)\varphi x.$

[1] A.N. Prior, 'Opposite Number', *Review of Metaphysics* (1957).

From this, by 8. it follows that it was the case the interval n ago that it would be the case the interval n later that this y is φ-ing, and from this and the converse of 9. it would follow that not only x but y is now φ-ing. But if x and y really have become distinct, it is perfectly possible that x should now be φ-ing and y not. To avoid the undesirable deduction, I suggested dropping 9., a suggestion which seemed plausible since there are independent reasons (connected with determinism) for questioning 9. anyway.

But this move, unfortunately, is not enough to prevent us from encountering other troubles. Let us suppose that the single individual x has become the two individuals y and z. If x has really *become* these two individuals, and has not simply ceased to exist and been in some sense replaced by them, then if anyone were to ask 'Where is x now?', one correct answer would be to say 'Here he is' and point to y. In other words, x is now y, and it would perhaps also be true to say that it is y who is now x, i.e. y is now x. But it would be equally correct to answer the question 'Where is x now?' by saying, 'Here he is', and pointing to z. In other words, x is now z; and, perhaps, z is now x. But from these premisses, the laws 6. and 7., above, would lead us to conclude that y is now z (this follows most straightforwardly, from $x=y$ and $x=z$, by the use of 7.). But *ex hypothesi*, y is *not* now z. We are therefore led to question not merely the rather dubious tense-logical principle 9., but even the fundamental identity principles 6. and 7., and therefore, of course, the still more fundamental 'Leibniz's law' 2., from which 6. and 7. immediately follow.

This seems to me in some ways a much more serious objection to Leibniz's law than a number which have been offered in recent years. For these other objections generally depend on replacing the individual variables x and y by *descriptions*, and the apparent breaches of the law can be eliminated by paraphrasing the descriptions away in the manner, say, of Russell. Instead of the examples normally used, drawn from modal logic or the logic of belief and knowing, we might here usefully consider a tense-logical example of substantially the same kind. Suppose that it is the case today that in a certain military unit the adjutant is the orderly officer ($x=y$). It is always the case that the orderly officer is the orderly officer (φx, where $\varphi \ldots$ = 'It is always the case that the orderly officer is $\ldots$'). But it does not follow that it is always the case that the orderly officer is the adjutant (φy). Here we simply have a couple of descriptions which sometimes apply to the same person and sometimes do not; what the first premiss really means is that someone is now both the adjutant and the orderly officer; the second premiss, in the only sense in which it is true, means that whoever is at any time the orderly officer is at that time the orderly officer; while in the only sense in which it yields the conclusion, the second premiss means that whoever is now the orderly officer is at all times the orderly officer, and in this sense it is false. What we do *not* have in this example is a couple of individuals who are sometimes the same individuals and sometimes not. Similarly, no startling departures from ordinary views of identity are involved in the statement that 'the orderly officer is a different individual every day'.[2] What this means, of course, is simply that on each day a different person is-the-orderly-officer, i.e. answers to that description.

Nothing so simple as this, however, is involved in the example we began by considering. Here we are supposing that a certain two individuals *were* at one time one and the same individual, and the *descriptions under which* they are presented at the different periods are quite irrelevant. And it now seems to me quite clear that the only way in which the ordinary logic of identity can be fully preserved is by maintaining that cases of this sort never occur or can occur, i.e. that it never is or can be the case that one individual thing becomes two individual things; and that whenever we are tempted to describe an empirical change in this way, what has really happened has been the ceasing to be of one individual and the beginning to be of two others, or else they were two all the time, only this was not apparent, or else they are still, in spite of appearances, one. This would be a reversion to the 'stark starting-to-be' which seems on the whole to be a rather *simpliste* notion, or to the theory that all genuine individuals are sempiternal.

Even if we are persuaded by these arguments that Leibniz's law is false, it remains obvious that something very like it is true, and we have to hunt for that. Here I content myself with two observations. In the first place, it may well turn out that the identity-functions for which we really do have a law like Leibniz's, and laws like $x=y \supset (x=z \supset y=z)$, are functions of higher order than identity of individuals. For example, if we have not a two-place predicate but a connective I such that Ipq may be read as 'The proposition that p is the very same proposition as the proposition that q', it may well be the case that for all p, q, and r, if

---

[2] I owe this example to E.J. Lemmon.

Ipq and *Ipr* then *Iqr*. Secondly, even at the level of identity of individuals, it would seem that *x* will only be both the very same individual as *y* and the very same individual as *z*, if *y* and *z* at least *have been* one and the same individual, or maybe also if they are going to be (I have confined myself to the case of fission; fusion presents similar problems, and perhaps others as well). This means that we do have at least

$$Ixy \supset (Ixz \supset (Iyz \lor PIyz \lor FIyz)).$$

We may, indeed, bypass all of these problems by simply dropping the notion of individual 'things' or 'continuants' which persist and act and interact as time goes on, in favour of the notion of four-dimensional objects which simply occupy so much time in the way that they occupy so much space; and we may suppose that some such objects have a branching structure in their temporal dimension. Or more precisely, we may suppose that the earlier temporal parts of a certain four-dimensional object are undivided spatially, while its later temporal parts are spatially divided. A rudimentary logic of the extension in time of 'objects' of this sort has been sketched by Carnap,[3] and something of the same sort is at present being developed by C. Lejewski. Lejewski's work is being done in the context of the Leśniewskian calculus, 'mereology', which deals with the part–whole relation between objects. On top of this he builds a discipline which he calls 'chronology', involving such conceptions as those of one object being wholly earlier than another, and of one object having a greater temporal extension than another.

The development of this new body of theory is something which is only to be welcomed, but to leave that matter there, and regard our problem as solved by presenting its data in 'chronological' terms, is unsatisfactory in at least two ways. In the first place, the 'chronological' solution is only a new variant of the solution according to which the two objects remain one even after the division. It is based on the 'mereological' thesis that for any pair of objects there is a third object which simply consists of the two of them together, and this third object remains such whether its parts are continuously connected or separate. More precisely, each of the later contemporaneous slices of our four-

---

[3] R. Carnap, *Introduction to Symbolic Logic*, Section 52.

dimensional object is as much a single object as each of its earlier slices, although the later ones have wholly distinct parts. There are no doubt senses of 'object' for which talk of this kind is appropriate, but they are not the senses in which the situation envisaged presents us with one object becoming two.

Secondly, and most seriously, to rest content with 'chronological' language as it stands would be to abandon the whole enterprise, which is one of the things that makes tensed predicate logic philosophically interesting, of exhibiting events and processes which are ordered and extended in time, and which can be conceived as having 'temporal parts', as logical constructions out of persisting and acting things or continuants. As was observed earlier, the successive phases of the history of a thing are in no sense parts of the thing itself; it is one and the same thing (the whole thing, so far as talk of parts and wholes is appropriate here) which at one time does or undergoes this and at another does or undergoes that, and at one time stands here and at another time – by which time it (the same thing) *has stood* here – stands there. It is within this framework that we must try to give the language of 'chronology' its meaning; not vice versa. This enterprise has been carried so far now that it is worth at least exploring the consequences of carrying it through to the end. But we cannot do this satisfactorily until much more work has been done, of the sort that is already beginning to be done, on the whole notion of an individual thing, and of 'the same individual thing'. If, even at this early stage, it appears that we shall be faced with the abandonment or at least the modification of Leibniz's law, we may reflect that this has been contemplated in recent years for quite trivial reasons, so we need not be too dismayed if we now have to contemplate it for serious ones.

X
RECENT ADVANCES IN TENSE LOGIC

1. *Lemmon's stratification.* By a 'tense logic' I mean a system with the following features: (a) it contains sentential variables (say p, q, r, etc.) which stand for sentences (like 'Socrates is sitting down') which in some cases are true at some times and false at others; (b) it contains the usual truth-functions (say $p \supset q$ for 'If p then q', $p \wedge q$ for 'p and q', $p \vee q$ for 'p or q', $p \equiv q$ for 'p if and only if q', $\sim p$ for 'Not p'), whose truth-conditions are given the obvious modifications, e.g. $\sim p$ is true *when* and only when p is false, $p \wedge q$ is true *when* and only when both its conjuncts are; and (c) it contains two additional functions (say Fp and Pp) which may be interpreted as 'It will be the case that p' and 'It has been the case that p', the former being true when and only when the plain p will be true later on and the latter when and only when the plain p has been true at some earlier time.

In my book *Past, Present and Future* (1967) and in the first edition of *Papers on Time and Tense* (1968) I gave some account of the main developments in this area that I then knew about; this article continues the story, mostly with notes on developments which either have occurred or have come to my notice since those books were written.

I shall, however, allow myself one major piece of recapitulation. Most of the developments I shall be discussing begin from the 'stratification' of tense–logic which was achieved in 1965 by the late E.J. Lemmon. Lemmon divided tense-logical postulates into those which could be regarded as simply reflecting the obvious truth-conditions of tensed sentences, and those which could be regarded as reflecting specific postulates about the earlier–later relation, e.g. that it is transitive, that it has no first or last term, etc. If we write $Ta(p)$ for 'It is the case at the instant a that p' and Uab for 'The instant a is earlier than the instant b', and use $\forall$ and $\exists$ for the universal and existential quantifiers, the times when the different principal kinds of complex are the case are given by the following equivalences:

T1. $Ta(\sim p) \equiv \sim Ta(p)$
T2. $Ta(p \wedge q) \equiv (Ta(p) \wedge Ta(q))$
T3. $Ta(Fp) \equiv \exists b(Uab \wedge Tb(p))$
T4. $Ta(Pp) \equiv \exists b(Uba \wedge Tb(p))$,

i.e. 'Not-p' is true at a if and only if p is not; 'p and q' is true at a if and only if p is and q is; 'It-will-be-that-p' is true at a if and only if there is some moment later than a at which p is true; and 'It-has-been-that-p' is true at a if and only if there is some moment earlier than a at which p is true. T1 and T2 yield further equations for other truth-functions, and if we define Gp (for 'It will always be that p') as $\sim F\sim p$ ('It will never be that not p') and Hp (for 'It has always been that p') as $\sim H\sim p$, T1–T4 yield the further equivalences

T5. $Ta(Gp) \equiv \forall b(Uab \supset Tb(p))$
T6. $Ta(Hp) \equiv \forall b(Uba \supset Tb(p))$.

From these, the truth-conditions of complexes like FHp, $FHp \supset p$, $p \supset FHp$, etc. can be worked out, and certain tense-logical formulae can be proved from T1–T4 to be true at any arbitrary instant a. These constitute Lemmon's lowest 'stratum' of tense-logical truths, his minimal system K_t. They turn out to be all those formulae which may be deduced by substitution, detachment and the rules

RG: $\vdash \alpha \rightarrow \vdash G\alpha$
RH: $\vdash \alpha \rightarrow \vdash H\alpha$

from propositional calculus plus the axioms

A1.1. $G(p \supset q) \supset (Fp \supset Fq)$
A1.2. $H(p \supset q) \supset (Pp \supset Pq)$
A2.1. $p \supset GPp$
A2.2. $p \supset HFp$.

(Alternative axiomatisations are possible, e.g. G and H may be taken as primitive, F and P defined as $\sim G\sim$ and $\sim H\sim$, and the A1s replaced by $G(p \supset q) \supset (Gp \supset Gq)$ and its image. The A2s, also, could be replaced by $PGp \supset p$ and $FHp \supset p$.)

Further tense-logical formulae can be proved to be true at any arbitrary instant a by adding special conditions on the relation U. It is additions of this sort – the ones that belong to Lemmon's second layer – that form the subject of the advances that I wish first to record.

2. *New postulates for nonbeginning and nonending.* One condition that we may wish to put upon the earlier–later relation U is that it has no first or last term, i.e. that for any term a there is a term b which is earlier, $\forall a \exists b U b a$, and for any term a there is a term b which is later, $\forall a \exists b U a b$. (With these formulae as theorems we can of course drop the initial $\forall a$, and assert them as $\vdash \exists b U b a$ and $\vdash \exists b U a b$). This addition to the minimal earlier–later calculus corresponds to the addition of the axioms $\sim Pp \supset P \sim p$ and $\sim Fp \supset F \sim p$ to K_t.

In earlier presentations of this result, at all events by me, it may not have been made sufficiently clear that these postulates mean no more than what has just been said, i.e. that the series of instants has no first and no last term. They do not express time's infinity in any quantitative or metric sense, i.e. they do not say that there is no maximum time *interval*, in either direction – they do not say that for any interval n, however large, every instant has an instant which is earlier than it by that interval, and every instant has an instant later than it by that interval. For the postulates of the last paragraph are quite consistent with the view that for each instant a there is some interval n such that no instant b is earlier than a by that much, though there are instants earlier than b by the whole continuous range of quantities *up to* (but not including) n, these instants having no earliest; and similarly on the other side. To distinguish this case from absolute quantitative infinity we would need a richer symbolic apparatus than the one so far described. On the earlier–later side we could do it if we had the form $U a b n$ for 'a is earlier than b by the interval n'. The weaker assertion of nonbeginning would then come out as $\forall a \exists n \exists b U b a n$, 'For every a there is an n and a b such that b is earlier than a by n', while the stronger assertion would come out as $\forall a \forall n \exists b U b a n$, 'For every a and for *every* n there is a b such that b is earlier than a by n'. If we define our original $U a b$ as $\exists n U a b n$, our earlier postulate $\forall a \exists b U a b$ will expand to $\forall a \exists b \exists n U a b n$, which is equivalent to the weaker assertion just made, while the stronger assertion has no exact equivalent in the dyadic U. On the tense-logical side, similar things are to be said about the relations between the forms $P(n)p$ and $F(n)p$ (for 'It was the case the interval n ago that p' and 'It will be the case the interval n hence that p') and our original Pp and Fp.

Endlessness without quantitative infinity is, of course, only possible if the series of instants is a dense one; in discrete time $\exists b U b a$ and $\exists b U a b$ *would* express quantitative infinity in the two directions. And whether time, if dense, has an intrinsic metric of a sort which makes the distinction between the two sorts of beginninglessness and endlessness an intelligible one, I am not at all sure. At all events the distinction cannot be drawn within the nonmetric tense–logic and earlier–later logic with which we are now concerned.

On the tense-logical side, it has been obvious for some time that $\sim\!Pp \supset P\!\sim\!p$ and $\sim\!Fp \supset F\!\sim\!p$ are by no means the only formulae we could use to express time's lack of a first and of a last instant respectively. For example, they yield by transposition $\sim\!P\!\sim\!p \supset Pp$ and $\sim\!F\!\sim\!p \supset Fp$, i.e. $Hp \supset Pp$ and $Gp \supset Fp$, and these in turn yield them by transposition. These formulae, again, can be shown to be deductively equivalent to $P(p \supset p)$ and $F(p \supset p)$, or to the rule that if α is any theorem then so are $P\alpha$ and $F\alpha$. An intriguing variant of the latter, due to C. Howard (1966), is the rule that if $G\alpha$ is a theorem so is α (this for no beginning), and the same for $H\alpha$ (for no ending). Given Howard's first rule, we can pass from $\vdash \alpha$ to $\vdash P\alpha$ via $\vdash GP\alpha$ (this from α by $p \supset GPp$, and $P\alpha$ from it by Howard's rule). And conversely, given that we may infer $\vdash P\alpha$ from $\vdash \alpha$, we may derive $\vdash \alpha$ from $\vdash G\alpha$ thus:

1. $G\alpha$
2. $(p \supset p) \supset G\alpha$ $[1, p \supset (q \supset p)]$
3. $P(p \supset p) \supset PG\alpha$ $[2, \text{RH}, \text{A1.2}]$
4. $P(p \supset p) \supset \alpha$ $[3, PGp \supset p]$
5. $P(p \supset p)$ $[p \supset p, \text{rule for } P]$
6. α $[4, 5]$.

But there are certain other principles which have been known for quite a time to fail if time had a beginning or end. McTaggart, for example, in a work published posthumously in 1927[1] having asserted that every event has 'all three' of the determinations past, present and future, adds in a qualifying footnote that 'If the time-series has a first term, that term will never be future, and if it has a last term, that term will never be past'. (Here McTaggart's 'will never be' seems to be doing duty for a tenseless 'at no time is'.) Nelson Goodman,[2] similarly, said in a work of 1951 that

---

[1] See McTaggart, *The Nature of Existence*, Vol. II, p. 20 n.

[2] See Nelson Goodman, *The Structure of Appearance*, 1951, p. 366.

A 'World War II was future' – if unaccompanied by any context determining what prior moment is being affirmed to precede World War II – says only what may be said about any event *that did not begin at the first moment of time*. Likewise, of any event *that does not run to the end of time*, we may truly say that it will be past. (Italics mine.)

So to say that *everything* that is the case 'has been future', and to lay this down as something always true, is in effect to say that time had no past moment, and to say (as something true always) that everything that is the case 'will be past', is in effect to say that time will have no end. This suggests $p \supset PFp$ and $p \supset FPp$ as axioms for nonbeginning and nonending respectively, and simple proofs of their deductive equivalence to $Hp \supset Pp$ and $Gp \supset Fp$ (given K_t) were found in 1967 by Storrs McCall. For the nonbeginning pair we have

1. $p \supset PFp$			1. $Hp \supset Pp$	
2. $Hp \supset PFHp$	$[1\ p/Hp]$		2. $HFp \supset PFp$	$[1, p/Fp]$
3. $PFHp \supset Pp$	$[FHp \supset p,$		3. $p \supset PFp$	$[2, p \supset HFp]$
	$RH, A1.2]$			
4. $Hp \supset Pp$	$[2, 3]$			

3. *Strong and Weak Futures.* There is one law in Lemmon's minimal system K_t which doesn't *sound* as noncommittal as all that, namely $p \supset HFp$, asserting that whatever is now the case has always been going to be the case. By contrast with its mirror image $p \supset GPp$ (whatever is now the case will always have been the case), this thesis has for many a flavour of determinism. There are various ways of removing this impression. We might say, for instance, that if determinism is false there is, at each moment, no *actual* future but only a number of alternative *possible* futures, so that Fp can only mean 'It will be the case in some possible future that p'. $p \supset HFp$ would then mean merely that if anything has in fact come to pass then it must always have been 'on the cards' that it would do so, and there is nothing deterministic about this. Genuine determinism would be the belief that there is only *one* possible future, and to express this you really do need to go beyond K_t and add a postulate for nonbranching of the future, e.g. $PFp \supset (p \lor Pp \lor Fp)$ ('Whatever has been "on the cards" either is the case or has been the case or is "on the cards" still').

If, however, in an indeterministic universe we read Fp thus, there must surely also be *another Fp* for which $p \supset HFp$ *would* have deterministic overtones – an Fp which means that p will be the case in *every* possible future. $\sim F\sim p$, i.e. Gp, is not exactly what we want here, for this goes too far; for since Fp means that p will be true *somewhere* in *some* possible future, $\sim F\sim p$ would mean that it will not be true *anywhere* in *any* possible future that not p, i.e. that p will be true *throughout* every possible future. What we want is something in between, which says that p will be true *somewhere* in *every* possible future.

My own past attempts to bring out this distinction have been via metric tense logic. If $F(n)p$ means that it will be the case the interval n hence in *some* possible future that p, then $\sim F(n)\sim p$ would mean that it will not be the case the interval n hence in any possible future that not p, i.e. that it will be the case the interval n hence in *every* possible future that p. In brief, if we read $F(n)p$ as 'It could be the interval n hence that p', we should read $\sim F(n)\sim p$ as 'It *is bound to be* the case the interval n hence that p'. We may then define the weaker of the plain Fps as $\exists nF(n)p$, 'It could be the case at some future time that p', and the stronger of the plain Fps as $\exists n\sim F(n)\sim p$, 'It is bound to be the case at some future time that p'.

This last piece of English, however, is still ambiguous, and it is to be feared that the meaning captured by my formula is the wrong one, i.e. not the kind of 'strong' or 'definite' future in which people who operate with 'definite' and 'indefinite' future tenses are most interested. For $\exists n\sim F(n)\sim p$ means that there is some specific interval n such that in every possible future p will occur after precisely that interval; and we have much less use for this than we have for the slightly weaker assertion that in every possible future p will be the case after some interval or other (*not* necessarily the same in each). We could only get this, one would think, if we had some way of quantifying over alternatives as well as over intervals.

In 1967, however, Storrs McCall cut this knot by digging back to the ordinary nonmetric earlier-later calculus, and putting forward a suggestion that amounted to the following: Use H, G and F as tense-logical primitives, with the truth-conditions of H and G given as usual by $Ta(Hp) \equiv \forall b(Uba \supset Tb(p))$ and $Ta(Gp) \equiv \forall b(Uab \supset Tb(p))$. Use P for $\sim H\sim$ but do not use F for $\sim G\sim$ but for a separate primitive whose truth-conditions are a little more complicated. If we write Iab for 'a is the same instant as b' and Bab for Iab ∨ Uab ∨ Uba, the latter will assert in effect that a and b are on the same branch. $Ta(Fp)$ is then equated with

$$∀b(Uab ⊃ ∃c(Bbc ∧ Uac ∧ Tc(p)),$$

i.e. Fp is true at a if and only if every later moment b has some moment c on the same branch, and also later than a, at which p is true. That is, Fp is true at a if and only if on every branch issuing from a there is some instant at which p is true. This is exactly what is needed. The weaker 'It will be that p', meaning only that p is true at some later instant on *some* branch, is of course given by ~G~p. It is now easy to assert $p ⊃ H$~G~p but deny $p ⊃ HFp$.

McCall has suggested certain postulates for an H-G-(strong)-F system in which it is assumed that the earlier-later relation is transitive and that time is dense, infinite both ways, and nonbranching in the past. The important and original part of McCall's list of postulates is, of course, the handful which involve the new F. These are

F1. $G(p ⊃ q) ⊃ (Fp ⊃ Fq)$
F2. $Gp ⊃ Fp$
F3. $Fp ⊃$ ~G~p
F4. $PFp ⊃ FPp$
F5. G~G~$p ⊃ GFp$
F6. $F(p ∨ Fp) ⊃ Fp$
F7. $Fp ⊃ G(p ∨ Fp ∨ Pp)$
F8. $F(p ∨ Fp ∨ Pp) ⊃ (p ∨ Fp ∨ Pp)$
F9. $(p ∨ Fp ∨ Pp) ⊃ H(p ∨$ ~G~$p ∨ Pp)$
F10. $G(p ∨$ ~G~$p ∨ Pp) ⊃ (p ∨ Fp ∨ Pp)$

Whether these are capable of further simplification, and whether they are complete, is not yet known. We may note that to prove Ta (F1) and Ta (F2) for any arbitrary a, nothing is required but the truth-conditions of G and F, i.e. F1 and F2 do not reflect any special conditions on U. (Whether the addition of F1 and F2 to K_t in G and H will yield *all* H-G-F theorems which are thus independent of special conditions on U, I do not know.) The presence of F2 in this 'noncommittal' group is a little surprising, for with the ordinary F, $Gp ⊃ Fp$ only holds if time is endless. F2 and F3 do indeed yield syllogistically one of the usual postulates for nonending, $Gp \supset \sim G\sim p$, but the 'kick' in this comes not from F2 but F3 (F3, though not F2, is true only in nonending time). The reason is that when there is no future Fp, like Gp, is vacuously verified. For the condition of its truth at a is that *if* along *any* path there is a later instant than a, then at some point on that path it is the case that p; 'some' here is governed by an 'every', and what begins with 'every X' is vacuously verified when there are no Xs.

If we add $\sim G\sim p \supset Fp$ to McCall's system, this with F3 equates Fp and $\sim G\sim p$, and gives $PFp \supset (p \vee Fp \vee Pp)$ (from F4 and F5) its usual interpretation as a postulate of nonbranching in the future.

4. *Density and circularity.* One condition which many would wish to impose on the earlier-later relation is that the series which it generates is a dense one. This condition is generally expressed by the postulate $Uab \supset \exists c(Uac \wedge Ucb)$, 'If a is earlier than b, there is a c which is later than a but earlier than b'. This enables us to prove the truth at any arbitrary instant a of all tense-logical formulae derivable from K_t enriched by any one of the axioms $HHp \supset Hp$, $GGp \supset Gp$, $Pp \supset PPp$, $Fp \supset FFp$ (weak F). If, however, time should happen to be circular, all of these postulates would be just as true if time were not dense but discrete. For in circular time every instant is both earlier and later than itself, i.e. we have Uaa as a law (and so $Uab \supset (Uaa \wedge Uab)$, and so $Uab \supset \exists c(Uac \wedge Ucb)$), and whatever has always been or will always be true is true now ($Hp \supset p$ and $Gp \supset p$, and so $HHp \supset Hp$ and $GGp \supset Gp$), and whatever is true now both has been true and will be true ($p \supset Pp$ and $p \supset Fp$, and so $Pp \supset PPp$ and $Fp \supset FFp$).

How, then, *can* we distinguish discrete and dense time even if time should be circular? It has been observed by K. Fine and J.R. Lucas that since in circular time U relates any pair of terms at all, it is impossible for this job to be done with the symbolic machinery employed in the last paragraph; Lucas has also indicated, constructively, what further devices are needed (1966). In the first place, a *metric* earlier-later calculus or tense-logic will do; for in the former we can say that if ever a is earlier than b by the interval n then there is some c which is both later than a and earlier than b by some smaller interval than n, and in the latter we can say that if it will be the case the interval n hence that p then for some m less than n it will be the case the interval m hence that it will be the case the interval n-m thence that p; neither of these being automatically true in circular time.

Alternatively, without introducing metric conceptions, we may introduce into the earlier–later calculus a certain triadic relation among instants which is not definable in terms of any dyadic one. I shall not here use the particular triadic relation selected by Lucas, but another one which can be more directly echoed by an undefined dyadic tense-function. The relation I shall use is what might be called 'directed betweeness', which must be distinguished both from undirected betweeness and from the directed betweeness which is definable in terms of earlier and later. If a, b and c are all points on a circle, each of them is in one way or another between the other two. If we speak of b being between a and c in a certain direction round the circle, there does seem to be a difference – Copenhagen is between London and Moscow if you're going eastwards but not if you're going westwards, and London is between Copenhagen and Moscow if you're going westwards but not if you're going eastwards. But if we define 'b is between a and c going east' as 'You can get from a to b and then from b to c, going east all the time', we don't capture this difference; for in this sense London *is* between Copenhagen and Moscow, even going east – we can go from Copenhagen right round the world eastwards (past Moscow) to London, and then from London round eastwards (past Copenhagen) to Moscow. If we define 'b is between a and c in the direction from earlier to later' as 'a is earlier than b and b than c', *this* 'betweeness' becomes similarly vacuous in circular time; for in circular time we can say of *any* instants a, b and c that a is earlier than b and b than c. It is the *undefined* directed triadic temporal betweeness that we need, i.e. the analogue of the relation whose terms are London, Copenhagen and Moscow in that order, but not in the order Copenhagen, London, Moscow. Given this, we can assert density even in circular time by saying that whenever a is earlier or later than c there is a term between them in earliness or lateness.

Similarly in tense–logic we could introduce a form, say Tpq, for 'It will be that p and then q' in the sense in which this is *not* just short for $F(p \wedge Fq)$, 'It will be that (p and it will be that q)'; and we could then assert density even in circular time by 'Whenever it will be that p then for some q it will be that q and then p', or by 'Whenever it will be that p, it will be that if-p-then-p and then p', $Fp \supset T(p \supset p)p$. We would, I think, want to have $Tpq \supset F(p \wedge Fq)$ (though not its converse) as a law even in 'noncommittal' tense logic, and this with the preceding would give the more usual density principle thus:

1. $Tpq \supset F(p \wedge Fq)$
2. $Fp \supset T(p \supset p)p$
3. $Fp \supset F((p \supset p) \wedge Fp)$ [1, 2]
4. $Fp \supset FFp$ $[3, F(p \wedge q) \supset Fq]$

5. *The logic of discrete future time.* As might be expected, axioms in P and F (or H and G) which are designed to express the view that time is *discrete*, like ones designed to express the view that it is dense, fail of their purpose if time is circular. However, we now know what axioms in P and F (or H and G) do express time's discreteness, to the extent that that is possible with these primitives. A set of postulates for infinite, nonbranching, discrete time (with the earlier-later relation transitive) is given by R.A. Bull.[3] There is no point in reproducing these postulates here, but it would be useful to axiomatise the purely future-tense part of this system, and I would conjecture that the following in G ($F = {\sim}G{\sim}$), subjoined to propositional calculus with substitution and detachment, would suffice:

RG: If $\vdash \alpha$ then $\vdash G\alpha$
G1. $G(p \supset q) \supset (Gp \supset Gp)$
G2. $Gp \supset Fp$ [for infinity]
G3. $Gp \supset GGp$ [for transitivity]
G4. $G(p \supset q) \supset (G(p \supset Gq) \supset$
       $(G(Fp \supset q) \supset (Fp \supset Gq)))$ [for nonbranching]
G5. $G((Gp \supset p) \supset (FGp \supset Gp))$ [for discreteness].

Ordinary transpositions easily equate G5 with

$$(F{\sim}p \wedge FGp) \supset F({\sim}p \wedge Gp),$$

which has been shown to yield (with the other postulates) the complete Diodorean modal logic (i.e. the modal logic with 'Possibly p' defined as 'It either is or will be that p') for discrete time. Moreover, when the mirror-images of these postulates are added, with the 'mixing axioms' $p \supset PGp$ and $p \supset HFp$, we obtain Bull's complete past-future calculus for discrete time. The key proof is this:-

[3] *Journal of Symbolic Logic*, March 1968 (not December 1967, as stated in the first edition of *Papers on Time and Tense*, p. 161).

1.	$HG(Gp \supset p) \supset H(FGp \supset Gp)$	[5, RH, H1]
2.	$HG(Gp \supset p) \supset (HFGp \supset HGp)$	[1, H1]
3.	$HG(Gp \supset p) \supset (Gp \supset HGp)$	[2, $p \supset HFp$]
4.	$HG(Gp \supset p) \supset (Gp \supset HHGp)$	[3, H3]
5.	$HG(Gp \supset p) \supset (Gp \supset HPGp)$	[4, H2]
6.	$HG(Gp \supset p) \supset (Gp \supset Hp)$	[5, $PGp \supset p$] = Bull.

These facts made the sufficiency of RG and G1–5 for their purpose a likely conjecture, but as yet that is all it is.

Verbally, my G5 asserts that if it will always be the case that (if it will always be that p then it is the case that p), then if it will be that (it will always be that p), then, right now, it will always be that p. If time is discrete, this is true, since we can use the antecedent to come back step by step from the future permanence of p to its present permanence. But if time is not discrete there may be a future first moment of p's permanent truth but no last moment of its falsehood, so that the steps backward cannot begin. Except that if time is circular we have $FGp \supset Gp$, and so G5, in any case.

6. *Yesterday and tomorrow.* Those features of the logic of time which underlie the *measurement* of temporal intervals have continued to be investigated by Hans Kamp. As was indicated elsewhere,[4] Kamp operates with two undefined functions of which one means that at some past time q was true, and p has been true throughout the interval between then and now (leaving it open whether p is true now; and whether q has continued to be true since the time in question); while the other is the future-tense analogue of this. The past-tense one, on which we shall concentrate here, he now reads as 'p since q', and symbolises as Spq. In 1965 he defined 'p the last time that q', and I later based on this an inductive definition of 'p the nth time ago that q'. Letting q mean 'It is midnight', 'p the last time that q' would mean 'p last midnight'. Kamp has now shown, in effect, how to define 'p at some time between last midnight and the one before', i.e. 'p at some time yesterday'. We first define 'p at some time today' as

---

[4] See *Past, Present and Future*, pp. 106–11.

'Not-q ever since (p-and-not-q, and not-q ever since q)',

i.e. $S(p \land \sim q \land Sq\sim q)\sim q$. We may abridge this, in words, to 'p at some time since the last time that q' and in symbols to $P(1)pq$. We can then define 'p at some time between the last midnight and the one before' as

'Not-q ever since (q and (p at some time since the last time that q))',

i.e. $S(q \land P1p \land q)\sim q$. And in general, '$p$ at some time between the $(n$-1)th midnight ago and the nth', or $P(n)pq$, may be defined as

'Not-q ever since (q and (p at some time between the $(n$-2)th midnight ago and the $(n$-1)th))',

i.e. $S(q \land P(n$-1$)p \land q)\sim q$. Kamp's own 'p at some time yesterday' is not, indeed, quite the same as our $P(2)pq$, as he counts last midnight as part of yesterday; but his function is obviously obtainable as the disjunction of our $P(2)pq$ and 'p the last time that q'. Similarly his 'p at some time during the day before yesterday' is the disjunction of our $P(3)pq$ and 'p the last time but one that q'.

This is still quite a far cry from 'p exactly 2 1/7 days ago', i.e. the $P(n)p$ of metric tense logic, but the further problems involved in reaching this goal can be expected to be increasingly those of the general theory of measurement rather than anything specifically tense-logical.

7. *Predication and existence*. All these developments concern tensed *propositional* calculi. In tensed *predicate* logic the main problem is, as it always has been, that of dealing satisfactorily with individuals which have existed or will exist, but do not exist now. This is one aspect of the more general problem of the relation between existence and quantification, a topic on which there is now a rapidly growing literature, with work by Cocchiarella, van Fraassen, Hintikka, Hughes, Lambert, Leblanc, Lejewski, Mates, Mayer, Routley, Scott, Thomason and others. I shall not go into details here, except to make an amendment to a system of my own.[5] Here free individual variables are

---

[5] This system is sketched on pp. 161–2 of *Past, Present and Future*.

allowed to stand for nonactual or nonpresent as well as for actual or present individuals, but bound variables for actual or present individuals only, and there are two sorts of predicate variables: ϕ, ψ, etc. for predicates quite generally, and f, g, etc. restricted to predicates which entail the existence of the individuals of which they are predicated. It is clear that with bound and free variables thus interpreted, the logic of quantification will not be quite standard, and we will not have either $\phi y \supset \exists x \phi x$ or $\forall x \phi x \supset \phi y$ without qualification. In the passage cited, however, I give what purports to be a proof that we do have standard quantification where the predicates are of the restricted sort, i.e. we do have $fy \supset \exists x fx$ and $\forall x fx \supset fy$. Mr. A. Trew has pointed out to me (1967) that the second of these (though not the first) is counter-intuitive. The antecedent says in effect that whatever exists has a certain existence-implying predicate, which might very well be the case; but in the consequent y could be a *non*existent individual, who *wouldn't* have any existence-implying predicate such as f; this would give the alleged logical implication a true antecedent but a false consequent. In fact my alleged proof of $\forall x fx \supset fy$ (though not that of $fy \supset \exists x fx$) is invalid; it makes use of the rule $\forall 1$, equivalent to the law $\forall x \phi x \supset \phi y$, which does not hold in this sort of quantification theory. Benson Mates, in a formalisation of the thought of Leibniz, has a law restricted to *atomic* predicates which makes these existence-implying, and his laws for these work out the same as for my fs.

I do not set much store by this system, as I am inclined not to regard sentences of the form fy as expressing propositions when nothing present or actual is named by y; but if systems allowing names of non-existents are to be developed, it is better that it be done properly. As I pointed out in *Time and Modality*, modal (tense-logical) systems which allow propositions of the form fy to be altogether absent from some possible worlds (at some instants) have to distinguish between 'necessarily (always) true' and 'not possibly (never) false'; and I sketched there a modal system Q in which this distinction was embodied. In the past two or three years this system has been very fruitfully worked upon by Dagfinn Føllesdal[6] and by Krister Segerberg.

---

[6] Dagfinn Føllesdal, 'A model theoretic approach to causal logic,' *Det Kgl. Norske Videnskabers Selskabs Skrifter* 1966 Nr. 2.

Segerberg[7] contrives to fit Q very neatly into current schemes of modal semantics.

[7] Krister Segerberg, 'Some modal logics based on a three-valued logic', *Theoria*, 33 (1967), pp. 53–71, and *Results in Non-classical Logic* (Lund, 1968), Paper III.

XI
TENSE LOGIC AND
THE LOGIC OF EARLIER AND LATER

W.V. Quine once wrote a paper entitled 'Three Grades of Modal Involvement'.[1] Tense logic, like modal logic, is something about which some philosophers have misgivings, and like modal logic, it may be presented in a more or less accommodating manner – it has, in Quine's terminology, its own 'grades of involvement'. I want to present here four such 'grades of tense-logical involvement', by presenting a series of calculi involving the notion of being true (or as Rescher says, 'realized') at an instant, making more and more controversial assumptions at each main stage.

1. *Tense logics and U-calculi.* We may begin from the juxtaposition of two calculi of E.J. Lemmon's, one a 'minimal' tense logic and one a minimal calculus of the earlier-later relation. Sometimes[2] the tense logic, called K_t, is axiomatized with F (for 'It will be the case that ...') and P (for 'It has been the case that ...') as primitive symbols, with G (for 'It will always be the case that ...') defined as $\sim F \sim$, and H (for 'It has always been the case that ...') as $\sim P \sim$. Here I take G and H as primitive, and define F as $\sim G \sim$ and P as $\sim H \sim$, the postulates then becoming

RG: $\vdash \alpha \rightarrow \vdash G\alpha$

RH: $\vdash \alpha \rightarrow \vdash H\alpha$

1.1. $G(p \supset q) \supset (Gp \supset Gq)$
1.2. $H(p \supset q) \supset (Hp \supset Hq)$
2.1. $\sim G \sim Hp \supset p$ $[FHp \supset p]$
2.2. $\sim H \sim Gp \supset p$ $[PGp \supset p]$,

these being subjoined to propositional calculus with substitution and

---

[1] Now printed in his *The Ways of Paradox* (1966), pp. 156–74.
[2] As in 'Stratified Metric Tense Logic' (Chapter XIII) and 'Tense–Logic for Non-Permanent Existents' (Chapter XIX).

detachment. In the associated earlier-later calculus, using $Ta(p)$ for 'It is the case at the instant a that p' and Uab for 'The instant a is earlier than the instant b', we subjoin to propositional calculus and quantification theory these postulates for T:

T1. $Ta(p \supset q) \supset (Ta(p) \supset Ta(q))$
T2.1. $Ta(\sim p) \supset \sim Ta(p)$
T2.2. $\sim Ta(p) \supset Ta(\sim p)$

and these for U:

UT1. $Ta(Gp \equiv \forall b(Uab \supset Tb(p))$
UT2. $Ta(Hp) \equiv \forall b(Uba \supset Tb(p))$.

In the T-calculus we may prove the converse of 1,[3] so that 1 and the 2s may be replaced by a pair of equivalences, and in the whole we may prove the formulae

$Ta(Fp) \equiv \exists b(Uab \wedge Tb(p))$ and
$Ta(Pp) \equiv \exists b(Uba \wedge Tb(p))$,

relating U to P and F, and giving us the postulates of the U-calculus appropriate to a system with these as primitive. Whether we use the one basis or the other, the tense-logical theses which are provable, preceded by Ta, in the minimal U-calculus (e.g. $Ta(FHp \supset p)$) are precisely those of the minimal tense logic K_t, and the addition of various special conditions on U (e.g. $\forall a \exists b Uab$, giving every instant a U-successor) makes possible the proof of new theses of tense logic, preceded by Ta.

Here the elementary forms $Ta(p)$ and Uab of the earlier-later calculus are what Rescher[4] calls 'chronologically definite' propositions, whose truth-value is independent of time; so of course are truth-functions and quantifications of these. If we regard these as propositions *par excellence*, the tensed formulae for which the variables p, q, r, etc. may stand may be regarded as *predicates* of the instants 'at' which they are (perhaps loosely) said to be true. Tense logic, we might say, is a

[3] *Editors' note.* In Chapter XV Prior corrected this.
[4] N. Rescher, 'The Logic of Chronological Proposition', *Mind*, Vol. 75, No. 297 (January 1966), pp. 75–96.

logic of pure predicates which are artificially torn away from their subjects and given a spurious independence. Its theses only make sense if we understand them to be implicitly preceded by a Ta, as they are explicitly in the U-calculus.

With this conception of the relation between the two calculi, we ought strictly speaking to use different symbols[5] for the implications and negations which occur inside and outside the T as; e.g. T1 ought properly to be written as $Ta(p \supset q) \Rightarrow (Ta(p) \Rightarrow Ta(q))$, T2.1 as $Ta(\sim p) \Rightarrow \neg Ta(p)$, and UT1 as $Ta(Gp) \equiv \forall b(Uab \supset Tb(p))$. Indeed, the four equivalences consisting of T1 and its converse, the T2s, and the UTs, may be replaced by *definitions* of the predicate-formers in terms of the proposition-formers, e.g. the T2s by

$$Ta(\sim p) = \neg Ta(p),$$

equating 'The instant a is (non-p)-ish' with 'It is not the case that the instant a is p-ish'; and UT1 by

$$Ta(Gp) = \forall b(Uab \Rightarrow Tb(p)),$$

equating 'The instant a is (p-for-evermore)-ish' with 'The instant a is earlier than none but p-ish instants'. T here expresses no more than the attachment of a predicate to its subject, and could be replaced by juxtaposition and bracketing, as in this further transformation of the T2s:

$$(\sim p)a = \neg(pa).$$

The expansion of pa, 'a is p-ish', to $Ta(p)$, 'It is true at a that p', is only a special case of the expansion we sometimes make of '$x\,f$s' to 'It is true *of* x that it fs'; 'at', we might say, is just this 'of'.

This is what I call the first or lowest grade of tense-logical involvement. Philosophers who are uneasy about tense logic will almost certainly find little in this amount of it to worry about. And there is a nice economy about it; it reduces the minimal tense logic to a by-product of the introduction of four definitions into an ordinary first-

---

[5] *Editors' note.* Prior is using script letters for proposition-formers. We are using $\Rightarrow$ and $\neg$ for proposition-formers and $\supset$ and $\sim$ for predicate-formers.

order theory, and richer systems to by-products of conditions imposed on a relation in that theory.

It is not *quite* to be taken for granted, however, that the U-calculus is philosophically simpler than a more substantial tense logic would be. For one thing, the U-calculus has two sorts of variables where tensed propositional logic has only one. And if it be replied that the extra ones are just name-variables, which will have to be introduced sooner or later anyway, the answer to that is that they are names of a very odd kind of entity. Some of us at least would prefer to see 'instants', and the 'time-series' which they are supposed to constitute, as mere logical constructions out of tensed facts. With this motivation, let us try going a little further.

2. *Assignments-to-instants as omnitemporal tensed propositions.* We may begin by ignoring the form Uab (we shall of course come back to it), and concentrating on the relations between the form $Ta(p)$, 'It is the case at the instant a that p', and the simple p. If we treat both of these as genuinely propositional, the form $Ta(p)$ will be simply a *special case* of the sort of thing for which the variable p can stand, and it will make sense to substitute such formulae for the ps and qs both of tense logic and of the U-calculus. $Tb(Ta(p))$, for example, will be as well formed as the simple $Ta(p)$, though there will be a certain vacuity about the initial Tb, since we may presume that if it is true at any time, e.g. now, that p is true at the instant a, this will be equally true at any other time. What this amounts to is that instead of ruling out such forms as $Tb(Ta(p))$, we explicitly lay it down that $Tb(Ta(p))$ is equivalent to the plain $Ta(p)$. Again, if forms like $Ta(p)$ and $\forall bTb(p)$ are on the same level as the simple p, they may occur as arguments of a single truth-function, as in, for example, $Ta(p) \wedge q$, $\forall a(Ta(p)) \supset p$.

Allowing ourselves these liberties (which represent the second grade of tense-logical involvement) we may add to T1 and the T2s the following further postulates for T:

RT: $\vdash \alpha \rightarrow \vdash Ta(\alpha)$
T3. $\forall aTa(p) \supset p$
T4. $\forall aTa(p) \supset Tb(\forall aTa(p))$
T5. $Ta(p) \supset Tb(Ta(p))$.

What we now have is equivalent to the system SI of Rescher. In the T-calculus thus enriched, it is easy to prove the converses of T4 and T5; and if we introduce the form $\Box\alpha$ as an abridgement of $\forall aTa(\alpha)$ in those cases where a does not occur free in α, we may prove for this $\Box$ the following:

R$\Box$: $\vdash \alpha \rightarrow \vdash \Box\alpha$

$\Box$1. $\Box(p \supset q) \supset (\Box p \supset \Box q)$ [from T1 by quantification theory and Df. $\Box$]

$\Box$2. $\Box p \supset p$ [from T3 by Df. $\Box$]

$\Box$3. $\sim\!\Box p \supset \Box\!\sim\!\Box p,$

the last a little tortuously (using T5). These are Gödel's postulates for the Lewis system S5, which we therefore have for this $\Box$.

If we now introduce the form Uab and draw upon UT1 and UT2, we may prove, for the above $\Box$, the theses

$\Box$4. $\Box p \supset Gp$

$\Box$5. $\Box p \supset Hp.$

For we obviously have

$\forall bTb(p) \supset \forall b(Uab \supset Tb(p))$ and
$\forall bTb(p) \supset \forall b(Uba \supset Tb(p)),$

and so $\Box p \supset Ta(Gp)$ and $\Box p \supset Ta(Hp)$ by UT1 and 2; from these we have $\Box p \supset \forall aTa(Gp)$ and $\Box p \supset \forall aTa(Hp)$ by $\forall 2a$, and finally $\Box$4 and $\Box$5 by T3.

We may also, drawing upon UT1 and 2, prove certain results about the prefixing of tense-operators to the form $Ta(p)$. It might be thought that, since $Ta(p)$ is 'omnitemporally' true, the forms $FTa(p)$, $PTa(p)$, $GTa(p)$, and $HTa(p)$ should all be equivalent to the plain $Ta(p)$, but it is not quite as simple as that. The key point is that UT1 and UT2 leave it quite open whether time has or has not a beginning or an end. If there *were* an end of time, $FTa(p)$ would be false at the end of time regardless of whether $Ta(p)$ itself were true or false, since anything at all beginning with 'It will be the case that ...' would be false then. In other words, $Ta(p) \supset FTa(p)$ might be false because although $Ta(p)$ *is* true, nothing whatever *will* be true, because there is now no future. And since Gp is equivalent to $\sim\!F\!\sim\!p$, $GTa(p)$ ($= \sim\!FTa(\sim\!p)$) would be vacuously *true* at the end of time regardless of the truth or falsity of $Ta(p)$. This means that we have $FTa(p) \supset Ta(p)$ and $Ta(p) \supset GTa(p)$ but not their converses, and similarly with P and H. It has already been observed that from T1, the T2s, and UT1 and 2 we have $Ta(Fp) \equiv \exists b(Uab \wedge Tb(p))$; hence we have

1.	$FTa(p)$	[assumption]
2.	$\exists b(Uab \wedge Tb(Ta(p)))$	[1]
3.	$\exists b(Uab \wedge Ta(p))$	[2, Conv. T5]
4.	$\exists b(Uab \wedge Ta(p))$	[3]
5.	$Ta(p)$	[4].

And for the other, we clearly have $Ta(p) \supset \forall b(Uab \supset Ta(p))$, and so, by T5, $Ta(p) \supset \forall b(Uab \supset Tb(Ta(p)))$, i.e. $Ta(p) \supset GTa(p)$. We may prove the converses, as we would expect, if we add the axiom $\exists bUab$, expressing time's forward infinity, and the converses of the corresponding theses in P and H if we add $\exists bUba$, expressing the infinity of the past.

To prove similar theorems about the form Uab, i.e. to prove $FUab \supset Uab$, $Uab \supset GUab$, and their images, it is necessary to add to UT1 and 2 the further postulate (analogous to T5)

UT3. $Uab \supset Tc(Uab)$.

The converse of this (like that of T5) is provable.

Finally, if we enrich the U-calculus in the ways suggested, any tense-logical formula which we can prove, preceded by Ta, in the U-calculus, we can now prove without this prefix, by passing from $Ta(f)$ by U.G. to $\forall aTa(f)$ and from this to f by T3. So we no longer have merely *parallel* tense logics and U-calculi; the tense logics now appear as *parts* of the U-calculi, and this may prepare the way for treating the U-calculi as parts of the tense logics.

3. *Alternative interpretation of the enlarged system*. The characteristic feature of the present enlargement of the T-calculus, the placing of $Ta(p)$ and the plain p in the same syntactical category, may well be felt by some to be *the* step which must *not* be taken. Certainly it is essential

to what I want to do next. But in itself it does not amount to much, and a person determined to treat tensed propositions as predicates could still do something with the present calculus.

To see what such a person might do with it, we should first observe that even from the point of view of such a person, the calculus of Section 1 has a certain insufficiency about it. It does not suffice to prove, for example, T3 preceded by Ta, i.e. $Ta(\forall aTa(p) \supset p)$; but surely even a person who regarded tensed ps as predicates of instants would want to say that it is true of any arbitrary instant a that it is 'p-ish if every instant is p-ish'. But the calculus of Section I does not even provide for the *formation* of predicates of this sort (i.e. ones like 'p-ish if every instant is p-ish'). In ordinary predicate calculus we may form complex predicates not only by truth-functionally combining simpler ones (as in the predicate 'stands and smokes'), but also by truth-functionally combining predicates and propositions, e.g. we might predicate of John that he 'is coming if and only if Mary is coming'. The predicate-of-instants '... is p-ish if every instant is p-ish', mentioned a few lines higher up, is clearly of this sort; another of the same would be '... is p-ish if the instant b is q-ish'. In defining predicate-formers in terms of proposition-formers we ought therefore to have not only

$$(p \supset q)a = (pa) \Rightarrow (qa)$$

but also

$$(p \supset \alpha)a = (pa) \Rightarrow \alpha$$

and

$$(\alpha \supset p)a = \alpha \Rightarrow (pa),$$

where the schematic letter α represents, any 'genuine' (i.e. chronologically definite) proposition. Or, doing it with a T-calculus, we could add to the axiom T1 the axiom-schemata

TS1. $\vdash Ta(p \supset \alpha) \equiv (Ta(p) \supset \alpha)$
TS2. $\vdash Ta(\alpha \supset p) \equiv (\alpha \supset Ta(p)).$

We could then obtain, for example, the above-mentioned thesis

Ta($\forall aTa(p) \supset p$) by TS2 from $\forall aTa(p) \supset Ta(p)$, which we have from quantification theory. And if, as is done in some systems of propositional calculus, we defined 'Not *p*' in terms of a constant false proposition 0, the equivalence of *Ta(~p)* and *~Ta(p)* asserted by our T2s would become simply that case of the schema TS1 in which *a* is 0.

But if someone wanted to replace the *schemata* TS1 and 2 by *axioms* for the key types of α that the system contains, he might well calculate that it would be less cumbersome to do it by running *p*s and αs together and preventing this confusion from doing any harm by the 'evacuating' postulates T4 and T5 (and UT3). This would mean regarding the theses of the enlarged calculus as all of them preceded by an unexpressed *Ta* (or $\forall aTa$) attaching to an arbitrary instant any ostensibly unattached 'predicates' *p, q, r*, etc. that a thesis might contain, the attachment to it also of 'genuine' propositions being a convenient but empty formality (rather like vacuous quantification).

4. *Instants as propositions.* That the last step forward is not a very sensational one, is sufficiently indicated by the fact that we are still left with variables ostensibly representing named or nameable instants as well as ones representing propositions. What I shall call the third grade of tense-logical involvement consists in treating the instant-variables *a, b, c*, etc. as also representing propositions. We might, for example, equate the instant *a* with a conjunction of all those propositions which would ordinarily be said to be true at that instant, or we might equate it with some proposition which would ordinarily be said to be true at that instant only, and so could serve as an index of it. When we do this we need of course to find some suitable interpretation for the form *Ta(p)*, as it scarcely makes sense to speak of one proposition as being true 'at' or 'in' another proposition. We might say, for example, that it is true 'at' or 'in' *a* that *p*, if the proposition *a* at all times implies that *p*; it can in fact be proved that *Ta(p)* is logically equivalent to $\square(a \supset p)$. (This follows from the postulates already given, plus two that will shortly be added to them.)

This sounds a highly artificial procedure, but remember that what lies behind it is the belief that 'instants' are artificial entities anyhow, i.e. that all talk which appears to be about them, and about the 'time-series' which they are supposed to constitute, is just disguised talk about what is and has been and will be the case. Certainly this revision of the concept of an instant turns quantification over instants into quantification over a certain sort of propositional variable, and it is important to notice that our third grade of tense-logical involvement commits us to this; but, while I shall not argue the pros and cons here, it seems to me, for reasons that have nothing specially to do with tense logic, that we have to admit such quantifications anyhow.

We take the instant-variables a, b, c, then, as propositional variables, substitutable in theses for the more general propositional variables p, q, r, etc.; though the converse substitution is not possible, since a, b, c, etc. stand only for those propositions which satisfy the postulates RT and T1–T5, together with two that are formulable now that instants are treated as propositions, namely

T6. $Ta(a)$,

i.e. one of the propositions that is true 'at' the instant a is always the instant-proposition a itself; and

T7. $Ta(p) \supset (a \supset p)$.

Of the theorems which are now provable, the most important are

T8. $\Diamond a$ $[= \sim\!\Box\!\sim\! a]$
T9. $\exists a a$
T10. $\Box(a \supset p) \supset Ta(p)$
T11. $Ta(p) \supset \Box(a \supset p)$.

T8 may be proved as follows:

1. $\forall b \sim\! Tb(a) \supset \sim\! Ta(a)$ [U.I.]
2. $\sim\! \forall b \sim\! Tb(a)$ [1, T6]
3. $\forall b Tb(\sim\! a) \supset \forall b \sim\! Tb(a)$ [T2.1, $\forall 1b$, $\forall 2b$]
4. $\sim\! \forall b Tb(\sim\! a)$ [3, 2]
5. $\sim\!\Box\!\sim\! a$ [4, Df.$\Box$];

T9 as follows:

1. $a \supset \exists a a$ [quantification theory]
2. $Ta(a) \supset Ta(\exists a a)$ [1, RT, T1]
3. $Ta(\exists a a)$ [2, T6]

4.	$\forall aTa(\exists aa)$	[3, UG]
5.	$\exists aa$	[4, T3];

T10 thus:

1.	$\Box(a \supset p)$	[assumption]
2.	$\forall bTb(a \supset p)$	[1, Df.$\Box$]
3.	$Ta(a \supset p)$	[2,U.I.]
4.	$Ta(\sim p) \supset Ta(\sim p \wedge (a \supset p))$	[3, $Ta(p) \supset$
		$(Ta(q) \supset Ta(p \wedge q))$]
5.	$Ta(\sim p) \supset Ta(\sim a)$	[4, $(\sim p \wedge (a \supset p)) \supset \sim a)$, RT, T1]
6.	$\sim Ta(\sim a)$	[T2.1, T6]
7.	$\sim Ta(\sim p)$	[5, 6]
8.	$Ta(p)$	[7, T2.2];

and T11 thus:

1.	$Tb(Ta(p)) \supset Tb(a \supset p)$	[T7, RT, T1]
2.	$Ta(p) \supset Tb(a \supset p)$	[1, T5]
3.	$Ta(p) \supset \forall bTb(a \supset p)$	[2, $\forall 2b$]
4.	$Ta(p) \supset \Box(a \supset p)$	[3, Df. $\Box$].

The addition of T6 and T7 also makes possible certain simplifications of the total system. For example, T3 can now be replaced by the shorter T9 ($\exists aa$), since T3 is provable from T9 and T7 as follows:

1.	$\forall aTa(p) \supset (a \supset p)$	[T7, $\forall 1a$]
2.	$a \supset (\forall aTa(p) \supset p)$	[1, prop. calculus]
3.	$\exists aa \supset (\forall aTa(p) \supset p)$	[2, $\exists 1a$]
4.	$\forall aTa(p) \supset p$	[3, T9].

We may also drop T4, though the proof of this is a little indirect. From S5 and quantification theory we can prove

$$\forall a\Box(a \supset p) \supset \Box(b \supset \forall a\Box(a \supset p)),$$

which is what T4 may be transformed into in virtue of the equivalence of $Ta(p)$ and $\Box(a \supset p)$ proved in T10 and T11. And T4 is not itself used in the proof of S5 for $\Box$ or of T10 and T11.

We may also prove $Ta(b) \supset Tb(a)$ and $Ta(b) \supset (Tb(c) \supset Ta(c))$, which with T6 $(Ta(a))$ show that when both its arguments are instant-propositions T behaves as an equivalence functor. Indeed we can prove (by T7 and induction on possible contexts of a and b) the metatheorem that $Ta(b) \supset (f(a) \supset f(b))$ holds for any function $f(a)$ constructible in the system, so that $Ta(b)$ can be used to express a certain sort of identity between instants $(Ta(b)$ means that precisely the same propositions are true at a as at b). We might, indeed, have introduced a propositional identity-function Ipq with the usual postulates $(Ipp$, and $Ipq \supset (f(p) \supset f(q))$) for all functions of the system, and laid down $Ta(b) \supset Iab$ instead of T7, thereby equating T (with instant-arguments) with this I (since T6, $Ta(a)$, is clearly equivalent by identity-theory to $Iab \supset Ta(b)$).

When we add the form Uab with its axioms UT1 and UT2, we can extend the above metatheorem $Ta(b) \supset (f(a) \supset f(b))$ to the new functions that we now have, either by introducing I and equating $Ta(b)$ with Iab, or (if we keep the original T7) by adding the further axiom

UT4. $Ta(b) \supset (Uca \supset Ucb)$.

$Ta(b) \supset (Uac \supset Ubc)$ then becomes provable (making possible the desired extension of the metatheorem). So does UT3, which we can therefore drop as an axiom. We can also, in this extended UT-calculus, prove the theses

T12. $Uab \supset Ta(Fb)$,
T13. $Ta(Fb) \supset Uab$.

T12 as follows:
1. Uab
2. $Tb(b)$ [T6]
3. $\exists c(Uac \wedge Tc(b)$ [1, 2, E.G.]
4. $Ta(Fb)$ [3, UT1].

T13 equates by UT1 to $\exists c(Uac \wedge Tc(b)) \supset Uab)$ which by quantification theory and UT4 yields $\forall c(Uac \wedge Tc(b)) \supset Uab$.

T12 and T13 mean that we could *define Uab* as *Ta(Fb)*, and if we do so we can replace UT1–4 by the last section's $\Box 4$ ($\Box p \supset Gp$) and $\Box 5$ ($\Box p \supset Hp$) and the tense logic K_t. Proofs of the UT's from these and a system which will shortly be shown equivalent to RT and T1–7, may be found in my *Past, Present and Future*. Moreover, when further tense-logical postulates are added to K_t, we can prove those conditions on *U* which make it possible to prove the added tense-logical postulates in the U-calculus; i.e. the traffic between tense logics and U-calculi, given the new T-calculus, is two-way. And since 'at' can no longer mean the predicational 'of', UT1 and UT2 cannot be replaced by definitions, and the movement from them to the tense logic K_t is less straightforward and natural than the converse one. U-calculi, in short, are now best thought of as by-products of the interaction of the T-calculus and tense logics.

We have still to derive these, however, from tense logic alone. As a step in that direction, but one which in itself commits us to no further 'tense-logical involvements', we shall develop the present T-calculus in slightly different form.

5. *Reformulation with $\Box$ primitive.* In view of T10 and T11, it is possible to develop the calculus sketched in the last section with $\Box$ instead of *T* as the one non-tense-logical primitive, defining *Ta(p)* as $\Box(a \supset p)$. This has in fact already been done in *Past, Present and Future*, using as postulates R$\Box$, $\Box$1–3, T8 ($\Diamond a$), T9 ($\exists aa$), and T2.2 (= $\sim\Box(a \supset p) \supset \Box(a \supset \sim p) = \Box(a \supset p) \lor \Box(a \supset \sim p)$). It is from these postulates, with K_t, $\Box 4$, $\Box 5$, and the definition of *Uab* as *Ta(Fb)* (= $\Box(a \supset Fb)$), that UT1 and UT2 are there derived; it remains to show their equivalence to those of the last section. The $\Box$ postulates were proved there and in the preceding section from the T ones, and as to the converse proofs,

(i)   given that *Ta(p)* $=\Box(a \supset p)$, it is easy to prove RT, T1 and T4–7 in S5;

(ii)   T2.1 follows from modal logic and T8 ($\Diamond a$);

(iii) T3 may be proved from T9 ($\exists aa$) as it was in the T-calculus (since we have the crucial thesis T7 by (i)); and

(iv) of the implications $\Box p \supset \forall a\Box(a \supset p)$ and $\forall a\Box(a \supset p) \supset \Box p$, jointly equivalent to the definition of $\Box$ in the T-system as $\forall aTa$, the first follows from modal logic and the second we prove thus:

1. $\forall a \Box (a \supset p) \supset p$ [T3]
2. $\Box(\forall a \Box (a \supset p)) \supset \Box p$ [1, R$\Box$, $\Box$2]
3. $\forall a \Box \Box (a \supset p) \supset \Box p$ [2]
4. $\forall a \Box (a \supset p) \supset \Box p$ [3],

where 3. follows from 2. by the 'Barcan formula' $\forall a \Box f(a) \supset \Box \forall a f(a)$, known to be provable from S5 and quantification theory, and 4 from 3 by $\Box p \supset \Box \Box p$, also known to be provable in S5. And if we define Iab as $\Box (a \equiv b)$, we may prove $Ta(b) \supset Iab$ from S5, T2.2 and T8, or (defining Uab as $Ta(Fb)$, i.e. $\Box(a \supset Fb)$) UT4 from S5, $\Box 4$, and K$_t$.

The *consistency* of the whole system may easily be shown by interpreting $\Box p$ as p, and the special variables a, b, c, etc. as standing for tautologies. The postulates then all become theses of the propositional calculus.

This $\Box$ system is stratified as well as the T system, but on a different principle. The T system divides its postulates into those (T1, T2.1, T2.2) which do not even assume that $Ta(p)$ is out of the same syntactical box as the plain p (and if U is added, UT1 and UT2 do not assume this either); those (RT, T3–5, UT3) which do assume this for $Ta(p)$ but not for the plain a; and those (T6, T7 – and when we add U, UT4) which assume it even for a. The postulates for the $\Box$ system, on the other hand, divide into those (R$\Box$, $\Box$1–3 and $\Box$4, $\Box$5, and K$_t$ when we add them) which do not require the special variables a, b, c, etc. for their formulation, and which thus apply to propositions generally, and those (T8, T9, T2.2) which do require these variables, and give in effect the conditions a proposition must meet to be substitutable for one of the special variables. It must be of such a sort that (i) any such proposition is at some time true (T8), (ii) at any given time some such proposition is true (T9), and (iii) such a proposition permanently implies either the truth or the falsehood of any given proposition (T2.2).

With a little modification of the $\Box$-system we can do without special variables in favour of a function Qp defined as

$$\Diamond p \land \forall q (\Box(p \supset q) \lor \Box(p \supset {\sim} q));$$

i.e. Qp asserts that p satisfies T8 and T2.2. We then drop these two postulates, and replace all formulae of the form $\exists a f(a)$ by $\exists p (Qp \land f(p))$, and all of the form $\forall a f(a)$ by $\forall p (Qp \supset f(p))$, and in theses with free special variables we replace these by ordinary propositional variables and conditions of the form $Qp \supset$ at the beginning of the thesis. For example,

T2.1. $\Box(a \supset p) \supset \sim(\Box a \supset \sim p)$

becomes

$Qq \supset (\Box(q \supset p) \supset \sim\Box(q \supset \sim p))$.

But we still need the postulate T9, in the form $\exists p(Qp \wedge p)$. This can be very slightly shortened by dropping from Qp, when expanded by its definition, the conjunct $\Diamond p$, which follows from the new conjunct p. A still shorter equivalent of $Qp \wedge p$ which may be used in this axiom is $p \wedge \forall q(q \supset \Box(p \supset q))$. The axiom as thus amended asserts that there is something which is now the case, and which is at no time true without everything that is now the case being then true also. (This would fit, for example, a conjunction of all the propositions that are now true; it would also fit a proposition which is true now but not at any other time; cf. our original account of 'instant-propositions' at the beginning of Section 4.) This modification of the $\Box$-calculus, however, we can ignore in what follows.

6. *The tense-logical definition of* $\Box$. We would reach a fourth grade of tense-logical involvement if we could give a tense-logical definition of $\Box$. As to this, it has been shown in *Past, Present and Future* that (i) if we are prepared to use a richer tense logic than K_t, quite simple tense-logical definitions of $\Box$ are possible, e.g. if we assume that time is like a single non-branching line and that the earlier-later relation is transitive, we may define $\Box p$, 'It is the case at all times that p', as $p \wedge Hp \wedge Gp$, 'It is and always has been and always will be the case that p'; and that (ii) even with the non-committal system K_t, if we enlarge our symbolic apparatus a little we can give a tense-logical definition of $\Box$, provided that we do not allow that there may be several distinct and independent time-series (in which case there would be 'times' which we could not locate from 'now' by any combination of 'will bes' and 'has beens'). But, under (ii), it is possible to improve a little upon the definition given in *Past, Present and Future*, and upon the proofs there given of the

postulates $R\square$ and $\square 1$–5.

We define the form $\square^n p$ inductively as follows:

$$\square^0 p = p$$
$$\square^{n+1} p = H\square^n p \wedge G\square^n p.^6$$

We then introduce quantifiers binding the ns, and obeying the usual rules, and define $\square p$ as $\forall n\,\square^n p$. This is equivalent to defining $\diamondsuit^n p$ inductively by

$$\diamondsuit^0 p = p$$
$$\diamondsuit^{n+1} p = P\diamondsuit^n p \vee F\diamondsuit^n p$$

and defining $\diamondsuit p$ as $\exists n\,\diamondsuit^n p$, i.e. we say that it is true at *some* time that p if and only if either p is itself true now or it is true preceded by *some* combination of 'will bes' and 'has beens'.

$\square^1 p$, it may be observed, is $Hp \wedge Gp$, and it is easy to show that for this functor, given K_t for H and G, we may prove all but $\square 2$ ($\square p \supset p$) of the postulates of the 'Brouwersche' modal system, i.e. $R\square$, $\square 1$, $\square 2$, and, instead of $\square 3$, the weaker $\sim p \supset \square\sim\square p$, which is equivalent to $p \supset \square\diamondsuit p$ or $\diamondsuit\square p \supset p$ (as $\square 3$ itself is equivalent to $\diamondsuit p \supset \square\diamondsuit p$ or $\diamondsuit\square p \supset \square p$). Given this result, it is not difficult to show, by induction and the rules for quantifiers, that we have at least the full 'Brouwersche' system *for* $\forall n\,\square^n$, i.e. for our defined $\square$. For $\square 2$ we have simply

1.	$\forall n\,\square^n p$	[assumption]
2.	$\square^0 p$	[1, U.I.]
3.	p	[2, Df. $\square^0$]

For $\square 1$, we clearly have

$$\square^0 (p \supset q) \supset (\square^0 p \supset \square^0 q) \qquad [\,= (p \supset q) \supset (p \supset q)],$$

and since we have

$$\square^1 (p \supset q) \supset (\,\square^1 p \supset \square^1 q),$$

---

^{6} For this abridgement of the definition used in *Past, Present and Future*, I am indebted to Mr. J.R. Lucas.

we may prove

$$\square^{n+1}(p \supset q) \supset (\square^{n+1}p \supset \square^{n+1}q)$$

from any

$$\square^{n}(p \supset q) \supset (\square^{n}p \supset \square^{n}q)$$

as follows:

1. $\square^{n}(p \supset q) \supset (\square^{n}p \supset \square^{n}q)$ [assumption]
2. $\square^{1}(\square^{n}(p \supset q) \supset (\square^{n}p \supset \square^{n}q))$ [1, R$\square$ for $\square^{1}$]
3. $\square^{1}\square^{n}(p \supset q) \supset \square^{1}(\square^{n}p \supset \square^{n}q)$ [2, $\square$1 for $\square^{1}$]
4. $\square^{1}\square^{n}(p \supset q) \supset (\square^{1}\square^{n}p \supset \square^{1}\square^{n}q)$ [3, $\square$1 for $\square^{1}$]
5. $\square^{n+1}(p \supset q) \supset (\square^{n+1}p \supset \square^{n+1}q)$ [4, Df. $\square^{n+1}$].

Hence we have $\forall n(\square^{n}(p \supset q) \supset (\square^{n}p \supset \square^{n}q))$, from which quantification theory takes us to

$$\forall n\square^{n}(p \supset q) \supset (\forall n\square^{n}p \supset \forall n\square^{n}q),$$

i.e. $\square$1 for our defined $\square$. $\Diamond\square p \supset p$ is provable similarly.

But in fact we have not only the ' Brouwersche' system but S5 for this $\square$. For Lemmon has shown that not only in S5 but even in the 'Brouwersche' system, supplemented by the usual rules for quantifiers, we may prove the 'Barcan formula' $\forall n\square f(n) \supset \square\forall nf(n)$. This enables us to prove, for our defined $\square$, the law $\square p \supset \square\square p$, thus:

1. $\forall n\square^{n}p \supset \square^{m+k}p$ [U.I.]
2. $\square^{m+k}p \supset \square^{m}\square^{k}p$ [provable by induction]
3. $\forall n\square^{n}p \supset \square^{m}\square^{k}p$ [1, 2]
4. $\forall n\square^{n}p \supset \forall k\forall m\square^{m}\square^{k}p$ [3, $\forall 2m$, $\forall 2k$]
5. $\forall n\square^{n}p \supset \forall k\square\square^{k}p$ [4, Df. $\square$]
6. $\forall n\square^{n}p \supset \square\forall k\square^{k}p$ [5, Barcan]
7. $\square p \supset \square\square p$ [6, Df. $\square$].

And it is known that the addition of 7 to the 'Brouwersche' system yields S5. Proofs of $\Box$4 and $\Box$5 are obvious.

The U-calculus now at last becomes simply a part of tense logic, and the minimal U-calculus is provable from the tense logic K_t, the axioms T8, T9, and T2.2 for the special variables (the $\Diamond$ and $\Box$ which appear in T8 and T2.2 now being seen as tense-logical functors), and quantification theory. From this basis we can in fact prove a little more than the minimal U-calculus; we can also prove a special condition on U, namely

UT5. $\forall a\, \forall b(U \cup \bar{U} \cup I)_* ab,$

i.e. every pair of instants is related by the ancestral of the logical sum of U, its converse $(\bar{U})$ and identity. This corresponds to the assumption that the time-series (whatever its shape) is unique, i.e. that all instants may be located from 'now' by some combination of 'will bes' and 'has beens'. This does not yield any new ordinary tense-logical formulae (i.e. without such symbols as our $\forall n\Box^n$) preceded by Ta; though it does strengthen the conditions on U that may be proved by adding various tense-logical axioms to K_t. And if we add UT5 to RT, T1–7, and UT1–4, we may prove not only K_t, T8, and T9 but the equivalence of $\Box p$ ($= \forall aTa(p)$) to the tense-logical $\forall n\Box^n p$, and so all the postulates used in the present section.

At this stage, however, there is no point in having U and T as primitives in addition to G and H. The latter, it should be noted, we *must* have at all stages but the first, for the formulation of UT1 and 2. At the first stage, these last are the definitions, and U is our only primitive constant. At the second, we need U, T, G, and H. At the third, we can get rid of U, and at the fourth of T also, leaving only G and H.

7. *Recapitulation.* The stages of our progress from what could be regarded as a pure earlier-and-later logic to what can be regarded as a pure tense-logic may be tabulated as follows (putting in parentheses those postulates which cease to be independent when a later stage is reached):

T-Postulates	*UT-Postulates*

System I.

T1. $Ta(p \supset q) \supset$ $(Ta(p) \supset Ta(q))$	UT1. $Ta(Gp) \equiv$ $\forall b(Uab \supset Tb(p))$
T2.1. $Ta(\sim p) \supset \sim Ta(p)$	UT2. $Ta(Hp) \equiv$ $\forall b(Uba \supset Tb(p))$
T2.2. $\sim Ta(p) \supset Ta(\sim p)$	

System II. Add to System I the following:

T3. $\forall a Ta(p) \supset p$	(UT3. $Uab \supset Tc(Uab)$)
(T4. $\forall a Ta(p) \supset Tb(\forall a Ta(p))$)	
T5. $Ta(p) \supset Tb(Ta(p))$	
RT: $\vdash \alpha \rightarrow \vdash Ta(\alpha)$	
$\Box p$ definable as $\forall a Ta(p)$	

System III. Add to System II the following:

T6. $Ta(a)$	UT4. $Ta(b) \supset (Uca \supset Ucb)$
T7. $Ta(p) \supset (a \supset p)$	

System equivalent to System IV: Add to System III the following:

$$\text{UT5. } \forall a \forall b (U \cup \bar{U} \cup I)_* ab$$

And the stages by which tense-logic so swells as to encompass the earlier-later logic may be tabulated thus (again bracketing those postulates which cease to be independent at a later stage):

System K_t

RG: $\vdash a \rightarrow \vdash Ga$	RH: $\vdash a \rightarrow \vdash Ha$
A1.1. $G(p \supset q) \supset (Gp \supset Gq)$	A1.2. $H(p \supset q) \supset (Hp \supset Hq)$
A2.1. $PGp \supset p$	A2.2. $FHp \supset p$
P defined as $\sim H\sim$, F as $\sim G\sim$	

System equivalent to System III. Add to K_t the following:
(R$\Box$: $\vdash a \rightarrow \vdash \Box a$)
($\Box$1. $\Box(p \supset q) \supset (\Box p \supset \Box q)$)
($\Box$2. $\Box p \supset p$)
($\Box$3. $\sim \Box p \supset \Box \sim \Box p$)
($\Box$4. $\Box p \supset Gp$)
($\Box$5. $\Box p \supset Hp$)
T8. $\sim \Box \sim a$
T9. $\exists a a$
T2.2. $\Box(a \supset p) \vee \Box(a \supset \sim p)$
$Ta(p)$ definable as $\Box(a \supset p)$, Uab as $\Box(a \supset Fb)$

System IV: Add to the above the following:

Df.$\Box^n$: $\Box^0 p = p$; $\Box^{n+1} p = G \Box^n p \wedge H \Box^n p$
Df.$\Box$: $\Box p = \forall n \Box^n p$.

8. *The uniqueness of the time-series.* I want, in conclusion, to look more closely at the beginning and the end of the movement I have sketched.

When the postulates of the tense-logic K_t are no longer regarded as just by-products of definitions in a first-order theory, but substantial assumptions in an independent discipline, it becomes intelligible to question whether they are all true. This possibility I shall not explore here;[7] but there is a converse point, namely that if we do not regard the postulate UT5, in the logic of the earlier-later relation, as a mere by-product of the definition of that relation in tense-logical terms, it becomes intelligible to question *that* postulate, and to wonder whether there are pairs of instants which are *not* connected, even indirectly, by the earlier-later relation. It is certainly intelligible to deny this postulate if we treat instants as genuine objects and the earlier-later relation as undefined; but perhaps we can also do it *without* falling into this 'Platonism' about instants.

Let me lead up to this last possibility by first observing that even if the earlier-later relation is only a logical construction out of tensed facts, we can give a good sense to the assertion that there are an infinity of different *logically possible* time-series. For this could be just a slightly

---

[7] I do explore it in Chapter XIX.

misleading way of saying that not only the futures that have issued from given past states, but the entire course of history, *might* without inconsistency have been different from what it has been and will be, i.e. it *might have been* that we had *d* and then *e* and then *f* instead of *a* and then *b* and then *c*; or *there would be no inconsistency in supposing* that we had *d* and then *e* and then *f*, instead of *a* and then *b* and then *c*. For even if all propositions are tensed, tense logic is not the whole of logic; there is also a logic of such functors as 'There would be no inconsistency in supposing that ...'. What we *cannot* say (if 'and then' is tense-logically defined) is that we *do* have a series *a*, *b*, *c*, and also a series *d*, *e*, *f* that is temporally unconnected with it.

Moreover, there is a logic of such functors as 'It appears from a certain point of view that ...', and one could therefore give a good sense to talk about an infinity of different 'apparent' time-series. I suspect that the infinity of 'local proper times' which figure in relativistic physics amount simply to what appears from various points of view, or in various 'frames of reference', to be the course of events. And given how the course of events appears from a certain point of view, your relativistic physicist will be able to calculate how it will appear from certain other points of view. He can also indicate what features of the course of events (what temporal orderings of those events) will be common to *all* points of view, and one can work out a 'tense-logic' for that too. (It turns out to be slightly different in the special and the general theories of relativity.) What the relativistic physicists *cannot* calculate from how the course of events appears from certain points of view is how, in all its details, the course of events actually is. It is not clear to me that there is anything surprising or unacceptable in this conclusion, or that we should be driven by it to renounce the use of forms like 'It appears from such-and-such a point of view that *p*', which assume that there is also a plain *p* which is or is not the case. Einstein himself once said to Carnap that

> the problem of the Now worried him seriously. He explained that the experience of the Now means something special for men,

something different from the past and the future, but that this important difference does not and cannot occur within physics.[8]

If my interpretation of relativistic physics is correct, he had something there.

We can, all the same, develop the logic of 'points of view' on the basis of a syntax which does *not* thus suggest that there is a 'real' (though only partly knowable) course of events which presents these various systematically related appearances. We might describe this alternative syntax in a very general way as follows: instead of using the plain *p* for a quite impersonal 'It is (really) the case that *p*', we use it for 'It appears (or is the case) from *this* point of view that *p*', or 'It is the case with *this* person or particle that *p*'. That is, the prefix 'It appears from *this* point of view that ...' or 'It is the case with *this* person or particle that ...' is one which has the same sort of vacuity in this language as 'It is *now* the case that ...' has in ordinary tense logic; it does not need to be expressed, but is understood in all that we say. We then describe what appears to be the case from other points of view, or what is the case with other persons or particles, by using quasi-modal operators which take us from 'this' point of view or particle to the other ones, very much as operators like 'It will be the case that ...' take us to other 'nows' from 'this' now.[9] They would, I think, be operators corresponding to the 'signal relation' of relativistic physics.[10] Associated with these other points of view or particles are other time-series. These, like 'this' time-series, are just logical constructions out of tensed facts, but they are reached from *our* 'now' not by tenses alone, but by tenses interrupted by the *other* quasi-modal operators that we use for getting from 'this' point of view or particle to the other ones; it is this that would make UT5 unprovable.

A language of this sort would have a solipsist ring to it which I find as hard to take as Platonism about instants, but it would have the

---

[8] As reported on p. 37 of *The Philosophy of Rudolf Carnap* (ed. Schilpp; The Library of Living Philosophers).

[9] A very crude language of this general type is sketched in Chapter XVI.

[10] See R. Carnap, *Introduction to Symbolic Logic and its Applications*, Chapter G. More accurately, we would need a conjunction corresponding to Carnap's relation C, in terms of which the signal relation is defined.

advantage of making scientifically unanswerable questions not even askable. This is perhaps one of those many cases where the logician's main philosophical function is to show that there is no escape from one or another of a group of not very palatable alternatives.

XII
THE LOGIC OF ENDING TIME

It is sometimes said that not only the universe but time itself will come to an end; and it is perhaps more often said that not only the universe but time itself had a beginning. I intend to concentrate on the first and perhaps less likely of these two hypotheses, but what I have to say will be easy to apply, with appropriate modifications, to the other one. It is sometimes suggested that the idea that time will come to an end is essentially incoherent; and so it would be if we had to express this supposition by saying that at all times after a certain time there will be no time at all. We do not, however, have to put it this way, and I shall begin by developing a perfectly consistent logical system embodying the assertion, in a quite clear way, that time will have an end. It is also sometimes said, contrariwise, that the supposition that there will be an end to change but not to time is incoherent, and that to suppose that after a certain time the total state of the universe will remain for ever unaltered, differs no more than verbally from the supposition that time will have an end. I shall look at this contention, and try and see if there is anything in it, in the later part of the paper.

Lemmon's minimal tense logic K_t, and the associated logic of the earlier–later relation. In developing a form of tense logic which embodies the belief that time will have an end, we shall naturally have to avoid postulates which imply that time will *not* have an end. Some systems of tense logic, for example, have as an axiom 'It will be the case that if p then p', and since axioms are taken to be true at whatever time there is, this one would mean that there will always be a future, and so that time will *not* end. 'It will *always* be the case that if p then p', it should be observed, need not commit us to this. If we use (as we shall be doing here) what might be called a *Boolean* 'always', i.e. if we so read 'It will always be true that …' as to make it equivalent to 'It will never be false that …' then 'It will always be that if p then p' doesn't commit us to there being any future; it only commits us to there being no future in which it is not the case that if p then p.

We can be sure of not having 'It will be the case that if p then p' either as an axiom or a theorem, if we begin from a system which E.J.

Lemmon discovered in 1965 to be 'minimal' in a sense which we shall shortly define, and which he called the system K$_t$. In this system G (for 'it always will be that') and H (for 'it always has been that') are taken as primitive, and F (for 'it will be that') and P (for 'it has been that') defined respectively as $\sim G\sim$ and $\sim H\sim$. We have the rules to infer $\vdash G\alpha$ and $\vdash H\alpha$ from $\vdash \alpha$ (RG and RH), and the following four axioms:

A1.1. $G(p \supset q) \supset (Gp \supset Gq)$
A1.2. $H(p \supset q) \supset (Hp \supset Hq)$
A2.1. $PGp \supset p$
A2.2. $FHp \supset p$

Among the theorems obtainable from this basis are

$G(p \supset q) \supset (Fp \supset Fq)$,
$(Gp \wedge Fq) \supset F(p \wedge q)$,
$(Gp \wedge Gq) \equiv G(p \wedge q)$,
$F(p \vee q) \equiv (Fp \vee Fq)$,
$p \supset GPp$,

and their images,[1] and we may also obtain the rules to infer $\vdash G\alpha \supset G\beta$, $\vdash H\alpha \supset H\beta$, $\vdash F\alpha \supset F\beta$, and $\vdash P\alpha \supset P\beta$ from $\vdash \alpha \supset \beta$ (RGC, RHC, RFC, and RPC).

This system is 'minimal' in the following sense: an alternative method of formalizing facts about time is to use the variables a, b, c, etc. for instants, the forms $Ta(p)$ for 'It is the case at the instant a that p', Iab for 'The instant a is the same instant as the instant b', Uab for 'The instant a is earlier than the instant b', and to lay down the following four axioms for U and T (with the usual laws for I):

U1. $Ta(\sim p) \equiv \sim Ta(p)$
U2. $Ta(p \supset q) \equiv (Ta(p) \supset Ta(q))$
U3. $Ta(Gp) \equiv \forall b(Uab \supset Tb(p))$
U4. $Ta(Hp) \equiv \forall b(Uba \supset Tb(p))$

These assert respectively that (i) it is true at a that not-p if and only if it

---

[1] *Editors' note.* The 'image' of a formula is obtained by simultaneously replacing F with P, P with F, G with H, and H with G.

is not true at a that p; (ii) it is true at a that p-implies-q, if and only if p's being true at a implies q's being true at a; (iii) it is true at a that it will always be the case that p, if and only if p itself is true at all instants later than a; and (iv) it is true at a that it has always been the case that p, if and only if p itself is true at all instants earlier than a. If we subjoin these postulates alone to propositional calculus and quantification theory (without adding any special conditions on U, e.g. that it is transitive), we can prove various tense-logical theses preceded by Ta, i.e. we can prove that various tense-logical formulae are true at any arbitrarily chosen instant a. For example, we can prove $Ta(F(p \wedge q) \supset Fp)$, 'It is true at any instant a that if it will be the case that both p and q, it will be the case that p'. What Lemmon has shown is that the tense-logical theses which are thus provable (preceded by Ta) in this 'minimal U-calculus', are precisely the theorems of the tense-logical calculus K_t. If special conditions are put on the relation U, further tense-logical theses become deducible, e.g. if we lay it down that U is transitive, $Uab \supset (Ubc \supset Uac)$, we can prove $Ta(Gp \supset GGp)$.

Proofs of tense-logical theses (preceded by Ta) in U-calculi are a fairly straightforward matter. But if certain further ideas and postulates are introduced, it is equally possible to prove U-calculus theses from tense-logical ones, e.g. $Uab \supset (Ubc \supset Uac)$ from the system K_t with the added axiom $Gp \supset GGp$. The essential trick is to treat the instant variables as a special sort of *propositional* variables, by identifying an 'instant' with the totality of what would be ordinarily said to be true *at* that instant, or indeed by identifying it with *any* proposition which would ordinarily be said to be true at that instant only. Formally, we begin from some tense logic, say K_t, and introduce (i) an operator $\square$, which means in effect 'It is true at all times that', and for which we lay down the modal system S5 plus the axioms $\square p \supset Gp$ and $\square p \supset Hp$; and (ii) the set of variables a, b, c, etc. to stand for such propositions as satisfy the following axioms:

A1. $\Diamond a$
A2. $\square(a \supset p) \vee \square(a \supset {\sim}p)$
A3. $\exists aa$.

$\Diamond a$ ($= {\sim}\square{\sim}a$) asserts in effect that the proposition a is true at some time; A2 that a is 'comprehensive' in the sense that for any proposition p, either a permanently implies that p or it permanently implies that not-

p; and A3, that for some 'world-state-proposition' a, that proposition is true right now. (The rule of necessitation from S5 enables us to pass from this to the theorem that at any time some such proposition is true.) Finally, we define $Ta(p)$ as $\square(a \supset p)$ ('It is the case at a that p' = 'The world state-proposition a permanently implies that p', i.e. p is one of the propositions 'in' that particular totality); Iab as $\square(a \equiv b)$; and Uab as $Ta(Fb)$ ('Instant a is earlier than instant b' = 'It is true at a that it will be the case that b').

If our tense-logical basis is K_t it is possible, given the enrichments just mentioned, to prove the minimal U-calculus postulates U1–U4,[2] and with appropriate additions to our tense logic we can prove the corresponding conditions on the earlier-later relation U. I shall not attempt even to sketch a proof of this here, but one or two observations on the 'world' calculus may be in order. In the system as given, the operator $\square$ is not a tense-logical one, but on any view of time except the view that there exist several totally unconnected 'time-streams', $\square$ is tense-logically definable, and on some views of time quite simply so, e.g. if time is infinite and non-branching in both directions, and the earlier-later relation is transitive, $\square$ is equivalent to GH or HG ('It is true at all times that p' = 'It has always been that it will always be that p', or vice versa). In any case, the basis given enables us to prove for $\square$ such theses as $\square p \supset \square Gp$, $\square p \supset G\square p$, $F\square p \supset \square p$, and $P\square p \supset \square p$. It does not, however, enable us to prove $G\square p \supset \square p$, i.e. 'If it will always be that p-at-all-times, then p-at-all-times', i.e. 'If it will never be false that p-at-all-times, then p-at-all-times'. And this is just as well, for if time will have an end, then *at* time's end the antecedent 'It will never be false that p-at-all-times' will be vacuously true for any p (for by then nothing at all is ever *going to be* false *or* true), but the consequent p-at-all-times is certainly not itself vacuously true for any p, even at the end of time.

Other easily provable theorems in the 'world' calculus include $(a \wedge p) \supset \square(a \supset p)$, or $(a \wedge p) \supset Ta(p)$, 'If the world-proposition a and the proposition p are simultaneously true, then p is one of the propositions which the world-proposition a permanently implies', i.e. one of the propositions true 'in' that world or 'at' that 'instant'; $(a \wedge Pa) \supset Fa$, 'If the present total world-state is one that we have had before, it

---

[2] Proofs of this, and of most of the other unproved assertions in this section, may be found in *Past, Present and Future*, Ch. V, § 6, and App. B, § 3.

is one that we shall have again'; $Ta(b) \supset Iab$, i.e. the only world-state proposition true at a is a itself; and $\forall a Ta(p) \equiv \Box p$, which could be used to define $\Box$ if we did not use the latter to define T. (Our actual procedure – taking $\Box$ as primitive instead of T – is only worth adopting if we regard $\Box$ as being tense-logically definable.) These particular theses require only K_t for the underlying tense logic. For instance, we prove $(a \wedge p) \supset Ta(p)$ thus:

1. a
2. p
3. $\Diamond(a \wedge p)$ $[1, 2, p \supset \Diamond p]$
4. $\sim\Box(a \supset \sim p)$ $[3, \Diamond(p \wedge q) \equiv \sim\Box(p \supset \sim q)]$
5. $\Box(a \supset p)$ $[4, A2]$

and $(a \wedge Pa) \supset Fa$ thus:

1. a
2. Pa
3. HFa $[1, p \supset HFp]$
4. $P(a \wedge Fa)$ $[2, 3, (Hp \wedge Pq) \supset P(p \wedge q)]$
5. $P\Box(a \supset Fa)$ $[4, \text{previous theorem, RPC}]$
6. $\Box(a \supset Fa)$ $[5, P\Box p \supset \Box p]$
7. Fa $[1, 6]$.

We may note also that the forms $Ta(p)$, Iab, and Uab could have been introduced as special cases of the forms $Tp(q)$, Ipq, and Upq, similarly defined. But if we did this, it might be better to define U a little differently. If we read Uab as 'The instant a is earlier than the instant b' it is perhaps natural to read the more general Upq as 'The event p is earlier than the event q'. McTaggart plausibly suggested[3] that 'The term P is earlier than the term Q if it is *ever* past while Q is present, or present while Q is future', i.e. if there is *any* time at which we have P past and Q present, or P present and Q future; and this goes into symbols as defining Upq, not as $\Box(q \supset Pp)$ or $\Box(p \supset Fq)$, but rather as $\Diamond(Pp \wedge q)$ or $\Diamond(p \wedge Fq)$. The alternatives in each case are easy to prove equivalent; for example, we get $\Diamond(Pp \wedge q)$ from $\Diamond(p \wedge Fq)$ thus:

---

[3] J.M.E. McTaggart, *The Nature of Existence* (Cambridge, 1927), § 610.

1. $\Diamond(p \wedge Fq)$
2. $\Diamond(GPp \wedge Fq)$ $[1, p \supset GPp]$
3. $\Diamond(FPp \wedge q)$ $[2, (Gp \wedge Fq) \supset F(p \wedge q), \text{RMC}]$
4. $\Diamond(Pp \wedge q)$ $[(3, \Diamond Fp \supset \Diamond p]$

and the reverse by a similar use of $p \supset HFp$. And if we do define Upq as $\Diamond(p \wedge Fq)$, this can be proved equivalent in the case of 'worlds' to our original definition, thus:

1. $\Diamond(a \wedge Fb)$
2. $\Diamond\Box(a \supset Fb)$ $[1, (a \wedge p) \supset \Box(a \supset p), \text{RMC}]$
3. $\Box(a \supset Fb)$ $[2, \Diamond\Box p \supset \Box p]$

And thus (for the converse):

1. $\Box(a \supset Fb)$
2. $\Box(a \supset (a \wedge Fb))$ $[1, (p \supset q) \supset (p \supset (p \wedge q)), \text{RLC}]$
3. $\Diamond(a \wedge Fb)$ $[2, \text{A1}, \Box(p \supset q) \supset (\Diamond p \supset \Diamond q)]$.

2. *Postulates for ending time.* One way of setting up a minimal logic for ending time is to add to the system K_t the one axiom $\sim Fp \vee F\sim Fp$, 'Either it *is already* the case that p will never be true, or it *will* be the case that p will never be true'. (Making this a thesis means, of course, laying it down as true at all times and for any p.) The first disjunct of this, it will be noticed, is something which is bound to be the case at the end of time; while the second is bound to be the case if the end of time is still ahead of us; so that if there *is* to be an end of time, the whole disjunction will be true throughout the whole of time (though neither it nor anything else will be true *after* the end of time). Indeed, 'after the end of time' is a self-contradictory description; but talk of time's having an end means that at a certain time, namely the last instant, all assertions to the effect that something *will be* the case, are false).

The postulate $\sim Fp \vee F\sim Fp$ is equivalent to $Fp \supset F\sim Fp$. In itself this simply asserts that if anything will be the case, then it will sooner or later be the case that *that* thing will never be the case. But we may deduce from it the apparently more general thesis $Fp \supset F\sim Fq$, asserting that if anything will be the case, then it will sooner or later be the case, not only with respect to that thing, but with respect to anything you please, that it will never be the case. The proof is as follows:

1. $Fp \supset F(p \supset p)$ $[p \supset (p \supset p),$ RFC]
2. $Fp \supset F{\sim}F(p \supset p)$ $[1, Fp \supset F{\sim}Fp]$
3. $Fq \supset F(p \supset p)$ $[q \supset (p \supset p),$ RFC]
4. ${\sim}F(p \supset p) \supset {\sim}Fq$ [3]
5. $F{\sim}F(p \supset p) \supset F{\sim}Fq$ [4, RFC]
6. $Fp \supset F{\sim}Fq$ [2, 5].

6. in turn easily equates to $Fp \supset FGq$.

Given this result, we may prove a further one in that fragment of this tense logic which constitutes a Diodorean modal logic. Diodorus defined 'Possibly p', $\Diamond p$, as 'It either is or will be that p', $p \vee Fp$, and 'Necessarily p', $\Box p$, as 'It is and always will be that p', $p \wedge Gp$. (These are of course a different $\Box$ and $\Diamond$ from those used in the 'world' calculus of the preceding section.) The Diodorean-modal thesis now to be proved for ending time is $\Box \Diamond p \supset \Diamond \Box p$, 'If it is and always will be that it is or will be that p, then it is or will be that it is and always will be that p'.[4] In endless time the antecedent of this could be true and the consequent false; this would be so if p were going to be true and false alternately for ever (it would then always be going to be true that p, but never going to be always true that p). But if time has an end, the antecedent will only be true if p is true at the end of time, and when this is so the consequent will be true also. In proving this implication from our axiom, note first that it expands by the Diodorean definitions to

$$((p \vee Fp) \wedge G(p \vee Fp)) \supset ((p \wedge Gp) \vee F(p \wedge Gp)).$$

Ordinary propositional logic will equate this with

$$(p \vee Fp) \supset (G(p \vee Fp) \supset ({\sim}(p \wedge Gp) \supset F(p \wedge Gp))),$$

---

[4] In D.C. Makinson's 'There are Infinitely many Diodorean Modal Functions', *Journal of Symbolic Logic*, vol. 31 (1966), pp. 406–8, this formula is mentioned as typical of a system D*, for the mirror-image of Diodorean modality in beginning time.

and in this, $\sim(p \land Gp) \equiv \sim p \lor \sim Gp$ (de Morgan), i.e. $\sim p \lor F\sim p$, and a commutation turns the whole into

$$(p \lor Fp) \supset ((\sim p \lor F\sim p) \supset (G(p \lor Fp) \supset F(p \land Gp))),$$

and this amounts (by $((p \lor q) \supset r) \equiv ((p \supset r) \land (q \supset r)))$ to the conjunction of the following four formulae:

1. $p \supset (\sim p \supset (G(p \lor Fp) \supset F(p \land Gp)))$
2. $p \supset (F\sim p \supset (G(p \lor Fp) \supset F(p \land Gp)))$
3. $Fp \supset (\sim p \supset (G(p \lor Fp) \supset F(p \land Gp)))$
4. $Fp \supset (F\sim p \supset (G(p \lor Fp) \supset F(p \land Gp)))$

Of these, 1. holds trivially because of its contradictory antecedents, and in the rest we may use either an antecedent Fp or an antecedent $F\sim p$ to obtain $FG(p \land \sim p)$ by $Fp \supset FGq$, and proceed as follows:

1. $FG(p \land \sim p)$
2. $G(p \lor Fp)$
3. $F((p \lor Fp) \land G(p \land \sim p))$ $[1, 2, (Gp \land Fq) \supset F(p \land q)]$
4. $F((p \land G(p \land \sim p)) \lor$
    $(Fp \land G(p \land \sim p)))$ $[3, (p \lor q) \land r) \supset ((p \land r) \lor (q \land r))]$
5. $F(p \land G(p \land \sim p)) \lor$
    $F(Fp \land G(p \land \sim p))$ $[4, F(p \lor q) \equiv (Fp \lor Fq)]$
6. $F(p \land Gp) \lor F(Fp \land G\sim p)$ $[5, (p \land q) \supset p, (p \land q) \supset q]$
7. $F(p \land Gp)$ $[6, \sim F(Fp \land G\sim p)]$.

Turning now to the U-calculus version of the theory of ending time, the condition on U which we need to add is

(A) $Uab \supset \exists c(Uac \land \forall d\sim Ucd),$

'If any instant is later than a, then some instant later than a has no instant following it'. If we were not leaving open the possibility of branching future, we might have used the simpler $\exists a \forall b\sim Uab$, 'Some instant has no instant following it', but with branching time this would be consistent with some branches *not* ending. The longer formula (A) ensures that every branch there may be has an end. (To see this, suppose some branch *hasn't* an end. Then, starting from some point a on this branch, there will be a point *b* further along for which we have the antecedent *Uab*, but no point *c* on the branch which is without any points *d* beyond it, i.e. no point *c* satisfying the consequent *Uac* ∧ ∀*d*~*Ucd*.) If (A) is a law (and so implicitly preceded by ∀*b*), the shorter formula will follow from it. For

(B)   ∀*b*(*Uab* ⊃ ∃*c* ∀*d*~*Ucd*)

follows from (A) in any case; we have by quantification theory ∃*bUab* ∨ ∀*b*~*Uab*; and ∃*c* ∀*d*~*Ucd* follows from (B) and ∃*bUab*, and from ∀*b*~*Uab* immediately.

The corresponding tense-logical formula   *Fp* ⊃ *FGq*, supposed true at *a*, is equivalent by U1–U4 to

(C)   ∃*b*(*Uab* ∧ *Tb*(*p*)) ⊃ ∃*c*(*Uac* ∧ ∀*d*(*Ucd* ⊃ ~*Td*(*q*))),

and this by quantification theory to

(D)   *Uab* ⊃ (*Tb*(*p*) ⊃ ∃*c*(*Uac* ∧ ∀*d*(*Ucd* ⊃ ~*Td*(*q*)))),

which we prove from (A) thus:

1.   *Uab*
2.   *Tb*(*p*)
3.   *Uac*   [1, (A)]
4.   ∀*d*~*Ucd*   [1, (A)]
5.   ∀*d*(*Ucd* ⊃ ~*Td*(*q*))   [4, ~*p* ⊃ (*p* ⊃ *q*)]

Conversely we obtain (A) from (D) by letting *p* and *q* in the latter be *p* ⊃ *p*, *Tb*(*p* ⊃ *p*) being detachable as a thesis, and *Ucd* ⊃ ~*Td*(*p* ⊃ *p*) being equivalent to ~*Ucd* (since it makes *Ucd* imply an absurdity).

Apart from the special axioms under consideration, the only tense-logical formulae used in all these proofs are ones provable in K$_t$.

It is of some interest to relate our formulae to McTaggart's characterization of beginning and ending time. What he says is that 'if the time-series has a first term, that term will never be future, and if it has a last term, that term will never be future, and if it has a last term, that term will never be past'.[5] Concentrating on the second clause, what first strikes one about it is that ending time, as characterized by McTaggart, does not obey the tense-logical law that was later enunciated by J.N. Findlay,[6] that whatever is or has been or will be the case, sooner or later will have been the case, $(p \lor Pp \lor Fp) \supset FPp$. The exception, in ending time, is anything that is true only at time's last instant; i.e. it is the last of the series of 'worlds'. If time is linear, then each instantaneous total world-state is something which is or has been or will be the case, i.e. we have $\forall a(a \lor Pa \lor Fa)$, but there is a world-state, the last one, which will never have been the case, $\exists a \sim FPa$. McTaggart's formula $\exists a \sim FPa$, i.e. $\exists aG \sim Pa$, follows in our ending-time system by

(A). $\rightarrow \exists a \forall b \sim Uab$
$\rightarrow \exists a \forall b(Uab \supset Tb(\sim Pa))$
$= \exists aTa(G \sim Pa)$
$= \exists a \Box(a \supset G \sim Pa)$
$\rightarrow \exists a \Box(Pa \supset PG \sim Pa)$
$\rightarrow \exists a \Box(Pa \supset \sim Pa)$
$\rightarrow \exists a \Box \sim Pa$
$\rightarrow \exists aG \sim Pa.$[7]

3. *The East-West and North-South views of time.* One variation of the ending-time theory is worth mentioning in passing. In 1965 C.L. Hamblin described a version of *circular* time according to which, if we go far enough into the future we shall find ourselves not in the future at all but in the past. He called this the 'East-West' conception of circular time, 'in the sense in which California is east but not west of Sydney, and west but not east of Manchester'. E.J. Lemmon then suggested that we might also have a 'North-South' conception of time, and this would be quite different, and not circular at all. The geometrical picture would be of this sort:

[5] *Op. cit.* § 329 n.
[6] In 'Time: a Treatment of Some Puzzles', in A.G.N. Flew's *Logic and Language*, First Series (Blackwell, 1951), pp. 37–54.
[7] Editors' note. There is a minor error in this proof, since the second occurrence of '=' should be replaced by an '$\rightarrow$'.

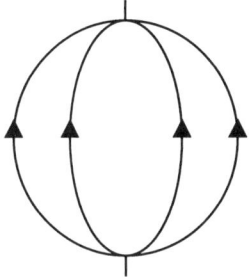

The North Pole would represent the end of time, and the South Pole would represent its beginning, and time would not be linear but branching, only the branches would all converge again. The usual formula for such convergence in the future is $FGp \supset GFp$, or in the U-calculus $Uab \supset (Uac \supset \exists d(Ubd \wedge Ucd))$, and for the past $PHp \supset HPp$ or $Uba \supset (Uca \supset \exists d(Udb \wedge Udc))$, but in the present case these formulae will not do. Concentrating on the future, the convergence U-formula says that if b and c are both later than a then they have at least one later moment in common; but if time also ends, one of them might have no later moment at all. This combination does not result in a strict contradiction, but it entails that no moment is later (and so none earlier) than any other, i.e. that there is no future and no past, and this is not the general 'North-South' picture, though it is a limiting case of it. Technically, if we combine either $Uab \supset (Uac \supset \exists d(Ubd \wedge Ucd))$ with ending, or the reverse convergence formula with beginning, we can deduce a contradiction from Uab, and so prove $\sim Uab$ as a theorem. Doing it the first way, we have

1. Uab
2. $\forall c(Uac \supset \exists d(Ubd \wedge Ucd))$ [1, convergence]
3. $\exists c(Uac \wedge \forall d \sim Ucd)$ [1, ending]
4. $\forall c(Uac \supset \exists dUcd)$ [2]
5. $\sim \exists c(Uac \supset \forall d \sim Ucd)$ [4].

Correspondingly, if we combine either $FGp \supset GFp$ and $Fp \supset FGq$ or $PHp \supset HPp$ and $Pp \supset PHq$, we can prove both $\sim Fp$ and $\sim Pp$ as theorems. Doing it the first way (using auxiliary theses from K_t)

1. $FGp \supset FG\sim p$ [$\dot{F}p \supset FGq, p/Gp, q/\sim p$]

2.	$FGp \supset {\sim}GFp$	$[1, FG{\sim} = {\sim}G{\sim}G{\sim} = {\sim}GF]$
3.	${\sim}FGp$	$[2, FGp \supset GFp,$
		$(p \supset {\sim}q) \supset ((p \supset q) \supset {\sim}p)]$
4.	${\sim}Fp$	$[3, Fp \supset FGq, q/p]$
5.	$HF(p \supset p)$	[prop. calculus, $p \supset HFp$]
6.	$Pp \supset P(p \wedge F(p \supset p))$	$[5, Hp \supset (Pq \supset P(q \wedge p))]$
7.	$Pp \supset PF(p \supset p)$	$[6, P(p \wedge q) \supset Pq]$
8.	$H{\sim}F(p \supset p)$	$[4, p/(p \supset p), \text{RH}]$
9.	${\sim}PF(p \supset p)$	$[8, H{\sim} = {\sim}P]$
10.	${\sim}Pp$	$[7, 9]$.

We have here, in effect, that trivialization of tense logic which consists in interpreting Gp and Hp as the tautological function $p \supset p$, and Fp and Pp as the contradictory function ${\sim}(p \supset p)$; i.e. $K_t + FGp \supset GFp + Fp \supset FGq$ is equivalent to the system obtained by adding these definitions to propositional calculus.

On the U-calculus side, the required amendment to the usual future-convergence formula is, I think,

(E) $Uab \supset (Uac \supset (Ubd \supset (Uce \supset \exists f(Uaf \wedge Ubf \wedge Ucf))))$,

i.e. if b and c are both later than a, then *if b and c have any later moments at all*, all three of a, b, c have a common later moment. (If we assume U transitive, the Uaf in the consequent is not needed.) This holds in non-trivial as well as trivial forms of 'North-South' time. The equivalent tense-logical formula is $F(p \wedge Fq) \supset (F(r \wedge Fs) \supset F(Pp \wedge Pr))$. The U-calculus translation of this is

$$\exists b(Uab \wedge Tb(p) \wedge \exists c(Ubc \wedge Tc(q))) \supset$$
$$(\exists d(Uad \wedge Td(r) \wedge \exists e(Ude \wedge Te(s))) \supset$$
$$\exists f(Uaf \wedge \exists g(Ugf(Tg(p)) (\exists h(Uhf(Th(r))))$$

which we may contract to

(F) $Uab \supset$
          $(Tb(p) \supset (Ubc \supset (Tc(q) \supset$
          $(Uad \supset (Td(r) \supset (Ude \wedge (Te(s) \supset$
          $(\exists f(Uaf \wedge$
          $\exists g(Ugf \wedge Tg(p)) \wedge \exists h(Uhf \wedge Th(r)))))))))))$.

We obtain this from (E) as follows[8]:

1. Uab
2. $Tb(p)$
3. Ubc
4. $Tc(q)$
5. Uad
6. $Td(r)$
7. Ude
8. $Te(s)$
10. Uaf [1, 5, 3, 7, (E)]
11. Ubf [1, 5, 3, 7, (E)]
12. Udf [1, 5, 3, 7, (E)]
13. $\exists g(Ugf \wedge Tg(p))$ [11, 2]
14. $\exists h(Uhf \wedge Th(r))$ [12, 6]

And we obtain (E) from (F) by making the substitutions p/b, q/c, r/d, s/e and proceeding thus:

1. Uab
2. $Tb(b)$
3. Ubc
4. $Tc(c)$
5. Uad
6. $Td(d)$
7. Ude
8. $Te(e)$
9. Uaf [1–8, (F)]
10. Ugf [1–8, (F)]
11. $Tg(b)$ [1–8, (F)]
12. Igb [11, $Ta(b) \supset Iab$]
13. Ubf [10, 12]
14. Uhf [1–8, (F)]
15. Thd [1–8, (F)]
16. Ihd [15, $Ta(b) \supset Iab$]
17. Udf [14, 16]

[8] Editors' note. Prior seems to have made a numbering mistake here going directly from 8 to 10.

then detaching the antecedents 2, 4, 6, 8 (i.e. $\Box(b \supset b)$, etc.) and dropping from the consequent all the conjuncts but 9, 13, and 17.

Summing up, 'North-South' time can perhaps be characterized by subjoining to K_t the axioms $Gp \supset GGp$ (for transitivity) with

$$F(p \wedge Fq) \supset (F(r \wedge Fs) \supset F(Pp \wedge Pr)) \text{ and } Fp \supset FGq$$

and their images.

4. *Ending time and 'dead' time.* Von Wright has observed that the apparently more restricted axiom for ending time, $Fp \supset F\sim Fp$, looks as if it might not express that view, but rather the view that the truth is endlessly changing – that if anything is true, it is not true more than once. It might seem, in short, to be compatible with the idea that every particular thing will indeed cease to be true, but only by being replaced by some different particular thing. But $Fp \supset F\sim Fp$ lays down this 'Everything will cease to be true' for *all* propositions, even logically true ones, and *these* surely could only cease to be true by time itself ending (their ceasing to be true would *be* time's ending). If the ps in the formula were confined to 'atomic' propositions, it might be susceptible of von Wright's interpretation; we would have something like it, too, if we replaced the ps by as. For logically true propositions are not substitutable for world-variables, and $Fa \supset F\sim Fa$ would indeed assert, not that there will be a last world-state, but that no future world-state will be repeated.

We come closer to ending time if we make an assumption that is in a way the opposite of von Wright's, namely that we will eventually reach a state which will never cease to be the world's total state, i.e. sooner or later time will 'stand still', in the sense that no further change will occur in anything whatever. Some philosophers have spoken as if there would be no more than a verbal difference between this state of affairs and time's coming to an end, and some have denied this. For example, McTaggart would apparently equate the two, since he says flatly that 'there could be no time if nothing changed'.[9] Locke, on the other hand, sharply distinguishes the regular motions which we use for *measuring* duration from the duration itself which is being measured, and insists that 'having from the revolutions of the sun got the ideas of certain

[9] *Op. cit.*, § 309.

lengths of duration, we can in our thoughts add such lengths of duration to one another as often as we please', and 'this we can continue to do on, without bounds or limits, and proceed *in infinitum*, and apply thus the length of the annual motion of the sun to duration, supposed before the sun's *or any other motion* had its being'[10] (last italics mine). And, presumably, after.

Formally, a short decision between these two positions would be that an end of change *can* be distinguished from an end of time. The U-calculus formula expressing the view that (on any branch that we may be on, if time has branches) we shall sooner or later reach an end of *change*, would be

(G) $\quad Uab \supset \exists c(Uac \land \forall d(Ucd \supset Icd))$,

which we may compare with

(A) $\quad Uab \supset \exists c(Uac \land \forall d{\sim}Ucd)$,

the formula for ending *time*. (G) follows trivially from (A), but not vice versa. The tense-logical counterpart of (G) is the thesis $Fp \supset F(q \supset Gq)$ ('If anything will be the case, then it will sooner or later be the case that whatever is true will be so for ever after'). Preceded by Ta, this expands to

$\quad \exists b(Uab \land Tb(p)) \supset \exists c(Uac \land (Tcq \supset \forall d(Ucd \supset Td(q))))$,

which is deductively equivalent to

(H) $\quad Uab \supset (Tb(p) \supset \exists c(Uac \land \forall d(Ucd \supset (Tc(q) \supset Td(q)))))$.

This may be proved from (G) as follows:

1.	Uab	
2.	$Tb(p)$	
3.	Uac	[from 1 by (E)]
4.	$\forall d(Ucd \supset Icd)$	[from 1 by (E)]
5.	$\forall d(Ucd \supset (Tc(q) \supset Td(q)))$	[from 4]

---

[10] *Essay Concerning Human Understanding*, Book II, Ch. XIV, §§ 23, 27.

Conversely, if in (H) we put b for p and c for q, we may detach $Tb(b)$ and $Tc(c)$ to obtain

$$Uab \supset \exists c(Uac \wedge \forall d(Ucd \supset Td(c))).$$

This yields (G) by $Td(c) \supset Icd$. And $Fp \supset F(q \supset Gq)$ is related to the ending-time tense-logical formula $Fp \supset FGq$ as (G) is to (A), i.e. it follows from it, but not vice versa. (If we let $Fp = Gp = Pp = Hp = p$, all of K_t, and $Fp \supset F(q \supset Gq)$, become propositional calculus tautologies, but not $Fp \supset FGq$.)

So far we seem to be with Locke and against McTaggart. It might nevertheless seem that the procedure adopted in our first section, of simply identifying an instant with the totality of what would be said to be the case 'at' that instant, immediately commits us to McTaggart's view that the end of change is only verbally different from the end of time. But the matter is not quite as simple as that. Certainly, given the way we use 'instant', we are committed to the view that, once an instant of 'dead' time is reached, there will be no *other* instant after this one; i.e. that there can only be one instant of 'dead' time. But, given the way we use 'instant', this means no more than that, once 'dead' time is reached, nothing will be true but what is true already. The question as to whether anything at all 'will' be true is still an open one, and one which, since 'it will be the case that' is not defined in terms of 'instants', it is perfectly possible to formulate, and to answer either way, without referring to 'instants' either in the above sense or in some more Platonistic one.

We could, indeed, immediately dismiss the idea of 'dead' but not ending time if we assumed that no instant is later than itself. This is intuitively obvious (given the above conception of an instant), and formally, if we make $\sim Uaa$ an axiom, we can deduce the ending-time formula (A) from the dying-time formula (G) as follows:

1.	Uab	
2.	Uac	
3.	$\forall d(Ucd \supset Icd)$	$[1, (G)]$
4.	$\forall d(Ucd \supset Udd)$	$[3]$
5.	$\forall d \sim Ucd$	$[4, \sim Udd]$.

But to say that no instant, in *this* sense of 'instant', is ever in its own future, is plainly to beg the question of whether dead but not ending time is possible, since it is just to say that no world-state is ever repeated. There are in fact consistent tense logics (ones for circular time) in which it is laid down that *every* instant is in its own future.

5. *Discreteness, denseness, and continuity.* There are, all the same, definite limits to our freedom to combine dying with non-ending time. In particular, too extreme an absolutism will be self-defeating. Locke, for example, seems to have held not only that there is a difference between time's going on but nothing happening, and time's not going on at all, but also that even in 'dead' time there is a difference between intervals in respect of their length. But if this is so, the instants of this supposedly 'dead' time, coming after a 'live' time, will not be identical in the above sense, since one thing that will be the case at any instant *a* of 'dead' time will be that the state of the world was something other than *a* such-and-such an interval ago, and these intervals will be different for each *a*, so that the *a*s will *not* all of them be quite the same proposition: indeed, no one of them will be quite the same as any other.

We have a special case of this when time is supposed to be discrete, since this gives us built-in units of temporal distance. In discrete time we just cannot without contradiction suppose an endless succession of identical world-states to follow after a state which is different from any of them; indeed, we cannot even get two. For one thing that will be true in the first state in this supposed succession, which we may suppose to be the state *a*, is that the immediately preceding state, whatever it was, was not *a*; but in the next state in the supposed succession, one thing that will be true is that the immediately preceding state *was a*; so these two states are not after all identical, and the supposition that they are is impossible. To formalize this reasoning, we may make use of a tense logic due to Dana Scott, in which the usual tensed forms are supplemented by *Tp* for 'It will be the case at the next instant that *p*', and *Yp* for 'It was the case at the instant just gone that *p*' and in which we have (among others) the following laws:

TG: $G(p \supset q) \supset (Tp \supset Tq)$
TY: $TYp \supset p$

(I select these two because in themselves they do not commit us either to time's infinity or its denial. Scott's complete system in fact contains the laws $Gp \supset Tp$ and $Hp \supset Yp$, which do commit us to time's infinity, but I shall not make use of these in what follows.) Given this much, we have the following proof, in which the antecedents express the assumptions that a is the case now, that it will be the case at the next instant, and that it was not the case at the instant just past:

1.	a	
2.	Ta	
3.	$Y{\sim}a$	
4.	$\Box(a \supset Y{\sim}a)$	$[1, 3, (a \wedge p) \supset \Box(a \supset p)]$
5.	$G(a \supset Y{\sim}a)$	$[4, \Box p \supset Gp]$
6.	$Ta \supset TY{\sim}a$	$[5, TG]$
7.	$TY{\sim}a$	$[6, 2]$
8.	${\sim}a$	$[7, TY]$,

in which the conclusion contradicts the hypothesis.

If time is *not* discrete, then if 'live' time is followed by 'dead' time, either (i) there is a first moment of 'dead' time but no last moment of 'live' time, or (ii) there is a last moment of 'live' time but no first or 'dead' time, or (iii) there is neither a last moment of 'live' time nor a first of 'dead' (the third alternative is only possible if time is dense but not strictly continuous). (i) can be easily excluded, since at the first moment of 'dead' time it will be the case that all previous moments were 'live', but at subsequent moments this will not be so, contradicting the definition of 'dead' time as time throughout which whatever is true at any moment is true at any moment future to that one. Or, more accurately, it entails that there can be *no* moment of 'dead' time which is future to the first (if there were the time would not be 'dead'), so that this kind of 'death' *is* identical with time's having an end. Formally the proof is:

1.	a	
2.	Ga	
3.	${\sim}Pa$	
4.	$\Box(a \supset {\sim}Pa)$	$[1, 3, (a \wedge p) \supset \Box(a \supset p)]$
5.	$G(a \supset {\sim}Pa)$	$[4, \Box p \supset Gp]$
6.	GPa	$[1, p \supset GPp]$

7.	$G{\sim}a$	$[5, 6, G(p \supset {\sim}q) \supset (Gq \supset G{\sim}p)]$
8.	$G(a \wedge {\sim}a)$	$[2, 7]$
9.	$G{\sim}p$	$[8, (p \wedge {\sim}p) \supset q, \text{RGC}]$
10.	${\sim}Fp$	$[9, G{\sim} = {\sim}F]$,

where p is any arbitrarily chosen proposition whatever.

It may be thought that in this last proof the antecedent (3) is stronger than our supposition warrants – we are only supposing that the time immediately leading up to the first 'dead' instant a is one throughout which a is false; we don't have to suppose a never to have been true before. But it can be shown that if we suppose a to have been true previously, with an intervening interval of falsehood, it will be inconsistent to suppose that a will be always true henceforward (where a is a world-state proposition). For we have

1.	a	
2.	$P({\sim}a \wedge Pa)$	
3.	$P(HF{\sim}a \wedge Pa)$	$[2, p \supset HFp]$
4.	$PP(F{\sim}a \wedge a)$	$[3, (Hp \wedge Pq) \supset P(p \wedge q)]$
5.	$PP\Box(a \supset F{\sim}a)$	$[4, (p \wedge a) \supset \Box(a \supset p)]$
6.	$\Box(a \supset F{\sim}a)$	$[5, P\Box p \supset \Box p$ twice$]$
7.	$F{\sim}a$	$[6, 1]$
8.	${\sim}Ga$	$[7, F{\sim} = {\sim}G]$.

Informally, if a completely characterized some previous world-state, part of its content would be that it was going to be false, so that if *this very same* a completely characterizes the present world-state, it cannot be that it will never be false again, i.e. that there will be no further alterations in the world.

If, however, we make supposition (ii) or (iii), above, i.e. if we suppose 'dead' time to be preceded by 'live' time but in such a way that between any moments of 'dead' and 'live' time there is an earlier moment of 'dead' time, the above proof of time's ending (two paragraphs back) cannot be constructed. Possibly, under these circumstances, some other line of proof will turn out to be available, but on the whole it looks as if we *can* distinguish between time's going 'dead' and time's coming to an end, provided that we do not (like Locke) suppose time to have an intrinsic 'metric' (in which case the supposition of time's going *completely* 'dead' is self-contradictory), and provided that we do not suppose there is a *first* moment of 'dead' time. If, finally, we redefine 'dead' time as time throughout which there is no change in the truth-value of those propositions which have no past or future-tense operators in them (a suggestion made to me by Dr. P. Nidditch), there would seem to be no *logical* incoherence in supposing 'live' time to be followed by an indefinitely long period of 'dead' time even *with* a first moment. For the negative results above depend entirely on the truths at a given instant including past-tense and future-tense ones.

XIII
STRATIFIED METRIC TENSE LOGIC

Statement of the problem. By a non-metric tense logic I mean propositional calculus enriched by the forms Fp for 'It will be the case that p', and Pp for 'It has been that case that p', with suitable postulates. By a metric tense logic I mean propositional calculus enriched by the forms $F(n)p$ for 'It will be the case the interval n hence that p', and $P(n)p$ for 'It was the case the interval n ago', with quantifiers binding interval-variables and manipulated according to the usual rules, and with suitable postulates for the special symbols. A certain amount of number-theory may be incorporated either in the metalogic or in the system itself.

Non-metric tense logic may be correlated with a theory of the earlier-later relation, in which the forms Uab, $a = b$, and $Ta(p)$ are used for 'The instant a is earlier than the instant b'; 'The instant a is identical with the instant b' and 'It is the case at the instant a that p' respectively, with the following postulates regarding the truth-conditions of tense-logical formulae:

U1. $Ta(\sim p) \equiv \sim Ta(p)$
U2. $Ta(p \supset q) \equiv (Ta(p) \supset Ta(q))$
U3. $Ta(Fp) \equiv \exists b(Uab \wedge Tb(p))$
U4. $Ta(Pp) \equiv \exists b(Uba \wedge Tb(p))$,

and with or without special conditions (e.g. transitivity) on the relation U. E.J. Lemmon has shown that if no such special conditions are laid down, the tense-logical formulae which may be derived, preceded by Ta, from propositional calculus, quantification theory, and the postulates U1–U4, are precisely those which may be derived by substitution, detachment, and the rules

$$\vdash \alpha \rightarrow \vdash \sim F \sim \alpha \text{ and } \vdash \alpha \rightarrow \vdash \sim P \sim \alpha$$

from propositional calculus and the axioms

1.1. $\sim F \sim (p \supset q) \supset (Fp \supset Fq)$
1.2. $\sim P \sim (p \supset q) \supset (Pp \supset Pq)$
2.1. $F \sim P \sim p \supset p$
2.2. $P \sim F \sim p \supset p.$

(The system defined by these postulates was called by Lemmon the system K_t.) It is useful to introduce the forms Gp ('It will always be the case that p') and Hp ('It has always been the case that p') as abbreviations for $\sim F \sim p$ and $\sim P \sim p$ respectively, turning the consequents of the rules into $\vdash G\alpha$ and $\vdash H\alpha$, and the axioms into $G(p \supset q) \supset (Fp \supset Fq)$, $FHp \supset p$ and their mirror images. Additional tense-logical postulates may be correlated with special conditions on U, notably

$FFp \supset Fp$ with transitiveness ($Uab \supset (Ubc \supset Uac)$),
$Fp \supset FFp$ with density ($Uab \supset \exists c(Uac \wedge Ucb)$),
$\sim Fp \supset F \sim p$ with non-ending,
$\sim Pp \supset P \sim p$ with non-beginning,
$(Fp \wedge Fq) \supset (F(p \wedge q) \vee F(p \wedge Fq) \vee F(q \wedge Fp))$ with non-branching in the future, and its image with non-branching in the past.

Postulates hitherto suggested for metric tense logic (e.g. by Rescher[1] and by myself[2]) do not have this 'stratified' character. For example, they include the rule that $\vdash \alpha \rightarrow \vdash F(n)\alpha$ and the axiom

$\sim F(n)p \supset F(n)\sim p,$

which assume non-endingness, the axiom

$F(n)\sim p \supset \sim F(n)p,$

which assumes non-branching in the future, and the axiom

$F(m)F(n)p \supset F(m+n)p,$

[1] In 'On the Logic of Chronological Propositions', *Mind*, vol. 75, No. 297 (Jan. 1966), pp. 75–96.
[2] E.g. in *Past, Present and Future*, Ch. VI.

which assumes the transitivity of the earlier-later relation. What I shall attempt here is to give a postulate-set for metric tense logic which makes no such assumptions, with the additions required to bring various assumptions in. I shall also devise a correlated earlier-later calculus, analogous to the U-calculus which is correlated with non-metric tense logic.

2. The metric U-calculus, and the minimal metric tense logic. Both in the metric U-calculus and in the metric tense logic, the interval-variables m, n, etc. will be taken as standing for positive numbers measuring the intervals used, and as much number-theory as we need will be incorporated in the calculus. If the range of numbers drawn upon is the integers, the calculus will be suitable for time considered as discrete; if the rational numbers, for time considered as dense; if the reals, for time considered as strictly continuous.[3]

In the U-calculus, in place of the non-metric Uab we shall use the form $Uabn$ for 'The instant a is earlier than the instant b by the interval n', and replace the original U3 and U4 by the pair

U3. $Ta(F(n)p) \equiv \exists b(Uabn \wedge Tb(p))$
U4. $Ta(P(n)p) \equiv \exists b(Uban \wedge Tb(p))$.

We also need a new postulate to cover quantification over intervals, namely

U5. $Ta(\exists n\alpha) \equiv \exists nTa(\alpha)$,

which is a schema covering the infinity of axioms in which (is replaced by any formula from the metric tense logic. We also need a postulate to make it clear that we regard an interval n as added to an interval m only if they are contiguous in the instant-series; i.e. we need

U6. $Uab(m+n) \supset \exists c(Uacm \wedge Ucbn)$.

---

[3] *Editors' note.* Here the first edition contains the sentence: 'The number-theory drawn upon in what follows will require no more, in the way of symbols, than the forms Imn for '$m=n$' and Smn for '$m+n$'.' To make this chapter as accessible as possible, we have replaced Prior's 'Smn' by '$m+n$'. Likewise we have replaced 'Imn' by '$m=n$'.

These postulates suffice to yield, preceded by Ta, all theses derived from the following postulates for metric tense logic, subjoined to propositional calculus, quantification theory (with quantifiers binding interval-variables), and that part of positive number-theory which is common to the integers, the rationals, and the reals:

$$\vdash \alpha \rightarrow \vdash \sim F(n)\sim\alpha, \vdash \sim P(n)\sim\alpha;$$

A1.1. $\sim F(n)\sim(p \supset q) \supset (F(n)p \supset F(n)q)$

A1.2. $\sim P(n)\sim(p \supset q) \supset (P(n)p \supset P(n)q)$

A2.1. $F(n)\sim P(n)\sim p \supset p$

A2.2. $P(n)\sim F(n)\sim p \supset p$

A3.1. $F(m)\exists nF(n)p \supset \exists nF(m)F(n)p$

A3.2. $P(m)\exists nP(n)p \supset \exists nP(m)P(n)p$

A4.1. $F(m)\exists nP(n)p \supset \exists nF(m)P(n)p$

A4.2. $P(m)\exists nF(n)p \supset \exists nP(m)F(n)p$

A5.1. $F(m+n)p \supset F(m)F(n)p$

A5.2. $P(m+n)p (P(m)P(n)p.$

It will suffice to show this for the left-hand columns. In the first place,

$\vdash Ta(\alpha) \rightarrow \vdash Tb(\alpha)$	[substitution; α not affected, as it contains no a]
$\rightarrow \vdash Uabn \supset Tb(\alpha)$	[by $p \supset (q \supset p)$]
$\rightarrow \vdash \forall b(Uabn \supset Tb(\alpha))$	[by U.G.]
$\rightarrow \vdash \sim\exists b(Uabn \wedge \sim Tb(\alpha))$	
$\rightarrow \vdash \sim\exists b(Uabn \wedge Tb(\sim\alpha))$	[by U1]
$\rightarrow \vdash \sim Ta(F(n)\sim\alpha)$	[by U3]
$\rightarrow \vdash Ta(\sim F(n)\sim\alpha)$	[by U1].

Then for A1.1, note first that $Ta(A1.1)$ expands by U1–U4 to

$$\sim\exists b(Uabn \wedge Tb(\sim(p \supset q))) \supset$$
$$(\exists c(Uacn \wedge Tc(p)) \supset \exists d(Uadn \wedge Td(q))),$$

which is in turn equivalent to

$$\forall c(\forall b(Uabn \supset (Tb(p) \supset$$
$$(Tb(q)))) \supset (Uacn \supset (Tc(p) \supset \exists d(Uad \wedge Td(q)))),$$

which we prove thus:

1. $\forall b(Uabn \supset (Tb(p) \supset Tb(q)))$
2. $Uacn$
3. $Tc(p)$
4. $Uacn \supset (Tc(p) \supset Tc(q))$ [1, U1]
5. $Tc(q)$ [4, 2, 3]
6. $\exists d(Uadn \wedge Td(q))$ [2, 5, E.G.].

$Ta(A2.1)$ expands to

$$\exists b(Uabn \wedge \sim\exists c(Ucbn \wedge \sim Tc(p))) \supset Ta(p),$$

which equates to

$$\forall b(Uabn \supset (\forall c(Ucbn \supset Tc(p)) \supset Ta(p)),$$

which we prove thus:

1. $Uabn$
2. $\forall c(Ucbn \supset Tc(p))$
3. $Ta(p)$ [1, 2].

$Ta(A3.1)$ expands to

$$\exists b(Uabm \wedge Tb(\exists nF(n)p)) \supset$$
$$\exists n\exists c(Uacm \wedge \exists d(Ucdn \wedge Td(p))),$$

in which $Tb(\exists nF(n)p)$ is equivalent to $\exists nTb(F(n)p)$ (by U5), and so to $\exists n\exists e(Uben \wedge Te(p))$, where the $\exists b$, $\exists n$, and $\exists e$ (introducing an antecedent) may be replaced by $\forall b, \forall n$, and $\forall e$ at the beginning of the whole,[4] which we may then prove thus (A4.1 being proved similarly):

1. $Uabm$
2. $Uben$
3. Tep

---

[4] *Editors' note*. Prior presumably had the following formula in mind:
$\forall b \forall n \forall e((Uabm \wedge Uben \wedge Te(p)) \supset \exists n\exists c(Uacm \wedge \exists d(Ucdn \wedge Td(p))))$.

4. $\exists d(Ubdn \wedge Td(p))$ [2, 3, E.G.]
5. $\exists c(Uacm \wedge \exists d(Ucdn \wedge Td(p))$ [1, 4, E.G.].

$Ta(A5.1)$ expands to

$$\exists b(Uab(m+n) \wedge Tb(p)) \supset \exists c(Uacm \wedge \exists d(Ucdn \wedge Td(p))),$$

which we prove thus:

1. $Uab(m+n)$
2. $Tb(p)$
3. $Uacm$ [1, U6]
4. $Ucbn$ [1, U6]
5. $\exists d(Ucdn \wedge Td(p))$ [4, 2, E.I.].

Whether the above $F(n)$-$P(n)$ postulates suffice to yield *all* the metric tense-logical theses that are obtainable, preceded by Ta, from our minimal metric U-calculus, has not been proved: I offer it as a conjecture that they do. They certainly suffice to yield Lemmon's minimal non-metric tense-logic K_t if we introduce the forms $F\alpha$ and $P\alpha$ as abbreviations for $\exists nF(n)\alpha$ and $\exists nP(n)\alpha$, where n does not occur free in α. Indeed, we can prove this much without drawing upon the A3s and A4s. We prove this rule to infer $\vdash \sim F\sim\alpha$ from $\vdash \alpha$ by taking an n which does not occur free in α and proceeding thus:

$\vdash \alpha \;\; \rightarrow \vdash \sim F(n)\sim\alpha$
$\quad\quad \rightarrow \vdash \forall n \sim F(n)\sim\alpha$ [by U.G.]
$\quad\quad \rightarrow \vdash \sim\exists nF(n)\sim\alpha$
$\quad\quad \rightarrow \vdash \sim F\sim\alpha$ [by Df.F].

And $\sim F\sim(p \supset q) \supset (Fp \supset Fq)$ thus:

1. $\sim F(n)\sim(p \supset q) \supset (F(n)p \supset F(n)q)$ [A1.1]
2. $\forall n \sim F(n)\sim(p \supset q) \supset$
      $(\exists nF(n)p \supset \exists nF(n)q)$ [1, quantification theory]
3. $\sim\exists nF(n)\sim(p \supset q) \supset$
      $(\exists nF(n)p \supset \exists nF(n)q)$ [2]
4. $\sim F\sim(p \supset q) \supset (Fp \supset Fq)$ [3, Df.F].

And $F{\sim}P{\sim}p \supset p$ thus:

1. $\forall n{\sim}P(n){\sim}p \supset {\sim}P(n){\sim}p$ $[p \supset p,\ \text{subst.},\ \forall 1 n]$
2. ${\sim}\exists n P(n){\sim}p \supset {\sim}P(n){\sim}p$ $[1]$
3. ${\sim}F(n){\sim}({\sim}\exists n P(n){\sim}p \supset {\sim}P(n){\sim}p)$ $[2,\ \text{Rule}]$
4. $F(n){\sim}\exists n P(n){\sim}p \supset F(n){\sim}P(n){\sim}p$ $[3,\ \text{A1.1}]$
5. $F(n){\sim}\exists n P(n){\sim}p \supset p$ $[4,\ \text{A2.1}]$
6. $\exists n F(n){\sim}\exists n P(n){\sim}p \supset p$ $[5,\ \exists 1 n]$
7. $F{\sim}P{\sim}p \supset p$ $[6,\ \text{Df.}F,\ \text{Df.}P]$.

The A3s, A4s, and A5s do not appear to yield, on their own, any further theses in non-metric tense logic, but they contribute to proofs in richer systems with axioms corresponding to special conditions on U. Before considering such systems, it is worth noting that the converses of the A3s are easily provable; that of A3.1 as follows:

1. $F(n)p \supset \exists n F(n)p$ $[p \supset p,\ \text{subst.},\ \exists 2 n]$
2. ${\sim}F(m){\sim}(F(n)p \supset \exists n F(n)p)$ $[1,\ \text{Rule}]$
3. $F(m)F(n)p \supset F(m)\exists n F(n)p$ $[2,\ \text{A1.1}]$
4. $\exists n F(m)F(n)p \supset F(m)\exists n F(n)p$ $[3,\ \exists 1 n]$.

We may also note that the procedure by which we just obtained 3. from 1. via 2. may be generalized, i.e. we may use the rule and A1.1 in succession to pass from $\vdash \alpha \supset \beta$ to $\vdash F(n)\alpha \supset F(n)\beta$; similarly with $P(n)$. We may call these derived rules RFC and RPC.

It should also be noted, before we pass on, that in the minimal system $Gp\ (={\sim}F{\sim}p)$ is not demonstrably equivalent to $\forall n F(n)p$. The definition of $\forall$ expands the latter to ${\sim}\exists n{\sim}F(n)p$, while the definition of F expands the former to ${\sim}\exists n F(n){\sim}p$; these can only be equated when the minimal system is supplemented by certain theses discussed in the next section. $Gp\ (={\sim}\exists n F(n){\sim}p)$ is, however, equivalent even in the minimal system to $\forall n{\sim}F(n){\sim}p$.

3. *Metric calculi reflecting special conditions on U.* We obtain richer calculi either by enriching the number-theoretical basis or by enriching the tense-logical postulates. To illustrate the first possibility, consider the effect of letting our intervals be measured by the real numbers, for

which we have, for any number n, the law $\exists l \exists m\ n=(l+m)$. We may then carry through the following proof:

1. $n=(l+m) \supset (F(n)p \supset F(l+m)p)$ $[m=n \supset (flm \supset fln)]$
2. $\exists l \exists m\ n=(l+m) \supset$
          $(F(n)p \supset \exists l \exists m F(l+m)p)$ [1, quantification theory]
3. $F(n)p \supset \exists l \exists m F(l+m)p$ [2, law for rationals]

From this we may deduce $Fp \supset FFp$ (one of the theses generally used in non-metric tense logic to express the density of the earlier-later series) thus:

4. $\exists n F(n)p \supset \exists l \exists m F(l)F(m)p$ $[3, \exists 1n, \text{A5.1}]$
5. $\exists n F(n)p \supset \exists l F(l) \exists m F(m)p$ $[4, \exists m F(n)F(m)p$
                                       $\supset F(n) \exists m F(m)p]$
6. $Fp \supset FFp$ $[5, \text{Df.}F]$.

Note the dependence of this proof on A5.1 as well as on the special postulate for density.

The converse of A5.1, namely $F(m)F(n)p \supset F(m+n)p$, is not provable in the minimal metric system as the converse of A3.1 is, nor does it have the same 'neutrality'. It yields, in non-metric tense logic, the thesis $FFp \supset Fp$, which expresses the transitivity of the earlier-later relation, and its own U-calculus derivation, preceded by Ta, depends on this 'law of summation' for the triadic U:

    $Uabm \supset (Ubcn \supset Uac(m+n))$.

The following point is also to be noted about this thesis: if $FFp \supset Fp$ is added to the minimal non-metric system K_t we may derive its own mirror image $PPp \supset Pp$, and vice versa. (Similarly with the density theses $Fp \supset FFp$ and $Pp \supset PPp$.) The same is true of the metric thesis $F(m)F(n)p \supset F(m+n)p$, added to the minimal metric system. To shorten the proof of $P(m)P(n)p \supset P(m+n)p$ from this thesis, we may first list some theses which are easily derivable in the minimal system, by various transformations and substitutions, from A2.1 and A2.2:

T1.1. $p \supset {\sim}F(n){\sim}P(n)p$
T1.2. $p \supset {\sim}P(n){\sim}F(n)p$

T2.1. $F(n)\sim P(n)p \supset \sim p$
T2.2. $P(n)\sim F(n)p \supset \sim p$.

We now give the main derivation:

1.	$F(m)F(n)p \supset F(m+n)p$	
2.	$\sim F(m+n)p \supset \sim F(m)F(n)p$	$[1, \text{p.c.}^5]$
3.	$P(m)\sim F(m+n)p \supset P(m)\sim F(m)F(n)p$	$[2, \text{RPC}]$
4.	$P(m)\sim F(m+n)p \supset \sim F(n)p$	$[3, \text{T2.2}]$
5.	$P(n)P(m)\sim F(m+n)p \supset P(n)\sim F(n)p$	$[4, \text{RPC}]$
6.	$P(n)P(m)\sim F(m+n)p \supset \sim p$	$[5, \text{T2.2}]$
7.	$P(n)P(m)\sim F(m+n)\sim P(m+n)p \supset$ $P(m+n)p$	$[6, \text{subst.}, \sim\sim p \supset p]$
8.	$P(n)P(m)p \supset P(m+n)p$	$[7, \text{T1.1}, \text{RPC}]$

(An analogous proof renders A5.2 superfluous as an axiom.)

For time's forward infinity we simply add $\sim F(n)p \supset F(n)Np$, from which the non-metric $\sim Fp \supset F\sim p$ is easily derivable. Time's backward infinity, $\sim P(n)p \supset P(n)\sim p$, does not of course follow, but must be laid down separately, if desired.

The converse thesis $F(n)\sim p \supset \sim F(n)p$ is the expression in metric tense logic of time's non-branching in the future; it corresponds to the U-condition $Uabn \supset (Uacn \supset b=c)$. Non-branching in the past, corresponding to $Uban \supset (Ucan \supset b=c)$, is expressed by $P(n)\sim p \supset \sim P(n)p$. Neither of these is derivable from the other, but we may concentrate on the one in F. Among the theses which become derivable when we add $F(n)\sim p \supset \sim F(n)p$ to the minimal metric system are

T1. $F(n)p \supset \sim F(n)\sim p$
T2. $P(n)F(n)p \supset p$
T3. $P(n)F(n+m)p \supset F(m)p$
T4. $F(n)p \supset (F(n)q \supset F(n)(p \wedge q))$
T5. $PFp \supset (p \vee Pp \vee Fp)$
T6. $(Fp \wedge Fq) \supset (F(p \wedge q) \vee F(p \wedge Fq) \vee F(q \wedge Fp))$.

---

^{5} *Editors' note.* The 'p.c.' stands for 'propositional calculus'.

The intuitive connexion between each of these theses and non-branching in the future is straightforward; we can see how each of them could have exceptions if there were no such thing as 'the' future but only a number of alternative possible futures. As a specimen, we prove T5, as follows:

1. $m=n \supset (P(m)F(n)p \supset P(n)F(n)p)$
2. $m=n \supset (P(m)F(n)p \supset p)$ [1, T2]
3. $m=n \supset (P(m)F(n)p \supset (p \lor Pp \lor Fp))$ [2, p.c.]
4. $m=(l+n) \supset (P(m)F(n)p \supset$
     $P(l+n)F(n)p)$
5. $m=(l+n) \supset (P(m)F(n)p \supset$
     $P(l)P(n)F(n)p)$ [4, A5.2]
6. $m=(l+n) \supset (P(m)F(n)p \supset P(l)p)$ [5, T2]
7. $\exists l\, m=(l+n) \supset (P(m)F(n)p \supset \exists l P(l)p)$ [6, quantification theory]
8. $\exists l\, m=(l+n) \supset (P(m)F(n)p \supset Pp)$ [7, Df.P]
9. $\exists l\, m=(l+n) \supset (P(m)F(n)p \supset$
     $(p \lor Pp \lor Fp))$ [8, p.c.]
10. $n=(m+l) \supset (P(m)F(n)p \supset$
     $P(m)F(m+l)p)$
11. $n=(m+l) \supset (P(m)F(n)p \supset$
     $P(m)F(m)F(l)p)$ [10, A5.1]
12. $n=(m+l) \supset (P(m)F(n)p \supset F(l)p)$ [11, T2]
13. $\exists l\, n=(m+l) \supset (P(m)F(n)p \supset \exists l F(l)p)$ [12]
14. $\exists l\, n=Sml \supset (P(m)F(n)p \supset Fp)$ [13, Df.F]
15. $\exists l\, n=(m+l) \supset (P(m)F(n)p \supset$
     $(p \lor Pp \lor Fp))$ [14, p.c.]
16. $m=n \lor \exists l m=(l+n) \lor \exists l n=(m+l)$ [number-theory]
17. $P(m)F(n)p \supset (p \lor Pp \lor Fp)$ [16, 3, 9, 15]
18. $\exists m \exists n P(m)F(n)p \supset (p \lor Pp \lor Fp)$ [17, $\exists 1n$, $\exists 1m$]
19. $\exists m P(m) \exists n F(n)p \supset (p \lor Pp \lor Fp)$ [18, A4.2]
20. $PFp \supset (p \lor Pp \lor Fp)$ [19, Df.P, Df.F].

4. *Comparisons with earlier systems.* Given the additions for infinity, we may abridge the A1s to

A1.1. $F(n)(p \supset q) \supset (F(n)p \supset F(n)q)$

and its image, and derive the rules to infer $\vdash F(n)\alpha$ and $\vdash P(n)\alpha$ from $\vdash \alpha$.

(We then get our original A1.1 by $\sim F(n)\sim(p \supset q) \rightarrow F(n)\sim\sim(p \supset q) \rightarrow$
$F(n)(p \supset q) \rightarrow F(n)p \supset F(n)q$.) Given the additions for non-branching,
we may make the shorter rules (to infer $\vdash F(n)\alpha$ and $\vdash P(n)\alpha$ from $\vdash \alpha$)
the primitive ones, and replace the A2s by the shorter T2 and its image.
These abridgements are the normal versions of these postulates, but
their adoption from the outset makes it difficult to see what depends on
what, and impossible to devise systems for those who find some of the
assumptions listed in the last section unpalatable.

In my earlier systems, a subtraction sign was introduced, the forms
$F(m{-}n)p$ and $P(m{-}n)p$ being considered well-formed in those cases in
which $m > n$, and such theses as

$$F(m)P(n)p \supset F(m{-}n)p$$

being laid down for those cases in which they are well-formed. Such
'conditional well-formedness' is, however, an awkward notion, and in
the present systems such notation is avoided. We can, however, define
'$m > n$' as $\exists l m = (l+n)$, and express the above thesis, without any
attached proviso to guarantee well-formedness, as

$$m=(l+n) \supset (F(m)P(n)p \supset F(l)p),$$

which is provable in any system that contains $F(n)P(n)p \supset p$. A minus
sign is really only worth having in a system like Rescher's, in which
intervals are represented by negative as well as positive numbers and
$P(n)p$ in effect defined as $F(-n)p$, but such an economy is only possible
in a fairly strong system, and removes all possibility of the stratification
here attempted.

The present system for 'alternative futures', i.e. the system without
$F(n)\sim p \supset \sim F(n)p$, is different from the 'Peircean' indeterminist metric
tense logic which I have sketched elsewhere,[6] though each may be
developed within the other. Broadly, the Peircean 'will' means
'necessarily will', whereas the present 'will' means 'possibly will'; the
present $F(n)$ is definable in the Peircean system as $\sim F(n)\sim$ – it is, in fact,
the $M(n)$ so defined in *Past, Present and Future*,[7] and the $MF(n)$ so

---

[6] In Chapter IV, and more fully in 'Postulates for Tense-logic' (*American
Philosophical Quarterly*, April 1966), and in *Past, Present and Future*, Ch. VII.
[7] *Past, Present and Future*, p. 132.

defined in Paper IV – and vice versa. Hence, for example, the absence of $F(n)\sim p \supset \sim F(n)p$ from the present system corresponds to the absence of its converse from the Peircean. As far as indeterminism goes there is little to choose between the two versions of it, but the present set-up yields more natural ways of questioning, e.g. time's infinity. We would, all the same, get very slightly neater postulates all round if we used $G(n)$ and $H(n)$ for our present $\sim F(n)\sim$ and $\sim P(n)\sim$, but made the former primitive and defined $F(n)$ and $P(n)$ as $\sim G(n)\sim$ and $\sim H(n)\sim$.

The minimal system would then be:

$$\vdash \alpha \to \vdash G(n)\alpha, \vdash \alpha \to \vdash H(n)\alpha$$

B1.1. $G(n)(p \supset q) \supset (G(n)p \supset G(n)q)$
B1.2. $H(n)(p \supset q) \supset (H(n)p \supset H(n)q)$
B2.1. $\sim G(n)\sim H(n)p \supset p$
B2.2. $\sim H(n)\sim G(n)p \supset p$
B3.1. $\forall n G(m)G(n)p \supset G(m)\forall n G(n)p$
B3.2. $\forall n H(m)H(n)p \supset H(m)\forall n H(n)p$
B4.1. $\forall n G(m)H(n)p \supset G(m)\forall n H(n)p$
B4.2. $\forall n H(m)G(n)p \supset H(m)\forall n G(n)p$
B5.1. $G(m)G(n)p \supset G(m+n)p$
B5.2. $H(m)H(n)p \supset H(m+n)p$

For transitivity we would add $G(m+n)p \supset G(m)G(n)p$, for infinity $G(n)\sim p \supset \sim G(n)p$ and its image, and for non-branching $\sim G(n)p \supset G(n)\sim p$ and its image. The system without $\sim G(n)p \supset G(n)\sim p$ (but with its image) would then be precisely the Peircean, with $G(n)$ for the Peircean $F(n)$.

XIV
'NOW'

The redundant present and the non-redundant 'now'. I have sometimes defended what might be called a 'redundancy theory' of the present tense, analogous to the redundancy theory of truth propounded by Ramsey and Ayer.[1] I have argued that, whatever the proposition that *p* might be, the proposition that *it is (now) the case that p* is the very same proposition as the proposition that *p*. For example, the proposition that *it is now the case that I am sitting down* is the very same proposition as the proposition that *I am sitting down*; and equally, the proposition that *it is now the case that I have been (or will be) sitting down* is the very same proposition as the proposition that *I have been (or will be) sitting down*. For this reason, in developing symbolic systems of 'tense logic', while I have introduced the form *Pp* for 'It has been the case that *p*' and *Fp* for 'It will be the case that *p*', I have introduced no analogous form for 'It *is* (now) the case that *p*', since I have taken the view that for this the plain *p* will do.

This position is, however, open to some criticism. I am not thinking of criticism from the point of view that the plain proposition *p* ought rather to be equated with the proposition that it is *timelessly* the case that *p*. This is so obviously not the case when we are considering *tensed* propositions that the point is not worth arguing about. I am thinking rather of criticism that could come as it were from *within* the enterprise of 'tense logic'. From this point of view it can hardly be denied that whatever the proposition that *p* might be, the proposition that it is now the case that *p* entails and is entailed by the proposition that *p*; or that any time at which it is correct to assert either of these propositions is bound to be a time at which it is correct to assert the other. To say, however, that they are *one and the same* proposition, is to say rather more than this; and in particular it is to say that whatever is true of either proposition is true of the other, e.g. if either of them has been or will be the case then the other also has been or will be the case. But is it really true that *it will be the case that it is now the case that I am sitting down* if and only if *it will be the case that I am sitting down*? And is it

---

[1] A.N. Prior, *Time and Modality* (1957), pp. 9–10; *Past, Present and Future* (1967), pp. 8–10, 14–15; 'On Spurious Egocentricity', Ch. III in this volume.

really true that *it has been the case that it is now the case that I am sitting down* if and only if *it has been the case that I am sitting down*?

The language in which these last questions have been formulated is not ordinary idiomatic English, and this makes them difficult to answer. Still, let us repeat the first pair of propositions and stare at them for a moment:

(A)   It will be the case that it is now the case that I am sitting down.
(B)   It will be the case that I am sitting down.

The point at issue may be clearer if we replace these by a slightly more specific pair, say these:

(C)   It will be the case *tomorrow* that it is now the case that I am sitting down.
(D)   It will be the case *tomorrow* that I am sitting down.

It would be natural to understand (D) as

(E)   It will be the case tomorrow that I am *then* sitting down.

We would assert this truly at a given time if and only if we could truly assert the plain 'I am sitting down' (or 'I am now sitting down') *on the following day*. But it would not be at all natural so to understand (C). The most natural way to take (C) is to take it as being true at a given time if and only if the plain 'I am sitting down' (or 'I am now sitting down') is true *at that same time*. We are, in fact, inclined to regard the following proposition as logically true:

(F)   If I am now sitting down, then it will always be the case that I am now sitting down,

though we are certainly not inclined to regard

(G)   If I am now sitting down, then it will always be the case that I am *then* sitting down,

as being logically true; and as to

(H) If I am sitting down, then it will always be the case that I am sitting down,

we probably hesitate, not being quite sure whether to read it as (F) or as (G).

There is surely no need for prolonged agonising about all this. For (i), as far as English idiom goes, it seems clear that constructions involving the word 'present' fit a redundancy theory fairly well, that ones involving the word 'now' do not fit it at all well, and that ones involving the plain present tense or the plain 'it is the case that' are in between. It will surely be agreed that what *will be present* is just what *will be*, and that what *has been present* is just what *has been*. 'It will always be that I am *now* sitting down', on the other hand, does not ordinarily mean the same as 'My sitting will always be present', or as 'I will always be sitting down', as on a redundancy theory of 'now' it ought to. And 'It will always be that I am sitting down' and 'It will always be the case that it is the case that I am sitting down' are just not quite ordinary English, and it is not clear whether an ordinary English speaker would equate them with 'It will always be that I am now sitting down' or with 'I will always be sitting down'. And (ii), as far as a formalised logical language is concerned, it is clear that we can use its forms in any way we please, and in particular, we can certainly invent a language in which the form 'It is the case that *p*', or even 'It is now the case that *p*', is used to express whatever proposition is expressed by the plain *p*, and no other proposition than that. Can we not just leave it at that?

Not quite; there are several reasons why the dialogue between the constructors of formalisms and the recorders of idioms must be taken a little further. In the first place, the fondness of the former for the merely redundant present is not an arbitrary preference, and the reasons for it should be appreciated. It is not quite right to say that the formalised languages of most current tense-logics have *no* present tense. The present is, on the contrary, the understood tense of any proposition that has no other specific tensing; and it is therefore the tense of the 'atomic propositions' or innermost kernels of all tensed constructions. There *has to be* such a tense if tense operators uniformly construct tensed propositions from tensed propositions; and moreover, this *has to be* a tense which every tensed proposition has even if it has no other. And it is natural for the tense-logician to go on to say, 'I must and do have *this* present tense in my systems; surely I need no other'.

He must do more than *say* this, however; he has to make a case for it – he has to show that whatever can be said with our idiomatic 'now', the 'now' for which $\varphi(p$–now) is *not* necessarily equivalent to $\varphi(p)$, can equally be said in his own language which contains no such operator. I believe that this can be done. How, I shall indicate in the next section, in which I closely follow Hector-Neri Castañeda. But until recently I would have gone further than this, and said that the formalist not only *can* do without the idiomatic 'now' but *must* do without it – that our ordinary use of 'now' has a certain fundamental disorderliness about it which makes it unamenable to formalisation (Section 3). Recently, however, I have been convinced to the contrary by Hans Kamp (Section 4), and have now myself produced an extension of tense-logic with a symbol corresponding fairly closely to the idiomatic 'now' (Section 5).

2. *The elimination of the idiomatic 'now'*. The essential point about the idiomatic 'now' is that however oblique the context in which it occurs, the time it indicates is the time of utterance of the whole sentence. In 'It will be the case tomorrow that my sitting down is present', the presentness referred to is a presentness that will obtain tomorrow, i.e. at the time to which we are taken by the tensing prefix. But in 'It will be the case tomorrow that I am sitting down now', the word 'now' indicates the same time that it would indicate if it occurred in the principal clause – the time of utterance.

In an earlier paper[2] I compared the word 'now' at this point with the word 'any', as opposed to 'every'. 'Every' gives universality to its immediate context (e.g. 'Not every man you meet is a liar' is a denial of 'Every man you meet is a liar', this subordinate sentence being universal but the whole sentence particular), but 'any', however obliquely it occurs, gives universality to the sentence as a whole (e.g. 'Not any man you meet is a liar' is not a denial of 'Any man you meet is a liar', but is, rather, equivalent to 'Any man you meet isn't a liar').

---

[2] *Editors' note.* Prior is presumably referring to the paper 'On Spurious Egocentricity', Ch. III in this volume.

Hector-Neri Castañeda has made a much more useful comparison of 'now' with 'I'.[3] The primary function of 'I' is self-reference, but in

(I)   I think Brown thinks I can help him,

the second 'I' does not indicate self-reference on the part of Brown, but rather on the part of the speaker of the whole sentence. Not, however, that the speaker has a thought that he would express by saying 'I can help him'; oddly (considering the words used), *no* one is depicted in (I) as having such a thought. Brown would be depicted as having such a thought, and as referring to himself, in the sentence

(J)   I think Brown thinks he can help me.

But not in (I). To express Brown's thought in (I) as Brown himself would express it, we would have to know Brown's way of referring to the speaker of the whole. The speaker of (I), however, does not profess to know what this is; what he does claim to know is something more indefinite that might be put thus:

(K)   I think that for some φ, (i) Brown thinks that (the only φ-er can help him), and (ii) I am the only φ-er.

Here the residual 'I' of clause (ii) is self-referential, and clause (ii) does express the speaker's thought (*Brown's* thought being one that he would express by something of the form 'The only φ-er can help *me*', this 'me' being also self-referential).

'Now', Castañeda observes, is an adverbial analogue of the pronoun 'I', and in

(L)   It is now the case that I will later be glad that I am φ-ing now,

the second 'now' does not refer to the presentness of my φ-ing at the time of my gladness, but rather to its presentness at the time when the whole sentence is true. Note, however, that the speaker is said to have at the time of utterance a thought that he would express by saying 'I am

[3] H.-N. Castañeda, 'Indicators and Quasi-indicators', *American Philosophical Quarterly*, vol. 4 (1967).

glad that I am φ-ing now'; indeed he is not said to have *that* thought at *any* time. He *would* have depicted himself as going to have that thought if he had said

(M)   It is now the case that I will later be glad that I am φ-ing *then*

(which is related to (L) as (J) to (I)). But not when he uses (L). To express the thought he depicts himself, when he uses (L), as going to have, we would need to know how he would refer, at the later moment when he is glad, to the moment when he uses (L). But in (L) itself he gives no indication of how he will later on think of that time. We may presume, however, that he will think of it as the only time at which some proposition or other is true (e.g. the time at which it is 6 o'clock GMT on April 10, 1968), so that (L) amounts to

(N)   It is now the case that for some proposition p which is true at one instant only, (i) it will be the case that I am glad it was the case that (p and I am φ-ing), and (ii) it is now the case that p.

Here both occurrences of 'now' indicate the time of truth of the clauses in which they immediately occur, and nothing is lost if both of them are dropped.

In some such way as this, it seems to me, we *can* dispense with the non-redundant 'now' in favour of the redundant one. In other words, the non-redundant 'now' *is* non-redundant only in the sense that you cannot *just* erase it from a sentence and leave the sense of the whole the same; you can, however, erase it and get something with the same sense by altering the rest of the sentence somewhat.

But do we *have* to dispense with the non-redundant 'now'? I shall indicate first why I formerly thought its introduction into tense-logic would have a quite explosive effect, and then why I now think it would not.

3. *The resistance of tense-logic to the idiomatic 'now'*. We had best start by setting up a simple tense-logical system. We shall not take as primitive the earlier-mentioned operators F (for 'It will be that') and P (for 'It has been that'), but will define these in terms of G (for 'It will always be that') and H (for 'It has always been the case that'). Using ~ for 'It is not the case that', we define Fp as $\sim G \sim p$ ('It will not always be

the case that not p'), and Pp as $\sim H \sim p$. Using $(p \supset q)$ for 'If p then q', $(p \wedge q)$ for 'p and q', $(p \vee q)$ for 'p or q' and $(p \equiv q)$ for 'p if and only if q', we assume some sufficient postulate-set for propositional calculus and then add the above definitions and the axioms

A1.1. $G(p \supset q) \supset (Gp \supset Gq)$
A1.2. $H(p \supset q) \supset (Hp \supset Hq)$
A2.1. $PGp \supset p$
A2.2. $FHp \supset p$.

Finally to the ordinary rules of substitution and detachment we add the following, for getting theorems from theorems:

RG: If $\vdash \alpha$ then $\vdash G\alpha$
RH: If $\vdash \alpha$ then $\vdash H\alpha$.

This system was called by the late E.J. Lemmon the system K_t.

It is possible to interpret the propositional variables of this system as if they were parts of *predicate* expressions in a first-order theory of the earlier-later relation. In this theory the individual variables, a, b, c, etc. are used for instants of time, the form Uab for 'a is an earlier instant than b' and the form $Ta(p)$ for 'It is true at a that p'. Where complex formulae of tense logic are preceded by Ta, the resulting formulae can be equated to ones in which all the complexity has been put *outside* whatever Tas may be left. Our propositional calculus operators $\supset$ and $\sim$ can be brought outside their Tas by means of the equivalences

UT1. $Ta(p \supset q) \equiv (Ta(p) \supset Ta(q))$
UT2. $Ta(\sim p) \equiv \sim Ta(p)$

and if our other propositional-calculus operators are defined in terms of implication and negation we can easily derive from these two such further equivalences as

$Ta(p \wedge q) \equiv (Ta(p) \wedge Ta(q))$
$Ta(p \vee q) \equiv (Ta(p) \vee Ta(q))$, etc.

For our tense-operators G and H, using $\forall b$ for 'for all b', we have

UT3. $Ta(Gp) \equiv \forall b(Uab \supset Tb(p))$
UT4. $Ta(Hp) \equiv \forall b(Uba \supset Tb(p))$.

From UT1–4 and the definitions of F and P, we can derive for these latter, by ordinary quantification theory, the equivalences

$$Ta(Fp) \equiv \exists b(Uab \wedge Tb(p))$$
$$Ta(Pp) \equiv \exists b(Uba \wedge Tb(p)).$$

Ordinary quantification theory also suffices for the proof of various tense-logical formulae preceded by Ta, e.g. $Ta(PGp \supset p)$. That is, we can prove in this system that anything of the form $PGp \supset p$ is true at any arbitrary instant a. We can prove this, in fact, for all thoerems of K_t; and if we assume nothing about the earlier-later relation U except UT1–4, we can *only* prove it for theorems of K_t. And UT1–4, we might well say, are not assumptions about the relation U at all; they are rather about the predicate-fragments $p \supset q$, $\sim p$, Gp and Hp, and tell us under what conditions these are true at an instant a.

If we add further postulates which really are about the relation U, e.g. the postulate $\forall a \exists b Uab$, asserting that U has no last term, we may be able to attach to our arbitrary instant a the theorems of some richer tense-logic than K_t. The addition just mentioned in fact enables us to attach to any arbitrary instant a all the theorems derivable from K_t plus the further axiom $Gp \supset Fp$.

For the present, however, let us simply consider the system K_t which is in a sense 'minimal'. It is as well to confine ourselves to this because I want to show that it is awkward to introduce into tense-logic an operator with the properties of the idiomatic 'now', but if the tense-logic into which I introduce this operator is richer than K_t it is too easy to suggest that the trouble arises from my having made rash assumptions about time in the first place. So, for G and H (and P and F) we stick, in the meantime, to K_t.

Suppose we now write Jp for 'It is *now* the case that p'. For this operator we do need the postulates

J1. $p \supset Jp$
J2. $Jp \supset p$

i.e. we do wish to say 'It is the case that p if and only if it is now the case that p'. On the other hand, we do *not* wish to say $Fp \supset FJp$ and $FJp \supset Fp$, 'It will be the case that p if and only if it will be the case that it is *now* the case that p'. Given K_t, however, these follow from J1 and J2. For RG will take us from J1 to $G(p \supset Jp)$, and in K_t it is easy to prove $G(p \supset q) \supset (Fp \supset Fq)$, so from $G(p \supset Jp)$ we can go to $Fp \supset FJp$; we reach $FJp \supset Fp$ from J2 by similar steps. Again, we want to say $Jp \supset GJp$, 'It is now the case that p it will always be the case that it is now the case that p' (the generalisation of proposition (F) in the first section); but K_t suffices to take us from this, with J1 and J2, to $p \supset Gp$, 'If p, it will always be the case that p' (the generalisation of proposition (H) in the first section, interpreted in the sense of proposition (G), which we certainly do not want).

In fact, given $Jp \equiv p$, $Jp \equiv GJp$ and $Jp \equiv HJp$, all of which seem desirable postulates for the idiomatic 'now', and given K_t for G and H, we can prove $p \equiv Gp$ and $p \equiv Hp$; indeed we can prove that p, Gp, Hp, Fp and Pp are all interchangeable in all tense-logical contexts, so that tenses are deprived of all usefulness. This result can, indeed, be tempered very slightly. A student of the idiomatic 'now' might well decide on reflection that he doesn't want to commit himself to so much as $Jp \equiv GJp$ and $Jp \equiv HJp$. For it will be evident on reflection that these postulates commit us not only to the standard properties of 'now' but also to the assumptions that time had no beginning and will have no end. For the 'always' in the 'will always be' of our system is a Boolean 'always', i.e. it is so used that Gp, 'It will always be that p' comes out as vacuously true (as Fp, 'It will be that p', comes out as vacuously false) if there is to be no future at all. Hence $GJp \supset Jp$ could be false if GJp is true not because it is now the case that p but merely because we are at the last moment of time. $HJp \supset Jp$ could be similarly false at time's first moment, if there were one. So the student of 'now' who didn't want to commit himself to time's having no beginning and no end would weaken $Jp \equiv GJp$ and $Jp \equiv HJp$ to the corresponding one-way implications $Jp \supset GJp$ and $Jp \supset HJp$.

This is enough, all the same, given the other postulates mentioned, to give us $p \supset Gp$ and $p \supset Hp$, and from these $Fp \supset p$ and $Pp \supset p$. Although these without their converses do not quite assert that there is no change at all, the only possible changes they would leave us with are those from the first moment of time (when everything of the form Pp is false) to later moments (when some things of this form are true) and to the last moment of time (when everything of the form Fp is false) from earlier moments (when some things of this form are true). This still makes tense operators *almost* vacuous, and it seems to have this effect even with a minimum of assumptions about the character of the earlier-later relation, so a tense logician could very well be pardoned for refusing to admit such an operator as J into his system.

The trouble can be pin-pointed a little more closely. None of the four K_t axioms A1.1–A2.2 are rendered any less intuitively acceptable when formulae containing J are substituted for their variables, but RG and RH are a different matter. Take, e.g. J1, $p \supset Jp$, 'If p then it is now the case that p'. This is all right, but the result of applying RG to it is $G(p \supset Jp)$, 'It will always be that if p then it is now the case that p', i.e. 'It will always be that if it is *then* the case that p it is *now* the case that p'. This, surely, is not all right at all. K_t, in other words, *could* accommodate J if we could drop RG and RH from it, or even if we could confine their operation to theorems in which J does not occur. This is still, however, a tall order if we are to think of K_t as embeddable in an earlier-later calculus in the usual way. For we can undoubtedly pass in such a calculus from $\vdash Ta(\alpha)$ to $\vdash Ta(G\alpha)$ as follows: From $\vdash Ta(\alpha)$ we obtain $\vdash Tb(\alpha)$ by substitution (α being unaffected by the substitution since it is a tense-logical formula and does not contain a), and from this we go to $\vdash Uab \supset Tb(\alpha)$ by $(p \supset (q \supset p))$, from this to $\vdash \forall b(Uab \supset Tb(\alpha))$ by universal generalisation, and from this to $\vdash Ta(G\alpha)$ by UT3. $\vdash Ta(H\alpha)$ is obtained from $\vdash Ta(\alpha)$ analogously.

4. *A revised earlier-later calculus to accommodate 'now'.* This last difficulty, however, is not insuperable. Hans Kamp devised in 1967[4] a consistent semantic interpretation for 'now' which can be presented, with slight modifications, as a new sort of UT-calculus, in which T ties each tense-logical proposition not to one instant but to two, i.e. our basic form is not $Ta(p)$ but $Tab(p)$. The proposition p is related to the instants a and b in different ways; the essential difference is that the elimination of complexities from what is put after Tab may take us to other instants than a, but never to other instants than b. And wherever we may have been taken from a by operators like G and H, the one place to which we are always immediately taken by J is the instant b, i.e. the instant

[4] In a multilith, 'The treatment of "now" as a 1-place sentential operator', circulated at the University of California at Los Angeles.

represented by the second argument of T. We might read the form $Tab(p)$ as 'From b it is the case at a that p', and 'From b it is the case at a that p – now' = 'From b it is the case at b that p'. So our basic equivalences are now

UT1. $Tab(p \supset q) \equiv (Tab(p) \supset Tab(q))$
UT2. $Tab(\sim p) \equiv \sim Tab(p)$
UT3. $Tab(Gp) \equiv \forall c(Uac \supset Tcb(p))$
UT4. $Tab(Hp) \equiv \forall c(Uca \supset Tcb(p))$

to which we add

UT5. $Tab(Jp) \equiv Tbb(p)$.

Substitution in UT1–4 will give us, it should be noted, the special cases

$Taa(p \supset q) \equiv (Taa(p) \supset Taa(q))$
$Taa(\sim p) \equiv \sim Taa(p)$
$Taa(Gp) \equiv \forall c(Uac \supset Tca(p))$
$Taa(Hp) \equiv \forall c(Uca \supset Tca(p))$.

And we seek for those tense-logical formulae which, when preceded by any arbitrary duplicated prefix Taa, are provable in the new calculus. It will be found that these include J1, J2, $Jp \supset GJp$ and all four of the *axioms* of K_t. But we cannot pass from $\vdash Taa(\alpha)$ to $\vdash Taa(G\alpha)$ by echoing the moves that formerly took us from $\vdash Ta(\alpha)$ to $\vdash Ta(G\alpha)$. For we cannot take the first step, which would be from $\vdash Taa(\alpha)$ to $\vdash Tca(\alpha)$ – that half-substitution is not legitimate. All the same, for any α *not involving* J for which we can prove $\vdash Taa(\alpha)$, we can also prove $\vdash Tca(\alpha)$ (by similar steps – apart from J, it does not matter whether the second instant is the same as the first or not), and so $\vdash Taa(G\alpha)$ and $\vdash Taa(H\alpha)$. We therefore have not only all the axioms but all the theorems of K_t, and also all substitutions in such theorems, including ones in which J occurs. But we do not have the G-ings and H-ings of J1 and J2.

Given this basis, what other tense-logical formulae (in G, H and J) can we prove to be attachable to any arbitrary Taa? What we want is of course a set of postulates for tense-logic in G, H and J from which all such formulae are deducible. I hope that what I say later (in Section 5, remarks (iv) to (vi)) will throw some light on this problem, but I want now to tackle what turns out to be a simpler one, which arises when we enrich our tense-logic with the further function 'p at all times'. We may write this as $\Box p$, and lay down the characterising equivalence

UT6. $Tab(\Box p) \equiv \forall cTcb(\Box p)$

(from which we get $Taa(\Box p) \equiv \forall bTba(\Box p)$. This addition immediately gives us, as preceded by any arbitrary Taa, whatever is derivable from the following postulates:

RL: $\vdash \alpha \rightarrow \vdash \Box\alpha$, provided that α does not contain J
L1. $\Box p \supset p$
L2. $\Box(p \supset q) \supset (\Box p \supset \Box q)$
L3. $\sim\Box p \supset \Box\sim\Box p$
L4. $\Box p \supset Gp$
L5. $\Box p \supset Hp$.

And we can now ask: what postulates in G, H, J and $\Box$ (not just G, H and J) will yield all those formulae which, preceded by an arbitrary Taa, are provable from quantification theory and UT1–6? I shall answer this piecemeal, noting now that (i) RL and L1–3 (subjoined to propositional calculus) are known to suffice for the pure $\Box$ portion of the required calculus, which is the modal system S5. (ii) From RL, L4 and L5 we can derive the modified RG and RH that we need for the G-H portion of our calculus. (iii) For the full $\Box$-G-H portion we need the above RL and L1–5, together with the four K_t axioms A1.1–A2.2. All that remains is to add the postulates for J, but before doing that I must digress again.

Kamp's is not the only way of modifying the UT calculus to obtain one that will accommodate J; though it is, so far as I know, the first solution offered to that problem. We might instead keep the simple form $Ta(p)$, and the postulates UT1–4 in their original forms, but introduce a *constant*, say n, for a particular instant, with the following equivalences for J and $\Box$:

UT5. $Ta(Jp) \equiv Tn(p)$
UT6. $Ta(\Box p) \equiv \forall bTb(p)$.

We then seek for those tense-logical formulae which can be proved attachable either to any arbitrary instant a, and so to n, or just to n. (Note that we cannot pass from ⊢ $Tn(\alpha)$ to ⊢ $Tb(\alpha)$, and so to ⊢ $\forall bTb(\alpha)$, because n is a constant.) These can easily be seen to be exactly the same formulae as those which are attachable in Kamp's revision of the UT calculus either to any arbitrary $Ta(b)$, and so to those in which the two instant-arguments are the same, or just to these latter. The use of a constant, however, has the advantage of having been tried before for another purpose. It was into just such a modification of the 'property calculus' that C.A. Meredith, round about 1953, embedded his modal logic with a contingent constant n for 'the world', in the sense of 'everything that is the case'. And we do know how to axiomatise that.[5]

5. *A tense-logic with 'now'.* We may begin by incorporating n not only into our UT calculus as an instant-constant but also into our tense-logic itself as a *propositional* constant, standing for some proposition (any proposition) which is true at this moment only. Since our calculus is designed to yield as theorems whatever is formulable in the system's symbolism and is true at this moment (apart from truths arising from special properties of the earlier-later relation), the new symbol gives us also a new axiom, viz.

A3. n.

Let us now bring from the UT calculus into the tense-logic itself not only n but also the variables a, b, c etc., each of which may stand for any proposition which is true at one instant and at one instant only. For these we have the two axioms

A4. $\sim\Box\sim a$
A5. $\Box(a \supset p) \vee \Box(a \supset \sim p)$.

Using $\Diamond p$ ('p at some time') as short for $\sim\Box\sim p$, we can abridge A4 to $\Diamond a$. Finally, we define Jp either as $\Diamond(n \wedge p)$ ('At some time, p true together with NOW'), or as $\Box(n \supset p)$ ('p true at all times at which

NOW'), alternatives which the uniqueness of NOW makes equivalent; and we enlarge the restriction on RL to 'provided that a does not contain J or n'.

The postulates RL (modified), L1–5 and A1.1–A5, with the definition of J, will I think yield all the theorems in J that we want; and the definition of 'now' as expressing contemporaneity with some unspecified proposition which is true only at the time of utterance nicely formalises Castañeda's explanation of the use of 'now' in oblique contexts. It may be felt, however, that this system is too much of a hybrid between a UT calculus and a tense logic. So let us hedge no more: we drop A3–5 and the proposed definition of J, and give postulates for an undefined J to be added to RL, L1–5 and A1.1–A2.2 of K_t; namely the following:

J1. $p \supset Jp$
J2. $Jp \supset p$
J3. $\Box(\Box p \supset Jp)$
J4. $\Box(Jp \supset \Box Jp)$
J5. $\Box(J\mathord{\sim}p \supset \mathord{\sim}Jp)$
J6. $\Box(\mathord{\sim}Jp \supset J\mathord{\sim}p)$
J7. $\Box(J(p \supset q) \supset (Jp \supset Jq))$.

I show below that in fact these postulates may be reduced to J1, J2, and J4. That these postulates are complete is a conjecture. The following results, however, are certain:

(i) From RL, L1–3, and J1–7 we can prove all of the following permanent equivalences: $\Box(JJp \equiv Jp)$, $\Box(\Box Jp \equiv Jp)$, $\Box(\Box p \equiv J\Box p)$, $\Box(\mathord{\sim}Jp \equiv J\mathord{\sim}p)$, $\Box((Jp \supset Jq) \equiv J(p \supset q))$. These enable us, within this sub-calculus (i.e. the part without G or H), when all the variables in a formula fall within the scope of an $\Box$ or a J, to equate the whole with a formula in which the only J occurs right at the beginning and there we can strengthen it to $\Box J$ by J4. So RL applies to formulae of this sort as well as to ones with no Js in them at all. But when we bring G and H in we do not have either $\Box(GJp \equiv Jp)$ or $\Box(HJp \equiv Jp)$, but only the weaker $\Box(Jp \supset GJp)$ and $\Box(Jp \supset HJp)$ (from J4, L4 and L5); to get the converses, as we have noted earlier, we need to add tense-logical postulates (say $Gp \supset Fp$ and $Hp \supset Pp$) which assume that time has neither a first nor a last instant. Only when such additions are made can we extend RL to *all* formulae of the calculus in which every variable falls within the scope of an $\Box$ or a J (without them we have, e.g. $GJp \supset JGJp$, from J1, but not $\Box(GJp \supset JGJp)$.

(ii) Given RL, L1–3 and A3–5, all of J1–7 are deducible from the definition of Jp as $\Box(n \supset p)$, or from $\Box(Jp \equiv \Box(n \supset p))$, and conversely, $\Box(Jp \equiv \Box(n \supset p))$ from J1–7. (The Castañeda reduction is thus possible but optional.) We still have this result if instant-*variables* are dropped and A4 and 5 replaced by $p \supset \Box(n \supset p)$.

(iii) I have pointed out elsewhere[6] that we can bring the whole UT symbolism within tense-logic by defining $Ta(p)$ as $\Box(a \supset p)$ (or $\Diamond(a \wedge p)$) and Uab as $Ta(Fb)$. If we assume these definitions, quantification over the variables standing for 'instant-propositions', and the 'bridging postulates' A3–A5, then (a) UT1, 2 and 6 become provable from RL and L1–3, as well as vice versa; (b) UT3 and 4 become provable also when we add L4, L5 and the four K_t axioms A1.1–A2.2, as these do when we add UT3 and 4; and (c) UT5 becomes provable when we add either $\Box(Jp \equiv \Box(n \supset p))$ or J1–7 to the pure $\Box$ group, as these do when we add UT5 to it. Results (a) and (b) also hold if we replace A3 (n) by $\exists aa$, which of course follows from it.

I add some results in pure G-H-J.

(iv) Suppose we introduce the G-H forms $\Box^0 p$, $\Box^1 p$, $\Box^2 p$, etc. by the following definitions:

$$\Box^0 p = p$$
$$\Box^{n+1} p = (\Box^n p \wedge G\Box^n p \wedge H\Box^n p)$$

(hence $\Box^1 p$ is $(p \wedge Gp \wedge Hp)$; $\Box^2 p$ is $(\Box^1 p \wedge G\Box^1 p \wedge H\Box^1 p)$, i.e.

$$(p \wedge Gp \wedge Hp) \wedge G(p \wedge Gp \wedge Hp) \wedge H(p \wedge Gp \wedge Hp),$$

which in K_t is equivalent to

$$p \wedge Gp \wedge Hp \wedge GGp \wedge GHp \wedge HGp \wedge HHp;$$

and so on. In general $\Box^n$ contains all possible H-G sequences with up to n members.) This notation enables us to represent and assert an infinity

---

[6] *Editors' note.* E.g. in Chapter XI in this volume.

of tense-logical formulae at once; thus, e.g. $\Box^n p \supset p$ is a scheme that covers $p \supset p$ ($= \Box^0 p \supset p$), $(p \wedge Gp \wedge Hp) \supset p$ ($= \Box^n p \supset p$), and so on. If α is a theorem of K_t so are all formulae $\Box^n \alpha$ (cf. RL); and we have as K_t theorems all formulae of the forms

$$\Box^n p \supset p \qquad \text{(cf. L1)}$$
$$\Box^n (p \supset q) \supset (\Box^n p \supset \Box^n q) \quad \text{(cf. L2)}$$

and for $n \geq 1$,

$$\Box^n p \supset Gp \qquad \text{(cf. L4)}$$
$$\Box^n p \supset Hp \qquad \text{(cf. L5)}$$

but (except where $n = 0$) we do not have $\sim\Box^n p \supset \Box^n\sim\Box^n p$, the analogue of L3, but only the weaker $\sim p \supset \Box^n\sim\Box^n p$ (this corresponds to the weakening, in modal logic, of S5 to the 'Brouwersche' system). UT1–5 also verify (as attachable to Ta) all the $\Box^n$ analogues of J4–7. It may be added that the $\Box^n$ analogues of L3 and J3 are not provable in the richer system in which K_t is supplemented by the $\Box$ and J postulates in their original forms; though in this richer system we can prove all the $\Box^n$ analogues of J4–7. Whether these last could be proved from a finite set of axioms in G, H and J, verified by UT1–5, I do not know. They can be proved easily enough, however, and the $\Box^n$ analogue of L3 too, if we drop the condition 'verified by UT1–5'.

(v) If we use the form Iab for 'a is the same instant as b' we can (if we wish) add to UT1–5 the following special condition on U:

UT7. $(Uac \vee Uca) \supset ((Ubc \vee Ucb) \supset (Uab \vee Uba \vee a=b))$.

This states approximately that every instant is either earlier or later than every other instant in the same time-system. With this addition our U-calculus will verify, as attachable to any Ta, not only K_t but all theorems derivable in K_t with the added axiom

A6. $(p \wedge Gp \wedge Hp) \supset (GGp \wedge GHp \wedge HGp \wedge HHp)$.

(Conversely, adding A6 to RL, L1–5, A1.1–5, and the definitions of T and U, and of $a = b$ as $\Box(a \equiv b)$, enables us to prove UT7.) A6 can easily be shown equivalent to $\Box^1 p \supset \Box^2 p$, which by substitution yields

$\Box^l \Box^l p \supset \Box^2 \Box^l p$, and so $\Box^2 p \supset \Box^3 p$, and so by syllogism $\Box^l p \supset \Box^3 p$, and by repetition of these steps $\Box^l p \supset \Box^n p$ for any n. This means that if we lay down J4–7 with $\Box^l$ for $\Box$ we can now derive J4–7 with any $\Box^n$ for $\Box$. The addition of A6 to K_t also enables us to prove L3 (and so all of RL and L1–5) with $\Box^l$ for $\Box$. It is the weakest addition to K_t that will do this. (Given K_t, A6 implies but is not implied by $\Box^l p \supset (GHp \wedge HGp)$, which reflects time's nonbranching, and is implied by but does not imply that $Gp \supset GGp$, which reflects U's transitivity.)

(vi) If we add to UT1–5, instead of UT7, the rather stronger

UT8. *Uab v Uba v a=b*

which asserts straightforwardly that every instant is earlier or later than every other (ruling out the possibility of distinct time-systems), we can prove $Ta(p \wedge Gp \wedge Hp) \equiv \forall b Tb(p)$, equating 'It is and always will be and always has been the case that p' (true at some a) with 'p at all times', and making $\Box$ a superfluous symbol. The addition of $\Box^l p \supset \Box p$, or of the definition of $\Box$ as $\Box^l$, to RL, L1–5, A1.1–5 and the definitions of T, U and I, yields UT6–8 as well as UT1–4; and everything that can be proved of $\Box$ from UT1–6, including Ta(L3) and Ta(J3), can be proved of the purely G-H operator $\Box^l$ from UT1–5 + UT8.

Kamp has raised this further question: What postulates will suffice for G-H-J if we assume that U has the properties of the relation 'less than' among real numbers? I suspect that the answer is: To K_t (with restricted RG, RH) and J1–7 (with $\Box$ defined as $\Box^l$) add axioms for U's transitivity, e.g.

$Gp \supset GGp$

and for time's linearity, e.g.

$\Box^l p \supset (GHp \wedge HGp)$

infinity, e.g. McCall's[7]

---

[7] S. McCall, review of *Past, Present and Future* in *Dialogue*.

$p \supset (PFp \wedge FPp)$

and continuity, e.g. Bull's[8]

$GGp \supset Gp$
$HG(Gp \supset PGp) \supset (Gp \supset Hp)$
$GH(Hp \supset FHp) \supset (Hp \supset Gp).$

It can now be seen, also, that the Meredith paper cited at the end of Section 4 has more to our purpose than what we first found there, the constant n. Meredith's propositional-calculus primitives are $\supset$ and an impossible (or permanently false) constant 0 ($\sim p = (p \supset 0)$), and he has not only propositional variables but one (δ) for one-place connectives. He has these laws for $\square$, n and J:

M1. $\square(\delta((p \supset 0) \supset (q \supset r)) \supset \delta((r \supset p) \supset (q \supset p)))$
M2. $\square p \supset (\delta(p \supset q) \supset \delta q)$
M3. $\delta 0 \supset (\delta(0 \supset 0) \supset \delta(\square p))$
M4. n [=A3]
M5. $p \supset \square(n \supset p)$
M6. $p \supset Jp$ [=J1]
M7. $Jp \supset p$ [=J2]
M8. $\delta J(p \supset q) \supset \delta(Jp \supset Jq)$
M9. $\delta J0 \supset \delta 0$
M10. $\delta 0 \supset (\delta(0 \supset 0) \supset \delta Jp)$

Here M1–3, with substitution (for each sort of variable) and detachment, are equivalent to the whole of S5 (including propositional calculus) + $\square(p \equiv q) \supset (\delta p \supset \delta q)$. For n Meredith also has $\square n \supset p$, which denies that ours is the only possible world, or in tense–logic that now is the only instant; we omit it as out of place in a *minimal* system. He merely mentions M6–10 at the end of the article as being true of Jp defined as $\square(n \supset p)$; but as a group there is more interest to them than that. Given M1–5, they yield as well as being yielded by $\square(Jp \equiv \square(n \supset p))$ (or

[8] R.A. Bull, 'An Algebraic Study of Tense Logics with Linear Time', *Journal of Symbolic Logic*.

$\delta Jp \supset \delta\Box(n \supset p)$); and given just M1–3, they yield and are yielded by our own J1–7.

6. The original version of this paper[9] contained a mistake.[10] I stated[11] that my axiom J3, in the tense-logical form $\Box^n(\Box^n p \supset Jp)$, is not verified by the 'earlier–later' postulates UT1–5; and on p. 115 that it is not even verified by UT1–7. In fact it is, by both.

I shall not prove this directly, as it is an easy corollary of a more interesting result, namely that of my axioms J1–7 for 'now' (J), all but J1 ($p \supset Jp$), J2 ($Jp \supset p$) and J4 ($\Box(Jp \supset \Box Jp)$) are superfluous, given the 'Brouwersche' modal system for $\Box$ ('always'). I use this system rather than the stronger S5 at this point, as that is all that is verified by UT1–5 for the tense-logical functions $\Box^n$ (though all of S5 is verified when UT7 is added); I must therefore confine myself to the 'Brouwersche' system to be sure that the following proofs will go through when $\Box$ is replaced throughout by $\Box^n$:

1.	$p \supset \Box Jp$	[J1, J4]
2.	$p \supset \Box(\Box p \supset Jp)$	$[1, \Box p \supset \Box(q \supset p)]$
3.	$\sim p \supset \sim\Diamond\Box p$	$[\Diamond\Box p \supset p]$
4.	$\sim p \supset \Box(\Box p \supset Jp)$	$[3, \sim\Diamond p \supset \Box(p \supset q)]$
5.	$\Box(\Box p \supset Jp)$	$[2, 4, p \vee \sim p] = J3$
6.	$\Diamond Jp \supset \Diamond\Box Jp$	$[J4, \Box(p \supset q) \supset (\Diamond p \supset \Diamond q)]$
7.	$\Diamond Jp \supset Jp$	$[6, \Diamond\Box p \supset p]$
8.	$\sim Jp \supset \sim\Diamond Jp$	[7]
9.	$\sim Jp \supset \Box\sim Jp$	$[8, \sim\Diamond p \supset \Box\sim p]$
10.	$\sim p \supset \Box\sim Jp$	[J2, 9]
11.	$\sim p \supset \Box(J\sim p \supset \sim Jp)$	$[10, \Box p \supset \Box(q \supset p)]$
12.	$\sim\sim p \supset \Box\sim J\sim p$	[10]
13.	$\sim\sim p \supset \Box(J\sim p \supset \sim Jp)$	$[12, \Box\sim p \supset (p \supset q)]$
14.	$\Box(J\sim p \supset \sim Jp)$	$[11, 13, \sim p \vee \sim\sim p) (= J5)$
15.	$\sim p \supset \Box J\sim p$	[1]

---

[9] *Nôus*, vol. 2, no. 2, May 1968.
[10] Section 6 is an edited version of Prior's ' "Now" Corrected and Condensed', *Nôus*, vol. 2, no. 4, Nov. 1968.
[11] *Ibid.* p. 114.

16. $\sim p \supset \Box(\sim Jp \supset J \sim p)$ $[15, \Box p \supset \Box(q \supset p)]$
17. $p \supset \Box(\sim Jp \supset J \sim p)$ $[1, \Box p \supset \Box(\sim p \supset q)]$
18. $\Box(\sim Jp \supset J \sim p)$ $[16, 17, \sim p \vee p] \ (= J6)$
19. $q \supset \Box(J(p \supset q) \supset (Jp \supset Jq))$ $[1, \Box p \supset \Box(q \supset p), \text{twice}]$
20. $\Diamond Jp \supset p$ $[7, J2]$
21. $(\Diamond J(p \supset q) \wedge \Diamond Jp) \supset q$ $[((p \supset q) \wedge p) \supset q, 20]$
22. $\Diamond(J(p \supset q) \wedge Jp) \supset q$ $[21, \Diamond(p \wedge q) \supset (\Diamond p \wedge \Diamond q)]$
23. $\sim q \supset \sim \Diamond(J(p \supset q) \wedge Jp)$ $[22]$
24. $\sim q \supset \Box(J(p \supset q) \supset \sim Jp)$ $[23, \sim \Diamond(p \wedge q) \supset \Box(p \supset \sim q)]$
25. $\sim q \supset \Box(J(p \supset q) \supset$
          $(Jp \supset Jq))$ $[24, \sim p \supset (p \supset q)]$
26. $\Box(J(p \supset q) \supset (Jp \supset Jq))$ $[19, 25, q \vee \sim q] \ (= J7)$

   The remaining axioms J1, J2 and J4 are independent, even with the
full S5 for $\Box$. For J1 $(p \supset Jp)$, read J as (S5) $\Box$. For J2 $(Jp \supset p)$ read $J\alpha$
as $\alpha \supset \alpha$. For J4 $(\Box(Jp \supset \Box Jp))$, read $J\alpha$ as $n \wedge \alpha$, where n is a now-
true but not-permanently-true constant. The three of them amount to the
ut nunc equivalence $Jp \equiv p$ plus the permanent equivalence $\Box(Jp \equiv
\Box Jp)$ – a very neat basis for 'now'.
   There is, however, a genuine difference between J3 and my other
original axioms for 'now' (this is what misled me). To make the point
more simply, let us consider, not all of my functions $\Box^n p$ but just $\Box^I p$,
i.e. $(p \wedge Hp \wedge Gp)$, 'It is and always has been and always will be the
case that p'. Suppose that in my postulates J1–7 we do not replace *every*
occurrence of $\Box$ ('It is true at all times that …') by $\Box^I$, but only all
occurrences except an initial one, so that J3, for example, becomes
$\Box(\Box^I p \supset Jp)$, and J4 becomes $\Box(Jp \supset \Box^I Jp)$. Then UT1–6 will verify,
as 'true now', all the altered postulates except the altered J3, and UT7
will not verify this either. The non-verification arises because UT1–7
leave open the possibility that there are several quite unconnected 'time-
lines'. It will then be trivially true at the point NOW that if p is true at
that and all earlier and later points it is true now $(Tn(\Box^I p \supset Jp))$; but
not that it is true at every point on every time-line that if p is true at that
and all earlier and later points it is true now (i.e. we do not have
$\forall a T a(\Box^I p \supset Jp)$, i.e. $T n (\Box(\Box^I p \supset Jp))$, since NOW is neither
identical with nor earlier nor later than points on other time-lines. But
with *purely* tense-logical variants of J1–7, i.e. with $\Box$ replaced at *all* its
occurrences by $\Box^I$ (or other cases of $\Box^n$), J3 follows from the rest as
above.

Appendix:

Proofs of equivalences from RL, L1–3, J1–7:

1. $\Box J(p \supset Jp)$ [J1, J1, J4]
2. $\Box(Jp \supset JJp)$ [L2, J7, 1]
3. $\Box J(Jp \supset p)$ [J2, J1, J4]
4. $\Box(JJp \supset Jp)$ [L2, J7, 3]
5. $\Box(JJp \equiv Jp)$ [2, 4]
6. $\Box(\Box p \supset p)$ [L1, RL]
7. $\Box(\Box Jp \equiv Jp)$ [6 p/Jp, J4]
8. $\Box(\sim\Box p \supset J\sim\Box p)$ [L3, RL, J3]
9. $\Box(\sim\Box p \supset \sim J\Box p)$ [8, J5]
10. $\Box(J\Box p \supset \Box p)$ [9, transp.]
11. $\Box(\Box\Box p \supset J\Box p)$ [J3]
12. $\Box(\Box p \supset J\Box p)$ [11, $\Box(\Box p \supset \Box\Box p)$ from S5]
13. $\Box(\Box p \equiv J\Box p)$ [10, 12]
14. $\Box(\sim Jp \equiv J\sim p)$ [J5, J6]
15. $\Box(J\sim(p \supset q) \supset J(p \wedge \sim q))$ [$\sim(p \supset q) \supset (p \wedge \sim q)$, J1, J4, J7]
16. $\Box(J(p \wedge \sim q) \supset Jp)$ [$(p \wedge q) \supset p$, J1, J4, J7]
17. $\Box(J(p \wedge \sim q) \supset J\sim q)$ [$(p \wedge q) \supset q$, J1, J4, J7]
18. $\Box(J(p \wedge \sim q) \supset \sim Jq)$ [17, J5]
19. $\Box(J(p \wedge \sim q) \supset (Jp \wedge \sim Jq))$ [16, 18]
20. $\Box(\sim J(p \supset q) \supset \sim(Jp \supset Jq))$ [J6, 15, 19, $\Box((p \wedge \sim q) \supset \sim(p \supset q))$]
21. $\Box((Jp \supset Jq) \supset J(p \supset q))$ [20, transp.]
22. $\Box((Jp \supset Jq) \equiv J(p \supset q))$ [21, J7]

Add A3 and A5 to get:

23. $\Box(n \supset p) \supset p$ [A3, $p \supset (\Box(p \supset q) \supset q)$]
24. $\Box J(\Box(n \supset p) \supset p)$ [23, J1, J4]
25. $\Box(J\Box(n \supset p) \supset Jp)$ [L2, J7, 24]
26. $\Box(\Box(n \supset p) \supset Jp)$ [25, 12]
27. $p \supset \sim\Box(n \supset \sim p)$ [23, $p/\sim p$, transp.]
28. $p \supset \Box(n \supset p)$ [27, A5] (= M5)
29. $\Box(Jp \supset \Box(n \supset p))$ [28, J1, J4, J7, 10]
30. $\Box(Jp \equiv \Box(n \supset p))$ [26, 29]

Add M1–3 (from which Ext: $\Box(p \equiv q) \supset (\delta p \supset \delta q)$) and
Df. ~ to get:

31.	$\Box(J(p \supset 0) \supset (Jp \supset 0))$	[J5, Df. ~]
32.	$\Box J(0 \supset 0)$	[$p \supset p$, J1, J4]
33.	$\Box(J0 \supset 0)$	[31, 32]
34.	$\Box(0 \supset J0)$	[$0 \supset p$, RL]
35.	$\Box(J0 \equiv 0)$	[33, 34]
36.	$\delta J(p \supset q) \supset \delta(Jp \supset Jq)$	[J7, Ext.] (= M8)
37.	$\delta J0 \supset \delta 0$	[35, Ext.] (= M9)
38.	$\delta \Box Jp \supset \delta Jp$	[7, Ext.]
39.	$\delta 0 \supset (\delta(0 \supset 0) \supset \delta Jp)$	[M3 p/Jp, 38] (= M10)

Proofs from M1–3, 6–10:

40.	$\Box(J(p \supset q) \equiv J(p \supset q))$	[$\Box(p \equiv p)$]
41.	$\Box(J(p \supset q) \equiv (Jp \supset Jq))$	[M8, 40] (gives J7)
42.	$\Box(J(p \supset 0) \equiv (Jp \supset J0))$	[41]
43.	$\Box(J0 \equiv 0)$	[$\Box(J0 \equiv J0)$, M7]
44.	$\Box(J(p \supset 0) \equiv (Jp \supset 0))$	[42, 43]
45.	$\Box(J{\sim}p \equiv {\sim}Jp)$	[44, Df. ~] (= J5, J6)
46.	$\Box((J0 \supset J0) \equiv (0 \supset 0))$	[$\Box((p \supset p) \equiv (q \supset q))$]
47.	$\Box(J(0 \supset 0) \equiv (0 \supset 0))$	[41, 46]
48.	$\Box(J\Box p \equiv \Box p)$	[M3, 43, 47] (gives J3)
49.	$\Box(\Box Jp \equiv Jp)$	[M10; $\Box(\Box 0 \equiv 0)$ and $\Box(\Box(0 \supset 0) \equiv (0 \supset 0))$ from M1–3] (gives J4)

Proof from RL, L1–3, A4, 30, Df. T:

50.	$\Box(n \supset p) \supset \Box(a \supset \Box(n \supset p))$	[$\Box p \supset \Box(q \supset \Box p)$, in S5]
51.	$\Box(a \supset \Box(n \supset p)) \supset$ $(\Diamond a \supset \Diamond \Box(n \supset p))$	[$\Box(p \supset q) \supset (\Diamond p \supset \Diamond q)$, in S5]
52.	$\Box(a \supset \Box(n \supset p)) \supset$ $\Diamond \Box(n \supset p)$	[51, A4]
53.	$\Box(a \supset \Box(n \supset p)) \supset \Box(n \supset p)$	[52, $\Diamond \Box p \supset \Box p$]
54.	$\Box(a \supset \Box(n \supset p)) \equiv \Box(n \supset p)$	[50, 53]
*55.	$Ta(Jp) \equiv Tn(p)$	[54, 30, Df. T] (= UT5)

From A4–6 we obtain Ta(A6), from which with UT1–4, and the
definitions of T, U and = we may prove UT7 thus (employing the

lemma $Ta(Fb) \equiv Tb(Pa)$, which I have proved in *Past, Present and Future*):

1.	*(Uac v Uca)*	[assumption]
2.	*(Ubc v Ucb)*	[assumption]
3.	*~Uab* (i.e. *Ta(G~b))*	[assumption]
4.	*~Uba* (i.e. *Ta(H~b))*	[assumption]
5.	*(Uac ∧ Ubc) v*	
	(Uac ∧ Ucb) v	
	(Uca ∧ Ubc) v	
	(Uca ∧ Ubc)	[1, 2, prop. calculus]
6.	*Ta(~b) ⊃*	
	(Ta(G~b) ⊃	
	(Ta(H~b) ⊃	
	(Ta(GG~b) ∧ Ta(GH~b) ∧	
	Ta(HG~b) ∧ Ta(HH~b))))	[Ta(A6)]
7.	*Ta(~b) ⊃*	
	(Ta(GG~b) ∧ Ta(GH~b) ∧	
	Ta(HG~b) ∧ Ta(HH~b))	[3, 4, 6]
8.	*Ta(~b) ⊃*	
	(((Uac ∧ Ubc) ⊃ Tb(~b)) ∧	
	((Uac ∧ Ucb) ⊃ Tb(~b)) ∧	
	((Uac ∧ Ubc) ⊃ Tb(~b)) ∧	
	((Uac ∧ Ucb) ⊃ Tb(~b)))	[7, UT3, UT4]
9.	*Ta(~b) ⊃ Tb(~b)*	[5, 8, prop. calculus]
10.	*~Ta(~b)*	[9, Df. *T*, A4]
11.	*~Tb(~a)*	[10, Df. *T*, LC-transp.]
12.	*Ta(b) ∧ Tb(a)*	[10, 11, UT2]
13.	*a=b*	[12. Df. *T*, Df. =]

Proofs of other results noted in the text (where not already to be found elsewhere in this volume or in *Past, Present and Future*) may be left to the reader.

XV
TENSED PROPOSITIONS AS PREDICATES

Prima facie, we may divide propositions, or ostensible propositions, into two sorts. There are those, such as 'Socrates is sitting down' or 'Socrates was sitting down', of which it obviously makes sense to ask '*When* are they true?', though the answer may in some cases be 'Always' or 'Never'. And there are, on the other hand, those of which it does not so obviously make sense to ask this question; one sub-species of these would be exemplified by 'Two and two are four', and another by 'The date of the Battle of Hastings is 1066'. Rescher has suggested that propositions in the first major division (those of which at least some are true at some times and false at others) be called 'chronologically indefinite', while those in the second major division he calls 'chronologically definite.'[1] In what follows, I shall call propositions of the first sort 'tensed', and propositions of the second sort 'untensed'. One view of the relation between the two sorts of propositions is that 'untensed' propositions are improperly so called; they are simply tensed propositions which are so obviously either always or never true that to ask *when* they are true is socially (but not logically) inept. The most plausible alternative to this is to say that tensed propositions are not genuine propositions but predicates of instants ('Socrates is sitting down' really means 'Socrates is sitting down at ...'), the instants which form their subjects being unmentioned, but usually understood to be the time of utterance.

Of these two views about the relations between tensed and tenseless propositions, I am myself a determined adherent of the first, i.e. the view that so-called tenseless propositions are simply a sub-class of those tensed propositions which are always or never true. It is not my present purpose, however, to defend this view, but rather to see how far we can take the opposite view, i.e. the view that tensed propositions are not propositions at all, but predicates of instants. I shall take my departure from the paper on 'Tense Logic and the Logic of Earlier and Later',[2]

[1] N. Rescher, 'On the Logic of Chronological Propositions,' *Mind*, vol. 75 (1966), pp. 75–96.
[2] Chapter XI.

hereinafter called TEL, in which I outline a series of formal systems concerned with the notion of a proposition or quasi-proposition p being true at an instant a. In the system which I call System I, and also in a slight enlargement of it which is given no number in TEL but which I shall here call System I^+, tensed propositions are a fairly restricted class; in particular, propositions to the effect that such and such a tensed proposition is true at such and such a time are not themselves classed, in this system, as tensed propositions. Nor are propositions to the effect that such and such an instant is earlier than such and such another instant. These restrictions are removed in the system which I call System II. And in System III, instants themselves are treated as tensed propositions of a sort (each instant is identified with a tensed proposition which would ordinarily be said to be true at that instant only). Using Systems I and I^+, in which tensed propositions are syntactically separated from propositions about instants, it is plausible to regard these tensed propositions as predicates of the instants at which they are said to be true; but this way of looking at the matter is hardly consonant with the syntax of System II, and still less with that of System III. I therefore describe these systems, in TEL, as embodying increasing 'grades of tense-logical involvement'.

In the present paper I make both formal and philosophical revisions of TEL. In the first place, I make the syntax of the various systems more explicit than it is in TEL. Secondly I reaxiomatize them in a way which I hope will be more illuminating (and which will at two points be more correct) than the axiomatizations of TEL. Finally, I show that the view of tensed propositions as predicates, though I still think it misguided, can be carried further than is admitted in TEL. I do this last by making certain modifications to the more 'tense-logically involved' of my systems, and tracing some of their consequences. In the course of these manoeuvres, I hope that some new light may be thrown not only on tense logic but also on predicate calculus.

I. The Systems I, I⁺, II, IIIa, IIIb, IIIc⁺ and IIIc

The vocabulary of System I consists of the instant variables a, b, c, etc., the tensed propositional variables p, q, r, etc., and the undefined constants $\supset$, $\sim$, G, H, I, U, T, and $\forall$. Tensed propositions are defined as follows:

(i)   The variables p, q, r, etc., are tensed propositions.
(ii)   If ϕ and ψ are tensed propositions, so are $\phi \supset \psi$, $\sim\phi$, $G\phi$, and $H\phi$.

Informally, $\phi \supset \psi$ is to be read as 'If ϕ then ψ', $\sim\phi$ as 'Not ϕ', $G\phi$ as 'It will always be that ϕ', and $H\phi$ as 'It has always been that ϕ'. Other truth-functions, in particular $\phi \vee \psi$ ('Either ϕ or ψ'), $\phi \wedge \psi$ ('Both ϕ and ψ') and $\phi \equiv \psi$ ('If and only if ϕ then ψ'), may be defined in the usual ways, and $F\phi$ (for 'It will be that ϕ'), and $P\phi$ (for 'It has been that ϕ') as $\sim G\sim\phi$ and $\sim H\sim\phi$ respectively. Untensed propositions are defined as follows:

(i)   If u and v are instant variables, Iuv and Uuv are untensed propositions.
(ii)   If u is an instant variable and ϕ a tensed proposition, $Tu(\phi)$ is an untensed proposition.
(iii)   If α and β are untensed propositions and u is an instant variable, $\alpha \supset \beta$, $\sim\alpha$ and $\forall u\alpha$ are untensed propositions.

Informally, Iuv is to be read as 'u is the same instant as v', Uuv as 'u is earlier than v', $Tu(\phi)$ as 'It is the case at u that ϕ', and $\forall u\alpha$ as 'For all u, α'. $\supset$ and $\sim$ are for 'If' and 'Not', and the other truth-functions are definable in terms of them, as before; and $\exists u\alpha$, for 'For some u, α', is definable as $\sim\forall u\sim\alpha$.

All the theses of the system are untensed propositions, and the postulates consist of the following axioms subjoined to ordinary propositional calculus, quantification theory, and identity theory:

ET1. $Ta(p \supset q) \equiv (Tq(p) \supset Ta(q))$
ET2. $Ta(\sim p) \equiv \sim Ta(p)$
UT1. $Ta(Gp) \equiv \forall b(Uab \supset Tb(p))$
UT2. $Ta(Hp) \equiv \forall b(Uba \supset Tb(p))$.

Or in words:

ET1. It is true at *a* that if *p* then *q*, if and only if, if it is true at *a* that *p* it is true at *a* that *q*.

ET2. It is true at *a* that not *p*, if and only if it is not true at *a* that *p*.

UT1. It is true at *a* that it will always be the case that *p*, if and only if it is true at all instants later than *a* that *p*.

UT2. It is true at *a* that it has always been the case that *p*, if and only if it is true at all instants earlier than *a* that *p*.

As observed in TEL, the symbol *T* is superfluous in this system; we could write $Tu(\phi)$ as ϕu and regard the axiom as defining complex predicates in terms of propositional complications, thus:

ET1. $(p \supset q)a \equiv (pa \supset qa)$
ET2. $(\sim p)a \equiv \sim(pa)$
UT1. $(Gp)a \equiv \forall b(Uab \supset pb)$
UT2. $(Hp)a \equiv \forall b(Uba \supset pb)$.

Or in words:

ET1. '*a* is an if-*p*-then-*q*-ish instant' =
      'If *a* is *p*-ish then *a* is *q*-ish'.

ET2. '*a* is a not-*p*-ish instant' = '*a* is not a *p*-ish instant'.

UT1. '*a* is a *p*-for-evermore-ish instant' =
      'All instants later than *a* are *p*-ish'.

UT2. '*a* is a *p*-through-all-the-past-ish instant' =
      'All instants earlier than *a* are *p*-ish'.

It is also stated, erroneously, in TEL that the equivalence ET1 can be weakened to an implication; in fact this weakening is only possible in System II. The proof of ET1 from the corresponding implication requires the rule that if α is a thesis so is $Ta(\alpha)$; in System I either the α or the $Ta(\alpha)$ of this rule will not be an untensed proposition as above defined. However, for System I as now axiomatized we can prove the metatheorem that if the tensed proposition ϕ is tautological in form, $Ta(\phi)$ is a thesis. (Just use ET1 and ET2 to equate the tensed tautology, preceded by *Ta*, to an untensed one; e.g. $Ta(p \supset p)$ to $Ta(p) \supset Ta(p)$.) And, as mentioned in TEL and elsewhere, the addition of UT1 and 2 enables us to prove, preceded by Ta, all theses of Lemmon's minimal tense-logic K_t, the postulates of which I need not repeat here.[3]

In System I^+, we enlarge the class of tensed propositions by the following additions:

(a) If one of ϕ and ψ is a tensed proposition and the other untensed, $\phi \supset \psi$ is a tensed proposition.

(b) If u is an instant variable and ϕ a tensed proposition, $\forall u\phi$ is a tensed proposition.

And for these new tensed propositions, we add to the axioms of System I the following axiom schemata:

ET1.1. $Ta(\alpha \supset p) \equiv (\alpha \supset Ta(p))$
ET1.2. $Ta(p \supset \alpha) \equiv (Ta(p) \supset \alpha)$
ET1.3. $Ta(\forall b\phi) \equiv \forall bTa(\phi)$,

where ϕ is a tensed and α an untensed proposition. (The necessity for ET1.3 was overlooked in TEL.) These equivalences can also be replaced by definitions, and we can regard this enlargement as simply allowing us to form complex predicates not only from other predicates but from a combination of these with propositions. (This is normal procedure in predicate calculus.) And it may be noted that each of the schemata ET1.1–3 equates something which is ill-formed in System I with something which is well-formed there; thus $Ta(\forall bTb(p) \supset p)$ (e.g., 'It is true at a that if Socrates is at all times sitting down then Socrates is sitting down') is equated by ET1.3 with $\forall bTb(p) \supset Ta(p)$ ('If it is true at all times that Socrates is sitting down then it is true at a that he is').

In System II the entire class of untensed propositions is absorbed into the class of tensed ones, and tensed propositions are admitted as theses. This makes the syntactical enlargement of System I^+ redundant, and its postulates ET1.1–3 are also made redundant by the postulates which System II adds to System I, namely

RET: $\vdash \alpha$ if and only if $\vdash Ta(\alpha)$, for a not free in α.

ET3. $Ta(Tb(p)) \equiv Tb(p)$

---

[3] *Editors' note.* See p. 103 in this volume.

ET4. $Ta(\forall bTb(p)) \equiv \forall bTb(p)$

ET5. $Ta(Ubc) \equiv Ubc.$

These postulates are equivalent to those given for System II in TEL, and, as there observed, the ET portion of the system is equivalent to a system of Rescher's. We cannot now dispense with the functor T in favor of simple predication without using propositions as predicates, i.e. having forms like $(pa)b$ and $((pa)b)c$. However, each of the axioms above equates a formula which is ill-formed in System I with one which is well-formed there, and the rule has a similar function.

Finally, in System III, the class of tensed propositions absorbs even instants, and for instants considered as propositions we have the one further axiom (which makes ET5 redundant).

ET6. $Ta(b) \equiv Iab,$

asserting that the 'instant' b is 'true at' a if and only if it is identical with a. The identity function is of course taken to have its usual postulates (say Iaa and the schema $Iab \supset (\alpha \supset \beta)$ where β differs from α only in having a b in place of an a). In TEL, I is not thus used as a primitive, though the possibility of doing so is mentioned. System III seems as far removed as possible from the representation of tensed propositions as predicates of instants – instants as objects have just disappeared. But (1) ET6 is like earlier extensions of System I in equating a formula which is ill-formed in that system with one which is well-formed there, though the I of Iab must be re-interpreted as some sort of connective when a and b are read as propositions; and (2) a very slight modification to System III will make it much easier to interpret its tensed propositions as predicates.

The modification I have in mind consists in dropping the identification of an instant with a tensed proposition true at that instant only, and introducing a functor S which forms that proposition from that instant. The tensed proposition Sa may be read as 'It is a', in the sense of 'it is' in which we say 'It is 5 o'clock', 'It is Thursday', 'It is the 5th of June', etc. And instead of adding ET6 to System II, we add

S1. $Ta(Sb) \equiv Iab,$

'That it is b is the case at a if and only if a and b are the same instant.'

Moreover, the form Sa and the axiom S1 could be added, not to System II, but to System I^+ or even System I without doing violence to the syntax of those systems; though if the form Sa is introduced into System I as a tensed proposition, it is natural to introduce quantifications of tensed propositions, and with them ET1.3, into that system.

For these various possible new systems I propose to adopt the following names:

(1)   'System IIIa' for System III as above presented, i.e. System II with instants counted as tensed propositions and ET6 added to the postulates.

(2)   'System IIIb' for System II with the following added to the definition of a tensed proposition: 'If u is an instant-variable, Su is a tensed proposition'; and with S1 added to the postulates.

(3)   'System $IIIc^+$' for System I^+ with the same additions to the definition of 'tensed proposition' and to the postulates.

(4)   'System IIIc' for System I with the following added to the definition of a tensed proposition: 'If u is an instant-variable and ϕ a tensed proposition, Su and $\forall u\phi$ are tensed propositions'; and with ET1.3 and S1 added to the postulates.

In Systems $IIIc^+$ and IIIc, it may be noted, as in System I^+ and I, the symbol T can be dispensed with in favour of predication, and S1 replaced by the definition

$(Sb)a = Iab.$

II. Quasi-Modal Fragments of the Systems

Where ϕ does not contain free a, we may abridge $\forall aTa(\phi)$ ('It is true at all times that ϕ') to $\Box\phi$, and it is pointed out in TEL that for a $\Box$ thus defined we may prove in System II the Lewis modal system S5, and also $\Box p \supset Gp$ and $\Box p \supset Hp$. What is not investigated in TEL is the result of introducing this definition of $\Box$ into Systems I^+ and I. The most important point to note about this is that in these systems $\Box$ is a 'heterogeneous' functor, forming untensed propositions from tensed ones. $\Box(p \supset q) \supset (\Box p \supset \Box q)$, $\Box(p \supset q) \supset (\Box(q \supset r) \supset \Box(p \supset r))$, and (with $\Diamond$ for $\sim\Box\sim$)$\Box(p \supset q) \supset (\Diamond p \supset \Diamond q)$, $(\Box p \wedge \Diamond q) \supset \Diamond(p \wedge q)$ and

$\Box p \supset \Diamond p$ are examples of formulae which remain well-formed, untensed, and theses in these systems; but $\Box p \supset p$, $\Box p \supset Gp$, and $\Box p \supset Hp$ are ill-formed in System I (being implications with untensed antecedents and tensed consequents), while in System I[+] they are tensed and therefore not theses. However, $\Box(\Box p \supset p)$, $\Box(\Box p \supset Gp)$, and $\Box(\Box p \supset Hp)$ are theses of System I[+], and $\Box p \supset \Box Gp$ and $\Box p \supset \Box Hp$ even of System I.

The fragments of Systems I and I[+] which use only $\supset$, $\sim$, $\Box$, and tensed propositional variables may be regarded as notational variants of certain forms of predicate calculus without name-variables developed by G.E. Hughes and D.G. Londey. In their published textbook,[4] Hughes and Londey give a calculus in which predicates consist of predicate-letters f, g, h, etc., and truth-functional complexes of these, atomic propositions are formed by prefixing U or E (in effect universal and existential quantifiers) to these, and molecular propositions in the usual truth-functional ways. As postulates we have all tautologies formulable in the language, all tautological truth-functional complexes of predicates with the whole preceded by U, and the following axioms (for use with predicate-substitution and detachment):

A1. $U(f \supset g) \supset (Uf \supset Ug)$
A2. $Uf \supset Ef$.

Without A2 (which expresses the non-emptiness of the universe), this system would appear to be equivalent to an earlier one with the same syntax, namely von Wright's 'Quantified Logic of Properties'.[5] Von Wright also has the idea of classifying the operators U and E as 'modalities' ('existential' modalities).[6] At all events, a mere rewriting of the Hughes-Londey postulates in our symbolism will give a basis for the $\supset$-$\sim$-$\Box$-p portion of System I, namely: All tautologies formulable in the language, all tautological complexes of tensed propositions with the whole preceded by $\Box$, and the axioms $\Box(p \supset q) \supset (\Box p \supset \Box q)$ and $\Box p \supset \Diamond p$.

[4] G.E. Hughes and D.G. Londey, *Elements of Formal Logic* (New York, 1965).
[5] G.H. von Wright, *Logical Studies* (London, 1957), second paper ('On the Idea of Logical Truth (I)').
[6] G.H. von Wright, *An Essay in Modal Logic* (Amsterdam, 1951), Ch. II.

Hughes has also axiomatized[7] an extension of the above predicate calculus in which propositional as well as predicate variables are used in the formation of complex predicates (an implication of which one component is a predicate counts as a predicate). The axioms are all tautologies, all tautologously formed predicates (including those with propositional components) preceded by U, and the axioms

A1.1. $U(p \supset f) \supset (p \supset Uf)$
A1.2. $U(f \supset g) \supset U(Uf \supset g)$
A2. $Uf \supset Ef$.

This gives for the $\supset$-$\sim$-$\Box$-p fragment of System I^+: all tautologies, all tautologously formed tensed propositions preceded as a whole by $\Box$, the axiom schema $\Box(\alpha \supset p) \supset (\alpha \supset \Box p)$ (where α is untensed) and the axioms $\Box(p \supset q) \supset \Box(\Box p \supset q)$ and $\Box p \supset \Diamond p$. ($\Box(\Box p \supset p)$ is obtained from $\Box(p \supset p)$ and the first axiom, and $\Box(p \supset q) \supset (\Box p \supset \Box q)$ from the first axiom and the schema.)

Nested modalities like $\Box\Box p$ and $\Box\Diamond p$ are of course ill-formed in both these systems, but they are not simply modal logics with such nestings ruled out (of the sort studied, e.g., by J.L. Pollock,[8] and earlier but more sketchily by myself[9]), since even $\Box p \supset p$ is not propositional enough to figure as a thesis.

If we add the tense-operators G and H, the resulting enlarged fragments of both systems will contain all theses of the tense-logic K_t preceded as a whole by $\Box$, and may be axiomatized by adding to the above postulates, besides these $\Box$-preceded K_t theses, in System I $\Box p \supset \Box Gp$ and $\Box p \supset \Box Hp$, and in System I^+ $\Box(\Box p \supset Gp)$ and $\Box(\Box p \supset Hp)$ (from which $\Box p \supset \Box Gp$ and $\Box p \supset \Box Hp$ are obtainable by the schema $\Box(\alpha \supset p) \supset (\alpha \supset \Box p)$, with $\Box p$ for α and Gp and Hp for p). One way of obtaining the K_t theses preceded by $\Box$, in either system, would be to lay down a sufficient set of K_t axioms each preceded by $\Box$, and then derive the theorems (a) by using substitution, $\Box(p \supset q) \supset (\Box p \supset \Box q)$ and detachment, and (b) where K_t theses are

---

[7] See A.N. Prior, critical notice of Hughes and Londey's *Elements of Formal Logic, Australasian Journal of Philosophy*, Vol. 44 (1966), pp. 224–31.
[8] John L. Pollock, 'Basic Modal Logic', *Journal of Symbolic Logic*, Vol. 32 (1967), pp. 355–65.
[9] A.N. Prior, *Time and Modality* (Oxford, 1957), Appendix C.

obtained by using the rules to infer $\vdash G\phi$ and $\vdash H\phi$ from $\vdash \phi$, to obtain the corresponding $\Box$-preceded theses by $\Box p \supset \Box Gp$ and $\Box p \supset \Box Hp$. (Tautological tensed formulae preceded by$\Box$ could be similarly obtained by laying down $\Box$-preceded tensed propositional-calculus axioms and using substitution, $\Box(p \supset q) \supset (\Box p \supset \Box q)$ and detachment.)

There is not much advantage in using the richer syntax of System I^+, but there is a little. Suppose, for example, we wish to add to either of the systems the postulate that there is a unique time-series, and that a linear one. Using instant variables, we can express this in the *full* vocabularies of both systems by $Uab \lor Uba \lor Iab$, asserting of any instants a and b that a is either earlier than or later than or identical with b; or by $Ta(p \land Hp \land Gp) \supset \Box p$, asserting that if it is true at any instant a that it is and always has been and always will be the case that p, then p is true at all times. But in the vocabulary of System I^+ we can express this assumption in pure $\Box$-$\supset$-$\sim$-G-H-p, by$\Box((p \land Hp \land Gp) \supset \Box p)$.

In both systems, G and H are 'extensional' functions of their arguments, in the sense that we have $\Box(p \equiv q) \supset \Box(Gp \equiv Gq)$ and $\Box(p \equiv q) \supset \Box(Hp \equiv Hq)$. If we read these arguments as predicates, this means that G and H are extensional functions in the standard sense, since these laws just mean

$$\forall a(pa \equiv qa) \supset \forall a((Gp)a \equiv (Gq)a) \qquad \text{and}$$
$$\forall a(pa \equiv qa) \supset \forall a((Hp)a \equiv (Hq)a).$$

Considered as bits of predicate calculus without name-variables, the extensions with G and H are of some interest. The Hughes-Londey pedagogical program of delaying the introduction of name-variables as long as possible begins to run into difficulties when we move from one-place to two-place predicates (how, e.g., without using name-variables, do we distinguish between $\forall a \exists b Uab$ and $\forall b \exists a Uab$?), and in fact they make no attempt to carry it that far; but here *some* of the logic of the two-place predicate U is brought in via a pair of operators forming one-place predicates from other one-place predicates – in particular, forming '... has only p-ish instants following' and '... has only p-ish instants preceding' from the predicate-of-instants '... is p-ish'. The procedure may be generalized by replacing any relation R by operators, on a predicate f, forming '... is R only to what is f', and '... is R'd only by what is f'.[10] The $\Box$-$\supset$-$\sim$-G-H-p logics we have been considering give a general calculus for such pairs of operators, and some well-known extensions of this logic enable us to state, within this type of calculus, certain properties of the 'hidden' relation. For example, it is known that if we add to System I the postulate that U is transitive, we can prove not just the theses of K_t preceded by Ta but, preceded by Ta, the theses of $K_t + Gp \supset GGp$; and in the present fragment of System I, the transitivity of the unmentioned U may be expressed by adding the axiom $\Box(Gp \supset GGp)$. And the replacement of U by G and H can be taken still further in the Systems III.

III. The Tense-Logical Construction of the Earlier-Later Logic

In what I am now calling System IIIa, it was shown in TEL that we may prove $Ta(p) \equiv \Box(a \supset p)$, and that the function $\Box(\ldots \equiv \ldots)$ satisfies the normal postulates for identity within the system. This suggests a re-axiomatization with $\Box$ as primitive and T and I defined as follows: $Ta(p) = \Box(a \supset p)$ and $Iab = \Box(a \equiv b)$. With $\Box$, $\supset$, and $\sim$ primitive, and the definitions just given, we obtain a system equivalent to the T-I portion of IIIa if we add to S5 for $\Box$ three special postulates for 'instant-propositions', namely $\Diamond a$, $\Box(a \supset p) \vee \Box(a \supset \sim p)$ and $\exists aa$.

Further, in System IIIa, with UT1 and 2 included, we can prove $Uab \equiv Ta(Fb)$ and $Uab \equiv Tb(Pa)$ (a is earlier than b if and only if it is true at a that it will be that b, and if and only if it is true at b that it has been that a). This suggests dropping U as a primitive and defining Uab either as $Ta(Fb)$ ($\Box(a \supset Fb)$) or as $Tb(Pa)$ ($\Box(b \supset Pa)$). If we do this, and add K_t for G and H, with the mixing postulates $\Box p \supset Gp$ and $\Box p \supset Hp$, to the $\Box$-$\supset$-$\sim$ postulates just mentioned, or to the T-I postulates to which they are equivalent, UT1–2 become provable. Thus the elementary logic of the earlier-later relation U can be developed from the logic of the tenses G and H, given the above postulates for $\Box$ or for T and I. Moreover, those conditions on U which have 'reflections' in tense-logic can be proved from those reflections; and even those which have none can be reformulated in terms of G, H, and $\Box$.

---

[10] For beginnings of such generalizations, see Chapters XVI and XVII.

These manoeuvres, however, presuppose both the identification of instants with instantaneous tensed propositions (the peculiarity of System IIIa) and the identification of T, U, and I functions with omnitemporal tensed propositions (a feature of System II also). The question which we may now ask is: How far can these manoeuvres be reproduced in systems such as IIIc$^+$ and c, which do not have these peculiarities, and in which tensed propositions are in effect treated as predicates of instants (just as they are in I$^+$ and I)?

The fact that the postulates of the richer systems can be given as simply equating new forms with old is an encouraging sign for this enterprise, and it turns out that practically everything required can be carried out even in the least 'tense-logically involved' System IIIc. We can prove, even in System IIIc, $Ta(p) \equiv \Box(Sa \supset p)$, $Uab \equiv Ta(FSb)$, $Uab \equiv Tb(PSa)$, $\Diamond Sa$, $\Box(Sa \supset p) \vee \Box(Sa \supset {\sim}p)$, and $\Box\exists aSa$ (the plain $\exists aSa$, being tensed, is not suitable for a thesis in System IIIc). We can also prove, even in IIIc, the 'Barcan' schema $\forall b\Box\phi \equiv \Box\forall b\phi$; an important point because in System II (on which Systems IIIa and IIIb are based) this schema can be represented as a by-product of quantification theory and S5 for $\Box$, but it is not provable from quantification theory and the $\Box$-$\supset$-$\sim$-p fragment of System I (on which IIIc is based).

We can now rebuild IIIc in various ways. In the least radical way, we may dispense with T in favor of predication, i.e. replace $Ta(p)$ by pa, and (1) introduce into predicate calculus with identity the definitions $(p \supset q)a = pa \supset qa$, $({\sim}p)a = {\sim}pa$, $(Sb)a = Iab$; and then (2) instead of adding a primitive U (with no axioms) and defining $(Gp)a$ and $(Hp)a$ as $\forall b(Uab \supset pb)$ and $\forall b(Uba \supset pb)$, we could define Uab as $(FSb)a$ or $(PSa)b$, and for the undefined G and H lay down the axioms for K_t each predicated of an arbitrary instant a, and the further axioms $\forall bpb \supset (Gp)a$ and $\forall bpb \supset (Hp)a$ (cf. $\Box p \supset Gp$ and $\Box p \supset Hp$ in System II and its extensions); equivalences corresponding to the definitions of G and H are then provable. We gain very little, of course, by this; the U-primitive version of System IIIc is obviously more compact; the reshuffling merely helps to show the sufficiency of K_t for a tense logic presupposing no special conditions on U.

It is possible, however, to proceed quite differently, and more interestingly. We may present the System IIIc as indeed a disguised predicate calculus, but of an extended Hughes-Londey sort; that is, if we may so speak, a predicate calculus without predication. We shall have, indeed, instant variables and quantifiers binding them (our system could not be equated with IIIc without them), but these instant-variables will not figure as subjects of predication – we shall not represent $Ta(p)$ as a variant of pa; but differently. Instant-variables will occur only as constituents of predicates (or tensed propositions) of the form Su, and $Ta(p)$ will be defined as $\Box(Sa \supset p)$, i.e., in effect as the formal implication of the predicate p by the predicate Sa. Nor will S be defined by equating $(Sb)a$ with Iab; on the contrary, S will be one of our primitives and Iab defined as $\Box(Sa \equiv Sb)$, i.e. as the formal equivalence of the uniquely instantiated predicates Sa and Sb. $\Box$ will be primitive, and the only undefined way of constructing a genuine or untensed proposition from a predicate, i.e. tensed proposition, will be by prefixing $\Box$ to it.

We now build up the postulates of the system in the following steps:

(1)   We axiomatize the $\Box$-$\supset$-$\sim$-p fragment of System I as in the last section.

(2)   We introduce instant-variables, quantifiers binding them, and S, with the three axioms $\Diamond Sa$, $\Box(Sa \supset p) \vee \Box(Sa \supset \sim p)$, and $\Box \exists asa$; the schema $\forall u \Box \phi \supset \Box \forall u \phi$ (the converse being provable); and the rules

$\forall 1$: If $\alpha \supset \beta$ then $\forall u\alpha \supset \beta$

$\forall 2$: If $\alpha \supset \beta$ then $\alpha \supset \forall u\beta$, for u not free in α

$\Box \forall 1$: If $\Box(\phi \supset \psi)$ then $\Box(\forall u\phi \supset \psi)$

$\Box \forall 2$: If $\Box(\phi \supset \psi)$ then $\Box(\phi \supset \forall u\psi)$, for u not free in ϕ, (where α, β are untensed propositions and ϕ, ψ tensed).

(3)   We introduce the predicate-formers (tensed-proposition-formers) G and H with postulates as in the last section, i.e. $\Box$-preceded K_t, $\Box p \supset \Box Gp$ and $\Box p \supset \Box Hp$.

(4)   We define $Ta(p)$ as $\Box(Sa \supset p)$, Iab as $\Box(Sa \equiv Sb)$, and Uab as $\Box(Sa \supset FSb)(Ta(FSb))$.

All these postulates (including equivalences corresponding to the definitions) are provable in our original version of IIIc; and the latter (including Iaa and the schema $Iab \supset (\alpha \supset \beta)$, where α and β are untensed propositions of the system and β differs from α only in a replacement of a by b) is provable from them.

If we construct a similar version of System IIIc[+] (with (1) and (3) adjusted as in the last section, and with it understood that in $\Box \forall 1$ and

$\Box\forall 2$ *at least one* and possibly but not necessarily both of ϕ and ψ must be tensed), we can omit the Barcan schema as provable, though we still need $\Box\exists aSa$.

The predicates Su function in these systems like Quine's 'Pegasizes'. Their unique instantiation is guaranteed by their special axioms. $\Diamond Sa$ asserts in effect that at least one individual (instant) has the property Sa, and $\Box(Sa \supset p)$ $v\Box(Sa \supset \sim p)$ that for any property p either whatever has Sa has p or whatever has Sa lacks p, so that we never have one thing with Sa having p and another lacking it; i.e. at most one thing has Sa.

We could go further than this. To symbolize a uniquely occurring predicate (tensed proposition) as Sa still suggests something more like 'is Pegasus' than 'Pegasizes' (our first reading of this form was, in fact, something like 'is 5 o'clock', or more precisely 'is 5 o'clock G.M.T. on January 14, 1957'), and we could drop this suggestion of an internal structure by not using the symbol S at all and treating the us (unprefixed) as themselves the uniquely occurring predicates (their unique instantiation being, again, secured by the special axioms). This would give us a system, which we might call IIId, in which the 'tensed propositions' of System I *are* enlarged by treating instants as such propositions, but are enlarged *only* in this way, genuine or untensed propositions (such as $Ta(b)$, Uab, $\Box p$, and truth-functions and quantifications of these) being still syntactically segregated from tensed ones, and being alone capable of figuring as theses.

IV. Further Considerations Regarding System IIId

It is tempting to say that, as far as the removal of dubious presuppositions is concerned, in this last system, IIId, we contrive to get the best of both worlds. Tensed propositions are still resolutely treated as predicates rather than as genuine propositions (so that our 'tense-logical involvement' is still minimal); yet instants do not figure in the systems as named entities, so that we do not seem committed to their 'existence' in any serious sense. We seem, in fact, to have come up with a type of calculus which might very well suit people who say such things as that logic should detach itself from a thing-quality or substance-accident metaphysic, or that things should be regarded as logical constructions out of events rather than *vice versa*. Against this it might be argued that although Hughes-Londey types of predicate calculus do not *mention* individuals they presuppose them, and that if tensed propositions in particular are really predicates we cannot avoid, though we may symbolically gloss over, the question as to what they are predicates *of*. It may also be remarked that even in System IIId we still *quantify* over instant variables, and on some views this would suggest we are not taking their treatment as predicates very seriously.

My own view on these points is that (a) a thing-quality metaphysics is fine, but that (b) instants are not things, and (c) quantifying over instant-variables does not commit us to the view that instants *are* things. But I do not wish to argue for these positions here, but rather to note that formally System IIId, as well as System IIIc, *could* be interpreted by taking the thinghood of instants very seriously indeed, and reading its tensed propositions simply as *class* symbols, denoting *sets* of instants, namely the sets of instants 'at' which we would normally say that each proposition is true. This interpretation is possible because of the extensionality of the functions G and H, considered as functions of predicates. It will be simplest to begin by developing this interpretation of System IIIc.

On this reading $\sim\phi$ obviously denotes the Boolean complement of the set ϕ, and $\phi \wedge \psi$ the intersection of the sets ϕ and ψ. $\Box\phi$, which is 'genuinely propositional' in Systems IIIc and d, does not denote a set but is a sentence asserting that the set ϕ (i.e. the set of instants at which ϕ) is the universal set (the totality of instants); or in brief, that $\phi = 1$. The set $\phi \supset \psi$, i.e. $\sim(\phi \wedge \sim\psi)$, is the complement of the intersection of ϕ with the complement of ψ; i.e. that part of the totality of instants which lies outside that part of the set ϕ which does not overlap the set ψ, i.e. the union of the set ψ and the complement of ϕ ($\sim(\phi \wedge \sim\psi) = \sim\phi \vee \psi$). $\Box(\phi \supset \psi)$ then asserts that this set $\sim(\phi \wedge \sim\psi) = 1$, i.e. that $\phi \wedge \sim\psi = 0$, i.e. that no part of the set ϕ fails to overlap the set ψ, i.e. that ϕ is wholly included in ψ (the obvious set-theoretic version of the statement that all instants at which ϕ are instants at which ψ, or that whenever ϕ is true so is ψ). G and H are functions from sets of instants to sets of instants, such that $G1 = H1 = 1$, $G(\phi \wedge \psi) = G\phi \wedge G\psi$ and $H(\phi \wedge \psi) = H\phi \wedge H\psi$, i.e. the G-set of the intersection of ϕ and ψ is the intersection of the G-sets of ϕ and of ψ, and similarly for H. (These conditions are set-theoretically equivalent to laying down $\Box\phi \supset \Box G\psi$, $\Box\phi \supset \Box H\psi$, $\Box(G(\phi \supset \psi) \supset (G\phi \supset G\psi)$, and $\Box(H(\phi \supset \psi) \supset (H\phi \supset H\psi))$. Further, relating the two functions, we have $\Box(\sim G\sim H\phi \supset \phi)$ and $\Box(\sim H\sim G\phi \supset \phi)$. It can then be shown that there is a relation-in-extension U between the instants in our sets, for which $G\phi$ is the set of instants such that all instants U'd by them are in ϕ, and $H\phi$ is the set of instants such that all instants which are U to them are in ϕ; or in symbols,

$$G\phi = \{a: \forall b(Uab \supset \phi b)\} \text{ and } H\phi = \{a: \forall b(Uba \supset \phi b\}.$$

For this property will be possessed by the relation between instants a and b which consists in a being in the set $\sim G\sim Sb$, where Sb is the set of which b is the sole member.

In System IIId, U is not expressible as a relation between instants, since that system does not contain names for instants. However, it has the symbols a, b, c, etc., denoting the corresponding unit sets, and so has the function Uab which consists in the unit set a being included in the set $\sim G\sim b$ ($\square(a \supset \sim G\sim b)$), and for U thus defined we can prove that a unit set a is included in $G\phi$ if and only if $\forall b(Uab \supset \square(b \supset \phi))$ and in $H\phi$ if and only if $\forall b(Uba \supset \square(b \supset \phi))$.

This, on this interpretation of the system, is precisely what we prove when we derive UT1 and 2 from its postulates for G and H.

Thus interpreted, System IIId is an 'algebra' in the sense of some recent papers by E.J. Lemmon,[11] and its proofs of theses about U from theses about G and H are simply versions of completeness proofs using such algebras. An extensional predicate calculus without name-variables is after all just a version of set-theory without symbols for members or for membership, and that in turn is simply a Boolean algebra, though if members of sets are to be represented in it by their unit classes it must be an 'atomic' Boolean algebra, i.e. it must contain elements a such that $a \neq 0$ and for any ϕ, if ϕ is included in a then either $\phi = 0$ or $\phi = a$, and such that if any element is $\neq 0$ then some atomic element is included in it.[12]

---

[11] E.J. Lemmon, 'Algebraic Semantics for Modal Logics,' *Journal of Symbolic Logic*, Vol. 31 (1966), pp. 46–65, and pp. 191–218.

[12] Cf. Tarski, 'On the Foundations of Boolean Algebra,' *Logic, Semantics and Metamathematics* (Oxford, 1956), pp. 320–41, esp. 2. Tarski does not have special symbols for atoms, but a definition of atomicity and a postulate for it, as above. This corresponds to variants of our systems in which special instant-variables are dispensed with in favour of the function Qp, for 'p is true at one instant only' (cf. Chapter XI, p. 129 and Chapter XVII, last section).

The set-theoretical proofs will of course go through *whatever* the sets are supposed to be sets of, e.g. if their members are teacups, $G\phi$ is the set of teacups such that all more expensive teacups than these ones are in the set ϕ, and $H\phi$ is the set of teacups such that all *less* expensive teacups are in ϕ. This, to my mind, means that we do not need to take the 'instants' of the original interpretation terribly seriously after all; for formal completeness proofs we can happily use System IIIc or d and think of teacups, and for metaphysics we can paraphrase the instants away altogether by thinking of IIIc and d as System IIIa with certain not very illuminating types of well-formed formulae (e.g. $Ta(Tb(p))$) omitted.

XVI
QUASI-PROPOSITIONS AND QUASI-INDIVIDUALS

Egocentric logic. Practitioners of tense logic are often asked the question, 'If you admit as genuine propositions ones whose truth-value depends on *when* they are propounded, why not also admit ones whose truth-value depends on *where* they are propounded, or *by whom*, etc.?'

Why not, indeed? There are many sentences of ordinary speech which have precisely these peculiarities. The truth of 'It is raining here' does depend on where it is uttered, and so does the truth of 'It is raining five miles away' (and more generally of 'It is raining *there*'); and the truth of 'I am sitting down' does depend on who says it, and so perhaps does that of 'Eating bacon and bananas is nice' (= 'I like it') and 'Jones is very tall' (= 'He is much taller than I am'). Nor is it at all difficult to concoct a rigorously formalized language with similar features.

There could, for example, be a language in which there are no proper names or pronouns, but in which the ultimate subject of every sentence is understood to be the speaker. A man might, for example, just say 'Sitting' to indicate that he is himself sitting, i.e. his 'Sitting' would have precisely the force of the English sentence, 'I am sitting'. (There could be, perhaps even are, *games* in which ordinary English speakers arranged in a circle report on their activities in this subject-less fashion.) Lacking names and pronouns, the only way that a speaker of this language would have of describing the activities of other people would be by certain 'modalizings' of his sentences which presented the activities of others as being, in a sense, indirect activities of his own. He might, for example, use the form 'All-tall sitting' to mean that everyone taller than himself is sitting, i.e. *their* plain sitting is presented as *his* 'all-tall sitting', i.e. his having-everyone-taller-sitting. This form obviously parallels 'It will always be that *p*' in tense logic; 'It will always be that Jones is sitting' is equivalent to 'At all instants later than now, Jones is sitting', and his plain sitting at *those* instants is presented as his sitting-for-evermore at *this* instant. 'Some-tall sitting' would be similarly used for '*Someone* taller than me is sitting', and would parallel 'It will be that Jones is sitting' for 'At some instant later than now, Jones is sitting', which presents his sitting at some later instant as his future-sitting at the present instant. 'All-short-sitting' and 'Some-short-sitting' would analogously express the sitting of everyone and of someone *shorter* than the speaker, just as we use 'It has always been that ...' and 'It has been that ...' to indicate what goes on at *earlier* instants than the time of speech. Indeed, there is no reason why we should not symbolize 'All-tall p', 'Some-tall p', 'All-short p' and 'Some-short p' as Gp, Fp, Hp, and Pp, placing these prefixes in the same category as negation, just as we do when they are used for tenses.

Iterated quasi-modalities would of course express oblique obliquities. 'All-tall (some-tall sitting)', GFp, would mean 'It is true of everyone taller than me that someone taller than him is sitting', and 'Some-tall (all-tall sitting)', FGp, would mean 'It is true of someone taller than me that everyone taller than him is sitting'.

Sentences of this 'egocentric' language will not translate as sentences of a normal 'person-neutral' first-order theory, but will be more like the *predicates* of such a theory, the modalities then having the obvious translations (with Uab for 'a is shorter than b'):

T1. $(Gp)a = \forall b(Uab \supset pb)$
T2. $(Fp)a = \exists b(Uab \wedge pb)$
T3. $(Hp)a = \forall b(Uba \supset pb)$
T4. $(Pp)a = \exists b(Uba \wedge pb)$.

Egocentric truth-functions (asserted by a) analogously translate by

T5. $(\sim p)a = \sim(pa)$
T6. $(p \supset q)a = (pa) \supset (qa)$.

These 'translations', with ordinary quantification theory, will suffice to guarantee that 'egocentric logic' includes the following laws (i.e. that all substitution-instances in the following will be true whoever says them):

T7. $G(p \supset q) \supset (Gp \supset Gq)$,

e.g. if all-tall if-standing-then-uncomfortable, then if all-tall standing, all-tall uncomfortable;

T8. $p \supset GPp$,

e.g. if sitting then all-tall some-short sitting, or in English, 'If I am sitting, then it is true of anyone taller than me that someone shorter than him is sitting'; and of course their images

T9. $H(p \supset q) \supset (Hp \supset Hq)$
T10. $p \supset HFp$.

We will also have the rules

RG: $\vdash \alpha \rightarrow \vdash G\alpha$
RH: $\vdash \alpha \rightarrow \vdash H\alpha$,

i.e. what is logically true of me is logically true of everyone taller and of everyone shorter than me (e.g. not only I, but everyone taller than me, and everyone shorter than me, sits if he sits and stands if he stands). Further, because the relation of being shorter than is transitive $(Uab \supset (Ubc \supset Uac))$ we have the law

T11. $FFp \supset Fp$,

e.g. if someone taller than me has someone taller than him sitting, then someone taller than me is sitting.

There is, in short, a pretty detailed formal parallel between tense logic and this rather simple type of 'egocentric logic'. In fact, we can obtain something *more or less* like tense logic if we take *any* first-order theory whatsoever, treat its one-place predicates as if they were propositions, and treat an *(n + 1)*-place function with n predicate-arguments and one individual argument as an n-place function of propositions. That is, we equate something of the form

(1) $f(p_1, p_2, \ldots, p_n, a)$

with something of the form

(2) $f'(p_1, p_2, \ldots, p_n, a)$

and drop the a. Our (1) could be, for example, $\forall b(Uab \supset pb)$, which is a function of the one predicate p and the one name a (the other variable, b, is bound, and the remaining symbols are constants), and then we use

G for the resulting *f'* in (2). The formal manipulation is the same whatever the variables stand for, and whatever predicate-constants we employ in constructing the function *f*.

2. *Person-propositions.* An egocentric propositional logic with quasi-modal operators is a strange form for the theory of comparative height to take. Still, as we have just seen, it *can* be done that way. Does not this render completely trivial the fact that the theory of the earlier-later relation can be set out in this way too? We may well be inclined to say: *of course* the theory of the earlier-later relation can be developed by using quasi-modalities (tenses), for the theory of *any* relation can be developed that way; but why do it, either in this case or in any other?

One answer to this which we might think of making is that we can not only develop tense logic within the first-order theory of the earlier-later relation, but can equally develop this first-order theory within tense logic (enriched by a little higher-order quantification). For we can identify an instant with a tensed proposition, namely with the conjunction of everything that would ordinarily be said to be true *at* that instant; or alternatively, with something that would ordinarily be said to be true at that instant only. We can then interpret being true at an instant as being necessarily or omnitemporally implied by that instant (considered as a proposition), and one instant's being earlier than another as the futurity of the latter being true 'at' the former, i.e. with the former's necessarily or omnitemporally implying that the latter will be the case. The theory of the earlier-later quasi-relation will then become a part of tense logic rather than vice versa. (I say quasi-relation because if *a* and *b* are sentential rather than individual variables, the link in the form '*a* is earlier than *b*' is a two-place *sentential connective* rather than a two-place *predicate* expressing a relation between objects.)[1]

Does not the possibility of this reversal mark off tense logic from other calculi that may be presented as by-products of first-order theories? Or can this reversal be equally performed in these other cases too? I am afraid the answer is that it can. Consider again our 'egocentric' version of the theory of the Tall and the Short. Not only can this be 'explicated' as a by-product of the normal version of this theory, but the latter can also be 'explicated' as a by-product of the former. We

---

[1] Cf. Chapter XI.

can, to start with, identify a person with, or replace him in our system by, the conjunction of all the propositions that would ordinarily be said to be true *of* this person, or by some proposition that would ordinarily be said to be true of him alone. We can then interpret being true 'of' a person as being necessarily or 'omnipersonally' implied by him. And we can say that one person is shorter than another (i.e. we can define the relation U of the associated first-order theory) by saying that the former necessarily or omnipersonally implies some-tall the latter, i.e. that someone taller than him is the latter. These last definitions no doubt require a little explanation, but it is easy enough to give it.

The form 'a omnipersonally implies that p' is true if the egocentric statement 'If a then p' is true whoever says it. Suppose, for instance, that a is the only person sitting, and that he is also drinking (others may be drinking too). We can in these circumstances identify the person a with the proposition 'Sitting' (i.e. 'I am sitting'); and 'If sitting then drinking', i.e. 'If I am sitting then I am drinking', will be true whoever says it (true if a says it because he is drinking, and true if anyone else says it because he is not sitting – *ex hypothesi*, a is the only person doing that). So in these circumstances sitting omnipersonally implies drinking; and this ('Omnipersonally if sitting then drinking') is the proposition of our noun-and-pronounless language by which we may translate the ordinary 'a is drinking'. Again, if b is the only person smoking, and a is still the only person sitting, and b is shorter than a, then 'If I am smoking then someone taller than me is sitting' will be true whoever says it (true if b says it because a is sitting, and true if anyone else says it because anyone else is not smoking); i.e. smoking will omnipersonally imply some-tall sitting. And this ('Omnipersonally if smoking then some-tall sitting') is how we express 'b is shorter than a' within this language. (With $\square$ for 'omnipersonally', $Uba = \square(b \supset Fa)$.)

Finally, the mode 'omnipersonally' itself, i.e. 'It is true of all persons that …', is definable in terms of the modalities or quasi-tenses 'All-tall' and 'All-short', though we must construct this definition carefully. It will not do to define 'It is true of everyone that p' simply as 'p and all-tall p and all-short p', e.g. 'All-persons sitting' as 'I am sitting and so is everyone taller than me and so is everyone shorter'. For this does not cover persons of the same height as the speaker who are not identical with him. These can be brought in, however, if the defining formula is revised by the addition of 'All-tall all-short p and all-short all-tall p', i.e. 'Everyone taller than me has p being true of everyone shorter than him, and everyone shorter than me has p being true of everyone taller than him'. (This works, at least, so long as people are of at least two different heights.) At this point 'egocentric logic' is rather like the tense logic that might be extracted from the earlier-later relation of the special theory of relativity. (In that theory, 'now' is always 'here-now', and what 'is the case here-now and throughout the absolute past and throughout the absolute future' will not necessarily be the case throughout the whole of space-time; but what also 'is the case throughout the whole absolute past of every bit of the absolute future and throughout the whole absolute future of every bit of the absolute past', *will* be true throughout the whole of space-time. The point-instants that are not here-now but are not absolutely past or future either, are like the persons who are neither taller nor shorter than nor yet identical with the speaker.)[2]

Given this definition, in terms of our basic modalities, of 'omnipersonally', it is possible to state within the system what it is for a given proposition to be a person, or at all events what it is for a given proposition to be an individual (i.e. an object of which it makes sense to say that it is taller or shorter than another object). The first requirement is that for every egocentric proposition q, either the given proposition p omnipersonally implies that q, or it omnipersonally implies that not q. (This is how we state in Egocentric that every individual is either sitting or not sitting, either drinking or not drinking, either smoking or not smoking, etc.) But this criterion alone would not exclude propositions which apply to *no* individual, since these would omnipersonally imply *every* proposition. (The proposition 'Smoking and not smoking', for example, omnipersonally implies every proposition; i.e. 'If I am both smoking and not smoking then p' is true whoever says it, and whatever p may be.) So our second condition – for a proposition to be an individual – must be that it must *not* omnipersonally imply every proposition. Symbolically, if we write Qp for 'p is an individual', we define Q thus:

$$\Box p = p \wedge Gp \wedge Hp \wedge GHp \wedge HGp$$
$$Qp = \forall q(\Box(p \supset q) \vee \Box(p \supset {\sim}q)) \wedge {\sim}\forall q\Box(p \supset q).$$

If we introduce special propositional variables a, b, c, etc. for ps such that Qp, and write $\Box(a \supset p)$ as pa and $\Box(a \supset Fb)$ as Uab, we can

---

[2] Cf. *Past, Present and Future*, Appendix B, Section 5.

reconstruct the ordinary first-order theory of the Tall and the Short within the quasi-modal egocentric system.

3. *Formalism and ontology.* Philosophically, where do we go from here? We *could* turn the tables on the objectors to tense logic by saying that not only are 'instants' not genuine individuals but there are *no* genuine individuals, only certain propositions that can be formally treated *as if* they were individuals. I suspect that there would be fewer takers for this theory than for the theory that instants, or point-instants, *are* genuine individuals; though some of the things that Leibniz said suggest that he did think of a 'monad' as the conjunction of all the propositions that would ordinarily be said to be true of it. I remember, too, C.A. Meredith remarking in 1956 that he thought the only genuine individuals were 'worlds', i.e. propositions expressing total world-states, as in the opening of Wittgenstein's *Tractatus* ('The world is everything that is the case'). Or 'egocentric logic' might be thought of as formalizing the strange remarks that are made about solipsism in the *Tractatus* 5.62–5.6331 ('What the solipsist *means* is quite correct; only it cannot be *said*'. 'I am my world'. 'The subject does not belong to the world: rather, it is a limit of the world').

But why go to extremes, in either direction? The physicists' equation

$$PV = R\theta,$$

relating the pressure, volume, and temperature of a gas, can be used either to raise the temperature of a given volume of gas by increasing the pressure on it, or to increase the pressure it exerts by heating it; there is nothing in the equation that compels us to do either of these rather than the other, or prevents us from sometimes doing one and sometimes the other. Similarly with the philosophical use of the logical equation-form in Section I,

$$f(p_1, p_2, ..., p_n)a = (f'(p_1, p_2, ..., p_n))a.$$

So far as I can see, there is nothing philosophically disreputable in saying that (i) persons just *are* genuine individuals, so that their figuring as individual variables in a first-order theory needs no explaining (*this* first-order theory being, on the contrary, the only way of giving sense to its 'modal' counterpart), whereas (ii) instants are *not* genuine individuals, so that *their* figuring as values of individual variables *does* need explaining, and it is the related 'modal' logic (tense logic) which gives to the first-order theory what sense it has.

What I am propounding here is an alternative to Quine's account of what he calls 'ontological commitment'. The 'entities' which we 'countenance' in our 'ontology' do *not* depend, as Quine says they do, on what kinds of variables we are prepared to bind by quantifiers. They depend on what variables we take seriously as individual variables in a first-order theory, i.e. as subjects of predicates rather than as *assertibilia* which may be qualified by modalities. If we prefer to handle instant-variables, for example, or person-variables, as subjects of predicates, then we may be taken to believe in the existence of instants, or of persons. If, on the other hand, we prefer to treat either of these as *propositional* variables, i.e. as arguments of truth-functions and of modal functions, then we may be taken as *not* believing in the existence of instants, etc. (they don't exist; rather, they are or are not the case). To use another of Quine's phrases, ontological commitment varies inversely with modal involvement.

4. *The two problems of ontology.* This is not the whole story, however. Philosophers worry about 'ontology' for two main reasons. In the first place, they may be worried about the *abstractness* of certain alleged individuals or objects, e.g. instants or events. They are compelled to admit that there certainly are truths which appear to be about such objects, and yet hesitate to say that they really *are* objects in the sense in which things and persons are, or that they 'exist' in the sense in which things and persons do. It is in this context that 'logical grammar', of the sort that we have just been doing, can be helpful; we can show that certain apparent names need not be seriously regarded as names of objects, by producing paraphrases in which such names are dispensed with in favour of other parts of speech, or it may be of whole sentences.

But in the second place, philosophers may be worried about the fact that certain undoubted truths appear to be about objects which, though not in the least abstract, are merely fictitious, or are mere has-beens or will-bes (i.e. they have ceased to exist, or have not yet begun to). Quantification, it seems to me, *is* relevant to *this* worry, but not quite in the way Quine says it is; indeed in almost exactly the opposite way. Quine says in effect that non-existents cannot figure as the values of bound variables; I would suggest that, on the contrary, this is the only way in which non-existents of this sort *can* figure. I cannot directly refer to what does not exist but is merely imagined to exist, or is merely going to exist; but I *can* make purely *general* (i.e. quantified) statements about the imaginary or future denizens of the world. The quantification, however, must occur within a 'modality'. I may, indeed, imagine some real object to be a mermaid; we can then say that there is an x such that x is imagined by me to be a mermaid; but if what is involved is, as we say, a 'merely imagined' mermaid, then we cannot say that *there is an x such that I imagine that x* is a mermaid, but only that *I imagine that there is an x such that x* is a mermaid.[3] Analogously, it may be that some existing person is going to live so long as to rule England in A.D. 3000; more likely, however, the ruler of England at that date does not yet exist, in which case we cannot say that *for some x, it will be the case then that x* rules England, but only that *it will be the case then that for some x, x* rules England.

I want to say, in short, that 'It will be the case that something ϕs' does not entail 'There is something of which it will be the case that it ϕs', i.e. that $F\exists x\phi x \supset \exists xF\phi x$ is not a law. But if we subjoin ordinary quantification theory to the tense logic defined by the theses T7–10 and the rules RG, RH of our first section, we obtain $F\exists x\phi x \supset \exists xF\phi x$ as a theorem. The tense logic thus defined – the system called by E.J. Lemmon K_t – is, however, the weakest that we can obtain if we treat this logic as a by-product of a first-order theory of the earlier-later relation (it is obtainable without assuming *anything* about the character of that relation). Isn't *this*, at last, a sure-fire formal proof that tense logic is *not* a by-product of a first-order theory of the earlier-later relation? It approaches that, I think; but of course its underlying account of the relations between quantification and ontology won't convince everyone. There are always answers.

[3] Cf. G.E. Moore, *Commonplace Book*, pp. 243–5.

XVII
EGOCENTRIC LOGIC

1. *Two ways of locating occurrences in times.* Tensed sentences such as 'Brown is ill', 'Brown has been ill' and 'Brown will be ill', have the peculiarity of being true at some times and false at others. This has led some logicians to say that such sentences do not express genuine propositions but merely *predicates*, which can be thought of as *characterising* the times or instants 'at' which they would ordinarily be said to be true. We can at all events embed the propositions or quasi-propositions of a tensed language within a first-order theory of the earlier-later relation between instants, in ways which may be illustrated as follows:

1. That *Brown is ill* is the case at the instant a
= 2. a is a Brown-being-ill-ish instant

and

3. That *Brown has been ill* is the case at the instant a
= 4. a is a Brown-having-been-ill-ish instant
= 5. a is later than some Brown-being-ill-ish instant
= 6. Some instant earlier than a is a Brown-being-ill-ish one.

In stating these equivalences we employ an exterior untensed language which would be formalised as a first-order theory of the earlier-later relation between instants, and an (italicised) interior tensed language which might nowadays be formalised by means of a quasi-modal logic with prefixes such as 'It has been the case that' functioning in the way that 'It is possible that' does in modal logic proper. In passing from 1. to 2., or from 3. to 4., we replaced a tensed sentence ('Brown is ill' or 'Brown has been ill') by a predicate of instants ('Brown-being-ill-ish' or 'Brown-having-been-illish'); in passing from 4. to 5. we define the predicate 'Brown-having-been-illish' in terms of the simple 'Brown-being-illish' and the earlier-later relation, but still retain a wording which represents what we are reporting as the characterisation of the instant a; and in moving from 5. to 6. we show that what has been thus represented is 'really' a characterisation of a different instant.

7.   That *Brown will be ill* is the case at the instant *a*

can obviously be subjected to a similar series of transformations.

In our exterior tenseless language we assume that we have some way of referring to individual instants. In the interior tensed language no such instants are explicitly mentioned, but when we say the plain 'Brown is ill' it is understood what is being implicitly characterised as Brown-being-ill-ish is the (unmentioned) *time of utterance*, and when we say 'Brown has been ill' or 'It has been the case that Brown is ill' it is understood that it is again the time of utterance that is being characterised as a Brown-having-been-ill-ish one, and that to represent the time of utterance as being thus characterised is a way of saying that some time earlier than that one is plain Brown-being-ill-ish.

Consider now a more complex case:

8.   That *Brown will have been ill* is the case at the instant *a* =
9.   *a* is a Brown-going-to-have-been-ill-ish instant =
10.   *a* is earlier than some Brown-having-been-ill-ish instant =
11.   Some instant later than *a* is a Brown-having-been-ill-ish one =
12.   Some instant later than *a* is later than some Brown-being-ill-ish one =
13.   Some instant later than *a* has some earlier instant which is Brown-being-ill-ish.

We may also note that

11. = 14. Some instant later than *a* is one at which *Brown has been ill* is the case; and
13. = 15. Some instant later than *a* has some earlier instant at which *Brown is ill* is the case.

It is clear that although the interior tensed language *mentions* no instants there is a sense in which it *implicitly refers* to the time of utterance, and by tensing what is implicitly said of the time of utterance it can indirectly characterise other times also, though these are referred to rather indefinitely.

If tenses are formed by attaching prefixes like 'It has been the case that' to the present tense, or to a complex with a present tense 'kernel', it is not always true to say that what is in the present tense is understood as a characterisation of the time of utterance; rather, it characterises whatever time we are taken to by the series of prefixes. The *presentness* of an event, we may say, is simply the *occurrence* of the event, and that is simply the event itself. But every complete tensed sentence characterises the time of utterance in some way or other, and other times only through their relation to that one.

2. *Two ways of locating properties in individuals.* If I say, not 'Brown is ill' but 'I am ill', the truth of this depends not only on when it is said but on who says it. It has been suggested, e.g. by Donald Davidson,[1] that just as the former dependence has not prevented the development of a systematic logic of tenses, so the latter should not prevent the development of a systematic logic of personal pronouns. But the machinery of tenses is in some ways very different from that of personal pronouns, and to bring out both the similarities and the differences I shall invent a stylised logical language, which I shall call Egocentric, in which properties *are* located in individuals in the same way as events are located in times by means of tenses.

In at least the most elementary tensed languages, as we have seen, instants or times are not mentioned, but tensed propositions are understood as directly or indirectly characterising the *un*mentioned time of utterance. So in Egocentric, individuals must not be directly mentioned, but the propositions of Egocentric will be understood as directly or indirectly characterising the speaker. The propositions of Egocentric will in fact be subject-less predicates of common speech, and I shall represent them by participles, i.e. things like 'Standing', 'Sitting', 'Drinking' will be sentences of Egocentric, and on their own will mean what is ordinarily meant by 'I am standing', 'I am sitting', etc. We do sometimes use a language like this in subordinate clauses, as when we say 'I remember *being* at the meeting' (or 'I remember *having been* at the meeting') for 'I remember *that I was* at the meeting'.[2] So, formally, we have

16.   *Standing* is the case with *a*
= 17. 'I am standing' is true when said by *a*

---

[1] Donald Davidson, 'Truth and Meaning', *Synthese*, Vol. 17 (Sept. 1967).
[2] My attention was drawn to this suggestive way of talking by a lecture by Miss J. Rountree.

= 18. *a* is standing.

To obtain oblique predications analogous to past and future tenses, we must find some relation between individuals which we can exploit in the way that tensed languages exploit the earlier-later relation between instants. Any relation which holds directly or indirectly between all individuals will do, but for simplicity's sake I shall assume with Leibniz that all individuals are arranged in a scale of comparative perfection, and use the form 'Inferior-to-standing' or 'Someone-more-perfect standing' to mean that I am less perfect than someone who is standing, i.e. that someone more perfect than me is standing. That is, we have the equivalences

19. *Inferior-to-standing* (or *Someone-more-perfect standing*) is the case with *a*
= 20. 'I am inferior to someone standing' (or 'Someone more perfect than me is standing') is true when said by *a*
= 21. *a* is inferior to someone standing
= 22. Someone more perfect than *a* is standing.

The form 'Superior-to-standing' or 'Someone-less-perfect standing' is similarly understood. Here we have an exterior language, without the modalities 'Inferior-to-' and 'Superior-to-', in which individuals are mentioned in the normal way, which could be formalised as a first-order theory of the relation of comparative perfection between individuals; and an interior language (Egocentric) in which reference to individuals is achieved by those modalities which take us to and from the speaker. In passing from 19. to 21. the Egocentric *proposition* 'Inferior-to-standing' is replaced by the *predicate* 'inferior to someone standing', and in passing from 21. to 22. we see that what 21. represents as a characterisation of the speaker is what might be more straightforwardly represented as a simpler characterisation of someone else.

   In a more complicated case, we have

23. *Inferior to superior to standing* (or *Someone-more-perfect someone-less-perfect standing*) is the case with *a*
= 24. 'I am inferior to someone superior to someone standing' (or 'Someone more perfect than me has someone less perfect than him standing') is true when said by *a*

= 25. *a* is inferior to someone superior to someone standing
= 26. Someone more perfect than *a* (say *b*) has someone less perfect than him (i.e. than *b*) who is standing.

We may note also that

25. = 27. *a* is inferior to someone with whom *Superior-to-standing* (or *Someone-less-perfect standing*) is the case
= 28. *a* is inferior to someone who can say truly 'Someone less perfect than me is standing'; and

26. = 29. Someone more perfect than *a* (say *b*) has someone less perfect than him (i.e. than *b*) with whom *Standing* is the case
= 30. Someone less perfect than *a* (say *b*) has someone less perfect than him who can say truly 'I am standing'.

It is not true to say that such a form as 'Standing' is always understood as characterising the speaker; rather, it characterises whatever individual we are taken to by the series of prefixes. But every Egocentric sentence characterises the speaker in some way or other, and characterises other individuals only through their relation to the speaker.

3. *Derivation of other modes of temporal reference within tense logic.* Could Egocentric be an *adequate* language for talking about individuals? On the face of it not, since it has no devices for referring specifically to other individuals than the speaker. But could it be so enlarged, without losing its egocentric character, as to contain such devices?

There is a similar problem about tense logic; could that be so enlarged, without losing its tensed character, as to contain devices for referring to specific times? The answer is that it can, though what devices are available to us depends to some extent on the nature of the time-series. Quite simple devices are available if the series of instants is linear and if each instant has something which is true at that instant only; so to make our illustrations simple we shall adopt these assumptions.[3] We begin with some more equivalences:

[3] For solutions available on other assumptions, see my *Past, Present and Future*, pp. 190–5, and *Papers on Time and Tense* (this volume p. 131, ed.).

31.   That *p*, is the case at the present only
= 32.   *(It is the case that) p, but it has not been the case that p and will not be the case that p.*

(I italicise tensed propositions.) And

33.   That *p*, is the case at one instant only
= 34.   At some time (*p, and it has not been the case that p, and it will not be the case that p*)
= 35.   At some time, 32.
= 36.   *Either* 32. *or it has been the case that* 32. *or it will be the case that* 32.

A proposition of which 36. is true will serve to *identify* a particular instant in tense logic; we may say that an instant *is* such a proposition. Philosophically the most interesting proposition which is true at a given instant only is the conjunction of all the propositions which are then true, but for formal purposes any proposition true at that instant only will do as its tense-logical 'representative'. In what follows, I use *A* for the 'representative' of *a*, *B* for that of *b*, etc.

37.   That *Brown is ill* is the case at *a*
= 38.   At some time (*it is the case that*) both A and *Brown is ill*[4]
= 39.   *Either (both A and Brown is ill) or it has been that (both A and Brown is ill) or it will be that (both A and Brown is ill).*

And finally,

40.   The instant *a* is earlier than the instant *b*
= 41.   That *it will be that B* is the case at *a*
= 42.   At some time, *both A and it will be that B*
= 43.   *Either (both A and it will be that B) or it has been that (both A and it will be that B) or it will be that (both A and it will be that B).*

---

[4] In *Past, Present and Future*: pp. 89–90, and *Papers on Time and Tense* (this volume pp. 128, 142, 216, ed.), I use the equivalent form 'At all times, *if A then Brown is ill*'.

In passing from 31. to 32., from 33. to 36., from 37. to 39. and from 40. to 43., we start with propositions of our untensed 'exterior' language stage by stage to equivalent propositions of our tensed 'interior' language, until the latter encompasses the whole.

4. *Derivation of other modes of individual reference within Egocentric.* We may similarly build up non-egocentric modes of individual reference within Egocentric on the Leibnizian assumptions that individuals form a linear series in the order of their perfection, and that each individual has something which is true of him only, i.e. an egocentric proposition which is true only when *he* says it. Philosophically the most interesting proposition which is true of a given individual only is the conjunction of all the truths that concern him, but for formal purposes any proposition which is true of him only, i.e. any egocentric proposition which is true only when he says it, will do. As Castañeda has nicely put it, each of us can say in Egocentric, 'I am a true proposition and everyone else is a false one'. For example, if I am represented by the proposition *Priorising*, Brown by *Brownising*, etc., I can truly say 'Priorising but not Brownising and not Quinising, etc', i.e. 'I am Prior but I am not Brown and not Quine, etc.' We now have these equivalences:

44.   I alone Priorise =
45.   *Priorising* is the case with me only =
46.   *Priorising but not Inferior-to-Priorising and not Superior-to-Priorising.*

And

47.   Only one individual Priorises =
48.   *Priorising* is the case with only one individual =
49.   It is the case with someone that 46. =
50.   Either it is the case with me, or it is the case with someone more perfect, or it is the case with someone less perfect, that 46. =
51.   *Either 46. or Inferior-to-46. or Superior-to-46.*

Again,

52. Brown is standing =
53. *Standing is the case with Brown* =
54. *Browning and standing* is the case with someone =
55. *Browning and standing* is the case either with me or with someone more perfect or with someone less perfect =
56. *Either (Browning and standing) or Inferior-to-(Browning and standing) or Superior-to-(Browning and standing).*[5]

And finally

57. Brown is less perfect than Quine =
58. *Inferior-to-Quinising is the case with Brown* =
59. *Browning and inferior to Quinising* is the case with someone =
60. *Either (Browning and inferior to Quinising) or Inferior to (Browning and inferior to Quinising) or Superior to (Browning and inferior to Quinising).*

In passing from 44. to 46., from 47. to 51., from 52. to 56., and from 57. to 60. we begin with our ordinary ways of describing individuals, and finish with something in Egocentric. Each of our end-points 46., 51., 56., 60. is in fact an implicit characterisation of *the speaker*. For example,

56. = 61. *I* am either Browning and standing or am less perfect than someone who is doing so or am more perfect than someone who is doing so.

In this way a typical statement about Brown is reduced to one about me, and in a language with no other subject than me this one subject of all that I say can go unmentioned.

5. *Egocentric and the logic of personal pronouns.* Egocentric is not a very promising stylised language for the development of a logic of personal pronouns, since it is distinguished precisely by leaving these out. Nevertheless, some of the problems which do arise in understanding personal pronouns may be illuminated by translating certain English

---

[5] For a modification necessary with less simple assumptions, see *Papers on Time and Tense* (this volume p. 218, ed.).

sentences into Egocentric. H.-N. Castañeda[6] has recently drawn
attention to certain peculiarities of such inferences as

62.   Brown knows that he is ill; therefore he is ill.

This seems at first a simple instance of the valid inferential form '*x*
knows that *p*, therefore *p*'. However as Castañeda points out, the form
of words 'He is ill' is here being used very differently in the premiss and
the conclusion. In the premiss, 'Brown knows that he is ill', the
fragment 'he is ill' expresses Brown's *self*-knowledge, i.e. it expresses
what Brown would himself express by saying '*I* am ill'. The premiss
does not mean the same as 'Brown knows that Brown is ill', for Brown
might know that *he* was ill even if through some unhappy accident he
did not know that he was Brown. In the conclusion, however, we say
'He is ill', not to express any sort of self-knowledge, but just as a short
way of saying that *Brown* is ill. If we used the word 'Self' to mean 'I' in
a sentence on its own and the first sort of 'He' in reporting the self-
knowledge of someone other than the speaker, it would seem that the
inference

63.   Brown knows that self is ill, therefore self is ill

would genuinely be of the form '*x* knows that *p*, therefore *p*', but would
not be valid, since it would mean 'Brown knows that he is ill, therefore *I*
am ill'; whereas the inference

64.   Brown knows that self is ill; therefore Brown is ill

would give the force of the original inference, and would be valid, but
would not be of the form '*x* knows that *p*, therefore *p*'. On the other
hand,

65.   Self knows that self is ill, therefore self is ill,

i.e. 'I know that I am ill, therefore I am ill' would be both valid and of
the form in question. If, now, we translate 63., 64. and 65. into

---

[6] For example, in 'The Logic of Self-Knowledge', *Noûs*, Vol. 1 (1967).

Egocentric (using *Someone p* for *p or inferior-to-p or superior-to-p*), we get

66.   *Someone Brownising and knowing being ill, therefore being ill*
67.   *Someone Brownising and knowing being ill, therefore someone Brownising and being ill*
68.   *Knowing being ill, therefore being ill.*

Here the valid 68. alone is of the form 'Knowing *p*, therefore *p*'; 67. is still not of this form, but its validity is easily derivable from the validity of this form, and the invalid 66. is not of this form at all; in fact, *all* inferences that are *really* of the form 'Knowing *p*, therefore *p*', or of derivable forms, *are* valid when we have got them into this language.

6. *Egocentric as a key to the philosophy of Leibniz.* On the subject of *temporal* reference, the development of the logic of the earlier-later relation as a simple extension of tense logic, i.e. the development of which a simplified form is sketched in Section 3, seems to me much more than a symbolic dodge, for I find myself quite unable to take 'instants' seriously as individual entities; I cannot *understand* 'instants', and the earlier-later relation that is supposed to hold between them, except as logical constructions out of tensed facts. Tense logic is for me, if I may use the phrase, *metaphysically fundamental*, and not just an artificially torn-off fragment of the first-order theory of the earlier-later relation. Egocentric logic is a different matter; I find it hard to believe that individuals really are just propositions of a certain sort, or just 'points of view', or that the real world of individuals is just a logical construction out of such points of view. Nevertheless the fact that we can have a consistent and comprehensive egocentric logic as well as a logic of tenses does suggest that some sort of idealism or relativism is a more defensible philosophical position than it once looked. And in particular, when I drew upon certain elements from the philosophy of Leibniz when working out the details of Egocentric, this was not an arbitrary or accidental choice; it does seem to me that much in the work of that philosopher takes on a new significance when we think of him as a man who would have regarded the 'egocentric' account of the world as 'metaphysically fundamental'. I conclude by mentioning some detailed points which support this suggestion.

(a) For Leibniz, self-knowledge was the starting-point of his understanding of the world. He said, for example: 'Since I conceive that other beings have also the right to say *I*, or that it may be said for them, it is by this means that I conceive what is called substance in general.'[7] The parenthetical 'or that it may be said for them' is worth noting. In relating Egocentric to more 'objective' languages, I have constantly referred to *the speaker*; but no such person is mentioned within Egocentric itself, and the facts which may be stated in Egocentric (e.g. what I remember when I remember *being at the meeting*) might also go *un*stated; e.g. the fact which my pencil would express, if it could think or talk, by saying 'Someone more perfect than me is holding me'.

(b) 'In consulting the notion which I have of every true proposition', Leibniz says in a notorious passage, 'I find that every predicate, necessary or contingent, past, present or future, is comprised in the notion of the subject.'[8] So a subject is a conjunction of predicates, i.e. a compound egocentric *proposition*.

(c) But the most fundamental point is this: In tense-logic the totalities of tensed propositions which are true at different instants fit together into a *system*, so that although the total course of history will be differently described at different times, the description at one time will determine what the descriptions at other times will be. For example, because a certain past totality of truth included the proposition that the Battle of Hastings *is* occurring, the present totality of truth includes the proposition that the Battle of Hastings *was* occurring. Similarly the world as a whole will be differently described by different people using an egocentric language, but how it is described by one person will determine how it is described by another. For example, if *Inferior-to-drinking* or *Someone-more-perfect drinking* is how things are with me, then just *Drinking* ('I am drinking') is how things are with someone more perfect than me; and because *Drinking* is part of the totality of truth that makes up his being, *Someone-more-perfect drinking* is part of the totality that makes up *my* being. This, of course, is the 'pre-established harmony', whereby although 'every soul is as a world apart', yet 'each substance expresses the whole sequence of the universe according to the view or respect which is proper to it'.[9]

---

[7] Cited in Russell's *Philosophy of Leibniz*, p. 215.
[8] *Ibid.*, p. 206.
[9] *Ibid.*, p. 206.

(d) Leibniz notoriously had no place for genuine *relations* between individuals. 'Paternity in David is one thing, and filiation in Solomon is another, but the relation common to both is a merely mental thing.'[10] In Egocentric, two-place predicates like 'is less perfect than' disappear into modalisings of propositions, with one modalising of a proposition in one personal totality requiring an appropriate other modalising in another personal totality.

(e) Leibniz wavered in his egocentricity when talking about God. 'Every soul is a world apart' continues: 'independent of everything else but God', suggesting that *God*'s egocentricity is somehow not egocentric at all. This won't do. I once said that if God did not see the past as past, he would be unaware of the fact at which I am rejoicing when I say 'Thank goodness that's over', but only of the quite ungratifying fact that something is earlier than something else; Mr. Anselm Müller suggested that if these were distinct 'facts' so would be the fact at which I rejoice when I am glad at *having won a bet* and the person-neutral *Someone Priorising and having won a bet* (a conjunction at which I have no particular reason to be pleased); but surely, Müller argued, it is no limitation to God's omniscience that the only fact (of these two) that he can see is the latter. (For God, *having won a bet* is not a fact at all, since not he but I won it.) Well, a person, e.g. Leibniz, who took Egocentric as seriously as I take tenses would have to say that *having won a bet* really *is* a fact which God cannot see as one, just as no one can see a war as being over until it *is* over.[11] But Leibniz seems to try, inconsistently, to put God outside this relativity. McTaggart is a more consistent Leibnizian at this point.

(f) However, there is no reason why there should not be a 'Supreme Monad', i.e. one than which none is more perfect. (McTaggart too seems to admit this.[12]) There is a tense-logic for a time which ends; one of its laws is 'For any p, either it will not be the case that p (because it is already the end of time and nothing "will be the case") or it will be that it will not be the case that p (because it will be that nothing further "will be the case").' An egocentric logic with a Supreme Monad would analogously contain the law 'For any p, either not-inferior-to-p (because

[10] *Ibid.*, p. 207.
[11] Cf. H.-N. Castañeda, 'Omniscience and Indexical Reference', *Journal of Philosophy*, Vol. 64 (April, 1967), pp. 203–10.
[12] See, e.g. *The Nature of Existence*, Vol. II, pp. 182–3.

I am the Supreme Monad) or inferior-to-not-inferior-to-p (because someone more perfect than me is the Supreme Monad)'. This is, in fact, precisely how the existence of a Supreme Monad would have to be stated in Egocentric.

Egocentric is also relevant to some more modern philosophising. I am never quite sure what is being affirmed or denied when people debate the possibility of a private language; but there is surely *some* sense of 'private language' in which Egocentric is one, although it is a language in which we can quite effectively communicate with one another because of the correspondences mentioned above under (c). Moreover, it offers a consistent development of the view that no one is directly acquainted with, or can directly talk about, any 'particular' but himself; our derivation, in Section 4, of ordinary ways of speaking with egocentric ones suggests how something like a common world *can* be built up from essentially private experience. Egocentric logic could also be exploited in defence of the Wittgensteinian thesis (if it is one) that 'I am in pain' has a different logical form from 'Brown is in pain'.

7. *Modality, quantification and individuality in Peirce.* There are also hints of some of the above lines of thought in C.S. Peirce.

(a) Peirce has a persistent habit of treating quantification as a special sort of modality, and quantification over individuals as a special sort of quantification over states of affairs, rather than *vice versa*. We encounter this subsumption of individuals under 'worlds', for example, in one of his expositions of his 'logical graphs', in which conjunction is expressed by juxtaposition and negation by bracketing, i.e. he uses AB for 'A and B' and '(A)' for 'Not A'. We can read such diagrams, he says, in two ways. In the simplest way we take them to relate to 'a single state of the universe, like the present instant'. This is in effect how current tense-logic proceeds. But we may also read an unmodified proposition as meaning 'that it is sometimes or possibly true', so that the compound AB signifies that A and B are each of them 'at some quasi-instant true', and (A) that A is true at no quasi-instant. Peirce then enriches the symbolism, taken this second way, not with names of particular states of affairs or instants, but with 'lines of identity', so that A-B means that A is true at some instant and B at *the same* instant ('Simultaneously A and B'), or that they are true in *the same* possible state of affairs, i.e. that they are 'compossible'. Peirce then says – and this is, for our present purpose, the 'punch line' – that 'our quasi-instants may be individuals', in which special case his second reading equates A with 'Something is A', (A) with 'Nothing is A', AB with 'Something is A and something is B', A-B with 'Something is both A and B' and so on.[13]

(b) Elsewhere Peirce suggests that individual terms are just general terms with a particular special feature. 'Individuals are either identical or mutually exclusive, and cannot intersect or be subordinated to one another as classes can'. 'The logical atom, or term not capable of logical division, must be one of which every predicate may be universally affirmed or denied. For example, let A be such a term. Then if it is neither true that all A is X nor that no A is X, it must be that some A is X and some A is not X, and therefore A may be divided into A that is X and A that is not X, which is contrary to its nature as a logical atom.'[14] This reduces the relation of a predicate to its subject, to a relation of a predicate to another predicate of a particular sort; and predicates are notoriously, for Peirce, just slightly damaged propositions,[15] so we have our own theory. And as to the particular feature of 'atomic' terms which Peirce singles out, it is like saying in tense-logic that if the tensed proposition A is an *instant*, then for any X, either A at all times implies X or A at all times implies not X; this is in fact provable in linear tense-logic when 'instant' and 'always' (i.e. 'not sometimes not') are defined as in our 32. and 36. above.[16] Similarly it should result from adequate egocentric definitions of 'individual' and of 'everyone' that if A-ing is an individual or individuating proposition, then for any X, either it is true of everyone that (his) A-ing implies (his) X-ing, or it is true of everyone that (his) A-ing implies (his) not X-ing; e.g. either everyone who Brownises is ill or everyone who Brownises is not ill.[17]

(c) After giving this account of a 'logical atom', Peirce goes on immediately to say that 'such a term can be realised neither in thought nor in sense', and that 'absolute individuality is merely ideal'. Not that we cannot guarantee terms that satisfy the condition of atomicity just mentioned, for any *empty* term will satisfy it trivially (if there are no As,

---

[13] C.S. Peirce, *Collected Papers*, 4.376, 385. For a formal system based on these diagrams, see J. Jay Zeman, 'A System of implicit quantification', *Journal of Symbolic Logic*, Vol. 32 (Dec. 1967), pp. 480–504.

[14] *Ibid.*, 3.92–3.

[15] *Ibid.*, 2.344, 4.572.

[16] Cf. *Past, Present and Future*, p. 83.

[17] Cf. *Papers on Time and Tense* (this volume, p. 218 ff., ed.).

then *both* all *A*s are *X* and no *A*s are *X*, whatever *X* may be); but non-emptiness is another condition of individuality, and we cannot guarantee that there are any terms that satisfy this and Peirce's condition as well. At all events, it is possible to produce a modal theory of possible-world-propositions, a tense-logical theory of instant-propositions, or an egocentric theory of individual-propositions, which does not assume that any actual proposition satisfies the definition of an individual or instant or state-of-the-world. I conclude by sketching a simple calculus of this sort, in three versions.

8. *A calculus of worlds (instants, individuals).* We use the symbols $\supset$, $\wedge$, v, $\sim$, $\equiv$ for 'if', 'and', 'or', 'not', 'iff', and use $\Box p$ for 'Everywhere p' and $\Diamond p$ ($= \sim\Box\sim p$) for 'Somewhere p', with the S5 laws:

RL: If $\vdash \alpha$ then $\vdash \Box\alpha$
L1. $\Box(p \supset q) \supset (\Box p \supset \Box q)$
L2. $\Box p \supset p$
L3. $\sim\Box p \supset \Box\sim\Box p$.

For 'p is an individual' (or an instant, or a possible total world-state) we write Qp. If we have propositional quantifiers, we can define Qp thus:

$$Qp = \Diamond p \wedge \forall q(\Box(p \supset q) v \Box(p \supset \sim q))$$

(Peirce's definition above, with the added conjunct $\Diamond p$ to exclude mere impossibilities). Using this, we can derive in quantified S5 the following:

Q1. $Qp \supset \Diamond p$
Q2. $Qp \supset (\Box(p \supset q) v \Box(p \supset \sim q))$
Q3. $Qp \supset \Box Qp$
Q4. $\Box(p \supset q) \supset (\Box(q \supset p) \supset (Qp \supset Qq))$.

Alternatively we may do without quantifiers and take Q as undefined with Q1–4 as its characteristic axioms. They are independent (to prove this for Q1 let $Q = \sim\Diamond$; for Q2, let $Q = \Diamond$; for Q3, let $Q\alpha = Q\alpha \wedge \alpha$; for Q4 – I owe this to Mr. K. Fine – use I for perfect identity, k for some constant, and read $Q\alpha$ as $Q\alpha \wedge I\alpha k$.) We can, however, replace Q1 plus Q4 by the one axiom $\Box(p \supset q) \supset (\Box(q \supset p) \supset (Qp \supset \Box Qq))$ (also due to K. Fine). If we just add propositional quantifiers with the usual rules, we cannot prove from this basis

Q5. $\Diamond p \supset (\forall q(\Box(p \supset q) \lor \Box(p \supset \sim q)) \supset Qp)$

(proof of independence: let $\Box\alpha = \alpha$ and $Q\alpha = \sim(\alpha \supset \alpha)$; K. Fine), which with Q1 and Q2 would be equivalent to the definition of Q in $\forall$ and $\Box$. But I do not know of any *quantifier-free* consequence of Q1–5 which does not also follow from Q1–4. For example, from Q1–4 we can prove $Qp \supset (\Box(p \supset q) \equiv \sim\Box(p \supset \sim q))$, $\Diamond Qp \supset Qp$, $QQp \supset (Qq \equiv \Box q)$ and $QQp \supset (q \equiv \Box q)$ (i.e. if Qp is itself a world, instant or individual, there is only one such).

If we use $O\,p$ for $\forall q\,(\Box(p \supset q) \lor \Box(p \supset \sim q))$, i.e. for the 'L-completeness' which worlds (instants, individuals) share with impossibilities, we can define O in a Q-primitive system as $\sim\Diamond p \lor Qp$, while in an O-primitive system we could define Qp as $\Diamond p \land Op$ and axiomatise by

O1. $\Box\sim p \supset Op$
O2. $Op \supset (\Box(p \supset q) \lor \Box(p \supset \sim q))$
O3. $Op \supset \Box Op$
O4. $\Box(p \supset q) \supset (Oq \supset Op)$

(where O1 is independent by $O\alpha = \sim(\alpha \supset \alpha)$ (J.T. Canty), O2 by $O\alpha = \alpha \supset \alpha$ (Canty), O3 by $O\alpha = \Box\sim\alpha \lor (\alpha \land O\alpha)$; O4 as Q4; but O3 + O4 may be replaced by $\Box(p \supset q) \supset (Oq \supset \Box Op)$). These are equivalent to Q1–4, and are to

O5. $(\forall q\,(\Box(p \supset q) \lor \Box(p \supset \sim q))) \supset Op$

as those are to Q5.

We can also axiomatise in W, where $Wp = p \land Qp$ $(p \land Op)$, meaning that p is the *actual* world, the *present* instant, the individual that I am. Q would be definable in this system as $\Diamond W$, and O in terms of Q as before. For axioms (yielding an equivalent system) we need only

W1. $Wp \supset p$
W2. $Wp \supset (q \supset \Box(p \supset q))$
W3. $\Box(p \supset q) \supset (\Box(q \supset p) \supset (Wp \supset Wq))$

(where W1 is independent by $W = \Box\sim$; W2 by $W\alpha = \alpha$ (Canty); W3 as Q4). These are to

W4. $\quad p \supset (\forall q(q \supset \Box(p \supset q)) \supset Wq)$

as Q1–4 (O1–4) are to Q5 (O5).

One formula which does not follow from W1–3 (Q1–5; O1–5) is

W5. $\quad \exists pWp \; (= Q6. \; \exists p(p \wedge Qp) = O6. \; \exists p(p \wedge Op))$

asserting that there is an actual world (present instant, individual that I am). Indeed, even $\exists pQp$ is not derivable from this basis, though $O(p \wedge \sim p)$, and so $\exists pOp$, follows easily enough from O1 and $\Box\sim(p \wedge \sim p)$. There is, certainly, no *finite* model satisfying W1–4 (Q1–5; O1–5) which would refute W5 (Q6; O6), since we can prove for any string of variables $p, q, r...$ the thesis

$$p \supset (q \supset (r \supset (...\exists s(s \wedge \Box(s \supset p) \wedge \Box(s \supset q) \wedge \Box(s \supset r)...))),$$

i.e. given any finite list of truths we can find a truth (namely their conjunction) which everywhere (always, necessarily) implies them all; and if these and their consequences were all the truths there are, their conjunction would satisfy the definition of W and so W1–4. But with an infinity of truths there might be no such conjunction. (To refute the weaker $\exists pQp$ we need only suppose that things are *always* like this.) There is perhaps a criticism of Descartes to be drawn from this. From 'I am thinking', i.e. 'Thinking' (p), egocentric logic does enable us to infer 'Thinking somewhere' $(\Diamond p)$, but not 'Thinking in some *individual*' $(\exists q(Qq \wedge \Box(q \supset p)))$, at least not unless 'There is an individual that I am' (Q6) is laid down as a special axiom.

When W5 (Q6; O6) is added to W1–3 (Q1–4; O1–4), it becomes possible to prove W4 (Q5; O5). In W the proof is

1.	p	[assumption]
2.	$\forall q(q \supset \Box(p \supset q))$	[assumption]
3.	Wr	[W5]
4.	r	[3, W1]

5.	$\Box(p \supset r)$	[2, 4]
6.	$\Box(r \supset p)$	[3, W2, 1]
7.	Wp	[5, 6, W3]

The addition of the weaker $\exists p Q p$ to Q1–4 (O1–4; W1–3) does not yield Q5 (O5; W4). (For independence, let n be the actual world and read $Q\alpha$ as $\Box(\alpha \equiv n)$; K. Fine.) But I do not know of any *quantifier-free* consequence of Q1–4 (O1–4; W1–3) with even the stronger W5 (Q6; O6) added which does not follow from the Q1–4 (O1–4; W1–3) alone; it would seem that the actual existence of worlds (instants, individuals) cannot be reflected in a postulate of the unquantified system.

XVIII
WORLDS, TIMES AND SELVES

1.1. We may axiomatise the modal system S5 by subjoining to all tautologies the special axiom-schema

A1. $\Box\alpha \supset \alpha$

and to the rule of detachment (*modus ponens*) the special rule

RL: $\vdash \alpha \supset \beta \rightarrow \vdash \alpha \supset \Box\beta$,

for every α that is 'fully modalised' (i.e. each of its propositional variables falls within the scope of some occurrence of $\Box$). $\Diamond$ ('possibly') is defined as $\sim\Box\sim$ ('Not necessarily not'). That these postulates yield exactly S5 was shown by Lemmon.[1]

1.2. It is well known that S5 may be interpreted as a fragment of ordinary predicate calculus. To make this interpretation obvious, we may construct the relevant fragment of predicate calculus as follows: We employ a single individual variable x, and an unlimited set of predicate variables p, q, r, etc. If φ is any predicate variable, φx is a well-formed formula. If α and β are well-formed formulae, so are $\alpha \supset \beta$, $\alpha \vee \beta$, $\alpha \wedge \beta$, $\alpha \equiv \beta$, $\sim\alpha$, $\Box x\alpha$ and $\Diamond x\alpha$. $\Box x\alpha$ is read as 'For all x, α' and $\Diamond x\alpha$ as 'For some x, α'. Typical well-formed formulae are

> px, meaning 'x is p'
> $\sim px$, meaning 'x is not p'
> $px \supset qx$, meaning 'If x is p then x is q'
> $\Box xpx$, meaning 'Everything is p'
> $\Box x(px \supset qx)$, meaning 'Everything that is p is q'.

---

[1] E.J. Lemmon, 'Alternative Postulate-Sets for Lewis's S5', *Journal of Symbolic Logic*, vol. 21, No. 4 (Dec. 1956), p. 347.

We may axiomatise the system by subjoining to all tautologies the axiom schema

A1′. $\Box x \alpha \supset \alpha$

and to the rule of detachment the rule

RL′: $\vdash \alpha \supset \beta \rightarrow \vdash \alpha \supset \Box x \beta$,

for every α in which x is not free. $\Diamond x$ is defined as $\sim\!\Box x\!\sim$. We may call this the uniform monadic first-order predicate calculus. It is a system in which we can make statements that are either about everything (where x is bound), or about a particular privileged individual x (where x is free). There may be other individuals, but only this one can be referred to individually. It is clear that in this calculus the symbol x is not really needed, but can be omitted as understood throughout. If we thus erase it, we may then read

> p as 'x is p'
> $\sim\!p$ as 'x is not p'
> $p \supset q$ as 'If x is p then x is q'
> $\Box p$ as 'Everything is p'

and so on. And when thus re-written, the system simply becomes S5 as previously formulated.

1.3. Just what is going on here? What, in other words, do I mean by calling this an 'interpretation' of S5? In the first instance, just this: I have the symbolic calculus described in 1.1. Where did it come from? In fact, of course, it came from an attempt to set out symbolically the logic of necessity and possibility. But I could have obtained exactly the same symbolic calculus in quite a different way, namely by taking a certain fragment of predicate calculus, i.e. of the logic of 'all' and 'some', and symbolising it a little curiously – first writing p, q, r, etc. instead of f, g, h, etc. for predicates (what's so sacred about the shapes f, g, h, after all?), and $\Box x$ instead of $\forall x$ for the universal quantifier (what's so sacred about the shape $\forall$, after all?); and then deleting all occurrences of the name-variable x, which in this fragment of the predicate calculus I can safely do because no other name-variables occur. And then, behold, I have precisely the calculus described in 1.1.

2.1. These are, to be sure, *different* ways of arriving at the calculus described in 1.1. To introduce p, q, r, etc. as variables standing for propositions is one thing, to introduce them as variables standing for predicates is quite another thing; and again, to introduce $\square$ as a constant meaning 'necessarily' is one thing, and to introduce it as a constant meaning 'For all –' is quite another thing. *Quite* another thing? Suppose I arrive at the calculus by the procedure of 1.2, only I don't let my xs stand for any old individuals but for individuals of a very special sort, namely possible states of affairs or 'worlds'; the privileged individual represented by the one variable x when free being the *actual* world. Similarly, I don't let my ps, qs etc. stand for any old predicates but for predicates of the type '... has the proposition that p true in it'; i.e. px means 'The world x has the proposition that p is true in it', i.e. 'It is the case in the world x that p' (a predicate eminently suitable for this sort of subject). Then px, with x free, will mean 'It is the case in the actual world that p', i.e. 'It actually is the case that p', i.e. 'It *is* the case that p'; i.e. p. And $\square xpx$ will mean 'Every possible world has p true in it', i.e. 'It is the case in every possible world that p'; and this, according to Leibniz, is precisely what we mean when we say 'Necessarily p'.

2.2. So the original, normal or standard interpretation of the calculus sketched in 1.1, i.e. the interpretation of it as a logic of necessity and possibility, can be presented as just a special case of the interpretation of it as a mildly odd formulation of the uniform monadic lower predicate calculus. It *can* be so presented. But do we illuminate the subject of modal logic by so presenting it? To this I want to say, No; or at all events, Not much. It is, if you like, formally but not materially illuminating to present modal logic thus. The metatheory of predicate calculus is more fully understood than that of modal logic, so that the presentation of the latter as a special case of the former enables certain transfers of information to take place. But possible worlds, in the sense of possible states of affairs, are not *really* individuals (just as numbers are not *really* individuals). To say that a state of affairs obtains is just to say that something is the case; to say that something is a possible state of affairs is just to say that something could be the case; and to say that something is the case 'in' a possible state of affairs is just to say that the thing in question would necessarily be the case if that state of affairs obtained, i.e. if something else were the case. That is, the proper logical form of the statement that it is true in the state of affairs p and q, is just: 'Necessarily if p then q', $\Box(p \supset q)$. We understand 'truth in states of affairs' because we understand 'necessarily'; not *vice versa*.

2.3. Further, if what is 'really meant' by 'Grass is green' is 'The actual world is grass-being-green-ish', what this in turn 'really means' will have to be 'The actual world is the-actual-world-being-grass-is-green-ish-ish', and so on *ad infinitum*. Certainly to be the case is to be the case in the actual world; but this equivalence does not give the meaning of being the case, but rather of the phrase 'in the actual world'. To be the case in a possible world is to be possibly the case; to be the case in an imagined world is to be imagined to be the case; to be the case in a former world is to have been the case; and to be the case in the actual world is just – to be the case. (Cf. Ramsey on truth.) Here again it is the straight-forwardly modal calculus of 1.1, without the xs, that brings out the structure of the facts, and when the xs of the calculus of 1.2 are brought into modal logic as names of possible worlds, they are merely obfuscating. To use a distinction I once heard Quine insisting upon, what we have in the calculus of 1.2 may be a *model* for modal logic, but it is not an *interpretation* of the modal words.

3.1. Another special use of the calculus of 1.2 (the uniform monadic first-order predicate calculus) would be this: I don't let my xs stand for any old individuals, but neither do I let them stand for such recondite individuals as possible words; I let them stand, rather, for individuals of a *fairly* special sort, namely times or instants, the privileged individual represented by the one variable x when free being the *present* instant. Similarly I don't let my ps, qs, etc. stand for any old predicates but for predicates of the type '... has the proposition p true at it'; i.e. px means 'The instant x has the proposition p true at it', i.e. 'It is the case at the instant x that p'. The 'propositions' here referred to will of course have to be of such a sort that at least some of them will be the case at some instants but not at others; i.e. propositions like 'Nixon is President' and 'Johnson was President'. I call these 'tensed' propositions. The plain px will now mean 'The present instant is a p-ish one', i.e. 'It is the case at the present instant that p', i.e. 'It is now the case that p', i.e. 'It *is* the case that p'. $\Box xpx$ will mean 'Every instant is a p-ish one', i.e. 'It is the case at every instant that p', i.e. 'It is always the case that p', or for short 'p always'. $\Diamond xpx$ will mean 'At least one instant is a p-ish one', i.e. 'It is the case at some instant that p', i.e. 'p at some time'.

3.2. If, having given the xs this interpretation, we now drop them, again obtaining the calculus of 1.1, i.e. S5, this latter will now be read as a fragment of the logic of tensed propositions. In this, what 'is the case at the present instant' is simply what is the case, as contrasted with what has been or will be the case, what 'is the case at some instant' is what is or has been or will be the case, this complex of tenses being abridged to the simple modifier $\Diamond$. In a richer logic of tensed propositions we would of course have symbols for the separate components of this complex, say F for 'It will be that' and P for 'It has been that', and this richer tense logic could also be presented, formally, as a result of deletions from a first-order theory; but it would have to be from a richer theory than the uniform monadic first-order predicate calculus. I shall not go into the details of this, except to say that this richer first-order theory could still be one in which only a single *free* variable occurs, though others would have to occur as bound.

3.3. Given this interpretation of the calculi of 1.1 and 1.2, which is now the more metaphysically illuminating of the two – the calculus with xs, or the one without? Here too I want to say 'The one without'; but here, perhaps, I am swimming against a stronger stream. I think I know what I mean when I say 'Some things are not the case but merely have been or will be the case', better than I know what I mean when I say 'Some things are not the case at this instant but only at earlier or later ones', and certainly better than I know what I mean when I say 'This instant is not p-ish but some earlier or later ones are'. And I understand 'p for ever' better than 'p at all instants'. I take instants, in short, with the same grain of salt as I take possible worlds.

4.1. Logicians have tended to welcome the presentation of modal logic as an artificially truncated bit of predicate calculus because we know all about predicate calculus, or at all events know an enormous lot about it, whereas modality is a comparatively obscure and unfamiliar field. And even philosophically, it might be said, it is in general pretty clear what is going on in predicate calculus, but not very clear what is going on in modal logic, or even in tense logic. It is not as simple as this. What we can do with first-order predicate logic *in toto* is indeed plain enough; but its uniform monadic fragment? Formally, this fragment is no doubt of some interest; for example, unlike the full first-order predicate calculus, it is decidable. But what is its *philosophical* interest? That question, I think, partly boils down to this one: What would a *philosophically* privileged individual be? And to this question, modal logic and tense logic possibly provide an answer. It is not that modal logic or tense logic is an artificially truncated uniform monadic first-order predicate calculus; the latter, rather, is an artificially expanded modal logic or tense logic. We treat the propositions of modal logic or tense logic as if they were predicates; invent subjects for them, calling these 'possible worlds' or 'times'; make the strong modal or tense operator a universal quantifier, and the weak one a particular quantifier, binding variables standing for these quasi-individuals; the 'privileged' quasi-individual represented by the free variable being a kind of zero attachment to its proposition, so that 'It is the case with the privileged quasi-individual (i.e. in the actual world, at the present time) that *p*' amounts to the plain *p*. If modal logic or tense logic is 'blown up' in this way, what we get is uniform monadic first-order predicate calculus; that is what this calculus 'really is'.

4.2. Or let us say more circumspectly, those are two things that uniform monadic predicate calculus *could* be. There is also a less recondite possibility. In any language with the normal stock of personal pronouns, there is at least one individual with 'privileges' that are perhaps of philosophical interest, namely the speaker. In other words, what the free *x*s in the calculus of 1.2 might stand for is simply: 'I'. It is arguable, epistemologically, that this is in fact the only individual that any speaker is ever in a position to refer to directly or specifically; all the rest must figure both in his language and his thought as mere 'something-or-others', variously qualified. Or to put it another way, it is arguable that 'I' is the only 'logical proper name' in the Russellian sense of that phrase. If this is so, the use of a predicate calculus with only one name variable occurring free has some philosophical interest and justification.

4.3. Is 'I' in fact the only Russellian individual name? What's wrong with 'this', for example? One argument against 'this', which I owe to Dr. A.J.P. Kenny, could be stated as follows: If 'this' is a logically proper name, then when we say 'This is red', for example, we are simply ascribing redness to a certain individual object without otherwise describing that object in any way. Hence if we say 'This is red' on two different occasions, indicating the same object both times, we are *saying the same thing* on the two occasions. But we may indicate the same object on two occasions without knowing we are doing so; hence we may say the same thing on two occasions without knowing we are doing so, and this seems a little strange, certainly if we know what we are saying on each occasion and remember the first occasion on the second one. Dr. Kenny drew from this argument the conclusion that if there are any logical proper names in the Russellian sense, they can only name momentary objects. As I don't believe in momentary objects, this conclusion, if established by Kenny's argument, would on my view entail that there are no logical proper names in the Russellian sense. However, the indicator 'I' does not seem to me open to Kenny's objection; if I say 'I am in pain' on two different occasions, I cannot but know what object I am indicating, and cannot but know that I am indicating the same object on the two occasions, and therefore (since each time what I ascribe to the object is being in pain) that I am saying the same thing on the two occasions. But so far as I can see, 'I' is the only indicator that is not open to Dr. Kenny's objection.

4.4. So the uniform monadic first-order predicate calculus makes some sense, or has some *rationale*, if we take its one individual variable when free to indicate the speaker, i.e. to do duty for the first person pronoun. But we have seen that where only a single individual variable is used, that variable can be dropped from the calculus without any loss of intelligibility or necessary alteration in its meaning. So we have now a new interpretation of the calculus without the xs, i.e. of S5. We can read the axiom $\Box p \supset p$ as 'If everything is p then I am p'; p ($\Diamond p$ as 'If I am p then something is p'; and the more complicated S5 law

$$\Box(p \supset \Box q) \supset (\Diamond p \supset q),$$

being a contraction of

$$\Box x(px \supset \Box xqx) \supset (\Diamond xpx \supset qx),$$

will mean 'If everything is such that if it is p then everything is q, then if something is p, I am q', i.e. 'If everything could truly say "If I am p then everything is q", then if something could truly say "I am p", then I can truly say, "I am q".'

4.5. Is this last move – dropping the xs from the calculus of 1.2 when this is 'egocentrically' interpreted – just a formal dodge, or has it also some philosophical significance? I am inclined to think it is just a formal dodge; but it *could* have some philosophical significance, as there are philosophers who are as sceptical about pure egos, and perhaps about individuals generally, as I am about possible worlds and about temporal instants, and such philosophers might well argue that if 'I' is the only logically proper name then indeed there are no logically proper names, since 'I' is not in reality a name of any sort, and is an entirely dispensable expression. I do not wish to develop this point of view in any great detail, but one might sketch it thus: Statements like 'I am in pain', 'I am tall', might be less misleadingly expressed as 'It is hurting', 'The ground is a long way off'. In the former, the 'it' is no more a genuine subject than in 'It is raining', and in fact elementary propositions do not need subjects; the assumption that they do reflects an erroneous 'thing-quality' or 'substance-accident' metaphysic. Of course it is one thing for me to be hurt and another for you to be hurt – your pain is not my pain. But it is a 'remote' pain of mine in the sense in which a former pain or a possible pain is a remote pain, though the 'removal' is in a different direction. Your pain is not what I mean by 'It hurts', but 'It hurts you' is a modality of 'It hurts' in the sense in which 'It could hurt' and 'It did hurt' are modalities of 'It hurts'.

4.6. Of course your pain *is* what *you* mean by 'It hurts', just as my former pain is what I formerly meant, and my possible pain is what I might have meant, by 'It hurts'. But I cannot speak truly for you, any more than I can speak truly today as if it were yesterday. And in this 'I'-less yet egocentric language, *who* is speaking is determined by what is said. Each person is identified by a set of propositions which describe the world as it is from his point of view, i.e. by the set of propositions which are true when said by him; by any single proposition which is true *only* when said by him.

5.1. Whether or not we collapse our language about individuals from that of 1.2 to that of 1.1, and whether or not we regard such a collapsing as a metaphysically significant move, it seems true that each speaker or thinker is himself the only individual he can identify with any assurance, and the rest are, as I said before, mere 'Somethings' variously qualified. It is these 'qualifications' which I now want to examine. We may be aware, for example, not merely that something, but that something that is *p*, is *q*. How to symbolise this is obvious; using the *x*s, we render it as ◊*x(px* ∧ *qx)*, 'For some *x*, *x* is both *p* and *q*'. Without the *x*s, we have ◊*(p* ∧ *q)*, 'Somewhere *p* and *q* together', which we may compare with 'Possibly *p* and *q* together', i.e. '*p* and *q* are compatible', and 'At some time *p* and *q* together', i.e. '*p* and *q* simultaneously'.

5.2. We can also say, still more specifically, '*The* thing which is *p* is *q*', and '*q* at *the* time at which *p*', and perhaps also '*q* in *the* possible state of affairs in which *p*'. This, however, is more than can be symbolised in the uniform monadic predicate calculus; it needs at least two individual variables and the dyadic predicate of identity, *I*. Given these, we can render 'The thing which is *p* is *q*' as the conjunction of 'Something which is *p* is *q*' and 'There is exactly one thing which is *p*'. The latter comes out as ◊*x*□*y(py* ≡ *Iyx)*, 'For some *x*, for all *y*, *y* is *p* if and only if it is identical with *x*', i.e. 'There is an individual with which everything that is *p* is identical'. No additional *free* variables, however, are needed for this, and we would not even need extra bound ones if we introduced 'For exactly one *x*, ...' as a special undefined mode of binding variables. We could write it as *Qx*, so that *Qxpx* would mean 'Exactly one thing is *p*', and '*The* thing which is *p* is *q*' could be written as *Qxpx* ∧ □*x(px* ⊃ *qx)*, 'Exactly one thing is *p*, and everything that is *p* is *q*'. If we do enrich the uniform monadic first-order predicate calculus with this special quantifier *Q*, it will have to have its own special postulates, and it is now known what these must be, namely a set which I gave (without *x*s).[2] My conjecture that these were sufficient has since been verified, independently, by D. Kaplan, K. Fine and R.A. Bull.

5.3. We could also symbolise 'The (one and only) thing that is *p* is *q*' directly, say as *Txpxqx*. Here *Tx* is a quantifier which forms a sentence not from one but from two following sentences. *Qx*α could then be defined as *Tx*αα, 'Exactly one thing satisfies α' being logically equivalent to 'The one and only thing that satisfies α satisfies α'. This is

---

[2] This volume, Chapter XVII.

a bit like developing ordinary quantification theory with formal implication rather than the universal or existential quantifier as a primitive. We could use, say, $Fx\alpha\beta$ for 'For all x, if α then β', and define $\Box x\alpha$ as $FxFx\alpha\alpha\alpha$, 'For all x, α' being equivalent to 'For all x, α is implied by "For all x, if α then α"'. Dropping the xs, S5 necessity can be similarly defined in terms of strict implication, $\Box\alpha$ as $FF\alpha\alpha\alpha$; systems of this sort are discussed elsewhere.[3] That 'the' might be represented by an analogous 'dyadic quantifier' has already been suggested;[4] to this suggestion we may now add that within the single-name-variable fragment of predicate calculus that variable can be dropped from Q or T as well as from $\Box$ or F, and we have the same varied possibilities of interpretation. That is, we can read Tpq either as 'The thing that is p is q', or as 'In the state of affairs in which p, it is the case that q', or as 'At the instant at which p, it is the case that q'; the word 'the' being understood in each case as conveying uniqueness, i.e. Tpq is false if nothing or more than one thing is p, or if p is the case in no state of affairs or in several, or at no instant or at several.

6.1. For the function $T\alpha\beta$ I shall now set up postulates. I shall omit xs, as they are only in the way, and therefore subjoin the postulates to any sufficient set for the modal system S5. And as our calculus is purely propositional, it will be convenient to use axioms with substitution for variables, rather than schemata. The axioms are as follows:

T1. $Tpq \supset \sim\Box\sim p$; [i.e. $Tpq \supset \Diamond p$]
T2. $Tpq \supset (Tpr \lor Tp\sim r)$
T3. $Tpq \supset \Box Tpq$
T4. $Tpq \supset (p \supset q)$
T5. $\Box(p \equiv q) \supset (Tpp \supset Tqp)$

T1 asserts that if the thing that is p is q then something is p; or that if it is the case in the state of affairs at which p that q, then possibly p; or that if it is the case at the instant at which p that q, then at some time p. Its independence may be shown by reading $T\alpha\beta$ as $\Box\sim\alpha$. This turns

[3] C.A. Meredith and A.N. Prior, 'Investigations into Implicational S5', *Zeitschrift für Mathematische Logik*, vol. 10, No. 3 (1964), pp. 203–20.
[4] A.N. Prior, 'Is the Concept of Referential Opacity Really Necessary?', *Acta Philosophica Fennica*, fasc. 16 (1963), pp. 189–200.

T2–5, but not T1, into theses of S5. T2 asserts that if the thing that is p is q (and so, if there is such a thing as the thing that is p), then either the thing that is p is r, or the thing that is p is not r; or that if anything is the case in the one state of affairs in which p, then either it is the case in that state of affairs that r or it is the case in it that not r; or similarly with instants. The independence of T2 may be shown by reading $T\alpha\beta$ as $\Box(\alpha \wedge \beta)$. T3 asserts that if the thing that is p is q then it is true of everything that the thing that is p is q; and analogously. If it is understood that variables are 'modalised' by falling within the scope of a T as well as by falling within the scope of a $\Box$, T3 may be dropped as an axiom and derived by applying RL of 1.1 to $Tpq \supset Tpq$. Its independence, otherwise, may be shown by reading $T\alpha\beta$ as $\alpha \wedge \beta$ (which does not modalise). That T3 remains independent even when T4 is strengthened to $Tpq \supset \Box(p \supset q)$ (which is proved below, from the present basis, as T7), may be shown by reading $T\alpha\beta$ as $\alpha \wedge T\alpha\beta$, the interpreting T being normal. T4 asserts that if the thing that is p is q, then if I am p I am q; or that if it is the case in the world in which p that q, then if it is actually the case that p it is actually the case that q; or that if it is the case at the time at which p that q, then if it is the case now that p it is the case now that q. Its independence may be shown by reading $T\alpha\beta$ as $\Diamond(\alpha \wedge \beta)$. T5 asserts that if exactly the same objects as are p are q, then if the thing that is p is p so is the thing that is q; or, etc. Its independence may be shown if we use I for perfect identity, k for some constant proposition, and read $T\alpha\beta$ as if it were $T\alpha\beta \wedge Iak$. For consistency, read $T\alpha\beta$ as $\alpha \wedge \beta$ and $\Box\alpha$ as α; all the postulates (including the S5 ones) then become propositional-calculus theses. My remaining sections will be occupied with deductions from these postulates (and, at the end, from one other).

6.2. I begin by showing the sufficiency of these postulates by deriving from them the postulates for Q, whose sufficiency is known. I shall assume laws and rules of S5 without proof.

T6. $\Box Tpq \supset (\Box(p \supset q))$ [T4, $\vdash (\alpha \supset \beta) \rightarrow$
                                               $\vdash \Box\alpha \supset \Box\beta$]

T7. $Tpq \supset \Box(p \supset q)$ [T3, T6]

T8. $Tpq \supset (\Box(p \supset r) \vee (\Box(p \supset \sim r)))$ [T2, T7]

T9. $\sim Tp\sim p$ [T7,$\Box((p \supset \sim p) \supset \Box \sim p)$,T1]

T10. *Tpq ⊃ Tpp*   [T2 r/p, T9]
T11. *☐(p ≡ q) ⊃ (Tpp ⊃ Tqq)*   [T5, T10]
T12. *☐(p ⊃ q) ⊃ (Tpp ⊃ Tpq)*
Proof:
1.   *☐(p ⊃ q)*   [assumption]
2.   *Tpp*   [assumption]
3.   *Tp~q ⊃ ☐~p*   [T7, 1]
4.   *~Tp~q*   [T1, 3]
5.   *Tpq*   [2, T2, 4]

Defining *Qα* as *Tαα*, we now have

T13. *Qp ⊃ ◊p*   [T1 q/p, Df.*Q*]
T14. *Qp ⊃ (☐(p ⊃ q) ⊃ ☐(p ⊃ ~q))*   [T8 q/p, r/q, Df.*Q*]
T15. *Qp ⊃ ☐Qp*   [T3 p/q, Df.*Q*]
T16. *☐(p ≡ q) ⊃ (Qp ⊃ Qq)*   [T11, Df.*Q*]
T17. *Tpq ≡ (Qp ∧ ☐(p ⊃ q))*   [T10, Df.*Q*, T7,
                                                      T12, Df.*Q*]

Here T13–16 are the axioms Q1–4 given in a previous chapter,[5] and T17
corresponds to the definition of *Tαβ*, in a *Q*-primitive system, as *Qα ∧
☐(α ⊃ β)*.

6.3. Some further theses that are of some interest are the following:

T18. *☐(p ⊃ q) ⊃ (Trp ⊃ Trq)*
Proof:
1.   *☐(p ⊃ q)*   [assumption]
2.   *Trp*   [assumption]
3.   *☐(r ⊃ p)*   [2, T7]
4.   *☐(r ⊃ q)*   [1, 3]
5.   *Trr*   [2, T10]
6.   *Trq*   [4, 5, T12]

T19. *☐(p ≡ q) ⊃ (Tpr ⊃ Tqr)*
Proof:
1.   *☐(p ≡ q)*   [assumption]

---

[5] This volume, Chapter XVII.

2.	Tpr	[assumption]
3.	Tpp	[2, T10]
4.	Tqp	[1, 3, T5]
5.	Tqq	[4, T10]
6.	$\Box(q \supset r)$	[2, T7, 1]
7.	Tqr	[5, 6, T12]

T20.	$\Box(p \equiv q) \supset (Tpr \equiv Tqr)$	[T19, $\Box(p \equiv q) \equiv$ $\Box(q \equiv p)$]
T21.	$\Box(p \equiv q) \supset (Trp \equiv Trq)$	[T18, T18 p/q, q/p].

T20 and T21 show that necessarily (universally, permanently) equivalent formulae may replace one another both as first arguments and as second arguments of T. Note also that T5 is a substitution instance (r/p) of T19, which could therefore replace it as an axiom. On the other hand T19 does not *have to* replace T5 as an axiom; given the rest of the system, the apparently weaker T5 yields the apparently stronger T19, as well as *vice versa*. In this T5 is like certain formulae discussed by Sobociński,[6] and by Łukasiewicz.[7]

It would have been possible (though less elegant) to replace axiom T1 by the pair T9 ($\sim Tp \sim p$) and T12 ($\Box(p \supset q) \supset (Tpp \supset Tpq)$). When these are added to T2–5, independence of T9 may be shown by reading $T\alpha\beta$ and $\Box \sim \alpha$; and of T12 by reading $T\alpha\beta$ as $\alpha \equiv \beta$ and $\Box\alpha$ as α. (The latter as well as the former could be used, with the original axiomatisation, to show the independence of T1.) T10 having been proved from T2 and T9 as in the last section, T1 comes from T9 and T12 by this proof *ad absurdum*:

1.	Tpq	[assumption]
2.	$\Box \sim p$	[assumption]
3.	$\Box(p \supset \sim p)$	[2]
4.	Tpp	[1, T10]
5.	$Tp \sim p$	[3, 4, T12],

---

[6] P. 208 in B. Sobociński, 'An Axiom-System for (K_t, N)-Propositional Calculus Related to Simons' Axiomatization of S3', *Notre Dame Journal of Formal Logic*, vol. 3, No. 3 (July 1962), pp. 206–8.

[7] J. Łukasiewicz, *Z zagadnien logiki i filozofii*, Warszawa (1961), pp. 168–70.

contradicting T9. With this axiomatisation, T12 is related to T18 as T5 to T19.

7.1. Suppose we use the special variables a, b, c, etc. for those propositions which are true of exactly one individual (in exactly one world; at exactly one time). We may substitute these for the more general propositional variables p, q, r, etc. in theses but not *vice versa*; and in general if a and b are propositions of this special sort, $\sim a$, $a \supset b$, $\Box a$ and Tab will not be, so that such formulae will not be substitutable in theses for the special variables, though they will be substitutable for ordinary propositional variables. For the special variables we now lay down a single special axiom, namely

T22. *Taa* (i.e. *Qa*)

Adding this to T1–5, the following theses are now provable:

T23.	$\sim\Box\sim a$	[T22, T1]
T24.	$Ta\sim p \supset (Tap \supset \Box\sim a)$	[T7, $\Box(p \supset q) \supset$
		$(\Box(p \supset \sim q) \supset \Box\sim p)]$
T25.	$Ta\sim p \supset \sim Tap$	[T24, T23]
T26.	$\sim Tap \supset Ta\sim p$	[T22, T2]

T27. $Tp(q \supset r) \supset (Tpq \supset Tpr)$
Proof:

1.	$Tp(q \supset r)$	[assumption]
2.	Tpq	[assumption]
3.	$\Box(p \supset (q \supset r))$	[1, T7]
4.	$\Box(p \supset q)$	[2, T7]
5.	$\Box(p \supset r)$	[3, 4]
6.	Tpp	[2, T10]
7.	Tpr	[5, 6, T12]

T28.	$Tp(q \wedge r) \supset Tpq$	[T18]
T29.	$Tp(q \wedge r) \supset Tpr$	[T18]
T30.	$Tp(q \wedge r) \supset (Tpq \wedge Tpr)$	[T28, T29]
T31.	$Ta(p \wedge \sim q) \supset (Tap \wedge \sim Taq)$	[T30, T25]
T32.	$\sim(Tap \wedge \sim Taq) \supset \sim Ta(p \wedge \sim q)$	[T31, transp.]
T33.	$(Tap \supset Taq) \supset \sim Ta(p \wedge \sim q)$	[T32, $\sim(p \wedge \sim q) = p \supset q$]

T34. $(Tap \supset Taq) \supset Ta{\sim}(p \wedge {\sim}q)$ [T33, T26]
T35. $(Tap \supset Taq) \supset Ta(p \supset q)$ [T34, ${\sim}(p \wedge {\sim}q)$
                                                   $= p \supset q$, T21]
T36. $Ta{\sim}p \equiv {\sim}Taq$ [T25, T26]
T37. $Ta(p \supset q) \equiv (Tap \supset Taq)$ [T27, T35].

T36 and T37 are theses which figure prominently in theories about 'truth at an instant', or 'truth in a world'.[8] And the form $Ta\alpha$ may indeed be read as 'It is true in world a that α', or 'It is true at the instant a that α', if we follow the suggestion made in 2.2 that to be the case in a world or at an instant is to be the case when something else is the case, a given 'world' or 'instant' being now identified with a proposition of a particular sort, a 'state-description'.

7.2. The suggestion of 2.2 that to be true at or in a given state is to be necessarily or permanently implied by that state, is supported by the following deduction:

T39. $\Box(p \supset q) \supset (\Box(p \supset {\sim}q) \supset \Box{\sim}p)$ [S5]
T40. $\Box(a \supset p) \supset {\sim}\Box(a \supset {\sim}p)$ [T39, T23]
T41. $\Box(a \supset p) \supset {\sim}Ta{\sim}p$ [T40, T7]
T42. $\Box(a \supset p) \supset Tap$ [T41, T26]
T43. $Tap \equiv \Box(a \supset p)$ [T7, T42].

Note, however, that we cannot prove the more general $Tpq \equiv \Box(p \supset q)$. For independence of this, read $T\alpha\beta$ as $\alpha \wedge \beta$, $\Box\alpha$ as α, and let the special variables be restricted to tautologies. All theses of our system will then become tautologies, but $Tpq \equiv \Box(p \supset q)$ will become $(p \wedge q) \equiv (p \supset q)$, which is not one, being false when p is false. And even on the normally intended interpretation, 'Anything that is p is q' ($\Box(p \supset q)$) will be true, and 'The one and only thing that is p is q' will be false, if nothing is p. However, it is only where there is such a thing as 'the thing that is p' that propositions of the form 'The thing that is p is q' are of much interest, and in those cases, as T43 indicates, 'The thing that is p' *is* equivalent to 'Anything that is p', $T\alpha\beta$ to $\Box(\alpha \supset \beta)$. So dropping $T\alpha\beta$ in favour of $\Box(\alpha \supset \beta)$, and leaving the individualising to be done by the special variables, is a move with something to be said for it. If we

[8] This volume, Chapter XI.

do this, replacing T by $\square(\dots\supset\dots)$ throughout our formulae the axioms T3–5 and T22 will all become theses of S5, but not T1 and T2. These last could be replaced by T23 ($\sim\square\sim a$) and T26 in the form $\square(a \supset p) \lor \square(a \supset \sim p)$, laid down as special axioms for the as. Or we could use T36 in the form $\square(a \supset \sim p) \equiv \sim\square(a \supset p)$, or $\sim\square(a \supset \sim p) \equiv \square(a \supset p)$, or $\Diamond(a \land p) \equiv \square(a \supset p)$, as a single special axiom for the as. Or more clumsily, we could use T1 and T2 themselves, with p replaced throughout by a, as special axioms for the as. Whichever we do, we obtain all of T1–T43, either as they stand (thus T3–7, T10–12, T15–43) or with p replaced by a (thus the rest), and in some cases when T is replaced by $\square(\dots\supset\dots)$ we can replace a by one of the unrestricted variables, say s (thus T22, T24, and of course T42 and T43). Consistency of the system may be shown by reading $\square\alpha$ as α and confining as to tautologies, and if we axiomatise with T23 ($\sim\square\sim a$) and T26 ($\square(a \supset p) \lor \square(a \supset \sim p)$), independence of the latter may be shown by reading $\square$ normally and confining as to tautologies, and of the former by reading $\square$ normally and confining as to contradictions.

XIX
TENSE LOGIC FOR
NON-PERMANENT EXISTENTS

1. *Tense logic, earlier-later logic, and modal logic.* By a 'tense logic' I mean a calculus in which the variables p, q, r, etc. stand for 'propositions' which may be true or false at different times, and in which the usual two-valued truth-functions $p \supset q$, $p \vee q$, $p \wedge q$, $p \equiv q$, $\sim p$, etc. are supplemented by the two forms Fp for 'It will be the case that p' and Pp for 'It has been the case that p'. The forms Gp, for 'It will always be the case that p', and Hp, for 'It has always been the case that p', are generally taken to be definable in terms of the others as $\sim F \sim p$ and $\sim P \sim p$ respectively.

It is sometimes argued that the 'propositions' of such a system are not properly so described, being in fact *predicates* of instants, its characteristic functors being used not to form propositions from propositions but to form predicates from predicates. We might use the variables a, b, c, etc. to stand for instants, and say that the theses of tense logic are all to be understood as predicable of any arbitrary instant a. We then write pa for 'a is a p-ish instant' or 'The pseudo-proposition p is true at the instant a', and read $(Fp)a$, $(Pp)a$, $(p \supset q)a$, and $(\sim p)a$ similarly. If we use $\Rightarrow$, $\neg$, and & for truth functors of which the arguments are genuine propositions, and $\exists a$ for an existential quantifier binding instant-variables, we might define our principal predicate-formers as follows:

$$
\begin{aligned}
(p \supset q)a &= (pa \Rightarrow qa) \\
(\sim p)a &= \neg pa \\
(Fp)a &= \exists b(Uab \,\&\, pa) \\
(Pp)a &= \exists b(Uba \,\&\, pa),
\end{aligned}
$$

where U is a two-place predicate which may be read informally as '... is earlier than ...'. The last two definitions assert that 'It is true at a that it will be the case that p' and 'It is true at a that it has been the case that p' respectively mean that p is true at some instant later, and that it is true at some instant earlier, than a.

If we incorporate these definitions in an appropriate first-order theory, we may prove that certain tense-logical theses are predicable of ('true at') any arbitrary instant a. E.J. Lemmon has found that the tense-logical theses which have this property are precisely those which are derivable by substitution, detachment, and the rules

$$\vdash \alpha \to \vdash {\sim}F{\sim}\alpha, \qquad\qquad \vdash \alpha \to \vdash {\sim}P{\sim}\alpha,$$

from some basis for propositional calculus and the four further axioms

1.1. ${\sim}F{\sim}(p \supset q) \supset (Fp \supset Fq)$
1.2. ${\sim}P{\sim}(p \supset q) \supset (Pp \supset Pq)$
2.1. $F{\sim}P{\sim}p \supset p$
2.2. $P{\sim}F{\sim}p \supset p$.

The tense logic defined by these postulates he called K_t. If certain conditions are imposed on the relation U, richer tense logics are obtainable (as predicable of an arbitrary instant a). For example, if we impose on U the following three conditions:

$Uab \supset (Ubc \supset Uac)$	(transitivity)
$Uab \supset (Uac \supset (Ubc \vee Ucb \vee b{=}c))$	(non-branching in the future)
$Uba \supset (Uca \supset (Ubc \vee Ucb \vee b{=}c))$	(non-branching in the past),

we may prove (as predicable of any arbitrary a) all the theses (and only the theses) of the tense logic obtained by adding to K_t the three further axioms

3. $FFp \supset Fp$
4. $PFp \supset (p \vee Fp \vee Pp)$
5. $FPp \supset (p \vee Fp \vee Pp)$.

In this strengthened system, if we define $\Diamond p$ as $(p \vee Fp \vee Pp)$, we obtain for this $\Diamond$ the modal logic S5, which Lemmon[1] has shown to be the system obtainable by subjoining to propositional calculus, with

[1] E.J. Lemmon, 'Alternative Postulate-sets for Lewis's S5', *Journal of Symbolic Logic*, Vol. 21, No. 4 (December 1956), pp. 347–9.

substitution and detachment, the axiom

$$p \supset \Diamond p$$

and the rule (call it RCM)

$\vdash \alpha \supset \beta \rightarrow \vdash \Diamond \alpha \supset \beta$, if every variable in α falls within the scope of an $\Diamond$.

(Lemmon proves this for slightly different postulates, the equivalence of which to these ones is obvious.)

2. *Modification of modal logic for contingent existents.* If we adopt a rather different view of tense logic from that sketched in the previous section and treat its 'propositions' as being just as properly so-called as those of the earlier-later calculus, it is possible to derive the latter from tense logic rather than vice versa. Moreover, if the postulates of the 'minimal' tense logic K_t are treated not as by-products of definitions in a first-order theory but as substantial assumptions, it is intelligible to question their truth. This is done, for example, in Chapter VIII of *Past, Present and Future*. The detailed arguments need not be reproduced here, but their upshot is as follows: when we introduce individual name-variables, and predicates attaching to them, it is arguable that before and after an individual x exists there are no such propositions as ϕx (though there may be propositions to the effect that there has been or will be *some* individual with such-and-such properties, viz. those of x). That is the way the matter is put by G.E. Moore;[2] I have myself sometimes put it by saying that at the times in question no such proposition is 'statable'. This latter locution has the disadvantage of suggesting that the difficulty here is simply with our mechanisms of reference; I want to say rather that there are no *facts* about x to be stated except when x exists. Moore's terminology, and my own alternative one about 'facts', has the disadvantage of suggesting that there are abstract entities called 'facts' and/or 'propositions' which exist as individuals do. The terminology does not matter, so long as the misleading suggestions are removed.

Formally, this line of argument makes it no longer plausible to

[2] G.E. Moore, 'Necessity', in *Lectures on Philosophy* (1966), pp. 129–31.

identify Gp, 'It will always be the case that p', with the mere $\sim F\sim p$, 'It will never be the case that not p', or H with $\sim P\sim$; and it would seem that although we have the rules

$$\vdash \alpha \rightarrow \vdash \sim F\sim\alpha, \qquad\qquad \vdash \alpha \rightarrow \vdash \sim P\sim\alpha,$$

we do not have

$$\vdash \alpha \rightarrow \vdash G\alpha, \qquad\qquad \vdash \alpha \rightarrow \vdash H\alpha;$$

and conversely, although we have $G(p \supset q) \supset (Fp \supset Fq)$ and its image, we do not have $\sim F\sim(p \supset q) \supset (Fp \supset Fq)$ or its image. And although we have $F\sim P\sim p \supset p$, $FHp \supset p$, and their images, we do not have $\sim G\sim Hp \supset p$, $\sim GP\sim p \supset p$, or their images.

The first problem I wish to pose is simply that of giving postulates for a minimal tense logic which will allow for this complicating factor. But before making a proposal here, I would observe that a partly similar problem arising in modal logic has already been solved. If we have individual name-variables in modal logic, it is arguable that in possible worlds in which the individual x does not figure, no proposition of the form ϕx can figure either, and this makes a difference between $\Box p$, 'Necessarily p', i.e. 'It is the case in all possible worlds that p', and $\sim\Diamond\sim p$, 'Not possibly not-p', i.e. 'It is not the case in any possible world that not-p'. In 1959[3] I gave some postulates which I conjectured would suffice for a modal logic which takes account of this possibility, and in 1964,[4] by drawing upon a result of R.A. Bull,[5] I proved this conjecture correct. The modal logic in question is called Q, and its axiomatization is as follows: beside the ordinary modal form $\Diamond p$, we introduce a form Sp, which may be taken as meaning 'In all possible worlds there is such a proposition as p', and we define $\Box p$ as $Sp \wedge \sim\Diamond\sim p$ (Sp then becomes provably equivalent to $\Box(p \supset p)$). For S we have the rules

[3] A.N. Prior, 'Notes on a Group of New Modal Systems', *Logique et Analyse*, No. 6–7 (Apr. 1959), pp. 122–7.

[4] A.N. Prior, 'Axiomatisations of the Modal Calculus Q', *Notre Dame Journal of Formal Logic*, Vol. 5, No. 3 (July 1964), pp. 215–17.

[5] R.A. Bull, 'An Axiomatisation of Prior's Modal Calculus Q', *ibid.*, pp. 212–14.

RS1. $\vdash S\alpha \supset Sp$, for any p occurring in α
RS2. $\vdash Sp \supset (Sq \supset (\dots \supset S\alpha))$, where $p, q, \dots$ are all the variables in α.

For $\Diamond$ we have the axiom $p \supset \Diamond p$ and the following modification of the rule given in the last section for S5:

RSM: $\vdash (\alpha \supset \beta) \rightarrow \vdash Sp \supset (Sq \supset (\dots \supset (\Diamond \alpha \supset \beta)))$ where all the variables in β fall within the scope of an $\Diamond$ or an S, and $p, q, \dots$ are all the variables in β that are not in α.

In the following sections, by introducing functors analogous to S, I shall propose modified postulates for the minimal tense logic K_t, and prove that if we strengthen this by adding suitable postulates for time's linearity and the transitiveness of the earlier-later relation, and again define $\Diamond p$ as $(p \vee Fp \vee Pp)$, and Sp in terms of the analogous functors, we obtain for this $\Diamond$ the modal system Q.

3. *Revised minimal tense logic.* We introduce, beside F and P, the functors T and Y (from 'tomorrow' and 'yesterday') such that Tp is true if and only if there will always be, and Yp if and only if there always has been, such a proposition as p. For these we need, to begin with, postulates analogous to RS1 and 2, expressing the notion that a complex proposition is 'stable' or 'there' if and only if all of its components are. That is, we have these schemata:

T1.	$\vdash T\alpha \supset Tp$,	where p is any variable in α
T2.	$\vdash Tp \supset (Tq \supset (\dots T\alpha))$,	where $p, q, \dots$ are all the variables in α
Y1.	$\vdash Y\alpha \supset Yp$,	where p is any variable in α
Y2.	$\vdash Yp \supset (Yq \supset (\dots Y\alpha))$,	where $p, q, \dots$ are all the variables in α.

We do not need any special form for 'It is *now* stable that p' or 'There is *now* such a proposition as the proposition that p', since this is tautologous, being itself only stable because p is. (Our whole logic, for this reason, must be developed in terms of what is now stable. To quote from an earlier article, 'Nothing can be surer than that whereof we cannot speak, thereof we must be silent, though it does not follow from this that whereof we could not speak yesterday, thereof we must be silent today'.[6])

For F and P alone we have

PF. $P{\sim}F{\sim}p \supset p$
RF: $\vdash \alpha \rightarrow \vdash {\sim}F{\sim}\alpha$
FP. $F{\sim}P{\sim}p \supset p$
RP: $\vdash \alpha \rightarrow \vdash {\sim}P{\sim}\alpha.$

For the combination of the two types of operators we need at least the following:

Df.G. $Gp = Tp \wedge {\sim}F{\sim}p$
Df.H. $Hp = Yp \wedge {\sim}P{\sim}p$
FT1: $\vdash Tp \supset (Tq \supset (\dots \supset {\sim}F{\sim}(\alpha \supset \beta) \supset (F\alpha \supset F\beta)))$
PY1: $\vdash Yp \supset (Yq \supset (\dots \supset {\sim}P{\sim}(\alpha \supset \beta) \supset (P\alpha \supset P\beta)))$,

where p, q, ... are all the variables in β that are not in α.

We need more than this, but before laying down further postulates we had better clarify some ambiguities in the forms Tp and Yp. Remember that we are at this stage trying to set up a *minimal* system, in which it is not assumed, for example, that time is infinite both ways, or that it is strictly linear. Consequently we must give a sense to Tp in the case in which we are at the end of time and there is *no* future, and also in the case in which we stand at a cross-roads and there is no such thing as *the* future but only a number of *alternative* futures, and similarly for Yp and the past. It is most convenient to use the Boolean 'always', making Tp vacuously true if there is no future; and in the matter of branching, it is convenient to take Tp as meaning that p will be statable throughout *all possible* futures; and analogously with Yp. Fp is simply false if there is no future, and true if it will be the case in *some* possible future that p; and Pp analogously.

Given this interpretation of our operators, we may consider various candidates for theses. $Tp \supset FTp$ is obviously excluded, since at the last moment of time, if there were one, Tp would be vacuously true and FTp

---

[6] A.N. Prior, 'Thank Goodness That's Over', *Philosophy*, Vol. 34, No. 128 (Jan. 1959), pp. 11–17.

false. The converse $FTp \supset Tp$ would be vacuously *true* (because of the falsehood of its antecedent and the truth of its consequent) at the end of time; but with a branching future it could be false if p were of the form ϕx and x might or might not be going to exist for ever, for this would mean that Tp is true in some possible futures (giving us FTp) but not in all (depriving us of the consequent Tp). If, on the other hand, there is only one future, $FTp \supset Tp$ is a reasonable thesis if we exclude the possibility that x, which must exist now for p $(= \phi x)$ to be now stable, may go out of existence and then start to exist again, this time for ever. (The realization of this possibility *would* give us FTp without Tp, even in linear time.) So we might wish to have $FTp \supset Tp$ in a calculus for linear time, though not in a minimal one. And even *without* excluding the possibility of intermittent existence,[7] we would have in linear time the weaker thesis $F(Tp \wedge Yp) \supset Tp$.

Consider now the pair $Tp \supset PTp$, $PTp \supset Tp$. There seems nothing to be said for the former, on any hypothesis; if x now exists for the first time, but will exist from now on, we have $T\phi x$ but not $PT\phi x$. On the other hand, $PTp \supset Tp$ seems certainly valid. Even with branching time, if it was true in some possible past that p would be stable throughout all futures then possible, it must be stable throughout all futures now possible.

Similar considerations apply to the group $Yp \supset PYp$, $PYp \supset Yp$, $Yp \supset FYp$, $FYp \supset Yp$.

In sum, we have the following two postulates to add to the basis set out above:

FY. $FYp \supset Yp$
PT. $PTp \supset Tp$.

This whole system, subjoined to propositional calculus with substitution and detachment, I shall call QK_t. It clearly collapses to K_t if we add the postulates $\vdash Tp$, $\vdash Yp$, or define both forms as $p \supset p$.

4. *Deductions in* QK_t. Examples of the schemata FT1 and PY1 include the following pair:

---

[7] For a discussion of this possibility, see *Analysis* Problem No. 11, in *Analysis*, Vol. 17, No. 6 (June 1957).

1. $\sim F \sim((p \wedge q) \supset p) \supset (F(p \wedge q) \supset Fp)$
2. $\sim P \sim((p \wedge q) \supset p) \supset (P(p \wedge q) \supset Pp).$

(Here, there are *no* variables in β that are not in α.) From $(p \wedge q) \supset p$, RF and 1, and from $(p \wedge q) \supset p$, RP and 2, we obtain

6. $F(p \wedge q) \supset Fp$
7. $P(p \wedge q) \supset Pp.$

(Numbers 3, 4, and 5 are already attached to some theses in Section 1, to which we shall later be returning.) For a more complicated proof, we have the following:

8. $\sim F \sim (\sim((p \supset q) \supset q) \supset \sim p)$ [RF applied to
                                                                   $\sim((p \supset q) \supset q) \supset \sim p$,
                                                                   a transposition of
                                                                   $p \supset ((p \supset q) \supset q)]$
9. $F \sim ((p \supset q) \supset q) \supset F \sim p$ [8, FT1]
10. $\sim F \sim p \supset \sim F \sim ((p \supset q) \supset q)$ [9, $(p \supset q) \supset (\sim q \supset \sim p)$]
11. $\sim F \sim p \supset (F(p \supset q) \supset Fq)$ [10, FT1]
12. $F \sim\sim p \supset Fp$ [$\sim\sim p \supset p$, RF, FT1]
13. $\sim Fp \supset \sim F \sim\sim p$ [12, $(p \supset q) \supset (\sim q \supset \sim p)$]
14. $\sim Fp \supset (F(\sim p \supset q) \supset Fq)$ [13, 11 $p/\sim p$]
15. $F(\sim p \supset q) \supset (\sim Fp \supset Fq)$ [14,
                                                                   $(p \supset (q \supset r)) \supset (q \supset (p \supset r))$]
16. $F(p \vee q) \supset (Fp \vee Fq)$ [15, p.c.]
17. $P(p \vee q) \supset (Pp \vee Pq)$ [analogously].

The converses of 16 and 17, however, are not theorems. The basic reason is that the formulae

$\sim F \sim (p \supset (p \vee q)) \supset (Fp \supset F(p \vee q)),$
$\sim P \sim (p \supset (p \vee q)) \supset (Pp \supset P(p \vee q))$

are not instances of FT1 and PY1 unless they are respectively preceded by '$Tq \supset$' and '$Yq \supset$'; hence we cannot use them (with RF, RP, and $p \supset (p \vee q)$) to prove $Fp \supset Fp \vee q)$, $Pp \supset P(p \vee q)$; we can only obtain $Tq \supset (Fp \supset F(p \vee q))$ and $Yq \supset (Pq \supset P(p \vee q))$. (A counterexample to the simple $Pp \supset P(p \vee q)$ would be 'If it has been that God alone exists, then it has been that either God alone exists or I don't exist'; here the antecedent, on the Christian hypothesis is true, but there is only such a proposition as 'Either God alone exists or I don't exist' when I do exist, both its disjuncts being then false, so this disjunction has never been true.)

However, FT1 and PY1 do enable us to lay down the simple

18. $\sim F\sim(\alpha \supset \beta) \supset (F\alpha \supset F\beta)$
19. $\sim P\sim(\alpha \supset \beta) \supset (P\alpha \supset P\beta)$

for all those αs and βs which contain the same variables. For such cases, therefore, we can deduce

20. $F\alpha \supset F(\alpha \vee \beta)$ $\qquad\qquad$ $[p \supset (p \vee q),$ RF, 18]
21. $F\beta \supset F(\alpha \vee \beta)$ $\qquad\qquad$ $[q \supset (p \vee q),$ RF, 18]
22. $(F\alpha \vee F\beta) \supset F(\alpha \vee \beta)$ $\qquad$ $[20, 21, (p \supset r) \supset$
$\qquad\qquad\qquad\qquad\qquad\qquad ((q \supset r) \supset ((p \vee q) \supset r))].$

(We also have $(P\alpha \vee P\beta) \supset P(\alpha \vee \beta)$ analogously from 19.) With this restriction, in fact, 18 and 19, with RF and RP, yield the rules

RFC: $\vdash \alpha \supset \beta \rightarrow \vdash F\alpha \supset F\beta$
RPC: $\vdash \alpha \supset \beta \rightarrow \vdash P\alpha \supset P\beta.$

If we now introduce the form $\Diamond p$ as an abbreviation for $p \vee Fp \vee Pp$, we may immediately prove the rule

RM: $\vdash \alpha \rightarrow \vdash \sim\Diamond\sim\alpha.$

For the consequent of this amounts to $\vdash \sim(\sim\alpha \vee F\sim\alpha \vee P\sim\alpha)$, which by de Morgan equates to $\vdash (\sim\sim\alpha \wedge \sim F\sim\alpha \wedge \sim P\sim\alpha)$, and we may prove each conjunct of this by $p \supset \sim\sim p$, RF, and RP. Again, for αs and βs which contain the same variables we have

23. $\sim\Diamond\sim(\alpha \supset \beta) \supset (\Diamond\alpha \supset \Diamond\beta),$

that is

$\sim(\sim(\alpha \supset \beta) \vee F\sim(\alpha \supset \beta) \vee P\sim(\alpha \supset \beta)) \supset$

$$((\alpha \vee F\alpha \vee P\alpha) \supset (\beta \vee F\beta \vee P\beta))$$

i.e. by de Morgan

$$((\alpha \supset \beta) \wedge \sim F\sim(\alpha \supset \beta) \wedge \sim P\sim(\alpha \supset \beta)) \supset$$
$$((\alpha \vee F\alpha \vee P\alpha) \supset (\beta \vee F\beta \vee P\beta)).$$

This is of the form $(\alpha \wedge \beta \wedge \gamma) \supset ((\delta \vee \varepsilon \vee \xi) \supset (\phi \vee \psi \vee \chi))$, where we have $\alpha \supset (\delta \supset \phi)$ (by $(p \supset q) \supset (p \supset q)$), $\beta \supset (\varepsilon \supset \psi)$ (by 18) and $\gamma \supset (\xi \supset \chi)$ (by 19), and we have from p.c.

$$(p \supset (q \supset r)) \supset ((s \supset (t \supset u)) \supset ((v \supset (w \supset x)) \supset$$
$$((p \wedge s \wedge v) \supset ((q \vee t \vee w) \supset (r \vee u \vee x))))).$$

From RM and 23 (where α and β have the same variables) we obtain the rule (with the same restriction)

RMC: $\vdash \alpha \supset \beta \rightarrow \vdash \Diamond\alpha \supset \Diamond\beta$.

This rule is freely used throughout the following series of proofs, where none of the theses contains more than one distinct variable:

24.	$p \supset \Diamond p$	$[= p \supset (p \vee Fp \vee Pp)$, from p.c.]
25.	$F\sim(p \vee Fp \vee Pp) \supset$	
	$F(\sim p \wedge \sim Fp \wedge \sim Pp)$	[de Morgan, RFC]
26.	$F\sim(p \vee Fp \vee Pp) \supset F\sim Pp$	[25, 6]
27.	$F\sim \Diamond p \supset F\sim Pp$	[26, Df. $\Diamond$]
28.	$P\sim\sim p \supset Pp$	[$\sim\sim p \supset p$, RPC]
29.	$\sim Pp \supset \sim P\sim\sim p$	[28, $(p \supset q) \supset (\sim q \supset \sim p)$]
30.	$F\sim Pp \supset F\sim P\sim\sim p$	[29, RFC]
31.	$F\sim \Diamond p \supset \sim p$	[27, 30, FP]
32.	$P\sim \Diamond p \supset \sim p$	[analogously]
33.	$\sim \Diamond p \supset \sim p$	[24, $(p \supset q) \supset (\sim q \supset \sim p)$]
34.	$(\sim \Diamond p \vee F\sim \Diamond p \vee P\sim \Diamond p) \supset \sim p$	[33, 31, 32, p.c.]
35.	$\Diamond\sim \Diamond p \supset \sim p$	[34, Df. $\Diamond$].

We also have, without any restrictions on α and β, the following schema:

SM. $Sp \supset (Sq \supset \ldots \supset (\sim\Diamond\sim(\alpha \supset \beta) \supset (\Diamond\alpha \ldots \Diamond\beta)))$, where p, q, $\ldots$
are all the variables in β that are not in α.

For given that $Sp = Tp \wedge Yp$, we may prove this from FT1 and PY1 by
the same steps that were used in proving 23 from 18 and 19, but with
added antecedents. And from this we may prove

36. $\Diamond(p \vee q) \supset (\Diamond p \vee \Diamond q)$

by steps analogous to those used in proving 16 and 17 from FT1 and
PT1.

Further, the definition of S, and the p.c. laws of $\supset$ and $\wedge$, obviously
take us from T1 and Y1 to RS1, and from T2 and Y2 to RS2.

5. *Deductions in* QK_t *with added assumptions.* I now want to consider
what further theses, particularly of a 'modal' sort, are obtainable when
we add to K_t the postulates 3, 4, and 5 of Section 1, for the transitivity
of the earlier-later relation and the linearity of time. We may note first
that from 3 $(FFp \supset Fp)$ and QK_t we may deduce the mirror-image of 3,
i.e.

37. $PPp \supset Pp$.

Lemmon noticed that this was deducible from 3 given K_t and the proofs
go through in QK_t also (basically because PPp and Pp contain the same
variables, namely the one variable p). Given this, we have the
following:

38.	$Fp \supset (p \vee Fp \vee Pp)$	[p.c.]
39.	$FFp \supset (p \vee Fp \vee Pp)$	[3, 38]
40.	$PFp \supset (p \vee Fp \vee Pp)$	[4]
41.	$(Fp \vee FFp \vee PFp) \supset$	
	$(p \vee Fp \vee Pp)$	[38, 39, 40, p.c.]
42.	$F(p \vee Fp \vee Pp) \supset$	
	$(p \vee Fp \vee Pp)$	[16, 41]
43.	$F\Diamond p \supset \Diamond p$	[42, Df. $\Diamond$]
44.	$P\Diamond p \supset \Diamond p$	[analogously, using 37 and 5]
45.	$(\Diamond p \vee F\Diamond p \vee P\Diamond p) \supset \Diamond p$	[$p \supset p$, 43, 44]
46.	$\Diamond\Diamond p \supset \Diamond p$	[45, Df. $\Diamond$]

47. $\sim\Diamond p \supset \sim\Diamond\Diamond p$ $[46, (p \supset q) \supset (\sim q \supset \sim p)]$
48. $\Diamond\sim\Diamond p \supset \Diamond\sim\Diamond\Diamond p$ $[47, \text{RMC}]$
49. $\Diamond\sim\Diamond p \supset \sim\Diamond p$ $[48, 35 \; p/\Diamond p]$
50. $(\Diamond\sim\Diamond p \vee \Diamond\Diamond q) \supset$
    $(\sim\Diamond p \vee \Diamond q)$ $[49, 46, \text{p.c.}]$
51. $\Diamond(\sim\Diamond p \vee \Diamond q) \supset$
    $(\sim\Diamond p \vee \Diamond q)$ $[36, 50]$
52. $\Diamond(\Diamond p \supset \Diamond q) \supset (\Diamond p \supset \Diamond q)$ $[51, \text{p.c.}]$.

We may now consider new theses in T and Y and also in S (where Sp = $(Tp \wedge Yp)$. But at this point it seems necessary to add new *postulates* involving these functions which become plausible when time is taken to be linear, namely the pair

FT2. $F(Tp \wedge Yp) \supset Tp$
PY2. $P(Tp \wedge Yp) \supset Yp$.

It is possible that these are provable when 3, 4, and 5 alone are added to QK_t, but I have not been able to prove them. It is also possible that QK_t is incomplete for its purpose, and that there ought to be further 'non-committal' axioms added to it which *would* yield FT2 and PY2 when 3, 4, and 5 are added. It would certainly be preferable to have FT2 and PY2 as a simple by-product of the addition of 3, 4, and 5. There is, however, no guarantee that they *can* be so derived, and there is independent evidence that making further assumptions about time may require the addition of special postulates involving T and Y. For example, one normal way of expressing the assumption that time will have no end is to lay down $F(p \supset p)$ as an axiom. From our present point of view, however, this will not do; for even if time *is* infinite in the future direction, i.e. even if there *is* going to be a future, $F(p \supset p)$ could be false because p has just reached the end of its statability. Something like $Tp \supset F(p \supset p)$ seems to be required here.

Given FT2 and PY2, the following proof becomes possible:

53. $F(Tp \wedge Yp) \supset Tp$ $[\text{FT2}]$
54. $F(Tp \wedge Yp) \supset FYp$ $[(p \wedge q) \supset q, \text{RF, FT1}]$
55. $F(Tp \wedge Yp) \supset Yp$ $[54, \text{FY}]$
56. $F(Tp \wedge Yp) \supset (Tp \wedge Yp)$ $[53, 55, \text{p.c.}]$
57. $FSp \supset Sp$ $[56, \text{Df. } S]$

58. $PSp \supset Sp$ [analogously]
59. $\Diamond Sp \supset Sp$ [$p \supset p$, 57, 58, Df. $\Diamond$].

We are now in a position to prove the rule RSM of the system Q. (We have already obtained RS1, RS2 and the axiom $p \supset \Diamond p$ in the last section, so this will complete the proof of Q in our enriched QK_t.) We shall adapt to this purpose the method used by Lemmon to prove the postulates given in Section 1 for S5, from a more usual basis.

Firstly, we prove the lemma that where every variable in α falls within the scope of an $\Diamond$ or an S, we have $\vdash \Diamond \alpha \supset \alpha$ The simplest way in which the condition that every variable falls within the scope of an $\Diamond$ or an S may be met, is by α to be itself of the form $\Diamond \beta$ or $S\beta$. In the first case $\Diamond \alpha \supset \alpha$ will be of the form $\Diamond \Diamond \beta \supset \Diamond \beta$, which is a theorem by 46, and in the second case it will be of the form $\Diamond S\beta \supset S\beta$, which we have by 59. More complicated cases arise either by α being of the form $\sim\beta$, where β meets the condition, or by its being of the form $\beta \supset \gamma$ where β and γ meet the condition. So we need to prove (i) that if we have $\vdash \Diamond \beta \supset \beta$ we also have $\vdash \Diamond \sim\beta \supset \sim\beta$, and (ii) that if we have $\vdash \Diamond \beta \supset \beta$ and $\vdash \Diamond \gamma \supset \gamma$ we also have $\vdash \Diamond(\beta \supset \gamma) \supset (\beta \supset \gamma)$. For the first, we proceed thus:

60. $\Diamond \beta \supset \beta$ [hypothesis]
61. $\sim\beta \supset \sim\Diamond\beta$ [60, $(p \supset q) \supset (\sim q \supset \sim p)$]
62. $\Diamond\sim\beta \supset \Diamond\sim\Diamond\beta$ [61, RMC]
63. $\Diamond\sim\beta \supset \sim\Diamond\beta$ [62, 49]
64. $\Diamond\sim\beta \supset \sim\beta$ [63, 33].

And, for the second, thus:

65. $\Diamond \beta \supset \beta$ [hypothesis]
66. $\Diamond \gamma \supset \gamma$ [hypothesis]
67. $(\beta \supset \gamma) \supset (\Diamond\beta \supset \gamma)$ [65]
68. $(\beta \supset \gamma) \supset (\Diamond\beta \supset \Diamond\gamma)$ [67, 24]
69. $\Diamond(\beta \supset \gamma) \supset \Diamond(\Diamond\beta \supset \Diamond\gamma)$ [68, RMC]
70. $\Diamond(\beta \supset \gamma) \supset (\Diamond\beta \supset \Diamond\gamma)$ [69, 52]
71. $(\Diamond\beta \supset \Diamond\gamma) \supset (\Diamond\beta \supset \gamma)$ [70, 66]
72. $(\Diamond\beta \supset \Diamond\gamma) \supset (\beta \supset \gamma)$ [71, 24]
73. $\Diamond(\beta \supset \gamma) \supset (\beta \supset \gamma)$ [70, 72].

From RM and the schema SM (proved in the last section) we immediately have the rule

$\vdash \alpha \supset \beta \rightarrow \vdash Sp \supset (Sq \supset (... \supset (\Diamond\alpha \supset \Diamond\beta)))$, where p, q, ... are all the variables in β that are not in α.

If we add the condition that all variables in β fall within the scope of an $\Diamond$ or an S, we will have, for this β, $\vdash \Diamond\beta \supset \beta$ (by the lemma just proved), and so, from the above rule, the original RSM of the system Q.

6. *Predicate calculi based on Q and QK$_t$.* Although the informal motivation of the systems Q and QK$_t$ has to do with the possibility of their propositions being of the form ϕx, the systems themselves, as developed above, are purely propositional calculi, with only propositional variables. We now consider the consequences of formally introducing individual-name variables and predicate variables, with quantifiers binding the former. It will be simplest to consider first what happens when we enlarge the modal system Q in this way.

For the quantifiers, postulates of the normal sort will suffice; for example, the two Łukasiewicz rules

∀1: $\vdash \alpha \supset \beta \rightarrow \vdash (\forall x\alpha) \supset \beta$
∀2: $\vdash \alpha \supset \beta \rightarrow \vdash \alpha \supset \forall x\beta$,

for x not free in α, with the definition of $\exists x$ as $\sim\forall x\sim$. From these we obtain in the usual way the derived rules

∃1: $\vdash \alpha \supset \beta \rightarrow \vdash (\exists x\alpha) \supset \beta$, for x not free in β,
∃2: $\vdash \alpha \supset \beta \rightarrow \vdash \alpha \supset \exists x\beta$.

And substitution is modified in the presence of quantifiers in the usual ways.

It is necessary also to make additions to the rule RS1, and to the conditions in rules RS2 and RSM, which take care of the presence of other variables than propositional ones, and of the possible binding of some of these. The operator S, for permanent or necessary stability, attaches to propositions only, so that Sx and $S\phi$ would not be well formed, but we could express the permanent or necessary existence of x, and of any object that may be mentioned in the predicate ϕ (which might be something like '... is taller than y'), by prefixing S to formulae containing x or ϕ as their sole free variables. For x it would be simplest to introduce a constant two-place predicate = (for identity), and use $S(x=x)$, and for ϕ, $S\,\forall x\phi x$ would do. We then add to RS1

RS1′: ⊢ $S\alpha \supset S\,\forall x\phi x$, where ϕ occurs in α,
RS1″:⊢ $S\alpha \supset S(x=x)$, where x occurs free in α,

and modify RS2 and RSM to

RS2′: ⊢ $Sp \supset (Sq \supset (... \supset (S\,\forall x\phi x \supset (S\,\forall x\psi x$
　　　$\supset (... \supset (S(x=x) \supset (S(y=y) \supset (... \supset S\alpha))))))))$,
　　　where p, q, ... , and ϕ, ψ, ... , and x, y, ... are all the free variables in α;

RSM′: ⊢ $\alpha \supset \beta \rightarrow$ ⊢ $(Sp \supset (Sq \supset$
　　　$(... \supset (S\,\forall x\phi x \supset (S\,\forall x\psi x ... \supset (S(x=x) \supset (S(y=y) \supset$
　　　$... \supset (\Diamond\alpha \supset \beta))))))))$,
　　　where all the variables in β (bound or free) are within the scope of an $\Diamond$ or an S, and where p, q, ... , and ϕ, ψ, ... , and x, y, ... are all the variables which occur free in β but do not occur free in α.

As an example of a formula which is provable in quantified S5 but not in quantified Q we may take the 'Barcan formula' $\Diamond\exists x\phi x \supset \exists x\Diamond\phi x$, asserting that if it could be that something ϕ's then there is (actually) something that could ϕ, or that if it is the case at some time that something ϕ's then there is now something that ϕ's-at-some-time. (In a universe of non-permanent objects this is clearly an undesirable theorem.) Even in S5 the following proof would not quite do:

74.	$\phi x \supset \Diamond\phi x$	$[p \supset \Diamond p]$
75.	$\phi x \supset \exists x\Diamond\phi x$	$[74, \exists 2x]$
76.	$\exists x\phi x \supset \exists x\Diamond\phi x$	$[75, \exists 1x]$
77.	$\Diamond\exists x\phi x \supset \exists x\Diamond\phi x$	$[76, \text{RCM}]$.

For in the consequent of 76 there is a variable not within the scope of an $\Diamond$, even though it is only one in a quantifier, so that RCM is not applicable. However, a more indirect proof *is* possible in S5, and also in the weaker 'Brouwersche' system, which may be axiomatized by the rule RM of Section 4, with the axioms 23 (unrestricted), 24, and 35. For we have

78.	$\Diamond \phi x \supset \Diamond \phi x$	[p.c.]
79.	$\Diamond \phi x \supset \exists x \Diamond \phi x$	[78, $\exists 2x$]
80.	$\sim \exists x \Diamond \phi x \supset \sim \Diamond \phi x$	[79, p.c.]
81.	$\Diamond \sim \exists x \Diamond \phi x \supset \Diamond \sim \Diamond \phi x$	[80, RM, 23]
82.	$\sim \Diamond \sim \Diamond \phi x \supset \sim \Diamond \sim \exists x \Diamond \phi x$	[81, p.c.]
83.	$\phi x \supset \sim \Diamond \sim \exists x \Diamond \phi x$	[82, $p \supset \sim \Diamond \sim \Diamond p$, from 35]
84.	$\exists x \phi x \supset \sim \Diamond \sim \exists x \Diamond \phi x$	[83, $\exists 1x$]
85.	$\Diamond \exists x \phi x \supset \Diamond \sim \Diamond \sim \exists x \Diamond \phi x$	[84, RM, 23]
86.	$\Diamond \exists x \phi x \supset \exists x \Diamond \phi x$	[85, $\Diamond \sim \Diamond \sim p \supset p$, from 35].

In Q, the move from 80 to 81 is blocked by the restriction on 23. Or, to put it another way, with our axiomatization of S5 we would proceed from 80 to 81 via

80′. $\sim \exists x \Diamond \phi x \supset \Diamond \sim \Diamond \phi x$ [80, $p \supset \Diamond p$],

from which 81 follows by RCM – but not when RCM is restricted as in Q; in Q we could only get

81′. $S(x=x) \supset (\Diamond \sim \exists x \Diamond \phi x \supset \Diamond \sim \Diamond \phi x)$.

It is also necessary, when quantifiers binding individual variables are introduced into Q, to modify the rule of detachment to

$$\vdash \alpha, \vdash \alpha \supset \beta \rightarrow \vdash S(x=x) \supset (S(y=y) \supset \ldots \supset \beta),$$

where $x, y, \ldots$ are all the individual variables which occur free in α but not in β. The effects of this modification are not very severe; for example, it does not block the usual derivation of the rules $\exists 1$ and $\exists 2$ from the rules $\forall 1$ and $\forall 2$ and the definition of $\exists$. What it does block is the derivation of the theorem $\exists x(x=x)$, which asserts in effect that the universe is not empty. Even this is possibly not undesirable; there would in fact be no point in using free individual-name variables if the universe *were* empty, as there would then be no facts or falsehoods directly about individuals. But one might very well want to say that the universe *might have been* empty, or that it once was or eventually will be; i.e. one might not want to preclude the possibility expressed by $\Diamond{\sim}\exists x(x=x)$, and we would be taken to the contradictory of this by RM if we had $\exists x(x=x)$ as a theorem. To put it another way: a formula is a thesis of this system if it is not only not actually false, or not now false, but is not possibly false, or not false at any time, for any values of its variables. (This is the consideration that legitimates RM.) And $x=x$ is not false at any time (i.e. it is true whenever statable – true so long as x exists); the same is true of $(x=x) \supset \exists x(x=x)$; but perhaps $\exists x(x=x)$ (which has no free variables that could stand for individuals whose non-existence would destroy its statability) was or will be or could be false. Hence the modification of detachment to block the derivation of the last from the former two. An alternative would be to admit as theorems all formulae of the system which are universally true *now*, and drop RM, or more accurately so modify RSM that RM is not derivable from it. But this is a type of system that has yet to be properly constructed.

The analogous modifications of QK_t are easy enough to work out. We need T1′, T1″, Y1′, and Y1″ analogous to RS1′ and RS1″; T2, Y2, FT1, and FY1 need to have antecedents in T and Y analogous to the additions in S to RS2 and RSM; and detachment must be modified exactly as in Q.

7. *Further problems.* Tampering with the allegedly 'minimal' tense logic K_t, as we observed at the outset, is only legitimate if we refuse to regard that calculus as a mere by-product of definitions introduced into the first-order theory of the earlier-later relation between instants. And if we do refuse to see things in this way, it is natural to go further and see them, positively, in the opposite way, i.e. to treat the first-order theory of the earlier-later relation as a mere by-product of tense logic. If our tense logic is K_t, we obtain the old 'definitions' of P and F in the form of equivalences. In detail, we introduce special propositional variables a, b, c for which we have

A1. $\Diamond a$
A2. $\Diamond(a \wedge p) \supset {\sim}\Diamond(a \wedge {\sim}p)$
A3. $\exists aa$,

and define the quasi-predication $(\alpha)a$ (where α is a proposition of tense logic) as $\Diamond(a \wedge \alpha)$ and Uab as $(Fb)a$. The $\Diamond$ used in these axioms and definitions is defined thus:

$$\lozenge^0 \alpha = \alpha$$
$$\lozenge^{n+1} \alpha = P \lozenge^n \alpha \vee F \lozenge^n \alpha$$
$$\lozenge \alpha = \exists n \lozenge^n \alpha$$

(in effect this equates $\lozenge p$ with 'p at some time'); and for this $\lozenge$, given K_t for P and F, we have S5, together with $Pp \supset \lozenge p$ and $Fp \supset \lozenge p$.

What kind of earlier-later logic do we get if we append these postulates, not to K_t, but to our new minimal tense logic QK_t? Do we, for instance, obtain the system Q for the $\lozenge$ just defined? And is there a case for adding the postulate Sa, or other postulates involving S which concern 'instant-propositions'?

That is one set of problems which still faces us. Another is this: there are many alternative solutions to the problem of devising a tense logic that is suitable for non-permanent existents. We might, for example, drop individual name-variables altogether and just use *general* names a, b, c, with an undefined individuating propositional form $\varepsilon' ab$, to be read as 'The only thing ever to be an a is a b'. For use with a 'name-logic' of this sort K_t seems unobjectionable; the complications can go into the name-logic. Given such an alternative, can QK_t be defined within it, or vice versa? If the answer is negative, either way, what further postulates might improve the situation?

XX
MODAL LOGIC AND
THE LOGIC OF APPLICABILITY

The modal system S5 may be axiomatised with ~ ('not'), ∧ ('and') and ◇ ('possibly') as primitives, with ⊃ ('if') and ≡ ('if and only if') defined in the usual ways, by subjoining to propositional calculus with substitution and detachment the rule RM to infer ⊢ ~◇~α from ⊢ α and the axioms

S1. ~◇~(p ⊃ q) ⊃ (◇p ⊃ ◇q)
S2. p ⊃ ◇p
S3. ◇~◇p ⊃ ~◇p.

The system may be thought of as embodying the notion of truth in possible worlds. If we write *Tap* for 'It is the case in the world *a* that *p*' we may lay down for this *T* the axioms

T1. *Ta~p ≡ ~Tap*
T2. *Ta(p ∧ q) ≡ (Tap ∧ Taq)*
T3. *Ta◇p ≡ ∃bTbp*,

where T3 states that it is the case in a world *a* that possibly-*p*, if and only if in some world it is the case that *p*. If these axioms are subjoined to first-order predicate calculus we can prove everything in S5 preceded by an arbitrary *Ta*.

Some time ago I proposed, and gave a matrix for, a modal system Q in which it is assumed that in certain worlds certain propositions simply do not occur, because they are directly about individuals which are absent from those worlds. This system has since been axiomatised by R.A. Bull, K. Segerberg and myself. A convenient axiomatisation to use here is the following: We introduce, beside ∧, ~ and ◇, a function *Sp* meaning that *p* occurs, or as I sometimes put it is 'statable', in all worlds, with the two schemata

RS1: $\vdash S\alpha \supset Sp$, for any p in α
RS2: $\vdash Sp \supset (Sq \supset (\ldots \supset S\alpha)$, where $p, q \ldots$ are all the variables in α.

For $\Diamond$ we have

M1. $p \supset \Diamond p$
M2. $\Diamond \sim \Diamond p \supset \sim \Diamond p$

and the rule

RM: $\vdash \alpha \rightarrow \vdash \sim \Diamond \sim \alpha$.

For $\Diamond$ and S together we have the axiom

MS1. $\Diamond Sp \supset Sp$

and the schema

RMS: $\vdash Sp \supset (Sq \supset (\ldots \supset (\sim \Diamond \sim (\alpha \supset \beta) \supset (\Diamond \alpha \supset \Diamond \beta))))$,

where $p, q \ldots$ are all the variables in β that are not in α.[1]

What postulates for Ta, consistent with the intuitions underlying the system Q, would yield everything in Q preceded by an arbitrary $\sim Ta\sim$? Note, first, that I do not say 'preceded by an arbitrary Ta'; this will not do because even logically true formulae of Q will contain variables which could stand for propositions which just do not occur in our arbitrary world a, so that the whole will not be true in a. However, a logically true formula will not be *false* in any world, and so should be provable in the required T-calculus preceded by $\sim Ta\sim$. (In the T-calculus for S5, the prefixes Ta and $\sim Ta\sim$ are of course equivalent, by T1.) In a preliminary discussion of this problem[2] I suggested that the required T-calculus would contain both $Ta(p \supset q) \supset (Tap \supset Taq)$ and $Ta(p \wedge q) \supset (Tap \wedge Taq)$ and their converses, but in fact the converse of the former, i.e. $(Tap \supset Taq) \supset Ta(p \supset q)$, is undesirable, for the substitution q/p in this would yield $(Tap \supset Tap) \supset Ta(p \supset p)$, and so (by

---

[1] A proof of an established set of postulates from these ones can easily be extracted from *Past, Present and Future*, pp. 155–6.
[2] *Past, Present and Future*, p. 157.

detachment of the tautological antecedent) $Ta(p \supset p)$; but in fact $p \supset p$ would not be true (or false) in a world a in which p did not occur. $Ta(p \supset p)$ can be regarded precisely as stating that p does occur in a, i.e. 'It is statable in a that p'. It will be convenient in what follows to abbreviate this to Sap, the distinction between this S and the monadic S which figures in Q itself being gathered from the context (e.g. in '$SaSp$' the second S is the S of Q and the first S our defined T-function, the whole abridging '$Ta(Sp \supset Sp)$').

The required T-axioms are

QT1. $Tap \equiv (Sap \wedge \sim Ta\sim p)$
QT2. $Ta(p \wedge q) \equiv (Tap \wedge Taq)$
QT3. $Ta\Diamond p \equiv (Sap \wedge \exists bTbp)$
QT4. $TaSp \equiv \exists bSbp$
QT5. $Sa\sim p \equiv Sap$
QT6. $Sa(p \wedge q) \equiv (Sap \wedge Saq)$
QT7. $Sa\Diamond p \equiv Sap$
QT8. $SaSp \equiv Sap$.

Of these, QT1 is equivalent to the three implications $Tap \supset \sim Ta\sim p$ ($= Ta\sim p \supset \sim Tap$, half of T1 in the S5 T-calculus), $Tap \supset Sap$ and $Sap \supset (\sim Ta\sim p \supset Tap)$ ($= Sap \supset (\sim Tap \supset Ta\sim p)$, a qualified version of the other half of T1). QT2 is exactly the same as T2 in the S5 T-calculus. QT3 is equivalent to the three implications $Ta\Diamond p \supset \exists bTbp$ (half of T3 in the S5 T-calculus), $Ta\Diamond p \supset Sap$ and $Sap \supset (\exists bTbp \supset Ta\Diamond p)$ (a qualified version of the other half of T3 – the qualification is needed because even if p is true in some world, it might not be true in a, because it might not be stable in a, that p is possible). In QT4 the conjunct Sap is not needed on the right-hand side, since it follows from what is already there. From this basis we can prove

$(Sap \supset Tap) \supset \sim Ta\sim p,$
$Ta(p \supset q) \supset (Tap \supset Taq),$
$Saq \supset (\sim Ta\sim(p \supset q) \supset (Tap \supset Taq)),$

and with their help all of Q preceded by $\sim Ta\sim$.

In both systems we could let the propositional variables stand for tensed propositions and the world variables for instants at which these are true. $\Diamond p$ will then of course mean 'At some time p'. The truth-conditions of the ordinary tensed forms Fp ('It will be that p') and Pp ('It has been that p'), and in the Q-like case of the forms Tp ('It will always be statable that p') and Yp ('It has always been statable that p'), can then be given in obvious ways by introducing the form Uab for 'a is earlier than b'.

In the T-calculus for S5, the symbol T is dispensable. We could simply regard modal propositions as *predicates* of the worlds 'in' which they are said to be true, and tensed propositions as predicates of the instants 'at' which they are said to be true. The equivalences T1–3 can then be transformed into definitions of complex predicates in terms of propositional complications, thus:[3]

T1.	$(\sim p)a = \neg(pa)$	Df.
T2.	$(p \wedge q)a = (pa \,\&\, qa)$	Df.
T3.	$(\Diamond p)a = \Sigma bpb$	Df.

An analogous interpretation of the T-calculus for Q is not so easy, since if we try it out we find that QT1 does not equate $(\sim p)a$ with $\neg(pa)$ but merely has the former implying the latter; similarly with QT3. $(\sim p)a$ is indeed equated with $Sap \,\&\, \neg(pa)$, i.e. $(p \supset p)a \,\&\, \neg(pa)$, but here the first conjunct still has a predicative rather than a propositional complication. I have sometimes used this fact to argue that the modal or tensed propositions of Q cannot be regarded as predicates at all;[4] but there is another possibility, recently aired by Storrs McCall,[5] namely that modal or tensed propositions may be regarded as predicates in a 'non-standard' or 'non-classical' type of predicate logic. I want now to explore this possibility a little further.

McCall mentions in particular the 'free logic' of Karel Lambert. This is not quite what is needed to cope with the present problem, but I shall mention to begin with a system due to Hughes and Londey, which resembles 'free logic' in being designed primarily to find a place for

---

[3] *Editors' note.* Here we use symbols of a semi-Russellian sort for functions of propositions.

[4] See, e.g. *Papers on Time and Tense* (1968) (this volume, pp. 220–1, ed.)

[5] S. McCall, review of *Past, Present and Future* in *Dialectica*, Vol. 6, No. 4 (March 1968), pp. 618–21.

'empty names'.[6] In this system (which at this point looks promising for our present purpose) the direct application of a predicate to a non-existent object is taken to be meaningful but always false, but the system is saved from the contradiction which would arise from having both pa and $\neg pa$ sometimes false, by distinguishing between $(\sim p)a$, which is false along with pa when a is non-existent, and $\neg(pa)$, which under these circumstances is true, along with $\neg((\sim p)a)$. In such a system $(p \supset p)a$ could be used to define 'a exists', $E!a$, and we would have such postulates as

H1. $pa = (E!a \, \& \, \neg(\sim p)a)$
H2. $((p \wedge q))a = (pa \, \& \, qa)$

corresponding to QT1 and QT2, H1 being equivalent to the three implications $pa \supset E!a$, $pa \supset \neg(\sim p)a$ and $E!a \supset (\neg(\sim p)a \supset pa)$, the latter two being equivalent to $(\sim p)a \supset \neg \, pa$ and $E!a \supset (\neg pa \supset (\sim p)a)$. Hughes and Londey do not, in developing this system, use the form Σapa, but just write Σp to indicate that p is instantiated. They show that although we have $pa \supset \Sigma p$, i.e. $pa \supset \Sigma bpb$, we do not have $\forall p \supset pa$, where $\forall p = \neg \Sigma (\sim p)$; i.e. we do not have $\neg \Sigma (\sim p) \supset pa$, i.e. $\neg \Sigma b(\sim p)b \supset pa$. Whether with an expanded symbolism we would have $(\neg \Sigma b \neg(pb)) \supset pa$, they do not consider, but I see no reason why we should not; $\Sigma b \neg(pb)$ would mean that something, maybe something that doesn't exist, fails to be p; its negation would mean that nothing, not even any non-existent thing, fails to be p (which would have as a side-consequence that nothing fails to exist), and this does seem to entail pa for any arbitrary a. The oddities of the non-existent are not here carried by the quantifiers but by the predicates; they are partly reflected in the form $\forall p$ because the negative predicate $\sim p$ is implicitly contained in this.

But while H1 and 2 above might do as interpretations of QT1 and 2, this system for empty names has something much stronger than the rewritten versions of QT5 and 6, i.e. than $(\sim p \supset \sim p)a = (p \supset p)a$ and $((p \wedge q) \supset (p \wedge q))a = (p \supset p)a \, \& \, (q \supset q)a$; namely $(p \supset p)a = (q \supset q)a$. This equivalence of all predicates of the form $\alpha \supset \alpha$ is precisely what justifies the abridgment of $(p \supset p)a$ to $E!a$, in which no predicate variables appear. We do not of course have $(p \supset p)a = (q \supset q)a$ in QT,

---

[6] See my *Past, Present and Future*, pp. 168–9.

since $p \supset p$ could be true in a but $q \supset q$ not true because not statable. What we have in QT is something more like a modification of predicate calculus to cope with a rather different problem, namely that of certain types of predicate being 'inapplicable' to certain types of subjects (e.g. colour-predicates to numbers). What we are now after is a 'many-sorted' predicate logic in which the burden of the many-sortedness is not carried by the name-variables we use in quantifiers but by our method of forming complex predicates. We say that a negative predicate $\sim p$ is 'applicable' to a subject a if and only if p is, and a conjunctive predicate $p \wedge q$ if and only if both p and q are. We do not say, however, that the attachment of a predicate to a subject to which it is inapplicable results in something which is 'senseless' in the sense of being ill-formed, non-propositional or without a truth-value, but only that it invariably results in something which is false. Thus pa may be false either because p and $\sim p$ are both applicable to a but it is $(\sim p)a$ which is true, or because p is inapplicable to a, in which case $\sim p$ will also be inapplicable, and we will have both $\neg(pa)$ and $\neg(\sim p)a$. For example, we might say that the number 4 is not prime because, although primeness and non-primeness are applicable to numbers, 4 is in fact non-prime; but 4 is not blue (it is not the case that it is blue) for a different reason, namely that blueness is not applicable to numbers, and for this reason 4 is not non-blue either (it is not the case that 4 is non-blue). We can call this second sort of falsehood 'senselessness' if we like, so long as we get its logic right, and don't deny that the negation of such 'nonsense' is meaningful and even true.

The predicate $\Diamond p$ is true of a subject a, i.e. we have $(\Diamond p)a$, if and only if p is applicable to a and is non-empty; for example 4 is 'possibly prime' because 4 is a number (and primeness is therefore applicable to it) and some numbers are prime; my tie is not possibly prime because primeness is not applicable to it, and not possibly both round and square because, although both roundness and squareness, and therefore roundness-and-squareness, are applicable to ties, nothing to which shape-predicates are applicable (nor, of course, anything else) is both round and square. If we adopt this interpretation, it might seem possible to take Sap, 'p is applicable to a', as an undefined function, and replace QT1–4 by the following definitions:

QT1. $(\sim p)a = Sap \ \& \ \neg (pa)$ Df.
QT2. $(p \wedge q)a = pa \ \& \ qa$ Df.

QT3. $(\Diamond p)a = Sap$ & Σbpb Df.

QT4. $(Sp)a = \forall bSbp$ Df.

and add $pa \supset Sap$ to the postulates for S. That $(p \supset p)a$, i.e. $\sim(p \wedge \sim p)a = Sap$, would be provable from the definitions and the other postulates. These definitions would not, however, be completely eliminative, as they would not eliminate $\sim$, $\wedge$, etc. from such forms as $Sa\sim p$, $Sa(p \wedge q)$, etc., but only from $(\sim p)a$, $(p \wedge q)a$, etc.

A 'categorial' predicate might be defined as one which is true of every subject to which it is applicable; or in symbols, $Cat(p) = \forall a(Sap \supset pa)$. For example, 'is a number' is true of every subject to which it is applicable. From this it follows that, although plenty of things are not numbers, nothing is a non-number. My tie, for example, is not a number, but because being-a-number is not applicable to it, it is not a non-number either, and it is not a possible number or a possible non-number. Only things which could be numbers are either numbers or non-numbers, and nothing which could be a number is a non-number, or even 'not a number'; whatever could be a number is one. In symbols, we can prove $Cat(p) \supset \neg(\Diamond\sim p)a$ and $Cat(p) \supset ((\Diamond p)a \supset pa)$. We do not, however, have $Cat(p) \supset (\sim\Diamond\sim p)a$, or even $Cat(p) \supset pa$; attributions of categorial predicates may be false, even though attributions of their negations are never true. Such attributions are like the 'structural propositions' which Johnson introduced as optional extra premisses in his expanded version of certain syllogisms.[7]

It is not difficult to present a predicate calculus of this sort as a set-theory, though this presentation raises a new problem. We can read 'pa' as 'a is in the set p', and associate each set with another set in which it is properly or improperly included, which we may call its A-set. The set $\sim p$ is then not the complement of p with respect to the entire universe over which the name-variables range, but only with respect to its A-set; i.e. the set $\sim p$ consists not of everything whatever that is not in p, but of all the members of p's A-set which are not in p. If the set p is empty so is the set $\Diamond p$, but if the set p is non-empty the set $\Diamond p$ coincides with p's A-set. As far as the formal development of the theory is concerned, A-sets can be arbitrarily selected from sets including given sets. For example, the A-set of the set of policemen could be the set of individuals who are either policemen or door-knobs; we would then say

[7] W.E. Johnson, *Logic*, II.i.6.

that while many things are-not policemen, only door-knobs (i.e. things that are either-door-knobs-or-policemen but not policemen) are non-policemen. And with this assignment of A-sets, all doorknobs are possible policemen and all policemen possible door-knobs. Some sets are no doubt more 'natural' than others for use as the A-set of a given set, but this consideration lies outside the formalism. It is arguable that only an *irreducible* use of modal words will give us a sense in which, *not* just relatively to an arbitrary assignment of A-sets, a fireman is a possible policeman but a door-knob is not.

Leaving aside this last small question, the use of 'possibly' and 'could' which is illustrated by the above explanation of '4 is not but could be prime, but my tie could not be prime' is one which might be expected to commend itself to those who wish to give an extensional sense to modal expressions. Moreover, the ordinary use of modal expressions could be represented as a special case of this one. If the object x is absent from the world a, this will mean that such a predicate as 'x-eating-chocolate-ish' is inapplicable to a, so that a is neither an x-eating-chocolate-ish world nor an x-not-eating-chocolate-ish one, i.e. it is neither p-ish nor (not-p)-ish where p is 'x is eating chocolate'. A world a is an x-possibly-eating-chocolate-ish world if and only if (i) the predicate 'x-eating-chocolate-ish' is applicable to it, i.e. x exists in a, and (ii) some world (a or another) to which 'x-eating-chocolate-ish' is applicable is one which is in fact x-eating-chocolate-ish. This is how we express in predicate-calculus terms the ruling that it is the case in world a that x is possibly eating chocolate if and only if (i) it is statable in a that x is eating chocolate, and (ii) in some world in which this is statable it is true. A similar representation is possible for tenses. An instant a is an x-at-some-time-eating-chocolate-ish instant if and only if (i) the predicate 'x-eating-chocolate-ish' is applicable to the instant a, i.e. x exists at a, and (ii) some instant to which 'x-eating-chocolate-ish' is applicable is one which is in fact x-eating-chocolate-ish, i.e. one at which x is eating chocolate.

I have said that modalities and tenses *could* be represented in this way. Whether they ought to be, for any purposes but the development of formal analogies, is another question. That modal systems can be given an extensional interpretation is now a commonplace; and as we have just seen, it is true even of the system Q. But I wonder whether anybody wants to put forward anything like the following as a piece of serious metaphysics: There really are such objects as possible worlds, and what we loosely describe as propositions of modal logic are in fact predicates of which these objects are the subjects. For example, to say that grass could have been pink is to say that there is – there really is – a world in which it *is* pink. To say that grass is green, without any modal qualification, would of course be, on this view, to predicate grass-being-green-ishness of the actual world, but this word 'actual' must not be taken as signifying that the world in question is in any way more 'real' than those other worlds in which grass is pink or purple. The word 'actual' must be regarded as having the concealed egocentricity which the temporal 'present' is sometimes said to have; the 'actual' world is just the world in which *we* figure. And even this is not quite right. For statements like, for example, 'I might have been a railwayman' must be taken to mean that there is – there really is – a world in which I *am* a railwayman. We all as it were perform on several stages at once, and in each world we are largely ignorant of our performances – real though they be – in others.

I say 'largely' ignorant because our knowledge of what we might have been doing would on this view be the way in which we are obscurely aware in one world of what we are doing in others. So the 'actual' world is not strictly identifiable as 'our' world – there are other worlds that are that too (though perhaps not *all* worlds are that). The 'actual' world is just the one we indicate by waving our arms about in a vague way and calling it 'this' world. Alternatively we could follow a suggestion of David Lewis[8] and say that each of us figures in one world only but may have a 'counterpart' or counterparts in other worlds, and that our knowledge of what we might have been doing is an awareness in one world of what our counterpart is doing in another.

In either of its forms, this seems a tall story, and as I have said, I doubt whether anyone seriously believes it. But plenty of people believe an exactly similar story about tenses, i.e. believe that tensed propositions are predicates of 'instants', and that to say that, for example, I have been drinking, is to say that there is – really is – an instant at which I unalterably 'am' drinking. I do not see much more reason for believing this story than the other one; but I must confess that there are fewer knock-down arguments against it – or for that matter against the taller story about modality – than I once thought; in

[8] David K. Lewis, 'Counterpart Theory and Quantified Modal Logic', *Journal of Philosophy*, Vol. 65, No. 5 (March 7, 1968), pp. 113–26.

particular a Q-like tense-logic is as amenable to this type of interpretation as less subtle ones are. In doing metaphysics there is still no
substitute for 'the choice of the soul'; or, if you like, prejudice. In any
case the modalities of Q are interpretable as qualifications of predicates
in the kind of predicate logic that I have described (the theory of
'applicability'). John Lemmon once said to me, not long after the
system Q had been invented and he was at work on its semantics, that
while this system could certainly be defended it could also be
trivialised; he offered me an 'awful' interpretation of Q to be set beside
what Łukasiewicz had called my 'awful' interpretation of his Ł-modal
system as a logic of deliberate ambiguity.[9] I think Lemmon had in mind
some such interpretation as the one I have sketched here.

All the same, a certain amount of argument, to bolster up the
prejudice, is still possible here. Suppose we introduce ordinary
individual variables, with quantifiers binding them, and also an identity
function with such variables as arguments, into our modal or tense logic,
i.e. suppose we have not merely a modalised or tensed propositional
logic but a modalised or tensed predicate logic with identity, still along
the lines of Q. The T-calculus for this would have to have some
additions, and if we abridge $TaIxx$ to Sax, the following suggest
themselves:

QT9. $Ta\exists xfx \equiv \exists xTafx$
QT10. $TaIxy \equiv (Sax \land Say \land Ixy)$
QT11. $Safx \equiv (Sax \land Sa\exists yfy)$.

I shall have something to say about QT9 and 10 shortly. QT11 states
that fx is statable in the world a, or at the instant a, if and only if this is
not prevented either by some fault in x or by some fault in f. The fault in
x would be x's non-existence in or at a, and this can be represented as
the failure in a of some formula, say Ixx, in which x is the only variable;
hence we define Sax, x's existence in a, as $TaIxx$, analogously to our
definition of Sap as $Ta(p \supset p)$. The fault in f would be its containing an
individual variable with the preceding fault, but formally it would
amount to the failure in a of some logical law in which f is the only free
variable, e.g. $\exists yfy \supset \exists yfy$. So the absence of such a fault is represented

[9] See my *Time and Modality*, p. 4, and article 'Logic, Many-valued' in the
Encyclopedia of Philosophy (Collier-Macmillan, 1967), Vol. 5, p. 4.

in QT11 by $Sa\exists yfy$, i.e. $Ta(\exists yfy \supset \exists yfy)$. These postulates would yield such desirable theorems as $\sim Ta\sim(fx \supset \exists yfy)$ and the schema $\sim Ta\sim(\alpha \wedge \exists xfx \supset \exists x(\alpha \wedge fx))$, where x is not free in α. Also, in identity theory they would yield the desirable $Tafx \equiv \exists y(Talxy \wedge Tafy)$. Further, these postulates would *not* yield such *un*desirable consequences as the Barcan formula $\Diamond \exists xfx \supset \exists x \Diamond fx$ preceded by $\sim Ta\sim$. We do indeed have, by ordinary quantification theory, $\exists a \exists x Tafx \supset \exists x \exists a Tafx$, and from this by QT9 $\exists a Ta \exists xfx \supset \exists x \exists a Tafx$, which in the T-calculus for S5 would be equivalent to $Ta \Diamond \exists xfx \supset \exists x Ta \Diamond fx$, and QT9 would equate this to $Ta \Diamond \exists xfx \supset Ta \exists x \Diamond fx$, and so to $Ta(\Diamond \exists xfx \supset \exists x \Diamond fx)$. In the T-calculus for Q, however, some of these moves are blocked. In words,

(1) (Possibly something f's) is true at a

= (2) It is statable at a that something f's, and (something f's) is true at some b

= (3) It is statable at a that something f's, and something (f's at some b),

where we go from (1) to (2) by QT3 and from (2) to (3) by QT9. But

(4) (Something possibly f's) is true at a

= (5) Something (possibly-f's at a)

= (6) Something (exists at a – where it is statable that something f's – and some f's at some b),

and this is not deducible from (3). The point is that it may be statable at a that something possibly-f's (and so – this does follow – there may be something of which it is statable at a that it possibly-f's), but with regard to the thing that does possibly-f, i.e. f's at some b, it may not be statable at a that *that* thing possibly-f's, and so not be *true* of anything at a that it possibly f's, i.e. not true at a that something-possibly-f's – even though it is true and statable at a that there is a b where something f's (the particular something in question not being mentionable at a).

When, however, we attempt to regard this extension of QT as part of a predicate calculus of the sort earlier sketched, we encounter serious conceptual difficulties. Let us begin, as before, by re-symbolising our postulates, thus:

QT9. $(\exists xfx)a \equiv \Sigma x(fx)a$

QT10. $(Ixy)a \equiv (Sax \ \& \ Say \ \& \ (x = y))$
QT11. $Safx \equiv (Sax \ \& \ Sa\exists yfy).$

Here f must be interpreted as a *two*-place predicate from which we form the one-place predicate fx by filling the first of its places with the name x, and the one-place predicate $\exists xfx$ by binding a variable in its first place. $Safx$ will mean that fx is 'applicable' to a, i.e. that a is a suitable second argument for f. QT9, on this interpretation, presents no problems. To say that 4 has the property of being divisible-by-something is equivalent to saying that for some x, 4 has the property of being divisible-by-x. (Here we read fxa as 'a is divisible by x', making f the 2-place predicate 'goes into', fx the 1-place predicate 'is divisible by x', and $\exists xfx$ the 1-place predicate 'is divisible by something'). But QT10 and 11 are not so easy. QT11 states that a is a suitable second argument for f provided that there is nothing about the other argument and nothing about f that prevents it. One can see how there could be trouble about f; suppose, for example, f were 'shaves' and a the number 4. Neither 'shaven', i.e. 'shaved by someone', nor 'unshaven', i.e. 'shaved by no one', seems applicable to 4, and this, as QT11 states, makes 'shaved by x' also inapplicable to 4. But could there be any trouble about x, that is to say about x *in itself*, or purely in relation to a? x might of course be an unsuitable *first* argument for f; but this would be expressed, if at all, by $Sxfa$, where f is the converse of the relation you first thought of; in fact the system has no way of expressing the unsuitability of predicates relative to xs, only relative to as. The conjunct Sax in QT11 says nothing about x in relation to f or to fa but only about x in relation to a; and its negation $\neg Sax$ would seem to mean that *no* relation with a for one of its terms could have x for the other. But do we ever have cases of this? There are obvious relations between the number 4 and, for example, my bed, e.g. the relation which consists in my bed having 4 legs; and it is hard to think of any pair of terms for which *some* applicable relating predicate could not be found. But we cannot do without Sax when QT is being used as a T-calculus for the modal system Q; the whole motivation for Q lies in fx being unstatable at a if x does not exist at a, i.e. if $\neg Sax$; the component $Sa\exists yfy$ is only necessary to exclude from statability at a an fx in which the f contains a z for which $\neg Saz$.

Formally, Sax is a definitional abbreviation for $(Ixx)a$, but this raises another problem when we treat QT as a predicate calculus. How can self-identity of x, or the identity of x and y, be regarded as a predicate of anything at all? How can identity, in other words, be assigned an additional argument beside its obvious ones, or treated as relative to some further object? This, of course, throws doubt on the very intelligibility of QT10.

When, on the other hand, we take QT9–11 seriously as part of a theory of worlds or instants, QT11 is not only (as we have seen) perfectly in order, but is the *only* one of the three postulates which is so. I don't mean that QT9 and 10 yield any theses of modalised or tensed predicate logic which are undesirable, though it may be that they do; but they are in themselves open to intuitive objection. Let us look first, from this point of view, at QT9; and to bring out the issues more clearly, let us first suppose that the interior calculus is a tensed rather than a modal one. QT9, as re-stated, employs an interior and an exterior existential quantifier, $\exists$ and Σ. The former is part of the tensed proposition $\exists x f x$, 'Something f 's', about which we can ask '*When* is this the case?' and 'Is it the case at the instant a?'. This second question amounts to 'Is there at the instant a anything which f 's?' It would be unnatural to regard an affirmative answer to this question as justified when f is 'will fly to Sirius', if *something which does not exist at a* is going to do so. Indeed, QT9 itself rules this out; '$\exists x(x$ will fly to Sirius)' is by QT9 true at a if and only if for some x it is true at a that x will fly to Sirius, and this is not true at a, since it is not even statable at a, if x does not exist at a. The quantifier $\exists x$, in short, is a 'tensed' quantifier. But not Σx. If we read Σx this way in QT9, i.e. if in effect we replace it there by $\exists x$, that formula becomes simply false (considered as assertable of any arbitrary a), for it will imply that whenever $(\exists x f x)a$, i.e. whenever it is true at a (which might not be now) that something f 's, then $\exists x(f x)a$, i.e. there is *now* something which f 's at a. This reading of QT9, moreover, would make it equate a tenseless proposition with a tensed one. No, Σx belongs to the 'exterior' theory to which Σa belongs, and ranges over objects regardless of when they exist, and can be used in stating timeless relations between these objects and the times at which they exist, and indeed between them and the times at which they don't exist; for we have in the system such formulae as $\Sigma x(\neg Sax)$, asserting that there 'is' an object of which it is not statable at a that it is self-identical, or concerning which there is no such proposition at a as the proposition that it is self-identical. All the same, there 'is' the proposition that $x = x$, a special case of the form '$x = y$' which occurs as part of the 'exterior' language of QT10, which apparently can be used at any time. Or can it? There 'is' this proposition that $x = x$, but there is no such proposition at a; and a could be now.

Similarly with modality. Where the interior language is modal, $\Sigma x(\neg Sax)$ will mean that there 'is' an object which does not exist in the world a, which could be the actual world; i.e. that there 'is' an object concerning which there is no such proposition in the actual world as the proposition that it is self-identical; and yet there 'is' – but not actually! – the proposition that $x = x$, where x is this object.

These are strange ways of talking. The trouble, I think, is this: The *form* of such propositions as the right-hand side of QT9, $\Sigma x(fx)a$, suggests that we are not only taking 'worlds' or 'instants' seriously as objects, but taking merely possible or merely past or future ordinary individuals seriously as objects too. But the *content* of the calculus, including QT9, suggests that these xs are after all just the individuals we know, which are nothing at all except when they are actual or present, and that is not in all worlds or always, still less outside all worlds or times. So one has the feeling that something has escaped from its modal or temporal cage, and appeared where it ought not to be. Of course quantifiers and identity, like truth-functions, have their place everywhere; we must have 'Σ' and '$=$' as well as '$\neg$' and '$\&$' in the outer framework we have provided for Q, just as we must eventually introduce '$\exists$' and 'I' as well as $\sim$, $\wedge$, etc. into Q itself; but the question is, what variables should the outer 'Σ' bind, and the outer '$=$' relate? Our ps and fs belong as it were within their brackets, tied to their as, and surely that is where our xs belong too; they have no business jumping over the fence into the timeless or super-modal framework, as they do in such forms as $\Sigma x(fx)a$ and the untied $x=y$. Nor do they appear there in QT11, but they do in QT9 and 10. So it seems to me that these last are a bit out of place in a T-calculus which is to preserve the ideas behind the system Q; such a calculus had better obtain its 'desirable theorems' in other (doubtless clumsier) ways.

We can indeed dissolve this distinction between the T-framework and the modal or tense logic that it encloses, and in so doing de-mythologise the former, by regarding its 'worlds' or 'instants' as modal or tensed propositions of a special sort, with special postulates, and defining Tap within the modal or tensed calculus as $\Diamond(a \wedge p)$ (to be true in or at a is to be possibly or at some time true along with a).[10] The distinction between '¬' and '~', and between '&' and '∧', will now disappear, and so will that between $x=y$ and Ixy. QT10 will in fact remain true on this interpretation, but will now mean that it is true *now* that Ixy is the case at a if and only if x and y both exist at a and x and y are *now* identical (a consequence of the fact that it is now statable that Ixy is the case at a if and only if Ixy is statable both at a and now). With the same interpretation, the '=' of $a = b$ will differ from the I of Ixy in being a connective rather than a two-place predicate (a and b being propositions), and $Σa$ will differ from $∃x$ simply in being a *higher order* quantification, just $Σp$ with a restriction on the range of p, and it might as well be written $∃a$ since the distinction lies not in the kind of quantification but in the kind of variable bound. But a supposedly timeless or super-modal $Σx$ will just not be definable at all, and therefore QT9 not formulable. QT9 would in fact be true in this wholly tensed or modal system if $Σx$ were replaced by $◇∃x$; but this will not do as a definition of $Σx$, since for the latter, ordinary quantification theory gives

$$(Sax \ \& \ Σyby) ≡ Σy(Sax \ \& \ Sby),$$

but we do not have

$$(Sax \ ∧ \ ◇∃ySby) ≡ ◇∃y(Sax \ ∧ \ Sby).$$

For here the left hand side means that it is now true that (x exists at a and it is at some time true that something exists at b), and this is compatible with nothing that exists at a existing at any time at which anything that exists at b exists. But if this last situation obtains, there is no time at which there is a y of which we can then truly say 'x exists at a and this (i.e. y) exists at b'; which contradicts the right-hand side.

At this point, then, what is desirable in a T-calculus for Q ceases to coincide with what is desirable in a 'logic of applicability'. For the former we want QT11 and perhaps QT10 but not QT9, and for the latter QT9 but not QT10 or 11.

One further point: In *epistemic* logic, it might seem plausible to regard statements about a person's beliefs as attaching predicates to his

---

[10] See Chapter XI and pp. 272–3.

'belief-world'. To say that a man believes in God, for example, may be to say that God exists in his belief-world (cf. Anselm's talk of God existing 'in the mind'), and this in turn to characterise his belief-world as 'theistic'. Perhaps in another man's belief-world God does *not* exist, i.e. that belief-world is 'atheistic'. Belief-worlds are in some ways easier to swallow than possible worlds; they are reminiscent of the 'private spaces' which figure in some of Russell's theories about perception, and perhaps they can even be given a neurophysiological interpretation. But it would seem that in many cases they are characterised neither by a given predicate nor by its contradictory; in plain language, a person may neither believe that *p* nor believe that not-*p*, since he may not have thought about the matter, and even if he has, may have arrived at no opinions about it. A belief-world may, for example, be neither theistic nor atheistic but agnostic. The T-calculus for Q could help us here; we could say that the predicate 'theistic', and therefore also the predicate 'atheistic', are just 'inapplicable' to certain belief-worlds, namely those of agnostics.

I am not inclined, however, to carry this line of thought very far, tempting as it is. For there are the following reasons against it:

(i) There are matters on which a person's beliefs may be not merely unformed but inconsistent, i.e. we do not have the analogue of $Ta\sim p \supset \sim Tap$, which would come from QT1. A much more serious modification of predicate logic than any we have so far contemplated would be needed to allow cases in which the predicates p and $\sim p$ are not merely false of the same subject, but true of the same subject.

(ii) We often need to compare a person's belief with what actually is the case; in particular, when we say that a person's belief that p is mistaken, we mean that he believes that p but it is not the case that p, and we mean that what he believes is *precisely* what is not the case. Hence if p is genuinely propositional in 'It is not the case that p' it must be genuinely propositional, and not merely predicative, in 'x believes that p'. To say anything less is to fail to take error seriously. Hence, conversely, if p in 'x believes that p' is to be construed as merely a predicate of a belief-world, so must it be on its own, or negated; but of *which* belief-world? We cannot identify the unqualified p or $\sim p$ with its being true of a selected one among a number of belief-worlds, as we might identify it with its being true in one of a number of possible worlds, or at one of a number of instants. The actual world isn't 'this' belief-world, in any sense of 'this'. At this point, so far as I can see, this theory can only be saved by taking one of two unplausible courses. We could introduce a new idealistic argument for theism, postulating a being with whose belief-world the actual world can be definitionally identified, i.e. defining the Truth as what God believes. Or we can say that there is no truth against which our beliefs are to be measured, and that simple assertion of a proposition is simply predicating it of *our* belief-world.

One might argue that there *is* one way of escaping these alternatives. There is nothing in the suggested representation of propositions about beliefs which ties the belief-worlds to *people* – they are just there, entities that we characterise. And one might introduce the actual world, call it n, as another entity of the same broad sort as the belief-worlds (n is substitutable in theorems for belief-world-variables), but with special features, e.g. though we do not in general have $\neg(pa) \supset (\sim p)a$, we do have $\neg(pn) \supset (\sim p)n$. (This brings out nicely the determinateness of what is actual by contrast with what is not.) 'a's belief that p is mistaken' would then come out as $pa \ \& \ \neg(pn)$, or the equivalent $pa \ \& \ (\sim p)n$. And we don't have to think of n either as God's belief-world or the speaker's; it isn't anybody's belief-world, but it is a world, and the belief-worlds are that too. This suggestion, however, still doesn't meet the first objection, or a third which we now state.

(iii) The system would make beliefs about people's beliefs inexpressible, since the form pa, i.e. 'a's belief-world is p-ish', *is* genuinely propositional and therefore not a possible characterisation of a belief-world. We have, indeed, the function $(\Diamond p)a$, but this will *not* mean that a believes that someone believes that p, but only that a has an opinion about p and someone believes that p, but only that a has an opinion about p and someone (a or another) does believe it. (Hintikka's system in *Knowledge and Belief*, which does at first sight look a bit like reducing assertions about beliefs to the ascription of predicates to belief-worlds, at this point precludes that interpretation, since in his system beliefs about beliefs are quite straightforwardly formulable.) To put this point another way: In the T calculus for Q the second quantification implicit in $(\Diamond\Diamond p)a$ is a vacuous one; the formula is equivalent to

$$(p \supset p)a \ \& \ \Sigma b(\Diamond p)b,$$

and this to

$$(p \supset p)a \ \& \ \Sigma b((p \supset p)b \ \& \ \Sigma cpc),$$

and this to

$$(p \supset p)a \ \& \ \Sigma b(p \supset p)b \ \& \ \Sigma b\Sigma cpc,$$

and this to

$$(p \supset p)a \ \& \ \Sigma cpc,$$

i.e. to $(\Diamond p)a$. In the T-calculus for S5 this is even more obvious; there

$$(\Diamond \Diamond p)a = \Sigma b(\Diamond p)b = \Sigma b\Sigma cpc = \Sigma cpc = (\Diamond p)a.$$

Intuitively this is right too, in tense and modal logic. 'It is true in a that it is true in some possible world that it is true in some possible world that p' is indeed equivalent to 'It is true in a that it is true in some possible world that p', and this (at least provided that p is statable in a) to 'It is true in some possible world that p'; and 'It is true at a that it is at some time true that p is true at some time' is equivalent to 'It is true at a that p is true at some time', and this (at least if p is statable at a) to 'p is true at some time'. But 'a believes that it is believed that it is believed that p' is not equivalent to 'a believes that it is believed that p', nor (as we have already noted) is this in turn equivalent, even if a has an opinion about p, to 'It is believed that p'.

Appendix 1

LIFE AND WORK OF ARTHUR N. PRIOR: AN INTERVIEW WITH MARY PRIOR

Given at Mary Prior's home in Oxford, Sunday 5th October 1997

Interviewer: Per Hasle

Mrs. Prior, you first met Arthur Norman Prior, your future husband, in 1943. Can you tell us about your first meeting, and something about your own and Arthur's backgrounds before that?

MP: It is now 53 years since Arthur and I met, and 28 years since Arthur died, so I am recalling the distant past. Sometimes it seems vivid and close, sometimes far off, another world, so my memory is very uneven. This is particularly true of Arthur's work, because though my initial training was in philosophy, even before Arthur's death I moved into history, and though during Arthur's life I could follow his work, I did not realize until after he died how much in his last years as his work got more technical I leaned on him to explain it. I had stopped standing on my own philosophical feet as I began to become preoccupied with finding my feet as a historian.

Arthur and I met on the last day of a Student Christian Movement conference in Christchurch. It was during the war and Arthur was stationed at a nearby Air Force Station. I had just finished my BA. He had graduated in the thirties, failing to gain the scholarship which would have led to postgraduate study abroad. He had nevertheless been to England. He belonged to a generation of students noted for their intellectual brilliance. I was very impressed. On this first occasion we talked almost non-stop for over five hours – philosophy, theology, gossip – lively and great fun. It was an immediate rapport of two people who saw their lives as very different. And yet our backgrounds were very similar. We both had nonconformist clergy in our families, doctors, nurses and missionaries.

Please tell us about your first years together, and Arthur's interests during that period.

We got engaged after meeting four times and married seven months later. After the birth of our son Martin, Arthur was posted as a wireless mechanic to the New Hebrides. Most reading matter was supplied by the American Navy. He read a lot of Herman Melville and Nathaniel Hawthorne and wrote love letters daily as did I. I don't know if he had any theological works with him, but he discussed theological problems in some of them.

On his return he applied for and got the job in Christchurch as a temporary assistant lecturer as a stop-gap for Popper, who had just vacated the senior lectureship. Before we moved to Christchurch our house burnt down and we lost all our possessions. A few precious books were rescued in a charred condition and rebound.

Christchurch was a wonderful place to be in those earliest years. Returned servicemen and former conscientious objectors filled the classrooms along with people straight from school. The distinction between staff and students can never have been less. It was a period when everyone was catching up on lost years. For Arthur it meant preparing courses of lectures in logic, ethics, and specialist options on the philosophy of Plato and Aristotle; of Locke, Berkeley and Hume, Mill and other 19th century English speaking philosophers. Philosophy was then part of a joint Psychology and Philosophy course, in which Logic and Ethics and one year of psychology were common to psychologists and philosophers. More advanced logic and a specialist subject – e.g. Plato and Aristotle – were taught to third year and MA-students. The special subject rotated. As all the philosophy teaching fell to Arthur he refused to teach a Kant and Hegel option. He did not speak German and had a distaste for Hegel. Interestingly, two of his abler students Jonathan and Gillian Bennett (née Quentin-Baxter) were to develop a strong interest in German philosophy!

During this period 1946 to early 1949 we lived in Macmillan Avenue on Cashmere Hill. Every Saturday morning Arthur took a tutorial lecture with his class, as did a neighbour Henry Broadhead. Usually Arthur biked to work, but on Saturdays Dr. Broadhead and Arthur drove together in Dr. Broadhead's car and then came back to our flat for coffee. Broadhead and Popper had been friends and I have no doubt their conversation was largely on Greek philosophy. Broadhead was about 15-20 years older than Arthur, and had I think been to Cambridge. I suspect Arthur's interest in early philosophy was fuelled by Broadhead.

In 1949, Arthur Prior was writing a book called 'A History of Scottish Theology'.[1] But that same year your flat burned down and the manuscript was damaged (one can still see the signs of burns on the manuscript now deposited in the Bodleian Library). You have yourself characterised this occasion as a turning point, after which Arthur Prior gave up that project, and increasingly turned his interest towards logic. Can you tell us about the project which was given up, and how and why Arthur's interests changed from that time on?

At this time Arthur was writing *Logic and the Basis of Ethics* [Prior 1949], which drew on material from the courses he was teaching. Although he still from time to time returned to his History of Scottish Theology, work coming out of his teaching commitments was taking over. The main thing I remember him doing connected with the History was ordering and reordering the table of contents. What was to be the order of God's Decrees for instance? I don't think he ever came to a conclusion. When a second fire once again destroyed our property together with others in the pleasant old wooden house in which we lived, material for the book was destroyed, and the project was never resurrected. A few somewhat charred remnants of material from this period survives in the Bodleian. Scottish theology remained however part of the mulch which nourished his work.

One important occasion in Arthur Prior's intellectual development was obviously his participation in the 1951 Philosophical Congress in Sydney. Please give us some impressions from the conference, and tell us about its influence on Arthur.

In 1949 we moved house twice before buying a house in Grange Street, Opawa. Arthur was able to present me with an advance copy of *Logic and the Basis of Ethics* on the morning our second child Ann was born. At this time we lived isolated from other philosophers, save by letter. Arthur found stimulation from his students, and this was to continue all his life even when no longer isolated. We scraped to go to the 1951 Meeting of the Australasian Philosophy and Psychology Society. There

---

[1] Link-path to information: see 'A History of Scottish Theology' under 'Boxes' → 'Box 1-11' → 'Contents of Box 7'.

were no grants towards such things in those days. We were amazed when Jack Smart, freshly out from Oxford, strode across the room to congratulate Arthur on *Logic and the Basis of Ethics*, which he announced was being much discussed in Oxford. At this conference we met many Australian philosophers, and became aware of the division between Andersonian philosophers in Sydney and Melbourne philosophers.

In Adelaide Jack [Smart] lived outside the storm centre, as did Arthur. We formed long lasting friendships with Jack and with John Mackie (the independent minded Sydney philosopher). I still keep in touch with Jack and Joan, John's widow, whom I meet regularly. This conference ended a period of near isolation. Jack, then a bachelor, came to several NZ philosophy conferences, several other Australian philosophers came occasionally. The first NZ conference was held in Christchurch in 1953. Through Jack, Arthur was also put in touch with English philosophers, and when Jonathan Bennett went to Oxford to do a B. Phil. in 1954, his long gossipy letters made them live. In late 1954 Gilbert Ryle visited NZ and brought in his pocket an invitation.[2]

Already in 1951, there were a few suggestions in Arthur Prior's manu-scripts to the effect that there could be a 'logic of time-distinctions'. But evidently it was not till 1953 that he started working on this project, which was to become his most noted achievement. Apparently a footnote by Findlay inspired him to take up this issue in earnest. Please tell us about this event.[3]

The idea of a logic of time distinctions may well have simmered in Arthur's head long before 1951, for it was in the Australasian Journal, December 1941, that John Findlay's paper 'Time: A Treatment of Some Puzzles' [Findlay 1941] first appeared. However, it became more wide-

---

[2] An invitation for Arthur Prior to give the John Locke lectures in the University of Oxford in 1956.

[3] John Findlay was the professor of Philosophy at Otago University, where Arthur Prior studied 1932-37. Findlay was the single-most formative source in Prior's early academic development, and Prior was later to remark of him 'I owe to his teaching, directly or indirectly, almost all that I know of either Logic or Ethics' [Prior 1949, p. xi]. (While this was true in 1949 it obviously does not hold for the later stages of Prior's career.)

ly available when it was reprinted in Tony Flew's *Logic and Language*, 1951 [Flew 1951]. But it was probably as late as in 1954 or early 1955, perhaps when he was working on the John Locke lectures, that he came and sat on the bed in high excitement. He read the all important footnote.[4] He felt he could formalise tense distinctions, drawing inspiration from this footnote of Findlay's. I date this from the fact that I have a vivid memory of the event occurring in a sunporch in the house we moved into in mid-1954.

The idea that logic and time should be related to one another was certainly a novelty at that time. What can be said about Arthur Prior's relation to mainstream logic and perhaps more generally, to analytical philosophy?

I hesitate to answer this, because I feel I may misrepresent Arthur, but I think I'm right in saying that Arthur initially accepted Russell and Whitehead as establishing the parameters of modern logic; developed doubts as he read more ancient and medieval logicians, and then sought to formalize a logic which would deal with tensed statements. As for analytical philosophy, he thoroughly enjoyed crossing swords with analytical philosophers – it was endemic in Oxford – and used to return home from dinner in Oxford colleges, when we were there, flushed with the pleasure of combat. His paper 'The Runabout Inference Ticket' [Prior 1960] is his most accessible thing on this subject, though perhaps I'm biased as I suggested the title.

Another notable feature of Arthur Prior's work in logic was his great historical awareness. He obviously had a comprehensive knowledge of Ancient and Medieval philosophers and logicians, and found their

---

[4] The footnote in question is found in [Findlay 1941], and reads:
'And our conventions with regard to tenses are so well worked out that we have practically the materials in them for a formal calculus... The calculus of tenses should have been included in the modern development of modal logics. It includes such obvious propositions as that

x present = (x present) present

x future = (x future) present = (x present) future;

also such comparatively recondite propositions as that (x).(x past) future; i.e. all events, past and future will be past.'

discussions fruitful also for a present-day study of logic. Can you tell us
more about his views on the importance of studying the history of logic?

I suspect that Findlay laid the groundwork of Arthur's interest in ancient
and medieval logic, and Broadhead furthered it. But it was fairly
dormant until the early 1950s, when he had papers in *Dominican Studies*
(1952), *Franciscan Studies* and *The New Scholasticism*.[5] I don't know
what set him going, probably the work of Bocheński, *La Logique de*
Theophraste 1947 [Bocheński 1947]. He was impressed by the rigorous
formalisation of medieval logic and by the work of the Polish School of
logicians (which included Bocheński) at roughly the same time. Articles
on both appeared in 1952, and marked a new departure. His work had
always taken the work of philosophers of the past as worth listening to,
and to be taken seriously. The past had a democratic right to speak to
the present. 1952 was the beginning. He had yet to meet others working
in that field, but he was in correspondence with them now.

1954 was a difficult year for your family, you yourself going to hospital
for some time, and your children being ill, too. What are your
recollections of that year?

Yes, 1954 was a difficult year. The family seemed to be always ill in the
years before that – measles, mumps, whooping cough. The things
children bring back from school in the first year or two. I was often ill.
It turned out that I had TB and passed it on to the kids. I spent 9 months
in a Sanatorium nearby, the children were nursed at home by a trained
nurse. Arthur fitted in when she was off duty and visited me faithfully
twice a week as well as lecturing and writing me daily letters. The
university was understanding and excused him all committee meetings.
How he coped I do not know. For the children being nursed at home
spared them the desolation of hospital life, and despite being confined to
bed they seemed to manage to have a jolly time. Arthur was a Pied Piper
with children, the two successive nurses were splendid and my parents
provided back-up from time to time. They lived 100 miles away in
Timaru.

In 1956, you went to Oxford, where Arthur Prior had been invited to

---

[5] See the Prior-bibliography, items 1952c, 1953b, and 1953c.

give the John Locke lectures that year. Many important contacts were made during that year, and in particular, Arthur Prior arranged the 1956 Oxford Logic colloquium. Please tell us about this year in Oxford, and the colloquium.[6]

When Gilbert Ryle visited Christchurch in late 1954, he brought an invitation to Arthur to read the John Locke lectures in Oxford. This unlocked many doors when we got there in 1956. Arthur was widely dined by established philosophers, mainly in the analytical tradition. Logicians were few on the ground. Dummett was away in America most of the year. However, contact was made with those around, like Bill and Martha Kneale. Some whose work was most important to Arthur were only marginally connected to the University: the Dominican monk, Ivo Thomas at Blackfriars, John Lemmon still a very junior fellow, Peter Geach, commuting between his job in Birmingham and Oxford, where his wife Elizabeth Anscombe had a fellowship at Somerville.

The John Locke lectures were formal occasions without any opportunity for discussion, so Arthur organised a discussion at our flat once a week, attended by Ivo, John, and Peter when he could manage it, plus occasional attenders, often postgraduate students.

Arthur met other logicians in the spring and early summer, and the idea of a colloquium in late summer was mooted. A small ad hoc committee was formed, and Marcus Dick arranged for a lecture room at Balliol. Almost everyone invited turned up. It lasted the best part of two days. At a punting party the last afternoon, Ivo, Arthur and John Lemmon and the Merediths from Dublin (Carew and David) started work on a paper (on calculi of implication) published in 1969 but circulated in MS form for many years, known as LMMPT – the initials of the authors [Prior 1969]. The conference ended with a party at our flat. So many people were meeting for the first time and talked logic with urgency. The decibel level was high. The flat was small in the gables of the house (8 Park Town) and sound bounced off the sloping walls. Tall men bent almost double. Much beer was drunk and Pat Lemmon and I rushed around with cheesy toast and twiglets. In those days – rationing was recently ended – entertaining was simple and undemanding.

[6] The plan for the Colloquium can be seen as 'Logic Colloquium Programme', at 'Boxes' → 'Box 1-11' → 'Contents of Box 11' (First Folder).

What was Arthur Prior's way of working, his attitude towards colleagues and students? How would you characterise him as a person?

Arthur worked intensely, often through the night. He seldom corrected a paper or made insertions. He might revise his opinion on a subject as he wrote, and would then be most likely to start again rather than fiddle with it. When he relaxed he wanted to do things which left his brain just ticking over. He never played bridge or other games involving thinking. He played with his children, went walking, and, after we came to England, engaged in canal cruising. Canal cruises often included friends like Tony Kenny (whom we got to know when we moved to Manchester). Tony at that time was a Roman Catholic priest in Liverpool, which is not far from Manchester – see Tony's *A Path from Rome* [Kenny 1985]. We bought a cottage in Shropshire and every summer exchanged visits with Peter Geach and Elizabeth Anscombe, who had a place at the other end of the county. A good deal of philosophy was often mixed in on such occasions. Arthur enjoyed philosophical conversations with colleagues enormously, and this included students as much as anyone else. He also enjoyed trying out philosophical puzzles on children. This tended to infuriate Ann who in frustration might punch him if it went on too long.

What sort of person was he? Spontaneous, very open. Formality made him impatient and pompous and manipulative people he despised. They were bullshit artists and dicky-lickers. Arthur retained from the airforce some ripe turns of phrase. He was a good friend but had a strong sense of the ridiculous and was no respecter of persons. He did not repress his feelings and occasionally lost his temper dramatically. He was not a stoic. Life with him was enormous fun. I think for this reason our fires and the TB episode ended up by being remembered largely for the bizarre situations they landed us in.

Before going on with milestones in your lives, we wish to discuss Arthur Prior's views and philosophical interests more closely. First of all, it seems that existential questions were for him a subject relevant to logic, and conversely. What was his conception of logic in general?

I find answering questions about the content of Arthur's thought particularly difficult. Partly this is because it is so long since I have been seriously involved in philosophy, and partly because I was so close to it, and it's hard to see the wood for the trees. For Arthur's thought and interests did change over time. I find too I now fumble for the right technical terms.

Jack Copeland prefaces his collection of essays on Arthur's legacy, *Logic and Reality* [Copeland 1996] with a quote from Arthur which in full reads: 'Philosophy, including logic, is not primarily about language, but about the real world.' Logic was a powerful tool, faulty logic led to error. 'One should always keep a-hold of nurse for fear of finding something worse.'[7] While a logic which ignored aspects of the real world was faulty or incomplete. I put this with the crudity of a layman, but I hope I don't misrepresent him.

The concept of time and the development of tense logic were, of course, central to Arthur Prior's work. How would you sum up his ideas on 'time'?

Arthur's ideas on time altered; developed, as I have already mentioned. He sought to extend the scope of logic to accommodate such statements as the state of affairs expressed in 'Thank Goodness that's over' – the title of a paper first published in 1959 [Prior 1959]. The last page of this paper shows Arthur at his controversial and funniest best.

In his early writings, before tense logic, Arthur Prior several times dealt with the Christian – and in particular Calvinist – idea of predestination. In a similar vein, the difficult question of God's foreknowledge versus human freedom was discussed by him – the latter question in fact also in his late writings. Can you tell us about the development of his views on these issues and how they influenced his thought? A related and lasting preoccupation within Arthur's work was the problem of free will. What were his views on this matter?

Yes, it is true that Arthur was preoccupied by the problem of free will. At first he saw it in a semi-theological context. I have never felt quite sure how seriously Arthur really took the Calvinism which intellectually attracted him. It was rigorous and logical, unlike the Methodism of his

---

[7] An allusion to the closing lines of Hilaire Belloc's cautionary tale 'Jim: who ran away from his nurse and was eaten by a lion'. Arthur Prior sometimes quoted this.

childhood. But its God lacked humanity. I think sometimes he entertained Calvinism in its various forms rather than quite believing it. He was very aware of the dilemmas it posed. Perhaps his failure to resolve them was a reason why despite so much preparation the book on Scottish Theology never came to anything. In his later work I think he was prepared to go where logic led him, but the idea of the future as open to choice, where the past and present were not, may also have had deeper emotional attractions. But here I speculate.

Recently, Arthur Prior's tense logic has been likened by some, notably Mogens Wegener,[8] to the philosophy of Søren Kierkegaard, who also considered the notion of the 'now' to be of crucial importance. Kierkegaard, of course, took a special interest in the existential implications, whereas tense logic rather naturally emphasises the logical importance of the 'now'. But we do know that Arthur studied Kierkegaard with interest as a young man, and also wrote a bit about him.[9] We wonder whether you can add something about Arthur's view on Kierkegaard, and the possible relation between Kierkegaard's thought and Arthur's.

I find Mogens Wegener's suggestion that Arthur's tensed logic can be likened to that sketched by Kierkegaard fascinating. It would be interesting to know whether Arthur had read the passages in Kierkegaard in which it was developed (*Philosophical Fragments* and the *Concept of Dread*) [Kierkegaard 1985/Kierkegaard 1980]. If he read them it was when he was reading Kierkegaard as a young man and it must have lain fallow. But he read him in the years before I met him. The only work of Kierkegaard I know he possessed was a translation of *Lidelsernes Evangelium (Gospel of Sufferings)* [Kierkegaard 1991] which appeared in 1955. It was translated by a friend, W.S. Ferrie, a Birmingham Presbyterian clergyman. I don't know how much was accessible to Arthur pre-1943 in English or French. In this period he read a lot of European philosophy and literature. Refugees from Nazi

[8] See [Wegener and Øhrstrøm 1997], which suggests this line of thought, albeit indirectly. The issue is further dealt with in a manuscript in Danish, as well as in an as yet unpublished English-language manuscript, both by Wegener.
[9] See [Prior 1940] and also 'Children of the Damned' under 'Boxes' → 'Box 1–11' → 'Contents of Box 6'. An interesting and more mature reference to Kierkegaard can also be found in [Prior 1956, p. 96].

oppression were flooding into England, and some even reached New Zealand providing a rich leaven to intellectual life.

Arthur Prior also had a strong political commitment to the cause of poor and otherwise oppressed people. What were his political views, and do they relate to his thought as a philosopher and logician?

Arthur was left-wing from his student days on. I think he would have felt something had gone very wrong with his philosophical and logical arguments if they had entailed a conservative viewpoint – that they had ceased to relate to the real world. Many of his friends were Marxists, but of course dialectic had no appeal because of its logical repercussions. However, I doubt if he realized this as a very young man. I think Clare, his first wife, was a card-carrying member of the Communist Party. She ended in middle age by emigrating to Russia.

In December 1956, you left Oxford and went back to New Zealand. About two years later, however, Arthur Prior was offered a professorship in Manchester, so in late 1958 you left NZ for good. Tell us about those last two years in NZ.

Although Arthur did not take up the Manchester Chair until January 1959 – we held Christmas 1958 at sea – he had been interviewed for a yet to be created second chair in Manchester in 1956.

The last two years in New Zealand were very much like earlier years save that Arthur's correspondence had increased enormously. We looked forward to moving back into the wider world. You must remember at that time flying was still prohibitively expensive, and the sea voyage took a month. Everything still moved at a slow pace. Now a logician in NZ is not cut off in the same way.

In this period, however, I think Arthur had become connected with the JSL [Journal of Symbolic Logic], perhaps still only one of the associate editors, and as a result received Kripke's first paper [Kripke 1959] for consideration. This was enormously exciting and was the highlight of these years. Arthur also had the stimulation during these years, and indeed, from the year or two before 1956, of meetings with John Mackie, who had come to the Dunedin Chair, and George Hughes to the Wellington Chair. They were external examiners for each other, and once the examining was done, philosophical talk continued until the small, or not so small hours. These occasions were looked forward to as much by me as Arthur – I mean the discussions – not the examining, of course.

I must correct you on one point here. We didn't leave NZ for good. Arthur lectured for the British Council for 2 months in 1965, and the rest of the family went out on a family visit.

What was it like, coming to Manchester?

Manchester? For Arthur it was very satisfying to get back to Britain, but for me it was rather lonely. One might say philosophy was more professionalized. There was less need to use our home as an auxiliary setting to the department. And Arthur had many invitations to give lectures in other departments, and even other countries – Poland and America. As a result, from this time on my knowledge of Arthur's work is less full than formerly – and this at a time when he was becoming increasingly productive, mature and fertile in his work. However, I did attend local seminars and some were held in our house, and we put up visiting lecturers.

The relationship between staff and undergraduates was not as informal and close as in New Zealand, but Arthur had some good postgraduate students – most notably Max Cresswell and Robert Bull – both New Zealanders. And of course the opportunities for discussion with other philosophers and logicians within the department and outside it was considerable. Tony Kenny was at Liverpool for several years at this time and we saw a lot of him. Kripke visited for a week – and you should have seen me struggling with Orthodox Jewish cooking, and Arthur with getting him anywhere on time – I wonder if that's still a problem. Alan Ross Anderson came for a year, and Arthur and he continued, face to face, arguments formerly carried on over some years by letter.[10]

In 1965, you both went to California. Apparently Arthur Prior's California lectures contributed significantly to the flourishing development in logic there at that time, and especially it seems to have

[10] The extensive correspondence between Prior and Anderson is found under the 'The Prior-Anderson Correspondence', 'Boxes' → 'Box 1-11' → 'Contents of Box 1'.

sparked off a great interest in tense logic. Please give us some impressions from the California tour.

The time in California followed on after our time in New Zealand – 1965 to early 1966. For Arthur this was a tremendously exciting period. As a visiting lecturer at UCLA he was the Flint Professor – photos of what the departmental secretary called 'Our Flints' adorned the walls of the department and Arthur's photo presumably is somewhere there. As well as lecturing there he read papers in various Californian universities including Berkeley. I did not usually accompany him on these one night stands. Who he met and talked to then, I hardly know. I think at Berkeley Dana Scott and Davidson. I'm not sure if he ever met David Lewis at this time or indeed ever, though he corresponded with him. The people I remember most clearly are John Lemmon and Richard Montague. John we had known of course from 1956 and Richard from the Helsinki conference on Modal Logic a few years later [1962]. We used to go to the Bel Air Hotel and drink beer under the trees. And logic flowered.

In 1966, Arthur Prior was elected a fellow of Balliol College, Oxford. He had to give up his professorship in Manchester in order to take up this position in Oxford. What were the special attractions of Oxford, and what was it like going there?

The special attraction of Oxford was that it was far more a centre for philosophy than Manchester could ever be, and Arthur came to the conclusion that postgraduate students got more stimulation there than in Manchester. And so would he.

This was perfectly true, and for Arthur the undergraduates as well as the graduate students were of the highest calibre, and then morale was high. The terrible creaming off that went on in English Universities (but not in NZ) meant that Manchester philosophy undergraduates often felt they had failed the grade. That they had not been good enough. I don't think this holds any more – certainly not in science or in history.

Please tell us about your Oxford years, colleagues and students, and Arthur's main interests during that period.

The short three years in Oxford were golden years for us both. I discovered the Bodleian Library and my involvement in philosophy and logic decreased as my absorption in social history increased. This was as well. Dons' wives were expected to be fellows of colleges in their own right or mind their own business. It is still the same – maybe more so. However we still did a lot of entertaining of students and logicians and philosophers, including many from abroad.

The usual form of entertaining students in Oxford seemed to be sherry parties in College. Students tended to linger and we used to sweep up the last half dozen and take them home to eat fish and chips bought on the way home, drink coffee and continue talking.

Oxford students – undergraduate and postgraduate – were as bright as the very brightest New Zealand ones. Amongst undergraduates I think of Sutdhisakdi Manibhandu, Andrew Saint (who moved into Art History) and Kit Fine. Many postgraduates were from abroad: Peter Roper and Anselm Müller, Greg Macleod, Roger Hughes (George's son), Robin Haack and his wife Susan, Bill Newton Smith (who succeeded Arthur at Balliol). There were others whose names escape me now. Kit was the most brilliant of these students. Not all remained in philosophy and logic, but I have not followed the subsequent careers of those who did, save those I continue to see.

Not all the time was spent in talking philosophy in closed rooms. Arthur learned to drive late. Philosophy and sightseeing were often mixed. He was an erratic driver though. I remember splendid drives with visiting philosophers, such as the Kotarbinskis from Poland. Several times we took a number of students and colleagues to the White Horse on the Berkshire Downs, where we flew kites.[11] The aim was to keep the kite aloft as it was walked from the White Horse to Wayland's Smithy along the Ridgeway. It wasn't easy as there were scrubby trees to be negotiated.

In 1969, you and Arthur Prior went to Norway on a lecture tour. On this tour, in Trondheim, Arthur Prior died on 6 October. Please tell us about your impressions of this tour, and the issues with which Arthur was concerned during this tour and the last year of his life.

Just before we left for Norway where he died we had a wonderful lunch party where we seemed to gather a herd of visiting scholars. I remember

[11] The 'White Horse' is a prehistoric figure cut in the chalk of the Downs.

Hugh Montgomery from NZ and Charles Hamblin from Australia, Dov Gabbay from Israel, R. Thomason from US, Kit Fine I think too, and several others. I think I only imagine Montague was there, as he ought to have been. Somewhere deeply buried is a postcard which everyone signed – but I cannot find it.

It was perhaps the last time Arthur was really able to forget the pains of angina and perhaps rheumatism, which dogged the last three months of his life.

On the way to Oslo he attended a conference at Oberwolfach whilst Ann and I brought the heavy luggage on to Oslo by boat.[12] He gave the first of the lectures at Oslo, but died before completing the course. He was in acute discomfort. He felt the cold, his coat felt heavy, walking up the short steep slope to our house gave him pain. He missed the very full life of Oxford so there was little distraction from his distress. The trip to Trondheim was broken on the way by a couple of days' rest and holiday when the pain lifted. They were happy days. On arrival at Trondheim we spent the evening with local philosophers and he died during the night.

Almost immediately after Arthur's death you and Peter Geach went through his papers, notes, correspondence etc. They were deposited in the Bodleian Library, and David and Steffi Lewis further organised the papers shortly after that. Please tell us about this material, how it was collected and ordered, and what has since happened with it – for instance, the posthumous publications.

After the memorial service in Oxford which took place about three weeks later people came back to the house for drinks, and Bill Kneale took me aside and suggested I ask Peter Geach to help me cope with Arthur's papers, as he had proved himself capable in such matters – he was one of Wittgenstein's executors. Peter was there and I asked him. The only window of opportunity for some time was that weekend, and so we went down to Arthur's room at Balliol and did a vast but rapid preliminary sorting of papers and correspondence. These letters were of course letters to Arthur. Collecting letters from Arthur was more difficult. I wrote around to most likely recipients, but of course few people keep letters to the extent Arthur did. They had for long been his

---

[12] In Oberwolfach Prior gave the talk which was published as [Prior 1970].

lifeline and were never destroyed. However, some of Arthur's letters were saved, though the only massive collection is from Alan Ross Anderson. Tony Kenny and Peter Geach put into publishable form one uncompleted book manuscript by Arthur, which appeared as *Objects of Thought* [Prior 1971]. They edited a collection of Arthur's papers posthumously [Prior 1976b], containing some unpublished papers as well as ones published in journals, and they also cannibalised sections of the *Craft of Formal Logic* [Prior 1951/Prior 1976a] of a historical and critical nature. The *Craft* was written in 1950 and 1951 and submitted to OUP, who wanted it cut. It was excessively long and it dealt too much with Aristotelian and medieval logic, too little with modern. It was very different from what appeared as *Formal Logic* [Prior 1955]. Kit Fine edited and supplemented the material for a book of which Arthur had left only one completed chapter. It draws on some of his last papers. The book, *Worlds, Times and Selves* [Prior and Fine 1977], continued to break new ground.

The archive has existed now for over 25 years. Only recently has it been much used, but it is a rich source not only of Arthur's work, but also because it contains so many letters from logicians and philosophers about their own work – letters written in the days when letters were the common method of communication over a distance.

Mrs. Prior, thank you very much for giving this interview.

Works mentioned in the interview:
Bocheński, I.M. (1947), *La logique de Théophraste*. Publications de l'Université de Fribourg en Suisse. Fribourg.

Copeland, Jack (1996), 'Prior's Life and Legacy'. In Copeland, Jack (editor): 1996, *Logic and Reality: Essays on the Legacy of Arthur Prior*, Oxford University Press/Clarendon Press, Oxford, pp. 1–40.

Findlay, J.N. (1951) 'Time: A Treatment of Some Puzzles'. *Australasian Journal of Psychology and Philosophy*, Vol. 19, 1941. (Reprinted in Flew 1951).

Flew, Antony (1951), *Essays on Logic and Language*. Basil Blackwell, Oxford.

Hasle, P. (1997), 'The Problem of Predestination – a Prelude to A.N. Prior's Tense Logic'. In Wegener, Mogens (editor): *Time, Creation and World-Order*. Aarhus University Press, pp. 139–59.

Kenny, Anthony (1970), 'Arthur Norman Prior (1914–1969)', *Proceedings of the British Academy*, Vol. 56, pp. 321–49.
——(1985), *A Path from Rome*. Sidgwick and Jackson, London.

Kierkegaard, Søren Aabye (1980), *The Concept of Anxiety*. (Formerly translated as *The Concept of Dread*.) Princeton University Press.
——(1985), *Philosophical Fragments – Johannes Climacus* (Kierkegaard's Writings, VII). Princeton University Press.
——(1991), *Gospel of Sufferings*. (Søren Kierkegaard, A.S. Aldworth, W.S. Ferrie). James Clarke & Co. Ltd.

Kripke, Saul A. (1959), 'A completeness theorem in modal logic'. *The Journal of Symbolic Logic*, 24, pp. 1–14.

Prior, A.N. (1940), 'Makers of Modern Thought (1): Kierkegaard', *The Student*, March 1940, p. 131–2.
——(1949), *Logic and the Basis of Ethics*. Clarendon Press, Oxford.
——(1951), 'The Craft of Formal Logic' (unpublished manuscript, 806 pages, 1951). Found in Prior's Papers, Box 22, The Bodleian Library. (See also Prior, A.N. 1976a).
——(1955), *Formal Logic*. Clarendon Press, Oxford, 1955.
——(1956), 'The consequences of actions', Proceedings of the Aristotelian Society, Supplementary volume 30 (1956), pp. 91–9.
——(1959), 'Thank Goodness that's over', *Philosophy*, Vol. 34 (1959), pp. 12–17.
——(1960), 'The Runabout Inference-Ticket', *Analysis*, Vol. 21 (1960), pp. 38–9.
Prior, A.N. (with E.J. Lemmon, C.A. Meredith, D. Meredith, and I. Thomas), 1969, 'Calculi of pure strict implication'. In *Philosophical Logic*, ed. J. W. Davis, D.J. Hockney, and W.K. Wilson, D. Reidel, Dordrecht, 1969, pp. 215–50. (Previously published in mimeograph form, University of Canterbury, 1957.) ('LMMPT')
——(1970), 'The notion of the present', *Studium Generale*, vol. 23 (1970), pp. 245–8. Reprinted in *The Study of Time*, ed. J.T. Fraser, F.C.

Haber and G.H. Müller, pp. 320–3, Springer-Verlag, 1972.

——(1971), *Objects of Thought*. Ed. P.T. Geach and A.J.P. Kenny, Clarendon Press, Oxford, 1971. Based on manuscripts by Prior.

——(1976a), *The Doctrine of Propositions and Terms*. Ed. P. T. Geach and A.J.P. Kenny. University of Massachusetts Press, Amherst, 1976. (A part of Prior's manuscript, 'The Craft of Formal Logic', 1951).

– (1976b), *Papers in Logic and Ethics*. Ed. P. T. Geach and A.J.P. Kenny. University of Massachusetts Press, Amherst/Duckworth, London, 1976.

——(1977), *Worlds, Times and Selves*. Ed. Kit Fine, University of Massachusetts Press/Duckworth, London, 1977. (Based on manuscripts by Prior with a preface and a postscript by Kit Fine.)

Wegener, Mogens and Øhrstrøm, P. (1997), 'A New Tempo-Modal Logic for Emerging Truth', in J. Faye et al. (eds.), *Perspectives on Time*, Kluwer Academic Publishers 1997, Boston, pp. 417–41.

Øhrstrøm, P. and Hasle, P. (1993), 'A.N. Prior's Rediscovery of Tense Logic'. *Erkenntnis*, Vol. 39, pp. 23–50.

Appendix 2

BIBLIOGRAPHY OF A.N. PRIOR'S WRITINGS

INTRODUCTION BY PER HASLE

Till now, two bibliographies of the work of A.N. Prior have been published, namely:

1. Flo, Olav (1970), 'Bibliography of Prior's Philosophical Writings', *Theoria* (36), pp. 189–213.
2. Øhrstrøm, P. and Flo, Olav (1996), 'Bibliography of A.N. Prior's Philosophical Writings'. In Copeland, Jack (ed.) (1996), *Logic and Reality: Essays on the Legacy of Arthur Prior*, Oxford University Press/Clarendon Press, pp. 519–32.

Flo was a Norwegian research-librarian, who compiled a comprehensive albeit not complete list of Prior's publications before Prior's lecture tour to Norway in 1969. It was on this tour Prior died, on the evening of 6 October 1969 in Trondheim. Thus it was obvious to make the list into a bibliography, and Flo did a very thorough piece of work on this. His bibliography appeared in *Theoria* in 1970, and for many years remained the authoritative bibliography of Prior's work.

Around 1990, Peter Øhrstrøm and I began a systematical investigation into Prior's *Nachlass*, which is deposited in the Bodleian library. Partly due to the publication after 1970 of posthumous editions of Prior's work, and partly due to the discovery of a few further papers in the Bodleian Library, Peter Øhrstrøm augmented Flo's bibliography. This led to the new version published in 1996. Flo had died in 1989 and did not partake in this work, but the bibliography was published in his name too. In his introduction to this new bibliography, Peter Øhrstrøm wrote 'In 1970, the year after Prior's death, the Swedish journal *Theoria* published a collection of papers in his honour. This collection also included a bibliography of Prior's philosophical writings compiled by the late Olav Flo, of the University of Bergen, Norway. An amount of Prior's works has appeared subsequently. It has also been possible to locate a small number of papers published prior to 1970 that were not included in Flo's bibliography. I have retained Flo's overall framework and his referencing system. Thus, for example, the reference '1937a' denotes the same paper in both the updated and the original bibliography.' (Copeland, p. 519).

With hindsight, the 1996 bibliography was premature. Work on the aforementioned *Nachlass* continued to add hitherto unnoticed items to a full bibliography. To be true, many of these are of lesser importance, but nevertheless they do add to a fuller picture of Prior's work and certainly belong in a full bibliography. The bibliography published in this volume is considerably extended when compared with the 1996 bibliography, and all significant publications traceable via the *Nachlass* are included in this version. Like the 1996 bibliography, the format found here follows Flo's framework and builds on his referencing system.

Prior's *Nachlass* in the Bodleian Library

Almost immediately after the untimely death of Arthur Norman Prior on 6 October 1969, his widow Dr. Mary Prior, aided by Peter Geach, went through his papers, notes, correspondence etc. This material was deposited in the Bodleian Library, Oxford. David and Steffi Lewis ordered the papers not long after they were deposited. The Bodleian Library now holds this *Nachlass* in 22 boxes, plus 7 further boxes found at the Philosophy Department Library, Oxford. A detailed description of the content of the boxes as well as access information can be found at the 'WWW-site for Prior-studies' (www.hum.auc.dk/prior).

The following researchers have at various times paid visits to work on the Prior *Nachlass*: David and Steffi Lewis, Roger Gallie, Olav Flo, Mary Cresswell, P.T. Geach, A.J.P. Kenny, Kit Fine, Jack Copeland, Peter Øhrstrøm, Torben Braüner, Tine Kleif, Per Hasle, and Thomas Müller. (There may, of course, have been other visits of which I am unaware.)

Some of the major results stemming from these visits should be mentioned. On the work undertaken by David and Steffi Lewis, Mary Prior has written: "David and Steffi Lewis were responsible for much of the ordering of the papers once they reached Bodley ... I shall always be grateful to them for the gift of their time during a sabbatical – I think the summer after the papers were deposited." P.T. Geach and A.J.P. Kenny twice edited and published a number of papers (cf. 1971a and 1976b). They also published one book based on Prior's manuscript *The Craft of Formal Logic* under the title *The Doctrine of Propositions and Terms*

[1976a]. Kit Fine edited some of Prior's manuscripts, which appeared as [1977a]. Peter Øhrstrøm and Jack Copeland edited and published a few more papers (in Copeland 1996).

Also a number of publications by Peter Øhrstrøm and myself have made use of material in the archives. The same applies to work by Torben Braüner, and Thomas Müller. And finally, the aforementioned Web-site for Prior-studies makes available our description of the entire *Nachlass* in the Bodleian Library.

1937

a.   'The Nation and the Individual', *The Australasian Journal of Psychology and Philosophy*, vol. 15, pp. 294–98.

1938

a.   Étienne Review of Etienne Gilson, *The Philosophy of St. Bonaventure, The Criterion*, vol. 18, pp. 141–3.

b.   'Beyond Tragedy', *The Contemporary Review*, September, pp. 377–8.

c.   'The Christian Pacifist Congress', *The Christian Quarterly*, October, pp. 137–8.

d.   'Dr. Lowrie on Kierkegaard', *The Evangelical Quarterly*, October, pp. 399–401.

e.   Review of G. van der Leeuw, *Religion in Essence and Manifestation, Purpose,* October, pp. 171–5.

f.   Review of Wm. Paton, *World Community, The Christian Quarterly*, October, pp. 143–4.

g.   'The Tragic Dilemma – The Christian Pacifist Congress', *The Church Times*, 30 September, p. 327.

h.   'World Calvinism at Edinburgh', *Theology*, September, pp. 176–8.

1939

a.   'Christian Youth in World Conference', *World Dominion*, October, pp. 369–72.

b.   Review of K. Barth, *The Church and the Political Problem of Our Day, International Affairs*, November, p. 809.

c.   'Karl Barth's Gifford Lectures', *The Evangelical Quarterly*, January, pp. 95–6.

d.   Review of Michael Roberts, *T.E. Hulme*, *Philosophy*, April, pp. 244–5.

1940

a.   'Makers of Modern Thought: Kierkegaard', *The Student*, March, pp. 131–2.
b.   'A Scot Seeks God', *The Churchman*, pp. 34–42.
c.   'A Calvinist Romantic', *Purpose*, January–March, pp. 15–21.
d.   'As Others See Us (2). A Presbyterian Looks at Quakerism', *The Friend*, 5 July, pp. 409–10.
e.   'Christian News', *Theology*, September, pp. 165–9.
f.   Review of O.E. Burton, *The Conflict of the Cross*, *The Churchman*, April–June, p. 145.
g.   'Infant Baptism in the Church of Scotland', *The Churchman*, April–June, pp. 135–45.
h.   'Missions and the Home Front', *International Review of Missions*, July, pp. 340–52.
i.   'A Modest Proposal', *The Presbyter*, August, pp. 1–3.
j.   'Speaking with Authority', *The Presbyter*, March, pp. 1–6.
k.   'Thinking Oecumenically', *The Presbyter,* April, pp. 1–6.

1941

a.   'Sense and Sentences', *National Education*, 8 March.
b.   'Fashionable Tribalism', *World Dominion,* May–June, pp. 151–53.
c.   'Revelation', *The Expository Times*, March, pp. 239–40.
d.   'Something to Read I: *Ulysses*, *The Student*, March, pp. 3–4.
e.   'Something to Read II: *The Organism of Christian Truth*, *The Student*, April, p. 4.
f.   'What May the Church Say to Men of Faith about their Political Responsibilities?', *The Presbyter*, January, pp. 1–6.
g.   'Who Is My Neighbour – The Teaching of Frederick Kohlbrigge', *The Congregational Quarterly*, April, pp. 165–70.

1942

a.   'Can Religion be Discussed?', *The Australasian Journal of Psychology and Philosophy*, vol. 20, pp. 141–51. Reprinted in Antony Flew and Alasdair Macintyre (eds.), *New Essays in Philosophical Theology*, S.C.M. Press, London, 1955, pp. 1–11.

b. Commentary on R.D. Whitehorn: *The Background of The Westminster Assembly*, *The Presbyter*, September, pp. 6–7.
c. 'The Church's Witness and the Church's Faith', *The Presbyter*, January, pp. 1–5.
d. 'The Forms of Thought of the Westminster Standards', *The Presbyter*, July–August, pp. 1–3.
e. 'Reader's Guide to Barth's Dogmatics', *Theology*, June, pp. 329–35.

1943
a. 'The Theology of James Joyce', *The Presbyter*, January.

1944
a. 'The meaning of good', *The Australasian Journal of Psychology and Philosophy*, vol. 22, pp. 170–4.
b. 'Bouquets and Brickbats from New Zealand', *The Presbyter,* August, pp. 12–13.
c. 'A Catena of Presbyterian Answers to Congregationalism: The Gathered Church', *The Presbyter*, June, pp. 10 f.
d. 'A Catena of Presbyterian Answers to Congregationalism: Ordination and Election', *The Presbyter*, July, pp. 6–10.
e. With Mary Prior, 'What is 'A Christian Novel'? Doctrinal Patterns in the Possessed', *The Presbyter,* December, pp. 8–10.

1945
a. 'The Subject of Ethics', *The Australasian Journal of Psychology and Philosophy*, vol. 23, pp. 78–84.
b. With Mary Prior, 'The Apocalypse of Ishmael', *The Presbyter,* November, pp. 27–30.
c. With Mary Prior, 'Easter Saturday (a Study of The Idiot by Dostoievsky)', *The Presbyter*, May, pp. 23–5.
d. With Mary Prior, 'Pro and Contra (a Study of The Bros. Karamasov by Dostoievsky)', *The Presbyter*, February, pp. 18–21.
e. 'Religion in Schools', *New Zealand Listener,* 5 January and 23 February, Wellington.
f. 'S.C.M. and the Church – Stage III', *The Student*, No. 8, October, p. 2.

1946

a.   'Eighteenth Century Writers on Twentieth Century Subjects', *The Australasian Journal of Psychology and Philosophy*, vol. 24, pp. 168–82.

b.   'The Reformers Reformed: Knox on Predestination', *The Presbyter*, February, pp. 19–23.

c.   'On the Outside Always Looking In', *The Student*, No. 1, March, pp. 9–10 and 15.

d.   'Tomorrow We Die', *The Student*, No. 5, August, pp. 1–2.

1947

a.   Review of Clive S. Lewis, *The Abolition of Man, Landfall*, vol. 1, pp. 63–67.

b.   Review of Karl R. Popper, *The Open Society and its Enemies, Landfall*, vol. 1, pp. 136–42.

c.   Review of D. Daiches Raphael, *The Moral Sense, Landfall*, vol. 1, pp. 314–318.

d.   'Supralapsarianism', *The Presbyter*, September, pp. 19–22.

e.   'The Open Society', *The Student*, No. 1, March, pp. 12, 14.

1948

a.   'Adam Gib and the Philosophers', *The Australasian Journal of Philosophy*, vol. 26, pp. 73–93.

b.   'Facts, Propositions and Entailment', *Mind*, vol. 57, pp. 62–8.

c.   'Disruption', *Landfall*, vol. 2, pp. 8–18.

1949

a.   *Logic and the Basis of Ethics*, Clarendon Press, Oxford. Second ed., 1956.

b.   'Argument A Fortiori', *Analysis*, vol. 9, pp. 49–50.

c.   'Categoricals and Hypotheticals in George Boole and his Successors', *The Australasian Journal of Philosophy*, vol. 27, pp. 171–96.

d.   'Determinables, Determinates and Determinants', *Mind*, vol. 58, Part I, pp. 1–20. Part II, pp. 178–94.

e.   Review of Signe Toksvig, *Emmanuel Swedenborg – Scientist and Mystic, New Zealand Listener,* 23 December, Wellington.

1950

a.   Letter to the Editor, *Landfall*, vol. 4, p. 266.
b.   Letter to the Editor, *Landfall*, vol. 4, p. 369–70.
c.   Review of H.A.R. Gibbs, *Mahommedanism, New Zealand Listener,* 13 January, Wellington.

1951

a.   'The Ethical Copula', *The Australasian Journal of Philosophy*, vol. 29, pp. 137–54. [Cf. 1976b.]
b.   'The Virtue of the Act and the Virtue of the Agent', *Philosophy*, vol. 26, pp. 121–30.
c.   Review of J.M. Bates, *A Manual of Christian Doctrine, New Zealand Listener*, 6 April, Wellington.

1952

a.   'In what Sense Is Modal Logic Many-Valued?', *Analysis*, vol. 12, pp. 138–43.
b.   'Łukasiewicz's Symbolic Logic', *The Australasian Journal of Philosophy*, vol. 30, pp. 33–46.
c.   'The Parva Logicalia in Modern Dress', *Dominican Studies*, vol. 5, pp. 78–87.
d.   'Modality De Dicto and Modality De Re', *Theoria*, vol. 18, pp. 174–80.
e.   'This Quarter', *Landfall*, vol. 6, pp. 49–53.
f.   Review of J.A. Passmore, *Ralph Cudworth: An Interpretation*, *The Australasian Journal of Philosophy*, vol. 30, pp. 133–37.
g.   Review of W.V. Quine, *Methods of Logic, The Australasian Journal of Philosophy*, vol. 30, pp. 200–2.

1953

a.   'Negative Quantifiers', *The Australasian Journal of Philosophy*, vol. 31, pp. 107–23.
b.   'The Logic of Negative Terms in Boethius', *Franciscan Studies*, vol. 13, pp. 1–6.
c.   'On some Consequentiae in Walter Burleigh', *The New Scholasticism*, vol. 27, pp. 433–46.
d.   'Three-Valued Logic and Future Contingents', *The Philosophical Quarterly*, vol. 3, pp. 317–26.

e.   'On Propositions neither Necessary nor Impossible', *The Journal of Symbolic Logic*, vol. 18, pp. 105–8.

f.   Review of Boleslaw Sobociński, 'L'analyse de l'antinomie russellienne par Leśniewski', *The Journal of Symbolic Logic,* vol. 18, pp. 331–3.

g.   Review of I.M. Bocheński, 'Non-analytical Laws and Rules in Aristotle', *The Journal of Symbolic Logic*, vol. 18, pp. 333–4.

1954

a.   'Entities', *The Australasian Journal of Philosophy*, vol. 32, pp. 159–68. [Cf. 1976b.]

b.   'The Interpretation of Two Systems of Modal Logic', *The Journal of Computing Systems*, vol. 1 (1952/54), pp. 201–8.

c.   'The Paradoxes of Derived Obligation', *Mind*, vol. 63, pp. 64–5.

1955

a.   *Formal Logic*, Clarendon Press, Oxford. Second rev. ed., 1962.

b.   'Curry's Paradox and Three-Valued Logic', *The Australasian Journal of Philosophy*, vol. 33, pp. 177–82.

c.   'English and Ontology', *The British Journal for the Philosophy of Science*, vol. 6 (1955–56), pp. 64–5.

d.   'Diodoran Modalities', *The Philosophical Quarterly,* vol. 5, pp. 205–13. [Cf. 1958h.]

e.   With Mary Prior, 'Erotetic Logic', *The Philosophical Review*, vol. 64, pp. 43–59.

f.   'Many-Valued and Modal Systems: An Intuitive Approach', *The Philosophical Review*, vol. 64, pp. 626–30.

g.   'Is Necessary Existence Possible?', *Philosophy and Phenomenological Research*, vol. 15, pp. 545–47.

h.   'Berkeley in Logical Form', *Theoria*, vol. 21, pp. 117–22. [Cf. 1976b.]

i.   Review of B.B. von Freytag Löringhoff, 'Zur Logik als Lehre von Identität und Verschiedenheit', *The Journal of Symbolic Logic*, vol. 20, p. 55.

j.   Review of Sadeo Shiraishi, 'The Structure of the Continuity of Psychological Experiences and the Physical World', *The Journal of Symbolic Logic*, vol. 20, pp. 169–70.

k.   Review of Arata Ishimoto, 'A Set of Axioms of the Modal
     Propositional Calculus Equivalent to S3', *The Journal of
     Symbolic Logic*, vol. 20, p. 169.
l.   Review of Shumpei Ueyama, 'Development of Peirce's Theory
     of Logic', *The Journal of Symbolic Logic*, vol. 20, p. 170.
m.   'Definitions, Rules and Axioms', *Proceedings of the Aristotelian
     Society*, vol. 56 (1955–56), pp. 199–216, with addendum. [Cf.
     1976b.]
n.   'Speaking about God', *The Student*, No. 5, September, pp. 7–10.

1956

a.   'Logicians at Play: or Syll, Simp and Hilbert', *The Australasian
     Journal of Philosophy*, vol. 34, pp. 182–92.
b.   'Modality and Quantification in S5', *The Journal of Symbolic
     Logic*, vol. 21, pp. 60–2.
c.   'The Consequences of Actions', *Proceedings of the Aristotelian
     Society*, supplementary volume 30, pp. 91–9. [Cf. 1968a.]
d.   Review of Jerzy Kalinowski, 'Teoria zdań normatywnych
     /Théorie des propositions normatives', *The Journal of Symbolic
     Logic*, vol. 21, pp. 191–2.
e.   Review of B. Sobociński, 'Studies in Leśniewski's Mereology',
     and of C. Lejewski, 'A Contribution to Leśniewski's Mereology',
     The Journal of Symbolic Logic, vol. 21, pp. 325–6.
f.   'A Note on the Logic of Obligation', *Revue Philosophique de
     Louvain*, vol. 54, pp. 86–7.

1957

a.   *Time and Modality, being the John Locke Lectures for 1955–56
     delivered in the University of Oxford*, Oxford University Press,
     London.
b.   'Is it Possible that One and the Same Individual Object Should
     Cease to Exist and Later on Start to Exist Again?', *Analysis*, vol.
     17, pp. 121–3.
c.   'The Necessary and the Possible', the first of three talks jointly
     entitled 'The Logic Game', *The Listener*, vol. 57, 627–8.
     'Symbolism and Analogy', the second of three talks jointly
     entitled 'The Logic Game', *The Listener*, vol. 57, pp. 675, 678.
     'Many-Valued Logics', the last of three talks jointly entitled 'The
     Logic Game' *The Listener*, vol. 57, pp. 717–19.

d.   'Opposite Number', *The Review of Metaphysics*, vol. 11, pp. 196–201. [Cf. 1976b.]

e.   Critical Notice of Alfred Tarski, *Logic, Semantics and Metamathematics*, *Mind*, vol. 66, pp. 401–10.

f.   Review of fourth edition of Lewis Carroll, *Symbolic Logic, Part I*, *The Journal of Symbolic Logic*, vol. 22, pp. 309–10.

g.   Review of Arata Ishimoto, 'A note on the paper "A Set of Axioms of the Modal Propositional Calculus Equivalent to S3" ', and 'A Formulation of the Modal Propositional Calculus Equivalent to S4', *The Journal of Symbolic Logic*, vol. 22, pp. 326–27.

h.   Review of Ronald J. Butler, 'Language Strata and Alternative Logics', *The Journal of Symbolic Logic*, vol. 22, p. 383.

1958

a.   'Escapism: The Logical Basis of Ethics', in A.I. Melden (ed.), *Essays in Moral Philosophy*, University of Washington Press, Seattle, pp. 135–46. Reissued as paperback, 1966.

b.   'Łukasiewicz's Contributions to Logic', in R. Klibansky (ed.), *Philosophy in the Mid-Century*, vol. 1, La Nuova Italia Editrice, Florence, pp. 53–5.

c.   'The Good Life and Religious Faith' (The East-West meeting in Canberra), *The Australasian Journal of Philosophy*, 36, pp. 1–13.

d.   'The Syntax of Time-Distinctions', *Franciscan Studies*, vol. 18, pp. 105–20.

e.   'Peirce's Axioms for Propositional Calculus', *The Journal of Symbolic Logic*, vol. 23, pp. 135–6.

f.   'Epimenides the Cretan', *The Journal of Symbolic Logic*, vol. 23, pp. 261–6. [Cf. 1976b.]

g.   'Time after Time', *Mind*, vol. 67, pp. 244–6.

h.   'Diodorus and Modal Logic: A Correction', *The Philosophical Quarterly*, vol. 8, pp. 226–30. [Cf. 1955d.]

i.   Review of Patrick Suppes, *Introduction to Logic*, and J.W. Blyth, *A Modern Introduction to Logic*, *The Australasian Journal of Philosophy*, vol. 36, pp. 146–50.

j.   Review of Robert G. Turnbull, 'A Note on Mr. Hare's "Logic of Imperatives" ', *The Journal of Symbolic Logic*, vol. 23, p. 442.

k.   Review of Walter Burleigh, *De Puritate Artis Logicae* (ed. Ph. Boehner), *The New Scholasticism*, vol. 32, pp. 127–30.

l.   Review of H.D. Lewis, ed., *Contemporary British Philosophy*, third series, *Philosophy*, vol. 33, pp. 361–4.

1959

a.   'Notes on a Group of New Modal Systems', *Logique et Analyse*, vol. 2, pp. 122–7.

b.   'Thank Goodness That's Over', *Philosophy*, vol. 34, pp. 12–17. [Cf. 1976b.]

c.   'Mr. Cohen on Thanking Goodness that *p* and *q*', *Philosophy*, vol. 34, pp. 362–3.

d.   'Creation in Science and Theology', *Southern Stars*, vol. 18, pp. 82–90.

e.   'Formalised Syllogistic', *Synthese*, vol. 11, pp. 265–73.

f.   Review of Alan Ross Anderson and Omar K. Moore, 'The Formal Analysis of Normative Concepts', *The Journal of Symbolic Logic*, vol. 24, pp. 177–8.

g.   Review of Alan Ross Anderson, 'A Reduction of Deontic Logic to Alethic Modal Logic', *The Journal of Symbolic Logic*, vol. 24, p. 178.

h.   Review of Alan Ross Anderson, 'The Logic of Norms', *The Journal of Symbolic Logic*, vol. 24, p. 178.

i.   Review of Frederic B. Fitch, 'Self-referential Relations', *The Journal of Symbolic Logic*, vol. 24, p. 240.

j.   Review of J. Porte, 'Deux systèmes simples pour le calcul des propositions', *The Journal of Symbolic Logic*, vol. 24, p. 247.

k.   Review of Jens Erik Fenstad, 'Notes on Normative Logic', *The Journal of Symbolic Logic*, vol. 24, pp. 247–8.

1960

a.   'The Runabout Inference-Ticket', *Analysis*, vol. 21, pp. 38–39. Reprinted in P.F. Strawson (ed.), *Philosophical Logic*, Oxford, 1967, pp. 129–31. [Cf. 1976b.]

b.   'The Autonomy of Ethics', *The Australasian Journal of Philosophy*, vol. 38, pp. 199–206. [Cf. 1976b.]

c.   'Identifiable Individuals', *The Review of Metaphysics*, vol. 13, pp. 684–96. [Cf. 1968a.]

d.   Review of Sören Halldén, *On the Logic of 'Better'*, *Philosophy*, vol. 35, pp. 359–61.

1961

a.   'Symmetry, Transitivity and Reflexivity', *Journal of the Philosophical Association*, vol. 7, pp. 67–9.

b.   'On a Difference between "Betweens" ', *Mind*, vol. 70, pp. 83–4.

c.   'On a Family of Paradoxes', *Notre Dame Journal of Formal Logic*, vol. 2, pp. 16–32. Reprinted in Steven J. Bartlett (ed.), *Reflexivity. A source-book in self-reference*, North-Holland Publishing Co., Amsterdam, 1992, pp. 97–113.

d.   'Some Axiom-Pairs for Material and Strict Implication', *Zeitschrift für mathematische Logik und Grundlagen der Mathematik*, vol. 7, pp. 61–5.

e.   Review of I.M. Bocheński: *A History of Formal Logic*, *Mathematical Reviews*, record 10899, vol. 22, p. 1854.

1962

a.   'Changes in Events and Changes in Things', University of Kansas, Lawrence, 13 pp. Reprinted in Robin Le Poidevin and Murray MacBeath (eds.), *The Philosophy of Time*, Oxford University Press, 1993, pp. 35–46. [Cf. 1968a.]

b.   'Nonentities', in R.J. Butler (ed.), *Analytical Philosophy*, Blackwell, Oxford, pp. 120–32. [Cf. 1976b.]

c.   'Quantification and Ł-Modality', *Notre Dame Journal of Formal Logic*, vol. 3, pp. 142–7.

d.   'Possible Worlds', *The Philosophical Quarterly*, vol. 12, pp. 36–43.

e.   'The Formalities of Omniscience', *Philosophy*, vol. 37, pp. 114–29. [Cf. 1968a.]

f.   'Limited Indeterminism', *The Review of Metaphysics*, vol. 16, pp. 55–61. [Cf. 1968a.]

g.   'Współczesna logika w Anglii' (Contemporary logic in England), *Ruch Filozoficzny*, vol. 21, pp. 251–6.

h.   'Tense-logic and the Continuity of Time', *Studia Logica*, vol. 13, pp. 133–48.

i.   'Some Problems of Self-reference in John Buridan', *Proceedings of the British Academy*, vol. 48, pp. 281–96. Reprinted in J.N. Findlay (ed.), *Studies in Philosophy*, Oxford University Press, 1966, pp. 241–59. [Cf. 1976b.]

j. Review of Andrej Grzegorczyk, 'The Systems of Leśniewski in Relation to Contemporary Logical Research', *The Journal of Symbolic Logic*, vol. 27, pp. 117–8.

1963

a. 'Is the Concept of Referential Opacity really Necessary?', *Acta Philosophica Fennica*, vol. 16, pp. 189–99. [Cf. 1971a.]
b. With C.A. Meredith, 'Notes on the Axiomatics of the Propositional Calculus', *Notre Dame Journal of Formal Logic*, vol. 4, pp. 171–87.
c. 'Indirect Speech Again', *Philosophical Studies*, vol. 14, pp. 12–15.
d. 'Rejoinder to Professor Lachs on Omniscience', *Philosophy*, 38, pp. 365–6.
e. With A. Kenny, 'Oratio Obliqua', *Proceedings of the Aristotelian Society*, supplementary volume 37, pp. 115–26. [Cf. 1976b.]
f. 'The Theory of Implication', *Zeitschrift für mathematische Logik und Grundlagen der Mathematik*, vol. 9, pp. 1–6. [Cf. 1965d.]

1964

a. 'Some Exercises in Epistemic Logic', in C.D. Rollins (ed.), *Knowledge and Experience*, University of Pittsburgh Press, Pittsburgh, pp. 21–7.
b. 'The Algebra of the Copula', in E.C. Moore and R.S. Robin (eds.), *Studies in the Philosophy of Charles Sanders Peirce*, second series, University of Massachusetts Press, Amherst, pp. 79–94.
c. 'Conjunction and Contonktion Revisited', *Analysis*, vol. 24, pp. 191–5. [Cf. 1976b.]
d. 'Two Additions to Positive Implication', *The Journal of Symbolic Logic*, vol. 29, pp. 31–2.
e. 'On the Unity of Professor Carnap', *Mind*, vol. 73, pp. 268–9.
f. 'The Done Thing', *Mind*, vol. 73, pp. 441–2.
g. 'Axiomatisations of the Modal Calculus Q', *Notre Dame Journal of Formal Logic*, vol. 5, pp. 215–17.
h. 'K1, K2 and Related Modal Systems', *Notre Dame Journal of Formal Logic*, vol. 5, pp. 299–304.
i. 'Indirect Speech and Extensionality', *Philosophical Studies*, vol. 15, pp. 35–8.

j.   With C.A. Meredith, 'Investigations into Implicational S5', *Zeitschrift für mathematische Logik und Grundlagen der Mathematik*, vol. 10, pp. 203–20.

k.   Review of Heinrich Scholz, *Concise History of Logic, Mathematical Reviews*, record 2959, vol. 28, pp. 576–7.

l.   Review of J. Dopp, 'Logiques construites par une méthode de déduction naturelle', *Philosophical Quarterly*, vol. 19, pp. 280–1.

m.   Review of M.A.E. Dummett and E.J. Lemmon, 'Modal Logics between S4 and S5', *Mathematical Reviews*, record 27, vol. 28, p. 6. [Cf. 1967n.]

n.   Review of Saul Kripke, 'The Undecidability of Monadic Modal Quantification Theory'. *Mathematical Reviews*, record 2975, vol. 28, p. 580.

1965

a.   'Existence in Leśniewski and in Russell', in J.N. Crossley and M.A.E. Dummett (eds.), *Formal Systems and Recursive Functions*, North-Holland, Amsterdam, pp. 149–55. [Cf. 1971a.]

b.   'The Cogito of Descartes and the Concept of Self-confirmation', in K. Ajdukiewicz (ed.), *The Foundation of Statements and Decisions,* PWN-Polish Scientific Publishers, Warsaw, pp. 47–55. [Cf. 1976b.]

c.   With C.A. Meredith, 'Modal Logic with Functorial Variables and a Contingent Constant', *Notre Dame Journal of Formal Logic*, vol. 6, pp. 99–109.

d.   'The Theory of Implication: Two Corrections', *Zeitschrift für mathematische Logik und Grundlagen der Mathematik,* vol. 11, pp. 381–2. [Cf. 1963f.]

e.   Review of B. Sobociński, 'On the Single Axioms of Protothetic', *The Journal of Symbolic Logic*, vol. 30, pp. 245–6.

f.   'Time, Existence and Identity', *Proceedings of the Aristotelian Society*, vol. 66 (1965–66), pp. 183–92. [Cf. 1968a.]

1966

a.   'Postulates for Tense-Logic', *American Philosophical Quarterly*, vol. 3, pp. 153–61.

b.   Critical Notice of G.E. Hughes and D.G. Londey, *The Elements of Formal Logic, The Australasian Journal of Philosophy*, vol. 44, pp. 224–31.

1967

a.   *Past, Present and Future*, Clarendon Press, Oxford.

b.   'Correspondence Theory of Truth', in Paul Edwards (ed.), *The Encyclopedia of Philosophy*, Collier-Macmillan, London, vol. 2, pp. 223–32.

c.   'Existence', *Ibid.*, vol. 3, pp. 141–7.

d.   'Logic, Deontic', *Ibid.*, vol. 4, pp. 509–13.

e.   'Logic, History of' (ed.), *Ibid.*, vol. 4, pp. 513–71. Within this section author of the following: 'Peirce, C.S.', pp. 546–9; 'The Heritage of Kant and Mill', p. 549; 'Keynes, John M.', pp. 550–1; 'Johnson, W.E.', p. 551; 'Polish Logicians', pp. 566–8; 'Bibliography', pp. 568–71.

f.   'Logic, Many-Valued', *Ibid.*, vol. 5, pp. 1–5.

g.   'Logic, Modal', *Ibid.*, vol. 5, pp. 5–12.

h.   'Logic, Traditional', *Ibid.*, vol. 5, pp. 34–45.

i.   'Negation', *Ibid.*, vol. 5, pp. 458–63.

j.   'Russell, Bertrand Arthur William', the section: 'Logic and Mathematics', *Ibid.*, vol. 7, pp. 244–51.

k.   With Paul Edwards and William P. Alston, 'Bibliography' (to Russell), *Ibid.*, vol. 7, pp. 256–8.

l.   'On Spurious Egocentricity', *Philosophy*, vol. 42, pp. 326–35. [Cf. 1968a.]

m.   'Stratified Metric Tense Logic', *Theoria*, vol. 33, pp. 28–38. [Cf. 1968a.]

n.   Review of M.A.E. Dummett and E.J. Lemmon, 'Modal Logics between S4 and S5', Iwao Nishimura, 'On Formulas of One Variable in Intuitionistic Propositional Calculus', and D.C. Makinson, 'There are Infinitely Many Diodorean Modal Functions', *The Journal of Symbolic Logic*, vol. 32, pp. 396–7. [Cf. 1964m.]

o.   Review of Keith Lehrer and Richard Taylor, 'Time, Truth and Modalities', *The Journal of Symbolic Logic*, vol. 32, pp. 401–2.

p.   Review of Storrs McCall, *Polish Logic*, *The Oxford Magazine*, vol. 8, pp. 111–12.

1968

a.   *Papers on Time and Tense*. Clarendon Press, Oxford. Reprints of 1956c, 1960c, 1962a, 1962e, 1962f, 1965f, 1967l, and 1967m, and the following new papers: 'Contemplation and Action', pp.

45–50; 'The Logic of Ending Time', pp. 98–115; 'Tense Logic and the Logic of Earlier and Later', pp. 116–34; 'Quasi-Propositions and Quasi-Individuals', pp. 135–44; 'Tense logic for Non-Permanent Existents', pp. 145–60.

b. 'Imperatives and Truth', *Akten des 14. Internationalen Kongresses für Philosophie*, Vienna, vol. 2, pp. 291–6.

c. 'The Logic of Tenses', *Akten des 14. Internationalen Kongresses für Philosophie*, Vienna, vol. 2, pp. 638–40.

d. 'Intentionality and Intensionality', *Proceedings of the Aristotelian Society*, supplementary volume 42, pp. 91–106. [Cf. 1976b.]

e. 'Fugitive Truth', *Analysis*, vol. 29, pp. 5–8.

f. With C.A. Meredith, 'Equational Logic', *Notre Dame Journal of Formal Logic*, vol. 9, pp. 212–26 [Cf. 1969j.]

g. 'Now', *Noûs*, vol. 2, pp. 101–19. [Cf. 1968i.]

h. 'Egocentric Logic', *Noûs,* vol. 2, pp. 191–207. [Cf. 1977a.]

i. ' "Now", Corrected and Condensed', *Noûs,* vol. 2, pp. 411–12. [Cf. 1968g.]

j. 'Time and Change', *Ratio*, vol. 10, pp. 173–7.

k. 'Modal Logic and the Logic of Applicability', *Theoria*, vol. 34, pp. 183–202. [Cf. 1977a.]

l. Comment on 'A Knock at Prelims Logic', *The Oxford Magazine*, vol. 9, pp. 68–9.

m. Review of Łukasiewicz, *Elements of Mathematical Logic*, *The Journal of Philosophy*, vol. 65, pp. 152–3.

n. Review of John Buridan, *Sophisms on Meaning and Truth, The Philosophical Review*, vol. 77, pp. 516–19.

1969

a. With E.J. Lemmon, C.A. Meredith, D. Meredith, and I. Thomas, 'Calculi of Pure Strict Implication', in J.W. Davis, D.J. Hockney, and W.K. Wilson (eds.), *Philosophical Logic*, D. Reidel, Dordrecht, pp. 215–50. (Previously published in mimeograph form, University of Canterbury, 1957.)

b. Critical Notice of Richard Gale, *The Language of Time, Mind*, vol. 78, pp. 453–60.

c. Review of Gerald Stahl, 'Le problème de l'existence dans la logique symbolique', 'Temps et existence', and 'Une formalisation du "dominateur"', *The Journal of Symbolic Logic*, vol. 34, pp. 140–1.

d. 'Worlds, Times and Selves', *L'Âge de la Science*, vol. 3, pp. 179–91. [Cf. 1977a.]

e. 'Tensed Propositions as Predicates', *The American Philosophical Quarterly*, vol. 6, pp. 290–7. [Cf. 1977a.]

f. 'The Possibly-True and the Possible', *Mind*, vol. 78, pp. 481–92. [Cf. 1976b.]

g. 'Propositional Calculus in Implication and Non-Equivalence', *Notre Dame Journal of Formal Logic*, vol. 10, pp. 271–2.

h. 'On the Calculus MCC', *Notre Dame Journal of Formal Logic*, vol. 10, pp. 273–4.

i. Review of G.H. von Wright, *Time, Change and Contradiction*, *The British Journal for the Philosophy of Science*, vol. 20, pp. 372–4.

j. 'Corrigendum to C.A. Meredith's and my Paper: "Equational Logic"', *Notre Dame Journal of Formal Logic*, vol. 10, p. 452. [Cf. 1968f.]

k. 'Self-perception and Contingency', *Analysis*, vol. 30, pp. 46–9. [Cf. 1976b.]

l. 'Recent Advances in Tense Logic', *The Monist*, vol. 53, pp. 325–9.

m. Review of G.E. Hughes and M.J. Cresswell, *An Introduction to Modal Logic*, *The Oxford Magazine*, vol. 10, pp. 50–1.

n. 'Extensionality and Propositional Identity', *Crítica*, vol. 3, No. 7, pp. 35–60. [Cf. 1971a.]

1970

a. '*I*', in B.Y. Khanbhai, R.S. Katz, and R.A. Pineau (eds.), *Jowett Papers 1968–1969*, Blackwell, Oxford, pp. 1–10.

b. 'The Notion of the Present', *Studium Generale*, vol. 23, pp. 245–8. Reprinted in J.T. Fraser, F.C. Haber and G.H. Müller (eds.), *The Study of Time*, Springer-Verlag, Berlin, 1972, pp. 320–3.

c. 'Logical Laws and Truth-Valueless Sentences', *Philosophical Studies*, Minneapolis, vol. 21, p. 95.

d. Review of G.H. von Wright, *An Essay in Deontic Logic and the General Theory of Action*, *Ratio*, vol. 12, pp. 175–8.

1971

a.   *Objects of Thought*, ed. by P.T. Geach and A.J.P. Kenny, Clarendon Press, Oxford. Based on manuscripts by Prior. Includes reprints of 1969n, part of 1963a, and most of 1965a.

1976

a.   *The Doctrine of Propositions and Terms*, ed. P.T. Geach and A.J.P. Kenny. Duckworth, London. (A part of Prior's unpublished 1951 manuscript *The Craft of Formal Logic*.)

b.   *Papers in Logic and Ethics*, ed. P.T. Geach and A.J.P. Kenny. Duckworth, London. Reprints of 1951a, 1954a, 1955h, 1955m, 1957d, 1958f, 1959b, 1960a, 1960b, 1962b, 1962i, 1963e, 1964c, 1965b, 1968d, 1969f, 1969k, and the following new papers: 'On Some Proofs of the Existence of God', pp. 56–63; 'It Was to Be', pp. 97–108; 'What is Logic?', pp. 122–9; 'What Do General Statements Refer To?', pp. 176–80; 'Things and Stuff', pp. 181–6.

1977

a.   *Worlds, Times and Selves*, ed. Kit Fine, Duckworth, London. Based on manuscripts by Prior with preface and postscript by Kit Fine. Reprints of 1968h, 1968k, 1969d, 1969e, and the following new chapters: 'The Parallel between Modal Logic and Quantification Theory', pp. 9–27; 'Supplement to "Egocentric Logic" ', pp. 46–50; 'Supplement to "Modal Logic and the Logic of Applicability" ', pp. 102–15.

1996

a & b.

      'Some Free Thinking About Time' & 'A Statement of Temporal Realism' (ed. Peter Øhrstrøm). In Jack Copeland (ed.), 1996, *Logic and Reality: Essays on the Legacy of Arthur Prior*, Oxford University Press/Clarendon Press, pp. 45–6 and pp. 47–51.

c.   With C.A. Meredith, 'Interpretations of Different Modal Logics in the "Property Calculus" ', in Jack Copeland (ed.), 1996, *Logic and Reality: Essays on the Legacy of Arthur Prior*, Oxford University Press/Clarendon Press, pp. 133–4. (Previously published in mimeograph form, University of Canterbury, 1956.)

INDEX